KENNETH MILTON CHAPMAN

Kenneth Milton Chapman at his desk in the Palace of the Governors,
c. 1915. (Courtesy of School for Advanced Research Archives, AC02 805d.)

KENNETH MILTON CHAPMAN

A Life Dedicated to

Indian Arts and Artists

JANET CHAPMAN

and KAREN BARRIE

UNIVERSITY OF NEW MEXICO PRESS ■ ALBUQUERQUE

12 11 10 09 08   1 2 3 4 5

Library of Congress Cataloging-in-Publication Data

Chapman, Janet, 1951–
Kenneth Milton Chapman : a life dedicated to Indian arts and artists /
Janet Chapman and Karen Barrie.
       p. cm.
Includes bibliographical references and index.
ISBN 978-0-8263-4424-3 (cloth : alk. paper)
  1. Chapman, Kenneth Milton, 1875–1968
  2. Anthropologists—New Mexico—Santa Fe—Biography.
  3. Archaeologists—New Mexico—Santa Fe—Biography.
  4. Museum curators—New Mexico—Santa Fe—Biography.
  5. Indian art—New Mexico—Santa Fe.
  6. Indians of North America—Antiquities—Collectors and
     collecting—New Mexico—Santa Fe.
  I. Barrie, Karen. II. Title.
     GN21.C485C53 2008
     301.092—dc22
         [B]
                                        2008015031

The authors wish to thank John Sheffield Chapman
for his generosity in assisting with the reproduction
of the color plates.

Designed and typeset by Mina Yamashita.
Composed in Minion Pro, an Adobe Original typeface
designed by Robert Slimbach.
Printed by Thomson-Shore, Inc. on 55# Natures Natural.

To my brightest lights, Damon and Jesse

Jesse would have been so proud

JC

For Jack and the synergistic best

of Barrie-Chapman love: Ward, Matt, SJ

KB

I tried several years ago to arouse the pride of the younger women in the good old designs of their own Pueblo and urged them to study and use them.

"But," they said, "[h]ow can we find out what kind of pottery our old people made? There is none left in the Pueblo. It is all gone; either worn out and broken, or it is sold to the 'Americanos' who buy things because they are old."

It was then that I saw the immediate need of giving the potters of each Pueblo a chance to study their own old decorative art, so that it might be revived in their hands if they really wished to use it.

—Kenneth M. Chapman

CONTENTS

LIST OF ILLUSTRATIONS / viii

PREFACE / xi

ACKNOWLEDGMENTS / xiii

CHAPTER 1: FORMING THE CLAY / 1

CHAPTER 2: A BEGINNING ARTIST / 22

CHAPTER 3: LAND OF ENCHANTMENT / 38

CHAPTER 4: AWAKENINGS / 69

CHAPTER 5: PASSIONS AND COMMITMENTS / 96

CHAPTER 6: ESTABLISHING AN IDENTITY / 118

CHAPTER 7: PROMISING DIRECTIONS / 144

CHAPTER 8: POTTERY AND POLITICS / 174

CHAPTER 9: CHAPMAN AND ROCKEFELLER / 202

CHAPTER 10: THE FOUNDING OF THE LABORATORY OF ANTHROPOLOGY / 228

CHAPTER 11: THE UNEXPECTED NAVIGATOR / 251

CHAPTER 12: THE EARTHEN VESSEL / 286

APPENDIX: A TAOS CREATION MYTH BY KENNETH MILTON CHAPMAN / 317

NOTES / 319

BIBLIOGRAPHY / 345

INDEX / 357

List of Illustrations

Chapman family portrait, 1892. / 3

Chapman family living room, c. 1892. / 12

Kenneth M. Chapman, c. 1898. / 34

Edgar Lee Hewett at Las Vegas Normal University, c. 1901. / 42

Frank Springer, c. 1915. / 45

Kenneth M. Chapman, 1915. / 53

Jesse L. Nusbaum and Alfred V. Kidder, 1908. / 64

Katherine "Kate" Muller, c. 1915. / 83

Staff and managing board of School of American Archaeology, c. 1910. / 86

Edgar Lee Hewett and staff at Rito de los Frijoles, c. 1910. / 87

Sylvanus G. Morley. / 102

Kate and Chap, c. 1915. / 109

Cartoon of 1916 Springer Expedition. / 122

Chapman with other painters on Palace of the Governors' patio. / 124

Tonita Roybal of San Ildefonso Pueblo, c. 1909–16. / 135

Julian and Maria Martinez, c. 1912. / 147

Chapman taking photos of pottery designs. / 160

The first Indian Fair, 1922. / 167

Chapman with his mother and daughter, c. 1925. / 197

John D. Rockefeller Jr. and Edgar Lee Hewett, 1924. / 211

Jesse L. Nusbaum, c. 1915. / 217

Alfred V. Kidder, c. 1920. / 229

Kenneth M. Chapman, 1929. / 239

Chapman supervising painting for Public Works of Art project, c. 1935. / 263

Chap and Kate, c. late 1930s. / 267

Kenneth M. Chapman and Maria Martinez, 1946. / 281

Chapman with his son, Frank Springer Chapman, 1952. / 300

Lucy Lewis of Acoma Pueblo and Kenneth M. Chapman, c. 1958. / 307

Members of the founding board of trustees of the Indian Arts Fund. / 310

Kenneth M. Chapman, self-portrait, 1962. / 313

Color plates follow page 194

Plate 1. Museum of Fine Arts watercolor, Kenneth M. Chapman, 1916

Plate 2. Conversion of St. Francis mural, painted by Kenneth M. Chapman, 1917

Plate 3. Cowkid, novelty card example, c. 1906

Plate 4. Silkscreen, undated

Plate 5. Chapman's line drawing on 1946 Centennial postage stamp

Plate 6. Gouache painting, Kenneth M. Chapman, 1903

Plate 7a. Detail from accession book for pottery by Kenneth M. Chapman for
 IAF catalog number 639, Santo Domingo bowl
  7b. Santo Domingo bowl (IAF.639), interior, artist unknown, c. 1900
  7c. Santo Domingo bowl (IAF.639), exterior, artist unknown, c. 1900

Plate 8a. Detail from accession book for pottery by Kenneth M. Chapman for
 IAF catalog number 9, Zuni water jars
  8b. Zuni water jar (IAF.9), artist unknown, c. 1880–90

Plate 9a. Detail from accession book for pottery by Kenneth M. Chapman for
 IAF catalog number 1166, San Ildefonso storage jar
  9b. San Ildefonso storage jar (IAF.1166), by Julian and Maria Martinez, 1926

PREFACE

The accomplishments of Kenneth Milton Chapman (1875–1968), artist and anthropologist, are as varied as they are significant: in his lifetime, he was recognized as the sole Anglo authority on the design elements of Pueblo pottery; he was a founding staff member of the Museum of New Mexico, the School of American Research, the Museum of Fine Arts, and the Laboratory of Anthropology in Santa Fe; he was the first professor of Indian arts at the University of New Mexico; and he was a leading force in the revitalization of Pueblo pottery in the 1920s, which led to the first Indian Fair (now Indian Market) and the founding of the Indian Arts Fund, one of the finest collections of Pueblo pottery in the world.

Our interest in Chapman was aroused in the early 1990s because of family connections: Janet is Chapman's grandniece and Karen is married to Chapman's grandnephew, Jack. We quickly recognized Chapman's importance in the fields of Indian arts and anthropology as well as in the history of Santa Fe. Chapman was a man of quiet strength and integrity with a handsome dose of humor. Our intent in this book is to convey the extent to which he lived his life by approaching professional issues with responsibility and awareness while at the same time pursuing, with a singleness of purpose, his personal passion for Indian arts.

Our biography covers Chapman's ancestry and his life from his early childhood in Indiana through his nearly seventy years in New Mexico. We have combined material from Chapman's unpublished memoirs (prepared during the 1950s when Chapman was in his seventies), his correspondence, and a thoroughly researched history of his life and times. Chapman was a fine writer, and his memoirs, in which he tells his own story to an unknown audience, are a special treasure. Deciding when to get out of his way and allow him to speak for himself was no easy task (we have chosen to use italics for quotations from Chapman's memoirs in the hope that this format will alert the reader to his voice while minimizing interruptions to narrative flow).

On balance, Chapman's memoirs contain much information about his early years and relatively little from the 1920s on. Thus we tend to quote more often from them in the early chapters of our book and have used them to establish the chronology of Chapman's life. Although the memoirs represent Chapman's hindsight, many other papers in Chapman's files contain substantial material that lends credibility to his powers of recall. For example, the files hold artwork from high school and afterward preserved by Chapman, notes written within hours or days of conversations, and multiple but nearly identical versions of troubling conflicts.

Not found in his memoirs are long ruminations about his family life or inner feelings. Chapman was an extremely private man. During the course of our research, we had occasion to look through boxes of Chapman's papers stored, at that time, with his son, Frank Chapman, in Albuquerque, New Mexico. The boxes contained a miscellany of articles, some significant and others that made us wonder why they had been saved. At one point, we pulled out a notebook. All of its pages were blank. "Is this his journal of emotions?" we asked. Frank laughed in agreement. Based on our sources, including our studies of private family papers, we believe that extensive personal information about Chapman is simply not available. For example, no letters survive from the mid-1910s, when he and his fiancée, Kate, were separated for several months. We do believe, however, that we have presented his character as best as we can determine through our interviews with his family and contemporaries as well as through our studies of correspondence with his friends and colleagues. The more we learned, the more pleased we were to be spending our time in the company of such a man.

ACKNOWLEDGMENTS

In many areas, shared authorship engendered nearly twice as many people to thank, as we both turned to respective resources as well as overlapping ones, which makes these acknowledgments a twice-blessed endeavor. While space does not permit identifying by name everyone who contributed to the creation of this book, we extend heartfelt gratitude to each and every person who helped us along the way, trusting you know you are appreciated even if you are not called out by name.

In that spirit, we wish first to thank Frank Springer Chapman and his wife, Jennie, who encouraged this book from its start in the early 1990s. We extend our deep appreciation to all with whom we spoke about Chapman's life and work. Their knowledge, wisdom, and wit added dimension to our portrait: Bruce Bernstein, J. J. Brody, David Caffey, Maria Chabot, John Chapman, Kay Chiba, John Conron, Kenneth Dauber, Carmelita Dunlap, Edwin Ferdon, Nancy Fox, Suzanne Newman Fricke, Barbara Gonzales, Frank Harlow, Peggy Harnisch, Michael Hering, Marjorie Lambert, Adam and Santana Martinez, Barbara Monroe, Nancy Parezo, Stewart Peckham, Bob Potter, Catherine Rayne, Sally Lewis Rodeck, Mary Lou Ross, Margaret Schmidt, and Fred Wendorf.

From coast to coast, librarians, curators, and staff assistants helped with tasks large and small: setting up appointments, providing guidance, pulling files, making copies, and performing myriad other services that made research efficient and energizing. We offer a special acknowledgment to Laura Holt, who led us to important files and extraordinary illustrations from the time we began our research (when she was a Laboratory of Anthropology staff member) up until we completed the final manuscript in 2007 (currently, she is librarian at the School for Advanced Research, Santa Fe). In addition, we were delighted to have met and worked with Jennifer Day, Estelle Rebec, and Christie Sturm (School for Advanced Research, formerly School of American Research); Sandra D'Emilio and Michelle Roberts (New Mexico Museum of Art, formerly Museum of Fine Arts, Santa Fe); Michelle Hiltzik (Rockefeller Archives, Pocantico Hills, Sleepy Hollow, New York); Diane Bird, Louise Stiver, and Willow Powers (Laboratory of Anthropology, Museum of Indian Arts and Culture, Santa Fe); Paul Benisek (Santa Fe Railroad, Schaumburg, Illinois); Tomas Jaehn, Oscar Romero, and Daniel Kosharek (New Mexico History Library and Photo Archives, Santa Fe); and Mima Kapches (Royal

Ontario Museum). Thanks also to Bob Willis of Albuquerque for his fine eye and illustration guidance during manuscript preparation.

Deep appreciation goes to our manuscript's reviewers, Bruce Bernstein of the Smithsonian Institution, National Museum of the American Indian, and Todd Bostwick, city archaeologist of Phoenix, Arizona, as well as to the editorial and design staff at University of New Mexico Press, particularly Maya Allen-Gallegos, MJ Devaney, and Mina Yamashita. Their fine input and oversight polished and beautifully set a rough-cut gem.

Finally, the authors extend profound love and gratitude to their ever-supportive family and friends, including Chap himself. Because of the discovery of his treasure trove, and the faith of those who shared the vision, this book came into being.

Thank you to one and all.

CHAPTER 1

FORMING THE CLAY

The Pueblo pot, stunning in its simplicity, is composed of the essentials. Clay from the earth. Paint from *guaco* (wild spinach). Heat from fire. The potter's hands mold it, form it, decorate it with stories that tell of rain clouds, feathered prayer sticks, serpents, and spider webs. The potter's heart brings to life the pot the clay has chosen. The clay is selfish, according to one Pueblo potter, saying, I want to be this, not what you want me to be. The clay forms itself, she says, but if the potter has a good intention and is one with the clay, the pot will please both the clay and the shaper. It will be an extension of the potter's spirit.[1]

A young Hoosier, twenty-five years old, Kenneth Milton Chapman is oblivious to these truths as he crouches in a canyon outside of Santa Fe in the early 1900s. His lanky body is bent close to the earth so that he can work his hands in the dirt, and he is thrilled when his long, slender fingers uncover sherds of ancient pottery. The pottery fragments tantalize him; they are like pieces to a puzzle. Bold black lines—waves of lines, spirals folding in on themselves—decorate rough gray clay. Chapman is immediately intrigued. The dig is led by Edgar Lee Hewett, president of New Mexico Normal University of Las Vegas, where Chapman teaches art. Chapman's inclination is to study these sherds with the appreciation of an artist and the precision of a scientist. He aches to define them. He cannot foresee that the sherds will also define him.

Chapman came to New Mexico in 1899, a twenty-three-year-old illustrator seeking a healthy climate for his fume-damaged lungs. By the time of his death in 1968, he had become "universally loved and esteemed in New Mexico."[2] In his lifetime, he was recognized as the sole Anglo authority on the design elements of Pueblo pottery and a major influence in the revitalization of potterymaking that took place in the 1920s. He was a founding staff member of the Museum of New Mexico, the School of American Research, the Museum of Fine Arts in Santa Fe, and the Laboratory of Anthropology, and he was the originator of Indian Fair, forerunner to today's Indian Market. He also cofounded the Indian Arts Fund (IAF), which amassed a comprehensive collection of Pueblo pottery and whose aims were to preserve the pottery of the post-Spanish period, to educate all in the artistic quality of the pottery, and to serve as a resource for Pueblo Indians.

Nearly seventy years of Chapman's quietly exceptional life were spent on south-western soil, but the clay on which he was raised was midwestern in origin—the black, fertile farmland of Indiana. Chapman was born on July 13, 1875, in Ligonier, a small town in northeast Indiana dotted with small lakes, green pastures, and the remains of ancient forests. He was the family's middle child, second son of Mary Cordelia White and John Milton "Milt" Chapman. His brother, Dwight, was two years older and his sister, Vera, six years younger.

The Chapman family enjoyed a relatively stable and comfortable life in northern Indiana. They made major moves twice as a family, both within the state—to Albion in 1876, four years after Mary and Milt were married, and then to South Bend in 1882. Milt Chapman was primarily a businessman. He was thereby not only following in the steps of his own father who spent his career as an entrepreneur but also placing him-self squarely in the Industrial Age in which he was raising his family. He engaged in several business ventures during his lifetime, such as brokerage, insurance, and small manufacturing (running, for example, a basket factory). Chapman remembered the basket factory particularly because of its business card, which bore the picture of a large shaggy dog. As children, too young to understand the subtleties of advertising, he and his brother, Dwight, had agreed that it was very thoughtful of their father to thus immortalize their own dog, Shep.[3]

Chapman's mother, Mary, painted. A competent student of art in her midtwenties, she continued to paint throughout her life, occasionally giving lessons to neighbors. Although Chapman did not recall his mother teaching him to draw, he recognized that her talent must have touched the family in many ways, not the least of which was in its strong influence on his own life's direction.

Both of Chapman's parents came from families who were longtime residents of the area, originally the Northwest Territory. This area, which came to include Ohio, Indiana, Illinois, Michigan, Wisconsin, and eastern Minnesota, had been first settled by the French, then won by the English, and finally acquired by the United States after the Revolutionary War. Settlers began to arrive in 1785. Milt's father, George Washington Chapman, was an Ohio native, born in Stark County, about fifty miles south of Cleveland, on February 18, 1818. Mary's ancestors were early pioneers of both Ohio and Indiana.

Settlement in the Northwest Territory brought Chapman's great-grandparents free-dom of movement, but with that freedom came the dangers and discomforts of the frontier. They were also witness to the disappearance of an entire culture. The Eastern Woodlands tribes, or Mound Builders, had flourished in the Mississippi Valley as early as the year 700 AD, building large monuments of earth as burial places and platforms for temples and houses of chiefs. Their arts and crafts are said to have rivaled those of ancient Mexico and Peru. But by 1830, they had vanished. The 1794 Battle of Fallen

Chapman family portrait, 1892: Dwight and Kenneth (standing), John Milton, Mary Cordelia, and Vera. (Courtesy of School for Advanced Research Archives, AC02 749c.)

Timbers in Ohio had led to the tribes' ceding southern Ohio and eastern Indiana to the United States. In 1830, Congress passed the Indian Removal Act, which allowed the government to move the remaining Indians west of the Mississippi River. By the time that Chapman's grandparents reached adulthood, the only signs of the early inhabitants that remained were the mounds they left behind.

George Washington Chapman, Chapman's paternal grandfather, was his only living grandparent. Chapman described him in his unpublished memoirs as a man who, *without being an out-and-out grocer, or hardware dealer, or any other particular kind of merchant,** kept stores.[4] He would purchase a store in one of the little northern Indiana towns, run it for a while, and then sell it at a profit. According to a family chart prepared by Chapman, his grandfather and first wife, Hannah McFarland, began their family in Ohio, where Chapman's father, Milt, was born on April 9, 1844, an underweight and slight child.[5] Milt was their firstborn, followed by three sisters, Sarah, Isabelle, and Josephine. The family moved to Roanoke, Indiana, in about 1850 where, unhappily, two new siblings, Harriet and Joseph, died in infancy, and where, when Milt was about ten, his mother passed away. He and his sisters remained with their father, who soon married Harriet Horton. Their daughter, Lillie, and son, Charley, were born in the 1860s, when Milt was in his teens.

In midlife, George used his talents to expand his opportunities. In Ligonier, he was ordained as a minister of the Protestant denomination Disciples of Christ, served a term as a state legislator—presumably Republican—and also began a new career as an investor in farm mortgages. Chapman remembered his grandfather dressing for the latter role, going about his business in a frock coat and high silk hat and carrying a gold-headed cane. Chapman maintained, however, that this elegance was the only resemblance to the heartless money-lending villain of the popular melodramas of the period. *Grandfather was mightily impressive, but a good man and well liked by his neighbors, including his clients*, Chapman recalled.[6]

Chapman's father grew to manhood in an area marked by increased settlement, as Indiana's economy blossomed because of the railroads' push into the state in the 1850s. Young adulthood found Milt facing the Civil War, which began three days after he turned seventeen in 1861. The North passed its draft law in March 1863—when Milt was close to celebrating his nineteenth birthday—which declared that all white men between the

---

* As noted in the preface, we have used italics for all direct quotes from Chapman's unpublished memoirs, archived at the School for Advanced Research (formerly the School of American Research). Chapman drafted these memoirs during the 1950s when he was about seventy-five; primarily, they cover his childhood, his early years in New Mexico, the difficulties he experienced in working with Edgar Lee Hewett, and his meeting with John D. Rockefeller Jr.

ages of twenty and forty-five were to be drafted. A year later, a bout with pneumonia left Milt weak and in ill health. To keep Milt out of war, his father paid the accepted fee of three hundred dollars in place of the draft and sent Milt to Butler College in Indianapolis for a year, where he studied geometry, algebra, and Greek—and admitted to feeling homesick. A diary that Milt kept at the time indicates a conscientious, precise, and sensitive young man with a decided flair for the dramatic:[7]

Wednesday, Jan. 11[,] [1865]

Arose at 6½, washed, commenced study, ate breakfast. studied, prepared for School . . . went to Legislature there was a joint session to elect an Agent of State, Publish printer, &c Republicans successful in every instance . . . Studied on Greek Algebra Geometry, all evening. retired at near eleven. the Moon peeped forth at an early hour in her full grown beauty, dispersed her radiant Charms in lavish profusion, as if her sympathies were enlisted in behalf of those nocturnal parties who enjoyed her radiant effulgence as the merry jingling bells, and outgushing of patriotic airs and the rapturous laughter of the passers by attested.

Friday, Jan. 13

Arose at 5–½, washed, studied, etc. . . . went to the City in afternoon, called on Chas Barnhart. Came home tryed to study. but had to pace the floor, all afternoon, while every nerve in my whole system seemed at times to quiver under the excrutiating tortures of the toothache. . . . retired at 10–20 hope I will get some sleep tonight.

Sunday, Jan. 15

Arose at 6¾, was awakened at about 5½ by a violent aching of my tooth. washed. ate breakfast nothing that ingenuity could suggest would appease my tooth I paced the floor suffering almost indescribable torment, my agony was so great that sweat exuded from the fires of my head, I resolved to have it pulled. started at 9½ for "Johnston" the dentist, gone to Church . . . waited, he came, went down to his office. he pulled it, very much of a gentleman, came home, tooth bled all afternoon & evening. . . .

Monday, Jan. 16

Arose at 6½. hail, all hail, the prominent feature of my diary for the past 2 or three days, viz that irrepressible toothache, shall never again be emblazoned in too legible characters to me. never again shall every nerve seem to be stretched to its utmost tension, and vibrate to the attuning hand of its excrutiating tune, never again shall the sun set in his gorgeous radiance, or the Moon march in her grand and queenly dignity through the barriers of clouds, and behold me in the throes of agony & pain from that tooth.

The following year—minus one tooth—Milt traveled to Poughkeepsie, New York, where he attended Eastman Business School for a year, returning in late 1866 to manage one of his father's businesses, a hardware store in Ligonier, Indiana. Possibly, he became acquainted then with Mary Cordelia White, a young woman of twenty-two, the same age he was, who lived and taught school in the county seat, Albion. Like Milt, Mary had lost a parent at an early age; but Mary's childhood seemed framed by loss. Before her seventh birthday, Mary had lost her father, mother, stepfather, and grandmother.

Mary's family had early settled in the area. Her father, Westley White, was born in 1812 to Mary Higley and John White II, a settler to Ashtabula in eastern Ohio from Granby, Connecticut. Westley was well educated for his time and pursued a career as a civil engineer. The success of the Erie Canal, completed in 1825 when Westley was thirteen, opened up the Great Lakes region to ships from the Atlantic Ocean and prompted a massive but short-lived burst of canal building in the country, which Westley later participated in as surveyor. Westley left home, on horseback, at age eighteen. His work meant days of traveling and rough conditions, which often ended in illness, including malaria. In April 1837, he wrote that "I am so weary with misfortune and hard tugged by disease that I would set my fortune on almost any chance to mend it or loose [sic] my all."[8] Fortune responded. Westley recovered, and in less than two years his life brightened when he met and married Jane Skinner of Noble County, Indiana.

Jane was the daughter of James Skinner and Harriet Beymer—two of Noble County's first settlers—and granddaughter to early Ohio pioneers. Her grandfathers Rueben Skinner and George Beymer II were pioneers together in New Haven, Ohio, in 1815. Beymer built the first schoolhouse in the township and established the first line of stages in Ohio, which ran from Wheeling, West Virginia, to Chillicothe, Ohio. James and Harriet must have become acquainted during those early frontier days; their marriage in 1819 was the township's first, and they raised at least six children there, including Jane who was born in 1822. But pioneering was in their blood, and James and Harriet chose to move to Noble County, in northeast Indiana, in 1836 where they, along with six other families, founded Jefferson Township. Perhaps Westley became acquainted with the family when his surveying work took him out of Ohio and into Indiana. The Skinners thought well enough of Westley to ask him to be their attorney.

After their marriage in 1839, Westley and Jane remained in Noble County, where their first child, Wilson (known as "Witt") was born in 1842. As they looked forward to the birth of their second child in 1844, thirty-two-year-old Westley was conscientious in caring for his family's welfare, combining his surveying career with the duties of county clerk, postmaster, and owner of a small dry goods store. Tragedy, however, arrived when an intense summer storm washed away a nearby bridge. A letter from twenty-year-old Jane, seven months pregnant, written in late September to Westley's father, John White II, tells of her heartbreak.[9]

> Dear Father,
>
> You will excuse me for my neglect of writing to you being unable to write in consequence of little Wilson being sick he has been very sick about four weeks with the chill and fever but is now getting better I have quit keeping house and sold off all of my things and am now at my Father's. . . .
>
> Since Mr. Whites death I have been incapable of doing my work my affliction seem to be so great to think I am deprived of one that I have taken so mutch comfort with one that was kind and willing to do anything for his family but he is gone and nothing have I to reflect on myself if I had ever been unkind to him I could not bear my affliction. . . .
>
> It seems if that was the time and place for him to die and therefore I feel more reconciled to give him up. In the morning he was very busy at work he came in and said he was agoing down to the river in which I insisted on him to stay at home but all of no avail He went down with several other men to save the bridge He and others was astanding on the bridge it started to go off and they crossed on the other side—they fixed a rope across and insisted on him to take hold but he thought he would try and swim without taking hold of it. It appeared that he could not swim when they saw that he was adrowning Several of the men went in after him but they could not get him. I would be glad to see you if you can a come out and see me at any time I would be glad to have you come . . . write to me often and I will endeavor to answer yours.

Within this sorrow, Mary Cordelia White was born on November 22, 1844, in her grandfather's home, where she grew into a toddler. Later, the grief her mother knew was transformed into hope by her acquaintance with William J. Engle, an innkeeper with a fervent desire to marry her. Engle was also widowed, with two children just older than Mary and Witt. Before the marriage, however, the families made a long journey—a journey that included two extended wagon rides, a canal ride through the locks near Toledo, and another boat ride on Lake Erie—to Ashtabula, Ohio, the home of Westley's father, because Jane "felt that she ought not marry again without consulting grandfather White."[10]

With White's blessing, Jane and William married on November 24, 1849. They moved into their home in Noble County, where five-year-old Mary spent Christmas. There was "a fireplace where the four pairs of stockings were hung—and Christmas morning I was happy with my first china doll—and firmly believed Santa had brought it by way of the chimney—and to further the delusion Father Engle made impressions of sled runner tracks upon the wood house roof in the snow."[11] Several months later, she awoke to find a "dear little half sister—named Harriet for our grandmother—but called Hattie—[who] grew to be very lovely with curly golden hair like our dear mother."[12] But the family's restored happiness was short lived. In May 1851, Mary and Witt lost both their mother and stepfather to a strep epidemic; within two days, they also lost their Grandmother Skinner. Completely orphaned, the children were separated. The Engle children went to their grandparents in Philadelphia, and the Ohio Skinners took in Mary and Witt. Mary's childhood was spent first with one of Jane's sisters on their farm. Later she returned to Albion, Indiana, where Grandfather Skinner lived until 1873. There, she lived with another aunt and taught in the local school.

It is not clear what prompted Mary to leave her teaching position at the age of twenty-four to spend a year at Granville Female Seminary in Ohio. But the school offered a drawing class, which so intrigued her that she transferred the next year to J. Insco Williams's art school in Cincinnati. There, Mary sat for a portrait by Williams, whose portrait and landscape paintings sold well, especially to a society that embraced the innovation of decorative items produced en masse by covering all available wall space. Williams urged Mary to remain in Cincinnati and make copies of his work for sale, but Mary chose instead to return to Albion in 1871. Perhaps this time the reason was love, for she and Milt married there on September 10, 1872. They set up house in Ligonier, where Milt was managing one of his father's hardware stores.

Their first child, Dwight, was born September 21, 1873. Kenneth—known as "Buddy" to his family—followed in July almost two years later.* In 1876, the family moved to nearby Albion. For Mary, it was a return to the town where her family had first settled. Her brother, Witt, also made his home there with his wife, Lou. During an era in which new industries were developing—when inventions like the typewriter (1867), telephone (1876), phonograph (1877), and electric light (1879) were radically changing business and its culture—Milt pursued several lines of business. In Albion,

---

* According to Chapman, the name of Kenneth, which was wished on him by one of his mother's aunts, was a headache from childhood on. He found it especially annoying after moving to South Bend, Indiana, from Albion (where he had been known as Buddy), because he had to explain it to "each and every new school mate, for such a name as Kenneth was unheard of in those days." To his great relief, he became known as "Chap" when he left Indiana to live in the larger cities, such as Chicago. In his memoirs, he relates that during his early years in Santa Fe, his wife met a totally deaf matron who said, by sign language, "I want a good name for our new boy. I like the looks of the name, Kenneth. Does it *sound* nice?" Chap regretted that he was not there to interpose with the sly gesture of pinching his nose.

among other professions, he served as local agent for the Studebaker wagons, which had evolved from a small South Bend blacksmith and wagon shop into the largest wagon manufacturer in the country.

Albion, with a population of less than two thousand, was Chapman's world until he was nearly seven. He recalled its *town square, bordered by stores with hitching-posts in front and dominated by the dingy brick bulk of the county courthouse in its center. Our house, a simple white frame cottage, was two blocks from the square. A barn and other outbuildings stood behind it, and beyond these the town commons stretched its flat expanse of blue-grass sod to the marshy banks of "Little Run," a small creek that for me . . . held all the watery wealth of the Mississippi.*[13]

Since Albion had no museum, preschoolers Dwight and Buddy, born at the dawn of the museum age (1875–1920), set about remedying the situation with their own collections at home. Like most collections-mad Victorian families, the Chapmans kept a curio cabinet in the parlor for the family's collectibles, and their mother assigned two shelves for the boys' less repellent specimens (the live snakes, frogs, and occasional fish worms were denied this top exhibition space). The assortment included a group of what Chapman described as *strange water-worn pebbles that, as I look back on it, must have been fossil corals from some beach at the north end of Lake Michigan, perhaps Petoskey.*[14] A part-time evangelist who worked for them occasionally as a carpenter had found the oddities under the front porch. The "God-stones," as the boys called them, were a proud feature of their collection.

Their preoccupations, however, were not always so exemplary; trouble found them easily enough. A whittling mishap of Buddy's caused a split thumb, which was attended to in his mother's absence by his father, who was inclined to faint at such sights. On several occasions, Buddy's inclination to go along with his friends' plans or Dwight's schemes led straight to mischief. He was about five when he fell into a deep muddy pool and had to be fished out with a long pole by his companions, who then took him home, hid him in the barn until his clothes were dry, and left him to explain to his skeptical parents that, completely untutored, he had learned to swim. An inspiration of Dwight's led to another adventure when he suggested that it would be interesting if Buddy were to be lowered to the ground by a rope from the barn's loft. Buddy was supposed to hang onto the rope with both hands but, as a safety precaution, Dwight tied the end of the rope to one of Buddy's ankles.

All went well until my hands reached the door-sill, then as the rope pinched my fingers I let go and fell head down. Luckily, my yelling as I dangled there by one foot brought a passing farmer on the run from his wagon, cursing heartily at Dwight and telling him to hold on to the rope. By then mother, too (and probably all the rest of Albion), had heard the commotion and reached us just as the farmer was lowering me to the ground. He was all for giving Dwight the paddling which both of us deserved, but finally accepted mother's thanks and went back to his waiting team, muttering his opinion about the sanity of Milt Chapman's young 'uns.[15]

More formal entertainment—fairs, circuses, vaudeville shows, and sporting events—found their way to Albion. Chapman recalled being taken to a one-ring circus by their housekeeper, Mrs. Wescott, when he was about four, and then *marching around and around our yard at home afterwards, carrying our pets in their cages in what seemed to us an entirely reasonable facsimile of a full-blown circus parade.*[16] An impressive event in the late summer of 1880 was the presidential campaign, which included torch-light parades, flag waving, and noise making, followed by Dwight and Buddy's version of such parades with six or eight Very Young Republicans toting candle-lit Chinese lanterns in the humid, grain-filled air of a midwestern evening.

Near tragedy struck when Chapman's father, who traveled in the country to farms and nearby towns on brokerage business, contracted typhoid fever. He was bedridden for many weeks, which surely worried Mary, who was too familiar with loss. Milt survived and as is so often the case, the seriousness of the situation did not impress itself on Chapman as a small boy. He remembered the illness mostly as an opportunity to try a taste of the tart fruit tamarind, which the doctor recommended to spark his father's diminished appetite.

In the summer of 1881, the family visited Milt's sister, Josephine Chapman Meagher, who lived with her husband, Edward, and three children in South Bend. Milt and Ed became interested in the development of the South Bend Malleable Iron Works, where Ed hoped to manufacture an improved wheeled plow, called Solid Comfort, which he had invented and patented. Returning from the more sophisticated South Bend, Chapman's parents might have been struck by Albion's relatively rural character. Their barn housed the family mare, Nellie, and a cow for the family's milk, butter, and cheese. There was plenty of fresh food from their garden and chickens enough for eggs and an occasional Sunday dinner. Squawks from the unhappy fowl selected by their hired man, Will Marshall, for the chopping block were the boys' signal to run to the barnyard to watch. According to Chapman, in September 1881, *when we were awakened by the familiar sound we jumped out of bed and ran to the barnyard. No Will, no signs of a sacrificed chicken! The squawking had ceased . . . and then father came out and herded us, still mystified, back to bed. After breakfast he led us into his and mother's bedroom for our first look at our new baby sister, Vera.*[17]

While their mother tended their infant sister, Dwight and Buddy started school together in a brick, four-room schoolhouse in Albion. Dwight had not been well, so his mother had taught him at home for a year. When he and Buddy entered grammar school in 1881, Buddy was six years old, and Dwight was just about to turn eight. They remained classmates throughout their schooling, which, given their age difference, probably meant they were always having to explain why they were together. Conceivably, the situation also aroused a competitive impulse in Chapman, for he says that he was especially determined to do well in high school after he overheard a neighbor tell his mother, *"Oh well, I suppose Buddy will find it hard to keep up with Dwight from now on. Two years difference in their ages does count a lot, you know." I said to myself then, "I'll show you."*[18]

In 1882, the family moved to South Bend, where Chapman's father and uncle joined in incorporating the ironworks as the Economist Plow Company along with a third partner, Leighton B. Pine. Milt held the position of secretary and treasurer. The teaming appeared to be successful; by 1886, the factory's employees numbered over two hundred. Chapman recalled that as boys he and Dwight could roam throughout the factory, provided they did not distract the workers, and that they took a lively interest in all the activity from the loading of the furnace to the pouring of the molten iron.

Buddy and Dwight were again classmates in South Bend, beginning the second grade together. Chapman recalled complaining often of stomachache throughout his grade school years, and though often genuinely ill, he used the excuse at least once to go fishing. Outside of school, Buddy and Dwight were both relatively free from chores and able to spend long hours with their "gang," which usually included cousins Mark and Ed *with their older sister Isabella sometimes taking a hand to keep us all on the paths of righteousness.*[19] They swam, skated, flew kites, played ball . . . and concocted imaginative tricks. Chapman recalled one summer evening, when

perhaps one of us had tried talking through our lawn hose and found that sound carried well through it. That gave us a new idea. We ran the hose from a front window, across the porch, and carefully beside the front walk to one of the gate posts, and up a foot or more behind it. The posts, built of boards, were nearly a foot square and perhaps five feet in height. When everything was set, we tested it and found that our voices would carry for several feet. So we trooped indoors, lay down at the window of our darkened living room, and when one of us spotted an approaching victim another opened up with, "Help! Help! Let me out!" There were various reactions: Some would stop and listen—then hustle away without stopping. Finally one man stopped, came up to the post and asked, "Where are you?" Then came the reply, "In this post. Aw Mister, please help me out o' here." He stared for a moment and then made a hasty get-away.[20]

John Milton, Mary Cordelia, Vera, and Kenneth in Chapman home,
South Bend, Indiana, c. 1892. Photograph by Dwight Chapman.
(Courtesy of School for Advanced Research Archives, AC02 749b.)

The Chapman family flourished in South Bend. They moved twice within the city,
and both homes were located in the city's best residential district.[21] The plow factory
grew steadily and, after the death of his brother-in-law from tuberculosis in 1886, Milt
assumed full supervision. He traveled to Pittsburgh and other cities to negotiate with
steel mills for materials, occasionally taking along either Dwight or Buddy. Chapman's
mother managed the household but also painted and offered drawing lessons to neighbors. She belonged to the Woman's Literary Club, for which she researched topics as
exotic as the flora of India. An avid bird lover, she also recorded her own bird lore.[22]

One night during, not unusual, sleepless hours, I heard stealthly [sic] footsteps upon the roof of my sleeping porch. Then silence—followed by an agonizing shriek from a mother bird, and the rapidly retreating steps of the prowler. Then I realized that a shocking domestic tragedy had overtaken my little feathered neighbors.

For days I had enjoyed the courting and nestmaking of two dear little house finches. The site they had chosen for their home was just under the eaves of my porch. As days went by there was great mutual happiness over the tiny eggs[,] . . . an omen of cherished hope and parental joy.

Many times a day the father bird, as he perched upon a nearby branch of a little tree in the patio, sang to his dear little mate, praising her for her patient devotion to her wifely duties—trying by his song, and provision of food, to shew his love and appreciation of her waiting, weary hours.

The next morning after the tragedy I heard the accustomed morning song—but there was no responsive "peep" from the nest. Thinking the weary mate was asleep, he quietly withdrew. These attempts to win the usual response from his mate continued for a day or two. Evidently he was unconscious of the awful desolation which had befallen his home, but at last he seemed to realize the futility of his efforts, and departed.

I had so admired his devotion and faithfulness that I must confess to a feeling of hopefulness the next spring that he might return with a new mate and set up housekeeping again in the vacant nest—But he never returned.

At home, the boys were well liked and popular, as was their sister, Vera, who enjoyed the status of a fancy tricycle. Chapman's strongest impression of the early 1880s is that they were simply starved for music. On their own, they took up instruments to entertain their parents and Vera, with Buddy switching from harmonica to fiddle to mandolin and finally settling on the guitar.

Chapman's memoirs relate a childhood rich in action—he and his friends tested their courage at the local swimming hole, experimented with used pistols (and managed to avoid catastrophe), hiked along the riverside, and built a boat seaworthy enough for a forty-mile trip down the river. He seemed to feel secure in these friendships; he was confident and open among his friends and enjoyed the company of others. But as he grew into his teens, he found himself becoming more and more self-conscious, especially in public recitations at school. In one instance, he talked his teacher into letting him play his harmonica instead of giving a speech. In another, he opted to write and recite a short story to the class in place of public speaking. *With full confidence that I had something on the ball, I marched up and read it off without a qualm. The applause, mainly from the boys, went far beyond my expectation. I felt myself blushing to the roots of my hair, and was glad to get back at my seat at the rear of the room.*[23]

Thus he seemed to gravitate toward activities that offered him an outlet for his curiosity and the chance to be with small groups of friends or even alone. Unlike Dwight, who was more extroverted, Buddy intensely disliked organized groups. He was not always a stellar student—he had to attend summer school for arithmetic and grammar to pass the eighth grade—but he had a lively intellect anytime his curiosity could be satisfied. History, and that of American Indians in particular, caught his imagination. Before the eighth grade, Chapman read and reread the opening lines of his history book on American Indians, even committing certain parts to memory. In later years when he came on a used 1885 edition of Barnes's *A Brief History of the United States*, he found he *was letter perfect with one short remembered sentence, "He apologized, therefore, to the animals he killed and made solemn promises to fishes that their bones would be respected."*[24]

The summer school course between eighth grade and high school taught him a lesson more valuable than the math and grammar credit he had to earn. After a sullen first day's performance, the "holy terror" Miss Tieche confronted him:

"Now Kenneth, I want you to sit up and look me straight in the eye. You're not dumb. Your report card shows you can learn if you want to. You're just plain stubborn. Your other grades were good. How on earth did you get a 98 mark in history?" "Because I liked it." "But you didn't learn your history by just liking it, did you?" "No, I studied hard because I liked it." "All right then," she said, "beginning today, suppose you start studying arithmetic and grammar the same way. First learn the few rules and definitions I have given you . . . and then try the examples. You may surprise yourself by finding that you are beginning to like what you have learned." Within a week I began to see the point, turned in satisfactory papers and even tried some extra work of my own.

. . . At the close of the term . . . Miss Tieche called me to her desk and said, "Kenneth, I want to tell you something. That first day I thought we were in for trouble. I know bad boys—mean boys, and I thought you were one of them. You scowled, you hardly spoke. But you are not really like that, and what's the use pretending that you are.

"We all have to do things that we don't like, and now that you have made a good start with two things you said you hated, I hope you will keep on until you really get to liking it. And one other thing. You will find in high school that nobody is going to tell you how or when to work. You will have to do the thinking for yourself. And if you fall behind—out you go! They're crowded already and haven't room for idlers."[25]

Pep talks come in various disguises. The coaching Buddy received that day stuck with him, apparently verbatim! It must have sustained him many times when he found himself saddled with a task to which he was not inclined.

Collecting continued to appeal not only because it was in fashion but also because it let him delve deeply into one subject. By the end of grade school, Buddy had at one time or another collected stamps, postmarks, tobacco tags, birds' eggs, seashells, fossil corals, and crinoid stems. But then his collecting turned to Indian relics. His interest in hunting for relics was aroused when he and some friends, on a Sunday hike down the river, passed a field where two men were strolling across a newly plowed field and occasionally stooping to pick up something of apparent interest. One of them showed the boys a good arrowhead he had just found. Buddy and the others tried for a few minutes without luck.

Later on, however, I tried it again, and was so much encouraged by my finds that I soon made hunting the main object of my hikes from then on. Time after time through spring, summer, and fall, I tramped through corn fields, wheat stubble and turnip patches, bordering the river paths, and soon as interest grew, I traded off my stamps, tobacco tags and miscellany and concentrated on Indian relics.[26]

He entered his collection of relics in the county fair, where all the collections were arranged in glass cases amid displays of needlework, jams, and cake. At the fair, he had occasion to study the collections of veteran relic hunters. The annual competition was keen—the winners earned prizes of $15 or more, a fabulous amount at the time. In the student category, Buddy twice won the first prize of $8.

Buddy also liked things he could "see." If Chapman's later sketches are any indication—renderings of pots and designs that were found in newspaper margins and on the backs of napkins—Buddy was probably drawing and doodling on any available surface at home. He attended his first drawing class when he was about ten—whether at his mother's urging or his own request is not known—which was conducted after school by Etta Sheehan. The class began with freehand drawing of parallel lines, triangles, squares, and then circles (the circles being more or less lopsided and angular in spots, recalled Chapman). Then they progressed to outline drawings of simple, familiar objects and finally to light and shade. *It was slow, exacting, and tedious work for a kid, for my drawings were made in a pretentious sketch-book, each page of which had to pass inspection before I was given the next problem. But it did develop a certain degree of patience, and a facility for drawing that proved very useful later on in my high school courses.*[27]

If Sheehan encouraged eye-hand coordination to the detriment of creativity, Buddy had found another way to express his ingenuity: *I seem to have had some way of putting things together,—rabbit hutches, a cage for a hawk with a broken wing, . . . and numerous contrivances such as a little lathe, built with odds and ends from old sewing machines, and other scraps from the pile at the factory.*[28]

Summer vacations with his cousins on a farm in Michigan, business trips with his father to the steel mills in Pittsburgh, and a pleasure trip to Chicago with his mother enlarged his worldview. His clearest recollection of a pre-1893 visit to Chicago was touring the World's Columbian Exposition building on the lakefront, before the fair opened, where there were band concerts at all hours and varied exhibits by merchants, including a curio dealer's collection of Indian relics and beadwork. A business trip with his father in 1889 brought them to Detroit, Niagara Falls, New York, Philadelphia, and Washington, DC.

In the nation's capital, Bud and his father toured the Smithsonian and the National Museum of Natural History. At the time of their visit, the Smithsonian was about forty years old. To foster its programs, the institute relied on support from members of the American Association for the Advancement of Science, such as Louis Agassiz, professor of geology and zoology at Harvard, and Lewis Henry Morgan, a railroad attorney with an interest in American Indians.[29] Morgan was a key player in the transition from ethnology to modern American anthropology, which occurred between about 1870 and 1910, alongside the emergence of natural history museums. Morgan's anthropological theories drove the field, including Southwest studies, for many years, and he supported John Wesley Powell, who led a significant survey of the West after the Civil War and formed the Bureau of Ethnology under the Smithsonian in 1879.[30] The bureau's first anthropology team (James Stevenson, Matilda Coxe Stevenson, John "Jack" K. Hillers, and Frank Hamilton Cushing) sent back wagonloads of specimens that represented the Hopi, Acoma, Zuni, and Zia cultures to the Smithsonian between 1879 and 1887.

Thus Bud and his father likely would have gazed at shelves of southwestern pottery. At the time, most eastern museums displayed their collections to educate immigrant and middle class audiences about Native societies, which the anthropologists believed were rapidly vanishing. Ironically, the museums themselves became implicit monuments to a dominant, expansionist, and scientific Anglo culture. Enthralled with the collections, Bud may not have realized that many specimens had not only been taken "in the dead of night," but had been transported from Southwest mesas to eastern museums solely to satisfy scientific curiosity even as contemporary native cultures were overlooked.[31] His most vivid recollection was envy. After viewing crowded case after crowded case of treasures, he told his father that he knew he would be sick when he returned to his little collection at home![32]

By high school, Bud was both enthused by learning and dismayed by the increasing demands that he assume a more public persona. He was happiest in his classes.

Mathematics plagued him still, but he did well in most courses—he was particularly fond of Latin, biology, and physics. This last, in particular, allowed him to put his originality and manual dexterity to use. He reveled in physics and its attendant equipment, and he helped to rig pendulums, devise scales, develop gadgets for innovative experiments, and even build an electric motor from improvised parts. And despite a poor showing in algebra, *in my senior year I made a top grade in the much dreaded plane geometry. That was something I could see!*[33]

Social situations—get-togethers, evening parties, hayrides—continued to make Bud miserable. As the years passed, he flatly refused to attend some gatherings, against Dwight's protests. Possibly his physical stature contributed to his discomfort. Bud, who was thin and well over six feet tall, describes himself as *reaching up to full Chapman height, but without the muscular strength to compete . . . in boxing, wrestling, and other usual outlets of youthful energy.*[34] He later commented that he *had stretched up too spindly to handle myself well,* and avoided team sports.[35] *When foot-ball was organized in our Junior year, the gang put pressure on me and ordered me out for a try-out. I made my first dash across the field and was given one slight sidewise push that twisted my left knee. That was enough; I limped across to the side line and handed in my resignation.*[36]

In his last year of high school, Bud was elected president of his class, which by then had dwindled from an initial sixty freshmen to twenty-one seniors. Though he generally shunned public recognition, he accepted because he fully expected that the job would entail only a few informal meetings without any parliamentary fuss. Several weeks passed before he realized what lay before him: a toast at the annual banquet, the address at commencement exercises, and officiating as toastmaster at class parties. The prospect made him miserable, but rather than resign, he tried to make the best of it. Recognizing that the social obligations of the office meant he had to have a partner, he asked a girl to accompany him to parties and events she *accepted the situation very sensibly and I hope was pleased to have done her bit for old times sake.*[37] Bud carried out his duties but felt burdened by a sense of failure. *I managed to somehow live through it all, but with the conviction that I had let them all down, the alumni, my classmates, and the girl by my side.*[38]

Bud's self-consciousness was accompanied by a tendency to perfectionism—perhaps fueled by his academic competition with Dwight—and a genuine need to remain private, which was manifest even at home.

One thing that I remember most clearly is my resentment at being reminded so often of my blunders. . . . Mother, in her old age, commented at times on the differences between Dwight and myself. Dwight, she said, was more dependent on affection, and confided more in her. . . . But I had little to say, and was inclined to block any move to invade my privacy. When displeased or distressed, I would show it by sulking and perhaps wandering off by myself, until some diversion brought me back into the circle, and the incident was soon forgotten.[39]

Hiking alone in the country appealed to Bud's sense of privacy, but the feelings of loneliness he experienced surprised him. Although he had always felt at ease walking alone at night to the library or park, he felt disturbed by his initial acquaintance with genuine silence.

Once I had planned a Saturday hike with Norm Harris, about Dwight's age, but for some reason he was needed at home. That left me with my lunch and "nowhere to go." It was then that I decided to try it alone. It was a new and somewhat startling situation. All went well until I passed the edge of town, but from there on, a strange silence fell, or rather, for the first time, I was made conscious of it. I would walk for some distance until I was overcome with an urge to turn and look behind. Meeting a few returning fisherman brought occasional relief, but the feeling of being followed did not leave me until I came to an open field where I planned to look for arrow heads. From then on, I seemed to forget it, and on the return trip, I began to test my ability to forge ahead to some landmark without turning.

    Gradually the feeling of loneliness wore off as I took other hikes, until, at the close of my high school years, I welcomed every chance to get away by myself. Out of it grew a feeling of independence that was to prove a useful asset in my years spent in the larger cities. I enjoyed congenial companionship perhaps even more, in contrast with solitude, but I was never at a loss for amusement when left to myself.[40]

Drawing became increasingly important to Bud. In the library, he became absorbed in pen drawings, spending hours poring over the comics of that time—*Puck, Judge,* and *Texas Siftings.* Most drawings were linecuts in pen and ink. Chap not only became absorbed in the techniques, given various twists by professional illustrators, but began to entertain serious ideas about a career in the field.[41] He applied skills learned in Sheehan's drawing class to his biology assignments, recording dissections of earthworms, crayfish, and grasshoppers through intricately detailed pencil drawings. A science teacher noticed Bud's drawing of a perch and proceeded to count the number of scales, from top to bottom, much to Bud's surprise. *"Pretty good,"* he said, *"You came within one or two of the correct number." I had done it by eye only, not realizing that each bass, pickerel, or sun fish has its own formula.*[42]

A practical application of his artistic skills came by way of their high school annual, *The Rubicon.* Bud worked as artist on it; a friend and classmate, Walter "Deffy"

Deffenbaugh, was editor; and Dwight took the job of business manager. Producing the magazine introduced Buddy to photoengraving. The local engraver who made the cuts was considered a pioneer in the craft, which further aroused Buddy's interest.

Graduating from high school in 1893, Bud leaned toward art as his future. Chapman's father gave each of his sons a deed to a city lot as a graduation present and also, as a more immediately rewarding gift, a two-week trip to the World's Fair. Dwight and Bud stayed with their Aunt "Dode" (Josephine, Ed Meagher's widow), exploring the fairgrounds every day. The 1893 World's Columbian Exposition marked the four-hundred-year anniversary of Columbus's discovery of America, and all of Chicago was elated, eager to show their city as "Second City" to none. The fair was one of only a handful of world fairs at the time—they were held just once per decade for no more than six months and were expected to educate and advertise. At the first World's Fair—the Great Exhibition of 1851 in London—the public not only exclaimed over the Crystal Palace but also over new products, such as the Colt revolver and the reaper. The telephone was heralded at Philadelphia's Centennial Exposition in 1876. The 1889 World's Fair gave us the Eiffel Tower.

The Chicago fair was a peculiar mix of classroom and freak show.[43] The boys had the opportunity to view the table on which the Declaration of Independence had been signed as well as the manuscript of Abraham Lincoln's inaugural address. They may also have searched out the 11-ton cheese or the 1,500-pound chocolate Venus de Milo. Located in Jackson Park, south of downtown Chicago, the fair buildings were set on two tracts, connected by the mile-long Midway Plaisance, where a 250-foot Ferris wheel— Chicago's answer to the Eiffel Tower—soared over the crowds.[44] Chapman later reported that *we rode on the original Ferris Wheel, marvelled at the stucco glories of the "White City," heard the bands and lined up regularly in front of the food exhibits, for free samples of foil-wrapped chocolate and other delicacies.*[45]

Bud's interest in collecting may also have prompted him to ferret out the fair's anthropology building, though it was tucked away in an almost secluded corner of the grounds. Frederic Ward Putnam, director of Harvard's Peabody Museum and former student of Louis Agassiz, was appointed chief of the fair's division of ethnology. The title Putnam came up with for the exhibit, "Anthropology—Man and His Works," was significant in establishing anthropology as the accepted term for the general science of humanity, with ethnology and archaeology as subdisciplines.[46]

Within the anthropology buildings were collections assembled by men whose names Chapman would come to know intimately. Franz Boas, who studied the Indian people of the Northwest coast (the artistically accomplished Haida, Kwakiutl, and Bella Coola tribes), was principal assistant and head of the physical anthropological section. He assembled an eye-catching assortment of masks and decorated tools.[47]

The Smithsonian anthropology exhibit featured a giant linguistic map of Indian tribes west of the Mississippi, prepared by John Wesley Powell. The exhibit itself, designed by Otis T. Mason, William Henry Holmes, and Frank Hamilton Cushing, replaced cases of artifacts with an innovative life-group and culture-area approach. Cushing was responsible for the southwestern Indian groups, which included Navajo silversmiths, a Hopi kitchen, and two Zuni women making pottery.[48]

The public gawked at the models of Acoma, Taos, and Hopi villages. In September, they pestered Richard Wetherill, a Colorado rancher and explorer, about his collection from Mesa Verde. Also on view was the Hemenway exhibit by Jesse Walter Fewkes, an anthropologist who would become known for his association with the Hopi-Tewa potter, Nampeyo.[49]

Dwight and Bud may also have been tempted to view Indian Village, where American Indians lived in traditional houses—whole villages were imported and meticulously rebuilt—and "made trinkets for sale." Native Africans, Germans, and Egyptians were among many groups invited to participate in nearly a hundred of these "living exhibits."[50] At the time, however, it is likely that such portents of Bud's future went unnoticed. His interests were captivated by more modern expressions of art:

> In the Fine Arts Building I saw the new, strange paintings of the Impressionists . . . and also saw the fair-going public stand longest before Hovenden's "Breaking Home Ties," an extremely conservative example of the pure story-telling school. But more than the paintings, I enjoyed the original sketches of the leading book and magazine illustrators, and when in another building I found one of them actually at work, in full view, I watched him for hours. This was Howarth, a staff artist for the humorous weekly "Puck," which had him turning out routine drawings as the main feature of its exhibit.
>
> Unchastened by the sight of all this top-quality work, I did some sketching of my own[.] . . . I stayed in South Bend for the rest of the summer, doing much sketching, hiking, and boating.

Fall's cooler weather—and probably a talk or two with his father—spurred Bud to try making his own way. By this time, the raw clay of Chapman's life had taken incipient form. He had developed a number of traits that would direct his life choices: comfort with silent observation; curiosity about the nature of things; a penchant for collecting; patience with detail; a preference for concrete data over abstract theory; and a decidedly inventive bent. In late October, he and his mother traveled again to Chicago. His mother's purpose was to visit, but Bud had come to stay. *While [my mother] and Aunt Dode did the Fair's closing days, and shopped, I went the rounds of the engraving and lithographing companies, looking for a job in an art department. Times were hard, in 1893, and although I had "openings," they were a little too open. The best of them offered only a place to work, with a dollar a week thrown in for carfare.*[51]

Given the economic times, a reasonable alternative was more schooling—but no more grammar or math! Bud wrote to his father about his failure to find a job as an artist and suggested additional training. His father understood. His return letter stated that he would pay Bud's expenses for a year's study at the Art Institute of Chicago.[52]

CHAPTER 2

A Beginning Artist

“I returned about an hour ago having attended the morning sketch class, which I thoroughly enjoyed,” Bud wrote to his family after his start at the Art Institute in November 1893. “We are also expected to hand in our best pencil sketches. I think that mine compare very favorably with the work of those who have been there since the school opened. Of course, I have that hurried manner which time alone will correct. But I am learning to work slower and take more pains.”[1]

The eighteen-year-old Chapman, discouraged by job hunting, began study at Chicago’s Art Institute a month after the term had officially begun. Perhaps he was anxious about the attention his late entrance would draw, but his fears were partly eased by the fact that instruction at the school was relatively fluid, and the teachers were accustomed to accommodating latecomers. Art Institute students numbered about two hundred in 1893, and Bud’s first classes included many more girls than boys (who numbered only a dozen or so). Because another student, Bert Chapman from Iowa, was known as “Chap,” the students quickly dubbed Bud “Little Chap,” a nickname he favored.

Beginners were outfitted with supplies for charcoal, pencil, and pen-and-ink draw-ing as well as *fresh rye-bread, pressed into convenient wads as erasers*, which the students shared the cost of.[2] Chap’s classes in the elementary form included outline drawing (“monotonous” according to Chap), a sketch class (“a welcome change”), and a daily anatomy lecture by the dean, John H. Vanderpoel (“a diversion”). Vanderpoel was an artist and illustrator known primarily for his mural decoration and easel painting; a later student of his, Georgia O’Keeffe, called him “one of the few real teachers I have known.”[3] Entrance into the school was not particularly difficult—the elementary form was open to anyone—but continued study into the next two divisions, preparatory class and top form, was possible only if the faculty considered a student’s subsequent work to be worthy.[4]

Chap found the first few assignments tedious—outline drawing with charcoal from plaster casts of monumental figure details: eye, ear, nose, and feet. However, in November he wrote his family that “the teachers are pleased to see me ‘sticking to my job’ on hands & noses and say that I will be able to do faces much better as a result. Most of them try difficult faces before studying the features separately, and they usually make sad failures. One of the teachers usually says 'that's good' when she criticises my work and another asked if I had ever studied before in an Art Institute. VanderPoel, the 'high muck a muck' came in our room on Friday. He said nothing while looking at my work but criticised a good many others."[5]

Chap's training at the school was distinctly European in style, with the basis of study being the human figure. The large and fine set of plaster casts from which Chap worked was acquired early in the school's history. Such a traditional art philosophy was in keeping with the school's supporters, who were the leading industrialists and merchants of the Midwest, such as Marshall Field. "It is interesting to note that in their businesses," writes author Donald J. Irving, the Chicago merchants "strove aggressively to shape and develop the most advanced, often high risk, endeavors, while in their cultural lives they sought traditional values, the ideal, the established."[6]

Originally founded by a group of Chicago artists in 1866 as the Chicago Academy of Design, the school nearly went under in 1878.[7] But Chicago, a town "burgeoning lustily, its free-wheeling profile aggressive and raw," was eager to establish itself as cultured.[8] The school was reincorporated in 1879 as the Chicago Academy of Fine Arts, and then renamed the Art Institute of Chicago in 1882. It had two objectives. The first was to establish a school with teachers from the best institutions in London, Munich, and Paris where young midwesterners might get first-rate instruction without having to go to Europe. The second was to open art galleries of old masters and contemporaries to students and the public.[9] Between 1882 and World War I, the school and museum matured together. They espoused similar values, curators were also faculty, and the programs of each were compatible with European tradition.[10] However, compared to late nineteenth- and early twentieth-century artists of the eastern seaboard, those trained at the Art Institute "seemed more conservative, less experimental, more deliberately moored to accepted practices."[11]

Chap's first classes were held in the Giles Building, but he and his class entered new quarters on the lakefront after returning from the holidays in January 1894. The building, where the gallery remains today, was a legacy of the Columbian Exposition of 1893, a permanent souvenir of the "City White."[12] The new classrooms were on the ground floor, and students had access to the galleries of paintings and sculpture, though Chap remembered that *neither . . . gave me much of a lift, for, shortsightedly, I was intent only on draftsmanship, for use in illustration.*[13]

Newcomers arrived as well, making Chap, now two months into study at the school, an old hand. Several failed to make the grade, with Chap noting that one girl's rendition of a human skull *might have served better as the portrait of an apple—not a very good apple at that, for the grinning teeth were most disturbing.*[14] Another student, who had nearly severed his left thumb as a former butcher's apprentice, had been sent to the school by his father who *decided to give him a try out at art, with the assurance that his tools—such as pencil and brush, would be less deadly. He, too, was soon advised to seek some other vocation.* Chap himself

> *found it discouraging to keep plodding along without definite indication of my progress, beyond an occasional, "Keep on—Keep on!" But within a few weeks, on returning, after lunch, to my easel, two girls who had preceded me were waiting to tell me of watching Mr. Vanderpoel, who had wandered through, glancing at the work here and there. Coming to mine, he stood some time and then sat down to compare my drawing with the cast. They said, "That's the first time he has ever done that!"*[15]

A sought-after award was the honorable mention, not only because such pieces hung for several weeks at a time but also because the award was an indication of a serious student who could advance at the school. And Chap was decidedly serious. His still-life composition of a fan, jar, and book was awarded an honorable mention in late winter. The drawing, the only one to receive an award for that group, exhibited for a full month. He received two more honorable mentions for his charcoal drawings of classical sculpture.

In a pattern that persisted throughout much of his life, Chap focused in Chicago on art rather than a social life. Although warmed by his aunt's family, with whom he lived, able to share a camaraderie with his fellow students, and interested in maintaining a correspondence with friends in South Bend, Chap's inhibitions still made social activities a poor second to art. He rarely went out and chose not to become involved with any of the girls he met. *At the Art Institute I was conscious of dozens of girls around me, and I believe that I had the average youngster's eye for pretty faces. But if there were any, I remember none, and as for other areas of attraction, in those days, everything from ankles up, was shrouded in mystery.*[16] One Sunday in January 1894, he visited the home of a teacher, Miss Hay. He wrote his family, "She is the teacher who takes considerable interest in me. She has three rooms in a dingy brick house at 35th St. but has as cosy quarters as anyone could wish for. There were four old maids, sculptors and modelers who worked at the fair, and a sister of one of the teachers and Miss Hay's younger brother aged 17. They seem to have been quite a literary family as she has about 600 books. . . . I spent a tolerably nice evening which is saying a good deal for me."[17]

Chicago, however, enlivened him by its sheer energy. Proud of its rise, phoenixlike, after the Great Fire of 1871, its one million citizens were equally enthralled with its 1893 World's Fair, which "roused Chicago to an exalted idea of what a city could be like."[18] But for every new building, a breadline half a block long crept toward relief. City life, which embraced a large and varied ethnic population, spread into the streets. Chap, in his five-mile walk to his aunt's during the early spring of 1894, passed hurdy-gurdy players and organ grinders, struggling to make a living.

Where passers-by were numerous they [Italian hurdy-gurdy players] made a stand near the curb, but farther out from the Loop, they roamed the streets, playing before apartment houses, where as windows opened, nickles [sic] would be dropped into the assistant's hat. . . . The then old-fashioned organ grinder and monkey were also out in numbers, making friends with the children. And added to these were lone violinists, some of them youngsters, who were kept on the alert, sometimes not missing a note as they hustled to plant a foot on a nickle before some scheming urchin grabbed it and ran.[19]

Chap's walks were his own antidote to the hours he spent sitting and sketching. As the weather grew milder, he and other students also tried to enjoy themselves on breaks at the school. Chap told his sister, Vera, in March that "we have played ball every day lately in front of the building but I think that they will put a stop to it for we act like little primary kids. The ball is nearly as large as a football. It goes into the street nearly every time we throw it and gets itself and our hands covered with black mud. Once it went clear across the street. A nicely dressed man was going to pick it up until he saw how dirty it was. So he gave it a hard kick and it hit a cab-horse in the neck."

"I am glad to hear that you are getting fat," he added. "I wish you could get a little for me. I haven't weighed myself lately. I am afraid to. I see a spool of black linen thread on my bureau and that reminds me that I ripped my trousers while playing ball yesterday. They gave away completely behind and it took several pins to repair the place. I got to my chair after I had pinned them and I sat there until 4 oclock. I didn't care to get up."[20]

School continued apace, sometimes cheering Chap with its honors and other times discouraging him by its few rewards. In January, Chap was given gallery privilege, which meant that he could choose his own model from among life-sized plaster casts of antique sculpture on the gallery floor, select the most favorable view, and set up an easel. Chap, however, wrote to this family that "as we have to furnish our own floor cloths and submit to the comments of the untutored public and free visitor's day, I don't count it much of a privilege."[21] Later, he continued,

Jim [fellow student] has been at home all of last week. He feels like me when he gets sick. Wants to see his Ma. Whenever I get discouraged, I usually break up the spell by thinking over his case. He is six years my senior and hasn't decorated the H.M. board but once and I reason that if he is hopeful and light hearted, I ought to be. White & I heard "Vandy" [Vanderpoel] talking the thing over with three life class fellows. They all get the blues, "Vandy" saying that he spoils everything he touches for weeks at a time. Sometime I think that I ought to be indexing letters or grinding plow points instead of spoiling charcoal paper. I am sure that I would find the work just as easy. It isn't difficult to mark on paper what you see on a cast. But the work lies in trying to see more than there is in the cast while a couple of your chums are having a good visit beside you and the sun is shining outside, trying to get your mind off "down the river." "We artists" have a tough time of it but I guess it is the same with every calling.[22]

In late March, Chap was preoccupied with his classes, striving continuously to improve and thus earn helpful criticisms from Vanderpoel, and looking forward to a visit from Vera and his mother, though she had just written to say that she was not feeling well. "I too have felt 'squeamish' for the past two days," he responded. "My stomach has given me considerable trouble. I have just finished dinner, having had a special diet of toast and tea. . . . Aunt Dode says to come and recuperate here rather than to disappoint Vera. . . . Hope that you will have recovered by this time."[23]

Graver news came in April, news so unexpected that Chap's stay in Chicago ended abruptly. *I was called out [of class at the Art Institute] to greet Mr. Greenawalt, a next-door neighbor in South Bend. He told me that my father was very ill, and that Mother thought I had better come home for a while. I might be away for some weeks, and perhaps I had better take my equipment with me, or possibly leave it at my aunt's apartment. We were ready to leave within a few minutes, and it was not until we had boarded a street car that he told me of father's sudden death.*[24]

Chap's memoirs reveal little of those first few days back in South Bend, where his father, who had just turned fifty, had died from an apparent lung hemorrhage—only that *we were all too stunned for a week or more to face the situation.* Mary, Chap's mother, could only have been driven back into a grief she had endured repeatedly as a child. The entire family must have struggled, missing both the comfort of Milt's love and humor and his dependability as a provider. Chap's father had successfully carried the Economist Plow Company through the Panic of 1893 and had been acquiring additional stock in the company since then. With Milt's death, leadership of the factory was turned over to Leighton B. Pine, the remaining owner, who also had charge of the case factory of the Singer Sewing Machine Company, then a major industry in South Bend. Because his association with Singer meant that he could give little attention to the plow factory,

Pine turned over management to his nephew, in what would turn out to be an ill-fated move for the company.[25]

Although the family expected to share in future profits, it was now essentially up to the boys to support their mother and twelve-year-old sister. Dwight, now twenty, would continue to work at the factory, where he had been helping in the office, so that his routine, at least superficially, remained intact. But Chap confronted a more dramatic change. His schooling had ended, and he had to find work. Despite his previous discouraging experience in looking for a drawing job, Chap persisted in trying to make a living through art. For most of May, Chap prepared sample drawings and then, on a whim, sent them to two farm weeklies that his father used to bring home from the factory: *Farm Implement News* in Chicago and *Farm Machinery* in St. Louis. Although the Chicago publication turned him down, he did receive a favorable reply from *Farm Machinery*, suggesting that they might have a place in the near future and asking if he were related to the late J. M. Chapman. Chap replied at once and then returned to practicing pen-and-ink techniques.[26]

In early summer, Chap traveled to his grandfather's in Warsaw, Indiana, intending to housesit for ten days or so while his grandfather went on a trip. But just before his grandfather's departure, Dwight arrived with the news that *Farm Machinery* had written, proposing terms for a three-year contract. *Grandfather, of course, took the news in his stride; said he could find some other help, and wished me well on my first venture away from home.*[27]

Chap arrived in St. Louis on a Saturday in early June, pleased with the prospect of a position as illustrator but curious about his job, for *Farm Machinery* printed few drawings and thus illustrating seemed unlikely to occupy him full time. *Farm Machinery's* editor and owner was C. K. Reifsnider, whom a staff member later characterized as someone who had missed his calling—instead of a newspaper publisher, he ought to have been the leader of a semi-occult religious group, because he had all of the persuasive ways and "front" necessary for putting it over on a grand scale.[28] Reifsnider welcomed Chap to his staff of seven, which included, to Chap's surprise, another full-time artist, Charles Champe. During the day, when Reifsnider returned to Chap the introductory sketches he had sent, Chap noticed Reifsnider's note on the back of the envelope: "He's a kid; wants room; about 18; nice boy; good family."[29]

Even more curious about his job, Chap was then introduced to Frank E. Richey, a St. Louis lawyer, who had teamed with Reifsnider to establish a weekly Populist magazine, *Vox Populi*. At the time, *Vox Populi* was one of literally hundreds of Populist newspapers with very small circulations sprouting up, serving as important vehicles for keeping reform issues before the people.[30] As the first modern reform movement of practical importance in the United States, Populism was challenging the Republicans and Democrats as a strong third party by taking the side of farmers against business interests. It was particularly popular in the southern and midwestern prairie states, and St. Louis was the site of significant Populist conferences. Richey hoped to use the Populist paper as a means of gaining influence with the party.

The middle class from which Chap originated, however, either ridiculed Populists or feared them, often taking seriously the hysterical literature that described them as anarchists or socialists. Chap's home state of Indiana and the other Northwest Territory states in particular had never embraced Populism.[31] Thus Chap was somewhat dismayed to discover that he had been hired not to illustrate *Farm Machinery* but to prepare drawings for *Vox Populi*. But young, fatherless, and anxious to prove himself, Chap's inclination was to look toward the opportunity rather than its shortcomings. During his first weekend in St. Louis as the invited guest of the Richey family, he listened to the lawyer's stories of the Populist Party, stories that suggested that *here was the chance of a lifetime. I should pitch into the fight and dedicate my life, like another Thomas Nast, to fighting corruption and oppression. I had my own ideas of a more congenial occupation, but a job was a job, and I was willing to give it a try, even though it might hold me through the three years of my contract.*[32]

The search for a room began on Monday, when the assistant editor, Buck, brought Chap to a boardinghouse on the south side of St. Louis run by a first-generation German family named Schmidt. In the mid-1890s, St. Louis was home to over half a million people, predominantly German, and about half of those were the children of immigrant parents. Most were crammed along the Mississippi River and near the edge of the expanding business districts.[33] Mrs. Schmidt, mother to two young girls, offered Chap a room to share with her twenty-five-year-old brother. Despite St. Louis's muggy, hot summers, Chap chose to walk the mile to and from work each day, inspired not only by the exercise but also by the hope of saving money for further art study. His route took him through St. Louis's business and residential areas, in which handsome brick-and-stone public buildings and islands of beautiful homes were interspersed with houses of the poor that were meaner, uglier, and more miserable than most, according to local writers and visitors at the time.[34] Chap complained to his mother about the room ("My room is small and not as neat as I had hoped for"), but he soon came to appreciate Mrs. Schmidt's excellent meals and her propensity for mothering. "They are nice people and take an interest in me," he wrote to his mother later that week. "She has given me advice as to diet. . . . So now all depends on my health and Mrs. S. says she is a good nurse and likes to take care of good boys, etc."[35]

At *Vox Populi*, his first assignments from Richey were to draw cartoons, a task that he found mechanical, with lots of copying. Joined with the tediousness was an anxiety about Champe; Chap worried not only that his being hired had somehow offended the older artist but also that Champe would look down on him for being a novice. His fears were eased only when he learned that Champe himself had recommended that a second artist be hired and that, though he recognized Chap's inexperience, he felt it would be *best for me to keep at it in my own way. I did little odd jobs leading up to tries at full page cartoons, and an occasional design or front page portrait, done in lithographer's crayon on Ross stipple board, for Farm Machinery. When out of work I kept practicing with pen and ink techniques, and all round sketching. But I had much of my few months' academic training to forget before I could loosen up and take things in my stride, as Champe did.*[36]

So Chap settled into his life in St. Louis as best he could. At the office he was once again known as Chap—the nickname he would always prefer to his given name Kenneth—which must have comforted him, a little, by its association with life in Chicago. Otherwise, as he neared his nineteenth birthday, he was surrounded by the unfamiliar: first job, new city, no family, no friends. Struggling with the loss of his father, burdened with the responsibility of making his own way, it must have been a deeply emotional time. But his letters home—embellished with amusing sketches—touch on these subjects only briefly, if at all. He writes of his room ("I am still satisfied with my roost"), his work ("The work is nothing that rushes one, but I find some of it pretty mechanical"), the weather ("Walked both ways today. It was hot so they say but I have felt it just as much at home"), and his hopes ("If I make some acquaintances this summer at church and elsewhere I will enjoy myself"). Meanwhile, his family in South Bend also was undergoing changes; he learned that his brother, mother, and sister would be moving to a new house. "So you are going to move?" Chap wrote to his sister, Vera,

> Well, I will have an easier time getting from the depot when I come home. From Mama's drawing, I should think it a nice house. . . . The young Schmidts are at home now. Poor kids they havent [sic] a very nice yard to play in. . . . The girls seem to be quarrelsome at times and both leak tears easily but they don't cry as loud as a girl used to, <u>what I used to know already</u>. Carrie the oldest put her arm around me the other day and said "Now you can think this is your sister standing by you." I didnt tell her that I would like to catch my sister putting her arms around boys she had known only a month.[37]

The office offered some companionship. He wrote his family that Richey was a jolly fellow (but not as jolly as Reifsnider); he could act wild, but "I have learned from contact with him that he is harmless[;] . . . we have lots of fun at Richey's expense, on the quiet."[38] He became better friends with Champe, with whom he spent an occasional Sunday afternoon, and enjoyed the antics of the staff. "Willie, our office boy, is a great one," he wrote home. "He seems to take considerable interest in me. Buck was blowing him up the other day for not going to the P.O. more often for exchanges and said 'I should think you would make that a *part of you.*' Willie said, 'Party! Where is they going to be a party?'"[39] In many ways, the job must have been ideal, exposing him to new illustration techniques in the unhurried atmosphere of the office and under the relaxed mentoring of Champe. And so, though the weeks dragged at first, they soon began to fly, especially as the political campaign began to heat up.

> *At times the whole force would get together with a few of Richey's hopeful hangers-on, for a rush job of mailing out campaign literature to the hinterlands. Once I tried to show them the trick I had learned as a kid in father's office, of folding a stack of a dozen sheets at once, but the Populist yearners were too busy airing their political views to consider any innovations, and kept at their easy going one-at-a-time pace.*[40]

The election ended up taking an unexpected turn. Generally Populists tended to align with Democrats when a compromise seemed practical, but Richey, after winning the nomination as Populist candidate, entered into a secret deal with the Republican nominee. Together, they challenged the Democratic party's incumbent to a triparty debate, sure that the Democrat would decline. When he did, they both harped on his refusal. Sometime that fall, Richey and his supporters switched to the Republicans, with the result that, in November 1894, St. Louis elected its first Republican Congressman. The Populist supporters swarmed to the office the following day, but both Richey and Reifsnider made themselves scarce. *After that Vox. Pop. went into a decline as Richey found it imperative to regain his law practice—possibly through some understanding with the new Congressman. But whatever the deal, we saw very little of him at the office from then on, and by December, he was out for good.*[41]

As Christmas drew near, Chap asked for a week off without pay to visit his family. The week turned into months as Chap caught a severe cold that kept him in bed and at home. Finally, in June 1895, he wired Reifsnider that he had recovered and would be returning to his job, but it appeared that with the decline of *Vox Populi*, Chap's job was also in danger. In an effort to renege on the contract, Reifsnider told Chap that he was fully prepared to show his illness had impaired his work. *With that to unnerve me, he produced a photograph of one of his advertisers and ordered me to make a full page portrait from it, for comparison with those I had made previously for Farm Machinery. I took a good look at the subject and was immediately struck with its suitability for an excellent job, so in good humor I went at it, determined to outdo myself.*[42]

Chap also took the precaution of contacting an acquaintance of his father, who in turn consulted a lawyer. The lawyer offered to confer with Reifsnider, who shortly agreed to compromise: he would pay Chap $5 per week for one-third of his time, Chap would have the use of a small room in the office with all facilities, and he would be free to pursue outside work. *I accepted the offer at once, and went back to a good room at my old boarding house. Mrs. Schmidt was shocked at my condition and immediately began force-feeding me. I needed little urging for within a week I had developed a raven-ous appetite. I ate everything in sight and for many weeks was the last to leave the table. . . . Gradually I regained my pep and had but little to remind me of my illness except a startling loss of hair.*[43]

Once settled, Chap began to market his work, showing samples to engraving and lithograph companies as well as newspapers. He soon found himself busier than before; he even began creating cartoons for the *Rolling Pin*, an old-fashioned comic weekly. *I held out [one cartoon] for a trial with the New York magazines, and sold it, "gag" and drawing to Truth for $4—my first contact with the big city! I kept for some time their accep-tance slip with the request, "Please deposit the enclosed check as promptly as possible." As if an artist would not grab his hat and rush out to the nearest bank or bar!*[44]

As summer progressed, Chap's health responded to Mrs. Schmidt's mothering and his spirits improved through the acquaintance of a new coworker, John Caskie. Caskie's lively personality was a magnet for the office, bringing a feeling of cohesiveness to the staff *(even Thompson, the dour, bespectacled and bewhiskered old Scotsman, began to smile)* and an emotional connection for Chap that he had not known since moving to St. Louis.

I was absorbed and uncommunicative when at work and [John] respected my ways. But gradually when I began to learn of his genuineness, I met him more than halfway and welcomed his interest. . . . Often at noon John would show me around the business section. . . . Two long-legged and lively youngsters could cover consid-erable ground in what was left of an hour after a quick lunch! . . . As I look back on those days, John, alone, made endurable those closing months in St. Louis. It was the beginning of a warm friendship between two youngsters, groping for something that neither could yet define. Whatever it was, it drew us together time after time through the sixty years that followed.[45]

Despite John's welcome friendship, Chap's life in St. Louis remained lonely *(in my stay of nearly 18 months in St. Louis, I made not one acquaintance socially with a girl)*, and he began seriously to consider returning to Chicago. He was drawn, perhaps, by the prospect of being closer to his family and, possibly, by the opportunity for further study at the Art Institute. He was also encouraged by Champe, who had left *Farm Machinery* for Chicago in October and quickly found work there. Torn between his dissatisfaction with St. Louis and the relative security of his current position, Chap struggled with his future. *On one of my trolley rides . . . at dusk [during the summer], I found the streets lighted by gas lamps. That gave me a nostalgic twinge for the South Side of Chicago. . . . [W]hen I had about decided to leave St. Louis, I rode down that way again just to clinch matters, and returned intent on making the break.*[46]

To Chap's deep satisfaction, looking for work in Chicago in late 1895 was much easier than it had been in 1893. Chap not only had over a year's experience but also a current Chicago contact. Champe was head of the art department for a humorous weekly called *Up to Date*, and he welcomed Chap to town.[47] Although *Up to Date's* publisher originally accepted Chap's cartoons for publication, he later decided (rightly, according to Chap) that his and Champe's cartoons were too similar to continue to publish them both. But this time Chap was not discouraged. *With* Up to Date *out of the picture, it was up to me to hunt a job! By then I had had another good taste of the brisk tempo of Chicago, as compared with the southern languor and conservatism of the German element in St. Louis. In those days it was said that even the clocks of the two cities reflected the contrasting attitudes; the pendulums of St. Louis, saying: "Ta-a-a-ke your t-i-m-e, ta-a-a-ke your ti-i-me," while in Chicago, they swung with, "Get bizzy! get bizzy! get bizzy!"*[48]

Within days, Chap was offered a job with the Illinois Engraving Company, which had just landed a contract with Montgomery Ward. *I accepted and asked, "When do I begin?" "Just as quick as you can get your coat off!" was the reply. So I hustled back for my outfit and was soon at work. . . . That was the last occasion I have ever had to hunt a job!*[49] Montgomery Ward was the first mail-order merchandiser in the country. Its stores stocked every possible product a farmer needed, plus many more he would want when he saw them in the catalog. Wards has been credited as perhaps the greatest single influence in increasing the standard of American middle-class living; its catalogs brought reduced prices to cities and farms, where millions of families were able to acquire quality goods.[50]

The catalogs, originally simply lists of items, had gradually incorporated sketches, with the first fashion illustration appearing in 1878. Chap's experience with *Farm Machinery* would have made a particularly favorable impression during his interview, because Wards' early advertising was concentrated in just such farm journals. By the 1890s, the catalogs ran over five hundred pages and contained about eight thousand illustrations. Chap soon discovered that his illustration experience in St. Louis had prepared him well. In particular, his experience with "stipple" paper, which allowed for shading gradations, transferred easily to catalog work. He used it to advantage in his attempts at millinery drawings, which so impressed the company that it began soliciting orders for millinery illustrations from the largest local manufacturers and wholesalers. Within a year, Chap was preparing all the millinery drawings for the Illinois Engraving Company. And yet Chap was aware that, despite his improved facility, his two years in Chicago were moving him farther and farther away from his goal as a magazine illustrator. Trying to remain true to his dream, Chap attended a life class at the Art Institute three nights a week and hoped for another chance at serious art study.

His social life remained unvaried, though he enjoyed the proximity to his family in South Bend and the comfort of his aunt's home, where he lived again with his three cousins, Mark, Ed, and Isabella. *Mark was by nature the more winsome of the two boys, loyal and considerate, and with it he had a line of blarney that made him welcome in any group. . . . Ed was another type; he was solidly built, seemingly sound, and inclined to loaf and dream. . . . Isabella had had a hard life under her mother's watchful eye. Aunt Dode was of the old school, girls stayed at home and waited for Prince Charming. She was petite and winsome, had many suitors, but none measured up to her ideal.*[51]

Meanwhile, however, the family's finances were faltering, and its need for support from Dwight and Chap's incomes became even more pressing. According to Chapman's memoirs, Pine's nephew, who had been put in charge of the factory, not only lost the confidence of his staff but also embezzled company funds to promote a real estate venture. The company folded in about 1896. The plant was appropriated for the Singer Sewing Machine Company, and the patent rights were sold to the Syracuse Plow Company. At the finish, neither Chap's mother nor his aunt retained a cent from that source.[52]

These family financial difficulties, combined with illness in 1897, disheartened both the Chapman and Meagher families. Mark, who had contracted tuberculosis, was in his final months. To maintain his own health, Chap spent an hour every other evening in the YMCA gym. But he was conscious that he was overextending himself, and he worried not only about his cousin Mark but also about the danger to himself in continuing to stay with his aunt. He was about to move to another neighborhood when a former coworker, Billy Aylward, wrote, asking him to move instead to another state. Aylward offered Chap a position with a new firm, the Cramer Engraving Company, which he had helped to establish in Milwaukee, Wisconsin. Taking up this serendipitous offer, Chap resettled in January 1898.

Milwaukee did not offer Chap startling new challenges in terms of his art skills, but it did give him the opportunity to show off his straightforward manner of business. He had no patience for colleagues who were all talk and no action, especially when their behavior reflected badly on his own work. Having been assigned to work with Milwaukee's clothing manufacturers, he soon asserted himself in a manner that foreshadowed his response to future work conflicts:

Kenneth M. Chapman, about twenty-three years old, c. 1898.
(Courtesy of School for Advanced Research Archives, AC02 750e.)

Within a few weeks I began to hear complaints from manufacturers that Richards [part owner of Cramer Engraving Company] was glib with promises to meet deadlines, but slow in making good. From there on, I reached an understanding with them that they deal directly with me. Since such matters could not be discussed by telephone they would ask me to come to their offices for "instructions" and then would accept my estimate of feasible delivery dates. Occasionally it meant overtime, evenings, Saturday afternoons and Sundays, but I appreciated their confidence in my square dealing,—my first contact of that sort.[53]

Chap must also have enjoyed his renewed friendship with Aylward, with whom he shared the dream of magazine illustration. Son of a shipping pioneer, Billy's passion was drawing ships. Later, Aylward would illustrate Jack London's "Sea Wolf" in addition to seafaring and shipping articles in leading magazines. But in Milwaukee, the two young men had to content themselves with mutual encouragement and moral support.

Ominously, despite Chap's move away from the tuberculosis threat in Chicago, he began to feel unwell in the early summer of 1898, plagued by a sensitive throat and chest pains. A Milwaukee doctor, recommended by Richards, found no signs of pulmonary trouble and suggested that Chap's trouble was indigestion. To recuperate, Chap vacationed in South Bend in June for two weeks, where he *loafed day after day in sunshine, and made numerous sketching trips up the river in Dwight's motor boat. Soon my throat trouble had disappeared and I returned to Milwaukee to find that their summer had really come at last.* Upon his return, Chap was invited to make his home with the Richards family at the northern edge of the city, from which he made frequent hikes and bike rides to the countryside. *As might be expected of an amateur archaeologist . . . I did a little hunting for Indian relics, in the fields near the river, but found little more than a few potsherds and broken arrow points.*[54]

And yet, despite the pride he felt in his manner of business and the apparently congenial working friendships with Billy and the Richards family, Chap still felt isolated. *I attended church and occasionally Sunday school in a mixed class, but as in Chicago and St. Louis, met no one who interested me.* Chap had also determined early on that his move would be temporary. *I had never felt that my stay in Milwaukee would be a prolonged one. I was saving all I could toward what I hoped would be an opportunity to give full time to study, maybe at the Art Students' League in New York where I would be in touch with publishers who might give me a chance at book and magazine illustrations. But before many months I was to find myself headed the opposite way.*[55]

In the late fall of 1898, Chap was keeping artistically fit with an evening sketch class and physically fit with a routine at the YMCA gym. But his throat and chest ailments returned and *in January of 1899, I woke one night with a slight hemorrhage. That "scared the living daylights" out of me, and remembering father's fatal bout with one, I resolved then and there to beat it to the Southwest.* Chap spoke first with an artist for the Milwaukee *Journal*, who had recently recuperated in Arizona and advised Chap to do the same. Meanwhile, at the recommendation of Dwight, who had consulted their family physician, Chap also toured a new tuberculosis sanitarium that had just opened on Milwaukee's lakeshore. *I visited the place and the director explained the cure—months in bed, force feeding, etc. It was a gloomy day, with a cold raw wind off the Lake. I shuddered at the thought of even a day in the place. Me for the Southwest and sunshine![56]*

Auspiciously, Chap had just come across an archaeological article by Frederick Webb Hodge about climbing Mesa Encantada (Enchanted Mesa) near Acoma, New Mexico. Hodge, who served as Cushing's field secretary on the 1887 Hemenway Expedition, joined the Bureau of Ethnology two years later.[57] In 1898, Hodge, after working in the field with Jesse Walter Fewkes and Walter Hough of the National Museum of Natural History, visited Laguna and Acoma Pueblos. He rode to Mesa Encantada, three miles from the pueblo and the traditional home of the Acoma people during prehistoric times. There, he found traces of an ancient pathway leading toward the summit and quantities of prehistoric ware, which had evidently washed down from the summit to the mesa.[58]

Chap was intrigued by the concept of living in an area where Indian culture had endured as a vibrant force.[59] More portents of a Southwest move came after his resignation from the Cramer Engraving Company, by way of an old South Bend acquaintance, Albert Folk, who had just returned from a year in New Mexico. *He said, "Keep away from the hot country. Head for Las Vegas, rest for a few weeks while you adjust to the altitude and get acquainted. Then take any outdoor job you can find."* A trip to the Southwest in his future, Chap coincidentally received further incentive from his grandfather. *I wrote my grandfather, telling him of my plans and asking if he would stake me to a return ticket if I couldn't make a go of it. He replied at once, "Better come here and meet the son of my next-door neighbor. He . . . will be leaving within a week for New Mexico."[60]*

His neighbor, Captain W. C. "Cliff" Reid, had lived in Las Vegas for several years before fighting with the Rough Riders in the Spanish-American War. When Chap spoke with him, he discovered that Reid indeed had plans to return to Las Vegas soon with his younger brother, Chester, who was recovering from typhoid fever, contracted in the army. And so Chap and the Reids arranged to meet in Chicago within a few days, where they would catch a train for New Mexico.

Many years later, looking back on my experience in Milwaukee, I came up with what I believe is the solution of my illness. . . . [T]he art department of the Cramer Engraving Company was in a corner of the engraving plant, and separated from it by a mere partition, about seven feet high, so that we were conscious of all that went on there—saws ripping into sheet metal, and the constant rumble and squeak of the rocking acid-baths for zinc and half-tone etchings.

I have no doubt that it was the fumes from the acid baths that affected me, and particularly during the winter months without proper ventilation. None of the others felt it but I happened to be allergic. Today [1950s] I presume that it is recognized as an occupational hazard among the engravers themselves, and that those who prove susceptible to it are advised at once to hunt some more congenial employment.[61]

But in March 1899, frightened by his ill health, Chap knew only that he must look for a more congenial location. Although his route to the Southwest would seem to be propelling him even further away from his dreams of a New York career, at least his experience up until then had prepared him, in many ways, for this moment. He had a varied and successful resumé, an acquaintance with starting fresh in new locations and, beyond his family, no binding social ties. The Southwest was farther away and more mysterious than any place he had tried so far. But, still, he was ready.

CHAPTER 3

LAND OF ENCHANTMENT

In the canyon outside Las Vegas, New Mexico, along the Gallinas River, Chap settles himself on the rocky bank, adjusting his shoulders into the boulder behind him. Nearly twenty-four years old, he is well over six feet tall and scarecrow thin. He looks serious, more serious than he feels usually, and good natured, which his handsome narrow face does a good job of expressing. He stretches out his legs and sits a moment, hypnotized by the water. Except for its rush and the rustling of pine branches, it is quiet, which Chap treasures. He has come to paint. It's late April; he's been in New Mexico for several weeks now, and already the pain in his lungs has lessened. He has started sketching the homes near the old plaza, adobe houses half a century old. He hopes to sell his artwork to tourists at La Castañeda, the Fred Harvey hotel by the station. But he's never worked seriously with color so he wants to experiment away from town, out of public view. He eyes a cluster of wild iris, sits up, and reaches into his knapsack for his watercolors.

Or so we might imagine. In his memoirs, Chap recalls his resolve to improve his painting skills. *I had never worked seriously with color[,] . . . and I was not for displaying my ignorance of the art in my sketching about town. So, as a tryout, I made a few trips up Gallinas Canyon.*[1] It worked. Only a few months after arrival, Chap was busy selling watercolors to travelers, who rode on the Atchison, Topeka, and Santa Fe Railway to marvel at all the Southwest had to offer. When the tourists requested a particular scene, Chap—true to his experience as a commercial illustrator—had no difficulty at all in creating art for their pleasure.

> *I soon learned that the paintings that sold readily, had all the essentials; an old adobe house on a hillside, with an outdoor oven, a string of chile peppers hanging beside the door, and for good measure, a native and a burro loaded with wood. All this of course, under a blue sky with a few fleecy clouds, and a background of distant mountains. This became the accepted formula, buyers would notice a missing detail in a composition that otherwise pleased them, and ask that it be inserted. Who was I to object? I did a thriving business that first summer.*[2]

Proud that he could support himself through painting, Chap settled easily into southwestern life. He took a room on North 5th Street with the Stoneroad family, made several acquaintances through his friendship with Cliff Reid, with whom he had traveled from the Midwest, and mastered his sales pitch. But that first summer, Chap became acquainted with something even more potent than financial success. In Las Vegas, Chap met destiny.

It took the form of two men whose names were Frank Springer and Edgar L. Hewett. In 1899, Springer, then president of the Maxwell Land Grant Company, was a powerful force in the territory. Renowned for his brilliance in law and revered for his sensibilities, "no one ever knew Frank Springer that did not love him," according to Reid, who worked in his office. "He was not a man of the world, not a mixer, but those who knew him had nothing but the highest respect for him. . . . He was a man of deep sympathy and of a wonderful and fine sense of humor; and possessed the kindest heart that was ever put into the bosom of man."[3]

Hewett, ten years older than Chap, was newly arrived in New Mexico from Colorado, having just accepted the position of Las Vegas Normal University's first president in August 1898. His was a forceful presence, full of vitality and charisma. Springer had advocated Hewett for the university position after becoming acquainted through a shared interest in archaeology. According to biographer Chauvenet, Hewett was popular with his students and "if he tended to moralize and even to preach, those qualities were expected in pedagogues. He also had a quiet humor and tremendous zest for life. He was searching history and philosophy for the truth about mankind."[4]

To Chap, these vibrant men were decisive influences. In Springer, Chap found a champion of his art and a fatherlike warmth and affection. In Hewett, he discovered the path to a lifetime career in the study of Indian art.

Their meeting place was Las Vegas, New Mexico, one of the last major Hispanic towns established in northern New Mexico. It was settled in 1835, officially named Nuestra Senora de los Dolores de las Vegas, only eleven years before the territory passed to the United States from Mexico. The emergence of the Santa Fe Trail quickly transformed Las Vegas from a rural village into a boomtown. The town became the center of the sheep and cattle industry, rivaling Albuquerque and Denver in population and industry. The coming of the railroad in 1879 further enhanced Las Vegas's position as a center of commerce, though it also created divisions where none had existed before.[5]

Las Vegas, then as now, was bordered by mountains to the west—where Chap experimented with his paints—leading into a wilderness that stretched for hundreds of miles. The prairies, from which the town took its name, formed its eastern boundary. The town harbored a similar dichotomy. Adobe homes radiated from the old plaza, West Las Vegas or "Old Town," built by the original settlers in conformance with Spanish traditions.

Despite the addition after 1846 of a few pitched roofs and a new Victorian-style hotel on the plaza, courtesy of American settlers such as Charles Ilfeld, the residents were faithful to their Hispanic culture. Chile *ristras* hung from the *portales*, for example, and outdoor ovens in the backyard were in frequent use.

In contrast, the eastern portion of Las Vegas was built after 1880 primarily by newly arrived settlers. New Town was centered about the railroad, which had been routed east of Old Town—not southwest of the plaza as originally anticipated. New Town was clearly midwestern in style, with its two-story Victorian frame homes built on grid-patterned streets reflecting the preferences and familiarities of its more recent settlers. Except for the New Mexican sky, which must have seemed closer and more vivid than any midwestern horizon, Chap might have mistaken his immediate neighborhood for an Indiana farm town.

Chap settled in Las Vegas simply because of Reid, who worked in Springer's law office. Chap originally intended only a short stay while his lungs recovered, before pursuing better opportunities in Albuquerque or El Paso. But instead, he later remarked, it was as if Springer and Hewett had been waiting there for his arrival.[6]

Chap was not formally introduced to Springer until summer, but he soon learned of him. A resident of Las Vegas since 1883, the Iowa-born Springer had made his fortune in northern New Mexico as attorney and then president of the Maxwell Land Grant Company, as attorney for the railroad, and through judicious investments. Chap's first glimpse of the famous lawyer came through Ralph Emerson Twitchell, an attorney, local historian, and publicist, who took an immediate liking to Chap. *I made my first real tryout with color, by copying a photograph of a picturesque old grist mill with a fine water wheel, on the Ruidoso far to the Southeast. . . . The photograph was loaned to me by Col. Ralph Twitchell, who was delighted with my work. He carried it about town, had the Daily New Mexican give it favorable mention and put it on exhibition at the Casteñeda. Las Vegas suddenly discovered that it had an artist in its midst.*[7]

A Michigan-born lawyer, Twitchell had arrived in the Southwest through the law offices of Judge Henry L. Waldo, solicitor for the railway. Twitchell's penchant for detail was valued, as were his skills as orator and lecturer. Twitchell also "loved the spectacular and the light of publicity."[8] The promotional pamphlets that the railway used to advertise Santa Fe had their origin and impetus in Twitchell.[9]

In April 1899, Twitchell, advertising chairman for the first annual Rough Riders reunion in Las Vegas, asked for Chap's help. The reunion celebrated the anniversary of the Rough Riders' engagement on land in the Spanish-American War. Because New Mexico volunteers comprised nearly half of the unit, they chose to hold the reunion in New Mexico. Las Vegas had successfully outbid other New Mexican towns for the celebration, which was to be attended by the Rough Riders' leader,

Theodore Roosevelt. To promote the event, Twitchell commissioned Chap for sketches and photographs for newspaper publication and asked him to attend the introductory meeting in April.

I arrived a few minutes before the hour and stood outside in a group, a few of whom I had met. At one side stood Mr. Springer, hands in his coat pockets, gazing at the steps below and evidently not listening to the discussion. The city engineer was telling the group that he had just finished his new map of the city, and asked if any of them would like to order a blue-print of it.

He then turned to Mr. Springer, and said, "Shall I put you down for one, Mr. Springer?" Then came a long embarrassing silence. Finally Mr. Springer turned to him and replied; "I'm sorry, I guess I wasn't listening. What is it?," and then learning what it was about, he said, "Oh, yes, of course, I want one."

The meeting soon came to order. . . . Frank Springer was chosen chairman of the finance committee[.] . . . He accepted . . . and then said, "I am glad to help with it, but before the committee can act, it must have an estimate of the total cost approved by all the sub-committees. Once that is in our hands, the finance committee will arrive at a fair and just assessment for each and every one in both Old and New Town, according to his ability, and his opportunity to profit by the celebration."

That gave me my first and lasting impression of Mr. Springer. Detached and so absorbed in his own interests that he was apparently unaware of what went on about him, yet in such a meeting, he was prompt and precise with his response.[10]

Soon after his arrival, Chap must also have learned of Hewett who, as Springer's protégé, was eagerly leading the new university toward excellence. A match for the fledgling institution, then at the close of its first year, Hewett, at thirty-three, was young, vital, and knowledgeable about subjects that interested his students. As president, he was enthusiastically putting into practice his teaching theories, which favored fieldwork over classwork and emphasized a one-on-one relationship between professor and student. In developing these theories, Hewett may have been exposed to the ideas of his contemporaries—for example, Francis Parker or John Dewey—who believed that the child, not the teacher, was the proper focus of instruction. These ideas had no place in the vast majority of classrooms in the late 1890s, however. More common were schools where the only voice was the teacher's, and textbooks were the students' main source of knowledge.[11]

Hewett rejected that style. His education and teaching positions in Missouri and Colorado led him away from the nineteenth-century models of drillmaster and

Edgar Lee Hewett at Las Vegas Normal University, c. 1901.
(Courtesy of School for Advanced Research Archives, AC02 822a.)

intellectual overseer and toward interpreter of culture. In conjunction, he also admired the teaching concept, apparently put forward by a Chicago waterfront tough, that the best way to teach boys to swim was to "push 'em off de pier."[12] Hewett wanted his staff to do the same.

Chap first met Hewett in May through a new acquaintance, Oscar Hanszen, who had also come to the Southwest for his health. Hanszen confided to Chap that when he felt well enough he hoped to introduce and direct a manual training department at the university. A few days later, Chap ran into Hanszen, who said he was on his way to meet Hewett and invited Chap along. When Hanszen introduced Chap as an artist, Hewett said he would be interested in examining examples of Chap's work. *I brought him a selection from my samples, including my recent sketches, which seemed to please him. He then asked if I had ever done any teaching, and I confessed that I had no experience. "Well," he said, "if you would like to give it a try, you are welcome to a room here during our vacation, without cost, and I believe you can interest enough of our pupils to make it worth while."*[13]

That first encounter made a huge impression on Chap, infused as it was with such spirit of generosity. He lost no time in acting on Hewett's largesse, quickly setting up a class in elementary art to complement Hanzsen's class in mechanical drawing.

> *We began our morning classwork a week following the close of the Normal's spring term. . . . Hanszen had three or four in his course, and I only five or six. . . . I was pleased with the results from the start, but before the close of our fourth week Hanszen had picked up a job, designing and supervising construction of a small business block and was obliged to abandon his class. By that time I was so familiar with his course that I agreed to carry on with it. Four of his pupils stayed through to the end, so that I was kept busy not only with the class work, but also with a Saturday morning sketch class, that drew a group of older students for the tours through Old Town.*[14]

At that time, coursework at Las Vegas Normal University, primarily a teachers college, led to a bachelor's degree of pedagogy and a life certificate to teach in any of New Mexico's public schools. Besides courses in math, English, history, and science, the university also offered classes in psychology, child study, and philosophy of education as well as opportunities for practical work in the schools. In addition, it offered postgraduate courses, the manual training department, and an academic program, which basically comprised high school classes. An important component of the teaching curriculum was a model school for grades first through eighth, created in conjunction with the Las Vegas Board of Education and taught by university faculty members.[15]

Hewett's educational convictions were even broader than the philosophy of education that led him to embrace the idea of the model school in which students could learn by doing. A consuming passion for archaeology and anthropology had emerged for Hewett nearly a decade earlier, and he was dedicated to the idea that a meaningful education should focus on such studies. Investigating how humans have lived over time would provide students with a solid base on which all other subjects could be understood, according to Hewett, who referred to his ideas as the "science of man."[16]

Hewett's initial fascination with archaeology had been conceived during a summer-long honeymoon in 1891 with his new bride, Cora Whitford. Leaving Missouri, they had camped from Yellowstone to Chihuahua in a wagon that Hewett designed. They were especially charmed by the West's ancient ruins. By the time Hewett took a position at the Teachers College in Greeley, Colorado, they were so intrigued that he and Cora continued to spend their summers traveling through the Southwest. They were particularly attracted to the ancient sites on the Pajarito plateau, the setting of Adoph Bandelier's *Delight Makers*. Over the years, Hewett gained a reputation as an amateur archaeologist.

In fact, his initial visit to Las Vegas had been at Frank Springer's invitation, when he was asked to lecture on the preservation of ancient ruins.[17]

During Hewett and Cora's summers in New Mexico, they visited Santa Fe where Hewett gravitated toward others captivated by ancient ruins and the descendants of the original inhabitants. About the time that he accepted the position in Las Vegas, Hewett had joined an archaeology society of like-minded acquaintances in Santa Fe. Judge John R. McFie, an associate justice of the Territorial Supreme Court, was the head of the Archeological Society of New Mexico, newly formed in 1900. The group was rich in experience and passion and numbered among its members Adolph Bandelier, who had been studying and publishing his work on ancient sites since the mid-1880s under the auspices of the Archaeological Institute of America (AIA), Charles Lummis, a journalist by trade who spent years living with and reporting on contemporary Indian societies, and Paul A. F. Walter, editor at that time of the *Santa Fe New Mexican* and, though a newcomer, already an influential force in local politics. Attorney Frank Springer shared their enthusiasm.

As university president, Hewett was able to combine his growing passion for archaeology and anthropology with his role as educator. The brochure for the 1898–99 school term notes that the university had set aside ample room for a museum. The brochure also touched on an emergent conviction that southwestern archaeology ought to be the province of regional scientists, who had its best interests at heart, rather than ruled from afar by eastern institutions. Hewett imagined a vital role for the museum in this area, which fed Chap's imagination. "In the lines of prehistoric interest, [New Mexico] stands alone: the richest field on the continent," wrote Hewett. "Large collections are annually leaving the Territory to be placed in eastern institutions. If centered in New Mexico, these would soon make one of the finest museums of anthropology in existence."[18]

For the 1900–1901 term, Hewett lectured on prehistoric archaeology using the results of his previous five years' experience in nearby fieldwork, including on the Pajarito plateau. By 1903, the lectures included an introduction to anthropology, prehistoric archaeology, and ethnology. In the ethnology lectures, Hewett explored the folklore and rituals of native peoples, their arts and industries, primitive societies, and languages.[19] By accepting Hewett's invitation to teach summer art classes at the university, Chap stepped into an environment rich in areas that had fascinated him since his childhood searches for arrowheads.

The summer classes were also the occasion for Chap's formal introduction to Springer. Hewett had mentioned to Chap that Springer might be interested in enrolling one of his daughters in the art class, so Chap called on him at his law office. *I . . . found him on his knees before an open safe, stacking some bundles of papers inside. . . . He sat*

Frank Springer, c. 1915.
(Courtesy of School for
Advanced Research Archives,
AC02 777b.)

down with me and on learning about my course, said he could furnish one and perhaps two
pupils, and added that if he were not so busy, he would like to enter the class himself.[20]

Springer's desire to join the class was not mentioned as a mere pleasantry. He was
a remarkable man with Renaissance-like interests. Originally from Iowa, born June 17,
1848, Springer chose to pursue a career in law, following in the footsteps of his father.[21]
Springer's subsequent career with the Maxwell Land Grant Company in New Mexico,
during which he drafted the principal provisions of the land grant law and pled a case
before the U.S. Supreme Court, proved his exceptional aptitude for legal issues.

But in Springer's heart beat another love—paleontology. In his last year at the
University of Iowa, Springer met Louis Agassiz, the foremost naturalist of nineteenth-
century America and an initial scientific resource for the Smithsonian. Agassiz was a
forceful figure in American science, known for raising money, careful research, and an
unyielding opposition to Darwin's theory of evolution. As director of the Museum of
Comparative Zoology at Harvard, Agassiz saw museums primarily as vessels of research,

intended to safeguard collections and provide a means for scholars to publish their find-ings. Serving as a vehicle to educate the public was decidedly secondary.[22] But he was also renowned for his ability to make nature study popular and appealing.[23] A. J. Abbot, a classmate of Springer's, remembered that on the tour

> Agassiz stood there, crayon in one hand and an eraser in the other, and, on a large black-board on the rear of the rostrum, the rock written history of the world's geologic periods grew out before us until we felt like exclaiming, It is the handwork of Him "who hath neither beginning of days nor end of life."
>
>   Then and there Frank Springer took the cue for his future career in science. . . . With Agassiz Springer enjoyed a personal acquaintance and a sincere friend-ship. It was due to his earnest advice that Springer did not, under the stress of law practice and business engagements, abandon the inviting, absorbing, and uplifting work in the paleontological field which was his specialty.[24]

Springer arrived in New Mexico in 1873 at the urging of another college classmate, W. R. Morley. Springer was then twenty-five years old and living in Burlington, Iowa, working as a county prosecuting attorney. At that time, Morley was vice president of the Maxwell Land Grant Company, which had purchased the grant from its original owner and was now confronted with serious problems concerning its title to nearly two mil-lion acres in northern New Mexico.[25] In theory, the land grant owner had rights to all resources: water, minerals, forests. But the vast holdings were difficult to manage and, soon enough, the company discovered that the grant was as rich in difficulties as it was in resources. Bloody encounters between the settlers and the "grant men" became com-mon. When Morley called on Frank Springer in the spring of 1873, citizens were bent on taking the law into their own hands.[26]

Springer, as attorney, pursued a legal solution for the company even as the "law of the West" reigned. Many settlers had lived on grant lands for decades, and some had already set up informal arrangements for rent with Maxwell himself. But they were angry about the new company and challenged the company's right to title. The company appeared to gain a victory in 1877, when Secretary of the Interior Carl Shurz issued a patent for the entire claim. Immediately, the company began to sue for possession of ranches. However, the U.S. attorney general set aside the patent in 1882, so Springer argued the case before the circuit court in 1886, which held that the patent was good and valid. The next year, when it was appealed to the Supreme Court, Springer argued the case again. The decision was upheld.

The Supreme Court victory was not only of extraordinary value to the Maxwell Land Grant Company but greatly enhanced the reputation of Frank Springer, who was commended by lawyers and company officials alike for his exceptional handling of the case.[27] For legal services, Springer had already received a large tract of land in north-eastern New Mexico, in which the town of Springer—named by the railroad company in 1879—was located.[28] In 1887, the Dutch board of directors conveyed sixteen thousand acres of land with water rights to Springer, who later purchased fifty-two thousand more. Five years later, Springer became president of the Maxwell Land Grant Company, a position he held until his death in 1927. He also served two terms in the territorial legislature.[29] Springer's reputation and holdings made him an influential figure in New Mexico, particularly in later years with regard to archaeology and the arts. Springer and his wife, Josephine M. Bishop, moved their family of seven from Cimarron to Las Vegas in 1883. Their two daughters—Eva, who later would become a noted miniaturist painter, and Ada—were among Chap's first students.

Family life, citizenship responsibilities, and outstanding achievements in the legal field, however, did not satisfy Springer's many-sided curiosities. Even on his busiest days, he continued paleontological research. In later years, Hewett noted that it was Springer's "habit to spend the greater part of the night with his scientific studies. A night worker myself, I knew the meaning of the light in his laboratory, and occasionally after midnight I dropped over to share the pleasure of a true lover of nature in contemplating some new aspect of ancient life. Often as the daylight approached I would hear the sound of his flute and knew that he had come to the end of a perfect day—a business day in the service of his profession, an evening with family or friends, a night of study or writing and then the harmony of sweet sounds."[30]

In the field of paleontology, Springer's work achieved the highest scientific level. His scientific career had coexisted with his legal work since 1867, when he and Charles Wachsmuth developed their research in fossil crinoids. Wachsmuth, a German lawyer, became attracted to fossil research in Burlington, Iowa, where he had moved for his health. After studying the crinoid collections in the British Museum, Wachsmuth resolved to devote all his energies to the elucidation of the crinoidea. Springer and Wachsmuth coauthored several monographs. With more money than time, Springer often contributed funds as his fair share.[31] After Wachsmuth's death in 1896, Springer continued the studies. A contemporary account of Springer's work states that "Frank Springer . . . has been able to produce the most elaborate and careful works in the intervals of a busy life as a lawyer—works which it may be remarked, are much better known in London than in New Mexico, where he resides."[32]

And so Springer's interest in Chap's art class was more than fanciful. He was in genuine need of clear and exacting illustrations of the fossils, particularly for a significant monograph currently in preparation, *Crinoidea Flexibilia*.[33] An excellent artist from Sweden, Georg Liljevall, had been assisting Springer, but exchanging instructions at such a distance was awkward at best. As the summer of 1899 drew to a close, Springer attended an exhibition of his daughters' artwork, at which he asked if Chap might be interested in trying some illustrations for one of his publications. According to Chap, who had collected a few crinoids himself as a youngster, "I had heard only in a vague way that he wrote books on geology and I was wholly unprepared for the thrill of his next visit when he opened before me the magnificent volume of plates illustrating Wachsmuth and Springer's monograph on the 'North American Crinoidea Camerata.' The superb drawings by Westergren, Ridgway, and other masters won my admiration. If I expressed any doubt as to my ability to qualify for such company, he must have dismissed it with the assurance that they, too, had once been beginners."[34] In time, Springer and Chap would foster in each other a father-son-like relationship, with a loyalty that never faltered.

That fall, in addition to being promised employment from Springer, Chap was also encouraged by Hewett to continue as art instructor for the university. He offered Chap a part-time position, contingent on recommendations to satisfy the board. Chap wrote to his former employers for references, as well as to a fellow student at Chicago's Art Institute, who now taught there. Certain that after six years' absence no one at the institute would remember him, Chap asked if he could at least send on his transcript. *He not only secured a transcript for me but laid my case before John H. Vanderpoel, dean of the school, who went all out to give me a holograph letter of recommendation that clinched the job. I regret that I have lost the letter, the tenor of which was that the Institute had suffered a severe loss at my enforced leaving in the midst of an outstanding career with them!*[35]

Thus, less than six months after moving to Las Vegas, Chap was illustrating Springer's scientific publications during the morning and conducting elementary art classes at the university each afternoon. He conducted his art classes primarily by individual instruction, similar to the way he had been taught at the Art Institute and consistent with Hewett's belief in the importance of the one-on-one relationship between instructor and student. Chap recalled that his *relations with Hewett were most cordial, at the Normal School. . . . In all those years I found him most dependable and considerate, as leader and companion.*[36] For the most part, the faculty, which totaled about fifteen instructors, was a close-knit group, loyal to Hewett and his ideas. Because of his part-time schedule, Chap generally met the other faculty members only at meetings held each Saturday night at Hewett's home. On Sundays, Chap went occasionally to a Baptist church, *but more often spent Sunday mornings on hikes to the foothills, several miles west of town. Perhaps nowhere else in the country, at that time and in so small a place, could I have held a position on the faculty of a teachers' college without regularly taking part in the activities of one church group or another.*[37]

In Las Vegas, Chap's social life was nearly as sparse as before, but he enjoyed visiting with the Stoneroad family, with whom he first roomed, and accompanied Elba Stoneroad, his landlady's daughter and a schoolteacher, to occasional picnics or winter skating parties. One Saturday afternoon in 1901, he and Elba journeyed in a rented carriage to El Porvenir, a popular resort sixteen miles west of town in Gallinas Canyon, for a weekend party. However, when they encountered the proprietor of the stable driving back from the party, he asked them to exchange their carriage for his rig because he would need the carriage the following morning. After making the exchange, Chap and Elba discovered that since the poor horse had already made the trip once, he was not enthusiastic about the change in plans. After dark, with no lantern at hand, the ungraded road was difficult to follow.

I trusted to horse sense to pull us through but hopped out at one point when our nag stopped suddenly, and found him standing at the end of a sheer bank of the creek! After that whenever he stopped I did more reconnoitering. Finally I used my last match, and from there on had to get out several times and actually feel the ground for yards ahead to make sure we were in the beaten track. For years after, I claimed to have pawed over more miles of road than anyone in the Southwest.[38]

During the summer of 1901, Chap visited his family in South Bend, where he was introduced to his brother Dwight's fiancée, Ethel Carpenter, who was, literally, the girl next door. After Dwight's marriage that summer, Chap's mother and sister joined him in Las Vegas where they shared a home. *Mother was ill at the time, but gradually recovered her health and later on took charge of the Carnegie Library. By that time, Vera had married, and within a few years found herself a widow with a young daughter.*[39] Feeling the weight of responsibility in their care, Chap rejected the idea of becoming serious about any of the young women he met.[40]

Other summers, Chap was employed by Hewett with mapping, sketching, and occasional photography at sites on the Pajarito Plateau, located in the Jemez Mountains outside Santa Fe. Sites such as Tsirege, where Chap worked in 1900, were filled with archaeological finds, including pottery sherds. Hewett's attempt to restore the pottery underscores the youthful naiveté of the archaeological field at that time. He and Cora used liquid glue and then stored the artifacts under a small tent at the camp. All went well until intermittent showers, followed by the hot sun beating down on canvas, resulted in a steam bath that melted the glue. Every mended specimen flattened out, and many labels could not be replaced on the proper bowls.[41] From then on, the pottery pieces were nested together until they could be shipped back to town where they would be repaired.

A particularly exciting opportunity for Chap came up in 1902 when Hewett asked Chap to accompany him on an extended trip to study the ancient Pueblo ruins of Chaco Canyon for the U.S. Department of the Interior. Besides Hewett, the party included his wife, Cora, Ruth Raynolds, and two university instructors, Margretta McNary, who taught Latin and Greek, and James G. McNary, a modern language and singing instructor. Because Cora's health had begun to deteriorate, Hewett prepared a sturdy spring wagon with a built-in bed, where Cora spent the greater part of each day. The other women slept in tents, while McNary and Chap slept on cots under the stars.[42] Chap remembered the trip fondly.

> *The others, I believe, shared in the expense of the trip but since I could not have left my summer's work for so extended a vacation, I was included at no expense, and I assume that I received some compensation for what little work I did with sketching, mapping, and photography. . . . Within a few days Jim [McNary] and I had a hand in all the daily chores and happily we found that each had his preference. Jim chose the horses and I took naturally to equipment, including the daily use of axle grease, the rustling of firewood, and a dozen other details. Because of Mrs. Hewett's condition we seldom made over twenty miles a day, and often much less, but this with the daily breaking and making of camp, the preparation and serving of three meals a day, and the endless chores of packing and unpacking, kept us busy six days a week from sunrise to sunset.*[43]

For Chap, the trip must have been an occasion of deep enchantment. They visited several pueblos, whose vivid culture and traditions were a far cry from the silent arrowheads he had spotted in the fields as a boy. The journey took them to Santa Clara Pueblo, where they also explored the ruins of Puyé, and Jemez Pueblo, where they photographed the only two surviving members of the Pecos tribe, who had abandoned their pueblo in 1838. (And where Ruth and Jim announced their engagement just before the group reached the Jemez hot springs!) The group appeared to enjoy a special camaraderie, laughing over jokes such as Chap's storing the kitchen utensils in an old box labeled "reloading tools" (it had formerly held shotgun shells) and their renaming of a horse they bought on the trail from "Chap" to "Chock" once Hewett pointed out that Chap had prior right to the name. Indeed, Chap was particularly impressed by

> *the cordial cooperation of each individual in the group, and the unfailing good humor and kindness with which they met every situation. In particular it was a privilege to be associated so closely with two such even-tempered, capable, and gracious young women as Ruth Raynolds and Margaretta McNary. To have prepared*

and served our three meals a day, under all conditions during the greater part of the two months' expedition was a major feat in itself, yet as I look back on it they seemed always to be leading a normal existence, and always ready to join in any diversion. . . . I learned much from my association with each member of the party, and still count it as one of the best examples of training in good citizenship that I have ever known.[44]

At Chaco Canyon, Hewett investigated the area while Jim and Chap measured the layout of several important ruins. Chap photographed the site, although he was disappointed to discover on his return that a camera piece had loosened along the trail, rendering all of the Chaco Canyon photos useless. Despite this, the trip had been a success and called for celebration, as far as Hewett was concerned. Chaco represented a recent victory for the regional archaeologists and an increase in importance for Hewett himself. Around the campfire, Hewett likely told Chap and the others of Chaco Canyon's treasure trove, which had been cleared by Richard Wetherill and the Hyde Expedition in 1896–97. The specimens, including over one hundred pottery bowls and a 1,214-piece turquoise mosaic, filled the entire railroad freight car that transported them to the National Museum of Natural History.[45] Hewett was probably also quick to point out his role in the government's investigation of Wetherill and the Hyde Expedition for its commercial activities. The result was significant: a permanent restraining order against the Hyde Expedition in 1902 (even though the Wetherills were exonerated) and a proposal to make Chaco Canyon a national park. Given a victory so fresh, author Snead suggests that Hewett made the trip to examine his prize.[46]

Chap might have counted as his treasure several encounters with Native Americans along the trail. At the Pueblo Bonito trading post, Chap became intimately involved with Indian art. At the time, paintings by Native Americans on paper with colored pencils or crayon were relatively rare, and, with a few exceptions, it was only the Plains Indians who used this medium.[47] *One of the clerks showed us some drawings of Navajo dance groups, made by a Navajo artist, with pencil, on cardboard salvaged from paper boxes. I gave the artist, Apie Begay, some good paper, and lent him my box of ten colored pencils, the first he had ever seen. Apie made three drawings for me that have been described and exhibited several times as the earliest known examples of Navajo art produced with white man's materials.*[48]

Also at Pueblo Bonito, a half dozen men—in everyday costume, with rattles improvised from tin cans and gravel—treated Chap and the others to their first Navajo dance. Firelight rendered it an exciting performance.[49] When Hewett, Cora, and Chap stopped at Zia Pueblo on their return trip, the whole pueblo was preparing for the annual dance. (Margretta, Jim, and Ruth had traveled on by train to the Grand Canyon.) They also visited Santo Domingo Pueblo, taking a side trip to Cochiti and the shrine of the Stone Lions, where they might have noticed potters at work. Perhaps Chap began to wonder then about the link between the few pots at these pueblos and the sherds he had handled at the ruins.

At that time, potters were producing pottery primarily for family or ceremonial use, although even family use had diminished with the abundance of metal cooking pans available. Some potters were just beginning to supply pottery to traders, such as Thomas Keam and Lorenzo Hubbell, who had begun to recognize its commercial potential by 1900, especially as the railroad began to carry tourists—like Ruth, Jim, and Margretta—deep into "Indian" country.[50] A few specialists were sensitive to the possibility that tourist demand for such souvenirs might offer an economic opportunity as well as a means of promoting traditional crafts. For example in 1902, William A. Jones, commissioner of Indian Affairs, instructed Indian office field matrons to encourage artisans to use traditional standards, materials, and techniques in an attempt to counter the growing mass production of cheap souvenirs.[51] Overall, however, the market for Indian art at the turn of the century was designed to enrich Anglos, not Indians. Traders paid for pots by the pound and dispatched barrelsful to buyers back east.

The sherds from ancient pottery that littered Tsirege and Chaco captivated Chap. He may have recognized in them the art of a master craftsman; the idea of the master craftsman was disseminated as part of the arts and crafts movement, which was at its height as Chap himself came of age. The movement had developed in reaction to the mass production of the Industrial Age. Sensitive to artistic paradigms, Chap would likely have evaluated the sherds and broken pots within the context of the movement's core principle, which declared that decoration must be true to the material and form of the object so that aesthetic and utilitarian components were perfectly balanced.[52] Pottery as craft—rather than fine art—would also have conformed to his perspective then. Although the arts and crafts movement helped to blur the distinction between fine art and craft, in general, popular perception still identified fine art as nonutilitarian and as the province of white males. Domestic art, or craft, was usually the work of minorities—women, laborers, or native peoples—and was functional only.[53] Chap brought Indian pots into his classroom at Normal, using them for forms in drawing and as decorative elements. "I can say truthfully I am probably the first one to use Indian art in school instruction in the United States," he noted in a 1965 interview.[54]

Normal University, with its innovative teaching practices, was also drawing national notice. According to the editor of the *Journal of Education* in January 1903, "it is one of the best normal schools in the country, and in the natural sciences especially, I have never seen it excelled. In ethnology and entomology, it is not approached in the whole

Kenneth M. Chapman in New Mexico, 1915. (Courtesy of School for Advanced Research Archives, AC02 766a.)

country, and the art department is superior."[55] Local residents, however, took a dimmer view. There are several accounts of why the board of regents abhorred Hewett. Hewett's biographer, Beatrice Chauvenet, explains that some observers were critical of a college that encouraged young people to traipse around the countryside in pursuit of education.[56] Fowler adds that Hewett's persistent efforts to get large tracts of public land set aside for national parks had angered powerful ranchers and landowners.[57] Bruce Ellis, assistant to Chap in the 1950s, noted in a 1971 paper that the board dispute originated over Sunday football at the university: Governor Miguel A. Otero Jr. and his friends were for football; Hewett and Springer, against.

Frank Springer's version is that local tensions with regard to Hewett's leadership were exacerbated in 1902 not only by his liberal academic ideas but also his unwillingness to play by the rules of local politics. According to Springer, Hewett refused to give all the university's printing to the Las Vegas *Record*, letting the work go to the lowest bidder as the law required instead. The policy aroused such hostility that Governor Otero, who disliked Hewett's methods, appointed a known opponent, Dr. W. B. Tipton, to the board of regents.[58] To arouse further bad feelings, Tipton charged that the under the current administration, the students were given "pernicious & immoral books." Springer used records to refute the accusation, but the incident had soured his commitment to the university.

Hewett had few friends on the board besides Springer, for during his years as president, he had engendered loyalty in his staff but had made little effort to cultivate relationships among the local business community. Chap ruefully noted that Hewett *spent most of his vacations out of town, on archaeological expeditions, and he had given a series of lectures on the subject in Santa Fe, but never one in Las Vegas!*[59] Harnessing the momentum gained from Tipton's appointment, the board of regents moved to oust Hewett, who announced his resignation at the January board meeting. Four days later, Springer resigned as regent "upon the ground that while willing to work for the institution he had no time for such squabbles."[60] Springer's resignation was a blow. Las Vegas leaders urged him to reconsider but to no avail.[61] *The faculty had counted on Mr. Springer's active support, but instead he had tendered his resignation as President of the Board, without entering one word of protest. Under such circumstances there was very little they could do for they too were not well enough acquainted with influential citizens to ask their support.*[62] In a dramatic statement, the entire faculty, Chap included, resigned en masse on commencement day.[63]

According to Chauvenet, Hewett "might have made a fight over the regents' decision, but he recognized that it would not be in the best interest of the school; even if he won, his future usefulness was impaired. He submitted his resignation without protest. It was the first serious defeat of his career."[64] Hewett was characteristically optimistic—when one door closes, another opens—and viewed the dismissal as an opportunity to advance his academic credentials by completing his doctorate, a survey of the ancient communities of the American Southwest. He and Cora traveled to Geneva, Switzerland, where Hewett attended the university in 1903. "Once when he mentioned to Frank Springer the failure of his presidency at Las Vegas, Springer rejected the idea, assuring Hewett that he had outgrown the college post and was ready to move on into his true life work. Springer was a source of steady support for Hewett's career."[65]

Chap, too, saw his resignation from the university as an opportunity rather than a setback. He intended to pursue other interests, admitting that he *was not greatly concerned over the outcome for Mr. Springer had decided to take an increasing portion of my time, and I was also eager to develop a very promising business in publishing my designs for use in greeting cards, calendars, and other novelties.*[66]

Chap appears to have been enthused about his novelty business (see plates 3 and 4), which combined his artistic talents and sly sense of humor. "Greetings from a Tenderfoot" heralded one card, decorated with a bandaged foot. He was also selling paintings to the Atchison, Topeka, and Santa Fe Railway for its Southwest promotions (see plate 6). But as Chap built up his business, he continued to illustrate Springer's work in progress, *Crinoidea Flexibilia*, rendering the fossils that Springer had brought with him to New Mexico. In 1905, Springer asked Chap to accompany him to Burlington, Iowa, for two months to work on specimens stored there that were too bulky or fragile to ship. By accepting, Chap was rewarded not only with work but, more importantly, an occasion to nourish a genuine friendship with Springer. In later years, Chap noted that

> *During my first five years, I had had no opportunity to become acquainted with the real Mr. Springer. He was not one to make friends readily; he was immured by his years of study, and by his dependence on only a few of his immediate associates. His legal and executive activities were exacting, and he spent much of his time out of town, so that often several weeks would pass before he could find time to review my work. It was not until the spring of 1905 that he found an opportunity to break away for several months' study at his little private museum in Burlington, Iowa, where he needed me to work on material that could not be well transported to New Mexico. It was on that trip that he disclosed his amiable qualities, and in our close association during that summer there developed a sort of father and son relationship that was to endure for the remainder of the nearly thirty years that I knew him.*[67]

Springer and Wachsmuth's collection—the world's greatest collection of fossil crinoids, according to an article in the local paper—was housed in Burlington, a town that Chap found most attractive. During walks with Springer, he saw well-kept homes, some with wide, unfenced lawns that stretched over an entire block.[68] To paleontologists, Burlington's attraction was its abundance of fossils, which could be found in the two-hundred-foot-thick limestone bed on which the town sat. Springer's collection nearly filled a small two-room building at the rear of the Wachsmuth residence, where Wachsmuth's widow still lived. According to Chap, "the cases had multiplied until they left scant room for our activities, but there in close quarters I was to settle down with [Springer] for the greater part of many years to come. . . . The little museum was an observation post for all the back door life of the neighborhood, from the bustle of washday to the last of Saturday's chores."[69]

At first, Chap's acquaintances included only Wachsmuth's friends, most of them sixty or older—nearly twice Chap's age—who lived well, but economically, and seemed satisfied with the standstill status of the old town. But by midsummer, Chap must have been indulging in romantic fantasies even as he labored over the crinoid sketches, for he'd met

"a Society girl," which in those days in the Middle-West seemed to mean one who was not working for a living.

My experience of six years in Las Vegas, with both "society" and working girls had left me with the conclusion that, with the responsibility of cooperation in sharing a home with my mother and sister, the girl question was not for me, and the situation had apparently been accepted by the girls themselves. But here in Burlington I was fancy free and lonesome. Here was a good natured and amusing girl, daughter of a staid well to do German family, alone, for her only brother was living in St. Louis. She had a most pleasing contralto voice, sang in a church choir, kept busy with choral society, charities, country club, and all such activities.

. . . Her speaking voice was a continual surprise. Between times, I couldn't explain it, but when I had taken counsel with myself and would resolve to slow down, saying to myself, "this is not for you,"—each time she found some special occasion to give me a ring. And then, at her "Hello!" my stern resolve turned weak in the knees![70]

After two months, Chap returned to his mother and sister in Las Vegas, and his new Burlington friend became "an obliging and amusing correspondent." Chap's novelty business was becoming more profitable, and he was also asked to compose illustrations—based on old drawings, historical data, and present conditions—for a New Mexico history, authored by his friend, Ralph E. Twitchell.[71] Chap continued making fossil sketches but saw little of Springer, who was busy in Raton with land grant affairs. Then, in the spring of 1906, the fifty-seven-year-old Springer suffered a severe heart attack. Returning to Las Vegas, he called Chap to his house

and there, in his family's absence and with the marks of his illness still upon him, he told me of his plight, of his splendid rally after a night of despair when he faced about and determined to die game. "We are going back to Burlington," he announced, "and we are going to fight this out to the finish!"

It was an anxious year for his family and friends. The memory of that summer [1906, in Burlington] will never leave me, for if I had never realized his gameness before, I saw it then. Once settled in his museum, he prescribed for himself a light but gradually augmented course of exercises. Progress was painfully slow for the first few months; indeed, it seemed at times as if it were a losing game. But he held on until, by fall, he could venture with me on a daily walk of several blocks. From then on, his improvement was rapid and the following summer saw us on frequent hikes of several miles over the hills of his boyhood, at a pace that kept me up to my best.[72]

During the summer of 1906, Chap was surely preoccupied not only with anxiety over Springer's condition but also over his growing affection for his Burlington companion, even as he realized the futility of a future together. Toward the end of the summer, the relationship *ended in the inevitable show-down. She accepted my point of view regarding my unpredictable future, but soon after my return to Las Vegas she availed herself of a girl's privilege, to change her mind, and wrote me, asking if we couldn't make a go of it. I did my best to measure up to it but could see no chance of taking on such a responsibility.*[73]

Looking to his financial future, Chap continued to expand his novelty business, which now included sculpture, postcards, and calendar designs. The business seemed very promising, though it demanded more and more of his time, which concerned Springer. To complete his monograph, he needed Chap's efforts full time for at least two years, so he appealed to Chap. "I might have held out but for the memory of his long struggle of the year before. I finally agreed and this led to an understanding between us absolutely unique in my experience and all the more significant, I have always felt, in that it rested solely on his confidence in me and on my absolute faith in his few words."[74]

The understanding was that Springer would reward Chap financially sometime in the future. *Mr. Springer told me that he could not then conveniently do all that he intended for me, but if I would agree to stand by him, he promised that I would never have reason to regret it. I gave my consent and thus, without one word on paper to confirm our agreement, seven years would pass before he made his promised settlement.*[75] However, Chap's agreement still left him without the means to pursue a more permanent relationship with the girl from Burlington. Before he returned in 1907 for his third summer in Burlington, she and her mother left for Europe. With a letdown in their correspondence, she returned to Burlington in September determined to end the affair.

She asked my forgiveness for the trouble her letter had caused me; said she saw it all from my view point, and intended to look up an old prospect in Chicago, get herself married and start raising a family. It was a relief no longer to face such an impasse, but losing our care-free companionship was the hardest blow I had ever had.[76]

Chap intended to spend the greater part of the next two years (1907–8) with Springer in Burlington, but he suffered a physical set back that "took several months of New Mexico sun light to bring me back to par." In his memoirs, Chap attributes his ailments to "the steady employment at such confining work," but one can only guess that heartbreak over the Burlington romance contributed to his ill health. At the same time, however, Chap was comforted by Springer's fatherlike affection. According to Chap, "once away from his business cares and settled in his museum, I learned to know him in his hours of relaxation and there began a friendship that was to grow from year to year. I was no longer an employee, but a co-worker. From then on it was 'we,' and our work went ahead on a new basis. I learned each day new depths of his resource-fulness, kindness, deep sympathy, his great generosity, and of the many other noble qualities that went to make him the great man he was. I have never ceased to marvel at his passion for work, at his physical and mental endurance and his wonderful power of concentration."[77]

Like the pioneer effort of his mentor Agassiz, which described more than seventeen hundred ancient species and was a model of exactitude, Springer's monographs, such as *Crinoidea Flexibilia* and *American Silurian Crinoids*, are remarkable examples of his own efforts to describe precisely the fossil groups.[78] Each monograph includes an overview of the fossils, followed by pages of specimens illustrated in painstaking detail. The faithful rendering was the result of Chap's combining photography with pen and ink. Though the camera is said never to lie, it often tells but half the truth, Chap noted. It was his duty to supply that other and important half by developing outline, light and shade, so that every feature of a drawing told its story of form and texture.[79] In his introduction to *Crinoidea Flexibilia*, Springer wrote that Chap had become "the master to whose pre-eminence the 75 beautiful plates of this work, as well as the numerous others in previous publications, bear convincing testimony."[80] Springer's method of scientific classification very much impressed Chap, who would imitate its systematic presentation in his own monographs on Indian art in the 1930s.

In Burlington, Chap worked alone in the mornings; around noon, Springer would join him. "But [Springer's] real concentration came late at night when, long after the neighbors' lights were out, it was his habit to work in seclusion until 2 a.m. or after."[81] In their daily interactions, Springer exhibited his natural and persistent curiosity in all things, which mirrored Chap's own inquisitive inclinations. "[Springer] allowed no interruptions from outside, and thanks to the care of Mrs. Wachsmuth, it was a rare occasion when a visitor broke in on his day's work. Yet, when a spider displayed her hundreds of infants on a web outside the museum door, his interest knew no bounds, and when the catbirds who nested in a lilac bush near by were in danger of losing their fledglings to a troop of neighborhood cats, he would spend hours guarding them and experimenting with improvised cages that would protect them until they could use their wings."[82]

Meanwhile, during Chap's Burlington years, Hewett had been building support for his dream—a southwestern archaeological institute. Having lost the affiliation with Las Vegas, where he had once hoped to establish "one of the finest museums in existence," Hewett now turned to Santa Fe. Hewett's vision was to lead American archaeological and anthropological research.

The major characters in the anthropology drama at the turn of the century had been brushing up against each other for nearly thirty years. Since 1900, several museums and universities had strengthened their anthropology departments, and many of the members of these departments were the same players who had contributed to the 1893 Chicago's World Fair: Franz Boas, Frank Hamilton Cushing, William Henry Holmes, Jesse Walter Fewkes, and Frederick Ward Putnam.[83] Nearly twenty years later, they had all grown in experience, in stature, and in a propensity for expressing firm opinions. They were making a name for themselves within a developing scientific field that operated like a small town and that, like any good soap opera, had its fair share of favorite sons and long-standing grudges.

In the Southwest itself, anthropologists included Charles Lummis, who practically invented the myth of the Southwest, and Adolph Bandelier, a longtime southwestern ethnologist. Both belonged to the Archaeological Society of New Mexico and so were acquainted with society president McFie as well as with Springer and Hewett. In addition to cultivating the support of this regional group, Hewett began to pursue the patronage of national figures such as Alice Cunningham Fletcher and William Henry Holmes after making their acquaintance in Washington, DC, in 1900. Fletcher, a Putnam protégé (like Boas), had been a founding member of the AIA. She was a staunch proponent of welfare for Indian peoples, supporting legislation and organizations such as the Women's Indian Association, and she held a lifelong fellowship at Harvard. Holmes, who had served as director of the Field Columbian Museum in Chicago and head curator of anthropology at the Smithsonian, ultimately succeeded John Wesley Powell as the Bureau of Ethnology's chief in 1903.

As the field of anthropology matured, developing both national and regional strains, Hewett saw an opportunity to establish a forceful presence by pursuing a passion of his own. He had long been critical of the lack of protection for American antiquities. Hundreds of thousands of specimens had been transported to the East from the Southwest, through trade or stealth, since the 1880s. To generate interest in Congress, Hewett invited Congressman John F. Lacey of Iowa to visit the Southwest in 1903, where they surveyed the situation on horseback. Hewett then prepared a comprehensive report on the problem in 1904 for the General Land Office that presented the case so clearly that Congress finally grasped the importance of the issue.[84] He continued to work tire-lessly for the bill, sponsored by Lacey, until its passage in 1906. Chap, who would have discussed the details with Springer, later noted "if [Hewett's] name in future years were to be associated only with that feat, he would still rank highly among the archaeologists of his generation."[85]

Hewett's accomplishment quickly amplified his archaeological network, while his professional energies sparked a lightninglike path to success. With family, however, he struggled with loss. In 1904, Hewett's father died in Hopkins, Missouri. The following year, Hewett suffered even more deeply as Cora's illness slowly took her from him; she died in Washington, DC, in 1905. Although she had become increasingly frail over the years, Cora had remained as devoted to Hewett as he had to her.[86] Losing Cora after fourteen years of marriage, Hewett succumbed to a profound grief. According to Chauvenet, "with Cora's death, something of his youthful exuberance went out of Edgar's life. . . . He had always worked long hours . . . and he now drove himself with a sort of desperation."[87]

The goal toward which Hewett drove himself was an American school sponsored by the AIA. In 1905, the AIA was still oriented toward Old World sites, as it had been since its founding in 1879. It had established schools in Athens, Rome, Jerusalem, and Baghdad, but some members, such as Harvard's Putnam, saw value in American archaeology and an Americanist committee had been formed. Most AIA members felt, however, that archaeological funds, always in chronic shortage, should be spent on tra-ditional expeditions and that little of cultural value could be found in the Americas. One ardent opponent of American research was Charles Eliot Norton of Harvard, a founding member of the AIA. Ironically, however, Norton's views on education coin-cided with Hewett's teaching theories, thus making him Hewett's unexpected ally. His and Hewett's shared educational ideas allowed Hewett to be first tolerated and then accepted by the other AIA founders. But the AIA continued to harbor doubts about southwestern fieldwork.[88]

Hewett's persistence in promoting the Southwest as a relatively untouched archaeo-logical treasure paid off with a $600 AIA fellowship in 1905. Well-meaning support-ers offered nearly as many ways to spend the fellowship funds as there were dollars. The chairman of the AIA's Americanist committee was Charles Bowditch, a contributor to the Peabody Museum and endower of a fellowship at Harvard, held then by Alfred Tozzer. Bowditch requested that Putnam be responsible for assigning duties to Hewett but then himself proposed that Hewett's energies be spent promoting the growth of local archaeological societies. William Henry Holmes believed that Hewett should investigate and report on Mesa Verde, in response to a mandate from the Department of Interior. Classical scholar Francis Kelsey asked Hewett to promote archaeological societies in

Colorado and California. Alice Fletcher urged Hewett to study the Indians as a people. Franz Boas wrote to Putnam that Hewett had proved himself as a self-starter and should choose his own activities. Finally Putnam told Hewett that he should make a comparative study of the culture—especially of the art and architecture—of the pueblo sites he already knew and those of ancient sites in Mexico to ascertain whether an ethnic connection existed between the two groups. Hewett tried to satisfy them all. He traveled to Santa Fe, Mesa Verde, and Denver, and then visited sites in Chihuahua, Mexico, where he gathered information for the comparative survey.[89] Hewett visited Alice Fletcher in Mexico, taking the opportunity to share his grand scheme of an archaeology school that would be located in the Southwest and reminding her that carrying out the mandate of the American Antiquities Act would require constant vigilance.

Late in 1906, Fletcher, who had replaced Bowditch as chairman of the AIA's Americanist committee, and Putnam, who had been impressed by Hewett's achievements in the field, persuaded the classicists that American research needed a full-time director. Hewett was appointed on January 2, 1907. One of the first things he did was organize summer fieldwork, asking Putnam, in the spring of 1907, to help recruit Harvard students.

A. V. Kidder, one of the initial recruits, recalled later he was trying to decide how to spend his summer when he saw the announcement in the *Harvard Crimson*. The article indicated that the AIA was looking for three men specializing in anthropology to volunteer for an expedition to the cliff-dwelling country. "That, if they'd take me, would solve my summer problem. Whether Anthropology 5 qualified me as a specialist was, I had to admit, dubious," he wrote in his memoirs.[90] Indeed, Tozzer, who was in charge of picking the recruits, did accept Kidder's application, as well as those of Sylvanus Morley and John Gould Fletcher (a poet and protégé of Amy Lowell)—an easy decision for Tozzer, as they were the only applicants.

Through Hewett, both Kidder and Morley would become close friends and colleagues of Chap's. Kidder, who would later enjoy a brilliant career in archaeology, vividly detailed his initiation into archaeology in his memoirs. His recollections bring to life the adventurous spirit and staunch friendships that fueled early archaeology in the Southwest:

> I can't remember that we were given any definite instructions, except that in early July we were to met [*sic*] Edgar L. Hewett . . . at a place called Bluff City, Utah.
>
> My diary says very little of what we looked out upon. I think I was dazed by that view [the mesa that separates the canyons of McElmo and Yellow Jacket in Utah], my first of such a vast desolation; naked red rock below and all about,

mesas, pinnacles, ragged canyon walls, sheer cliffs. I must, too, have been a bit overcome by what Mr. Hewett so casually told us we were to do. He waved an arm, taking in it seemed, about half the world, "I want you boys to make an archaeological survey of this country. I'll be back in about three weeks."[91]

Hewett put Morley in charge, as he was the only one of the three who knew what an archaeological survey entailed: assessing all the remains in an area and providing descriptions through notes, plans, and photographs as detailed as possible without excavating. Kidder was assigned to mapping and the journal, Morley wrote the notes, all three measured, and Kidder and Morley drew the plans of the structures.

Fletcher, whose fingers were all thumbs, turned out, though willing, to be of little use except to hold one end of the tape. . . .

Notwithstanding our primitive equipment, we did a pretty good job. But it was all due to Vay [Morley]. He was an indefatigable worker, full of energy, invariably cheerful, whistling and singing as he stumbled about among the ruins. Very nearsighted, it was a miracle that he didn't break a leg or pitch himself over any of the cliffs to the very edges of which many of the little canyon-head pueblos clung.[92]

Hewett was also delighted with their progress. Although initially concerned after receiving a "doleful" letter from Fletcher, Hewett recounts in his memoirs that he next heard from Morley and Kidder, who wanted to reassure Hewett that Fletcher's letter was a minority report. They were not infants, they told Hewett, and they would survive. Hewett was encouraged, observing that "it may be possible to live down a Harvard education."[93] When he visited their camp six weeks later, he was not only satisfied with their results but thrilled to hear them "testify that being thrown into the water without life preservers was the beginning of a real education for them."[94]

That summer, Alice Cunningham Fletcher visited Hewett in the Southwest and was charmed by all she saw. In December 1907, she pushed through a resolution at the annual AIA meeting to create a School of American Archaeology, with the location to be determined. Fletcher chaired the school's managing committee; other members were Boas, Fewkes, Kelsey, Lummis, and Putnam. Hewett then organized a second summer's field school. Apparently the 1907 survey had felt more like an adventure to Kidder and Morley than a hardship, because 1908 found them out West again, accompanied by Jesse Nusbaum, official photographer for the school under Hewett. Chap, who had been invited by Hewett, joined them in August for fieldwork at Rito de los Frijoles, having spent the earlier part of the summer in Burlington with Springer. The site, located in the rugged canyon and mesa country of northern New Mexico, had been on Hewett's list of sites to visit ever since he had read Bandelier's description of it in the *Delight Makers* in 1890.

> The Rito is a beautiful spot. Situated in a direct line not over twenty miles west of Santa Fé, it can still be reached only after a long day's tedious travel. It is a narrow valley, nowhere broader than half a mile. . . . Through the vale itself rustles the clear and cool brook to which the name of Rito de los Frijoles is applied. It meanders on, hugging the southern slope, partly through open space, partly through groves of timber, and again past tall stately pine-trees standing isolated in the valley. . . . In the cliffs themselves, for a distance of about two miles, numerous caves dug out by the hand of man are visible. Some of these are yet perfect; others have wholly crumbled away except the rear wall. . . . These ruins . . . bear testimony to the tradition still current among the Queres Indians of New Mexico that the Rito, or Tyuonyi, was once inhabited by people of their kind, nay, even of their own stock.[95]

The summer's expedition was funded by Harvard ($500), the New Mexico Archaeological Society ($500), and Frank Springer ($250). Professors Alfred M. Tozzer and Roland B. Dixon represented Harvard. Other members of the excavation team included the linguist John P. Harrington and eight or ten men from San Ildefonso. Kidder later remarked that the Tewa men "proved to be excellent shovelmen, who took a keen interest in everything they found. They helped us identify many specimens which would otherwise have been puzzling, and their comments on the pottery, and especially on the designs, was most illuminating."[96]

Chap met Kidder and Nusbaum for the first time at Buckman station, a stop on the Denver and Rio Grande narrow-gauge railway that ran from Utah through Colorado to New Mexico. Kidder and Nusbaum were en route from Bluff City, Utah, where they had been working in the field with southwestern anthropologist Byron Cummings, associated with the University of Utah, and his nephew Neil M. Judd.[97]

> As often before, the train was a few hours late and I was much relieved when Jesse Nusbaum and Alfred Kidder appeared with a great lot of luggage from their previous camps. . . . Like myself they had carried emergency rations so that we were well supplied for the three meals we would need there and enroute to camp.
>
> We spread our bed rolls near the D&RG track on ground used by Buckman for unloading logs hauled by wagons downgrade from the pine forests of the Pajarito Plateau. . . . I remember the lumber yard in particular for the depth of pine bark

Jesse L. Nusbaum (left) and Alfred V. Kidder, Mesa Verde, Colorado, 1908. (Courtesy of Palace of the Governors [MNM/DCA], 139157.)

chips made a dry and springy site for our bedrolls. But it was also used as a lunch room by numerous bark beetles. The chirping noise of one, directly under my head kept me awake for some time, but I fell asleep before I could decide how to silence him.

. . . In [the] morning by appointment a bearded native with team and wagon came to haul our impedimenta to Frijoles, across the old Buckman bridges. . . . On the way, walking and hitching a ride on down slopes, I had a good opportunity to compare notes with Kidder[;] . . . we were soon fast friends. We found the driver unusually friendly, and he spoke a little English and my smattering of Spanish helped fill the gaps. . . .

As we neared Frijoles canyon, we were on a woody road through Ancho canyon when we heard shouting, then the roar of falling rock and saw a pack horse tumble to his death from the cliff near by. Then came more shouting and on that Jess and Kidder recognized the voices of a party of three . . . headed by Sylvanus Morley who had made the journey by pack train from Mesa Verde.[98]

At Rito, Tozzer—who claimed years of field experience—had already arrived, and, according to Chap, was "fit to be tied," having waited nearly two days for the other members of the scattered group, when Chap, Nusbaum, Kidder, and Morley finally appeared. However, Hewett, who arrived the following day, then discovered that no one had brought a tape line for site preparation and so had to send for one from Santa Fe. According to Chap's memoirs, the dilatory start of the month's fieldwork left Tozzer and Dixon most critical of Hewett's casual modus operandi.[99]

Though a foreshadowing of criticism to come, disapproval from the eastern archaeologists probably did not discomfit Hewett at the time. After many years in New Mexico, it is likely that the Southwest's disrespect for time seemed more the norm to Hewett than any rigid schedule upheld by intellectuals from the East. More important, however, Hewett would simply have been in his element. Although still deeply grieving Cora, Hewett must also have felt a profound sense of satisfaction at the direction his life had taken: he was at work on the Pajarito Plateau and surrounded once again by students. The teacher in Hewett was always a powerful presence. Chap recalled that whenever he met former students of Hewett, *without exception, they said that they had not met one instructor from heads of departments-down who surpassed Mr. Hewett as an ideal teacher.*[100]

The summer's work at Frijoles marked a turning point for Chap as well. He, too, was in his element. His colleagues—Kidder, Morley, Nusbaum, and others—were bright, congenial, and able to laugh. During the month's fieldwork, Kidder and Chap discovered a mutual interest in Indian pottery. From Kidder, Chap learned about articles on prehistoric wares published by the Bureau of American Ethnology, including Fewkes's articles on ancient pottery, the Sikyatki style. Possibly for the first time, Chap may have given serious thought to a career in anthropology, which would combine his interests in art and Indian artifacts. Chap's task that summer was to create sketches of the site, including a panorama of the cliff's cave dwellings.

I had not yet recovered fully from an illness of the previous winter and I stepped around and climbed easy grades rather gingerly for a few days until I toughened up for the job ahead of illustrating the reports to be prepared by Mr. Hewett, the most exacting being the outline panorama of the mile and more of cliff with the remains of cave dwellings in group after group. One very easy and satisfactory way of doing the job would have been to await Nusbaum's photographing of the cliff from the opposite side of the canyon and to work from his enlargements. But as he could not get at this at once I finally climbed the trail to the top of the south cliff and set to work by hand and eye.

Holding a foot ruler at arm's length and sighting at the cliff from across the canyon, I located spots at its base where I might set up markers at the beginning of the next day's work, thus dividing the cliff into equal sections from end to end. Then sketching the details of each section on a separate sheet, it was easy to join them as continuous master sheet for tracing onto good drawing paper. Primitive though the method seems today, it sufficed for a semi-diagrammatic presentation of the several caves and house-groups in relation to intervening and almost inaccessible recesses in the cliff.[101]

A dramatic finding occurred during the summer's work of excavating Tyuonyi. A. J. and Ida Abbott, who were acquaintances of Springer and Hewett with homestead rights in the area, innocently followed a stray cow along a natural path one day. They spotted the large open-mouthed natural cave that Hewett and his staff had observed earlier in the summer. However, the Abbotts' vantage point permitted them to see that the cave held a roofless and partly filled pit of an ancient kiva. The Abbotts reported their sighting to Hewett, who had Nusbaum and several men from San Ildefonso hew hand- and toeholds in the rock the following day so the cave could be inspected for the first time.[102] The Ceremonial Cave, as it is now known, is a spectacular example of an ancient pueblo's spiritual site. Probably fearful of giving the eastern anthropologists ammunition with regard to his methods, Hewett made no mention of the Abbotts' contribution in his detailed account of the field sessions published in the *American Anthropologist*. Although the Abbotts said nothing to Hewett, they let Chap know that they were hurt by the omission.[103]

Nevertheless, the two field sessions proved Hewett more than capable of contributing to archaeology. Now he set about persuading the AIA's Americanist committee, and Alice Fletcher in particular, that Santa Fe should be the school's headquarters. In this effort, Hewett was backed by the New Mexican powerhouses of Springer, McFie, and Walter, who also supported the idea of housing the school in the old Palace of the Governors, which had been built to accommodate the Spanish government in 1610 and had been given to the United States as a national monument in 1907 by the territorial legislature.

Fletcher was partial to the notion of locating the school in Santa Fe, unlike Bowditch, the former Americanist chair, and also Boas and Tozzer, who feared that a center in Santa Fe would put at risk their campaign to locate an International School of American Archaeology and Ethnology in Mexico City. The Americanist Committee—Boas, Bowditch, Putnam, Fletcher, and Hewett—met to settle the matter in November 1908, making a three-to-two vote against Santa Fe likely (as Putnam would side with Bowditch and Boas). But Fletcher had mailed ballots to the committee's remaining four members, ensuring victory. Boas and the others took the outcome personally. Bowditch and Putnam assigned Tozzer the task of trying to get the committee vote overturned at the annual AIA meeting in Toronto, but he failed. The following year, they battled again at the AIA's annual meeting but lost. To make their point, they gave up their membership in the AIA.[104] Their fury, however, they held close.

The matter of where the school would be housed within Santa Fe was also resolved in 1909, when the New Mexico territorial legislature established the Museum of New Mexico (also vigorously promoted by Springer, McFie, and Hewett) and decreed that the old Palace of the Governors would be home to both the School of American Archaeology and the museum. Hewett was made director of both institutions, a formidable assignment. An AIA committee, composed of members from around the country, managed the school. The museum was a state-funded institution, under the control of a board of regents appointed by the New Mexico governor. However, the chairman of the museum's board of regents would also serve on the school's managing board to provide an interlocking directorate. The convoluted museum-school structure was reminiscent of the Smithsonian's—the Smithsonian housed and administered, on behalf of the government, a national museum, even though the museum and the institution were separate entities. The purpose in the Smithsonian's case was to prevent mixing of its private funds (from the 1829 Smithsonian bequest) and the museum's public monies.[105] In New Mexico, the founders of the museum-school had similar aims. Hewett and Springer's experience in Las Vegas had taught them that they would need to safeguard their vision against ruthless politicians.

As director of both institutions, Hewett could recommend appointments for each board. Las Vegas had also shown him the value of allies—Fletcher was chair of the school's managing committee, and most of its members were sympathetic to Hewett's views. Along with Fewkes and Holmes were eastern anthropologists Frederick Webb Hodge of the Bureau of Ethnology and Hermon C. Bumpus of the American Museum of Natural History. Congressman John Lacey, a friend to both Springer and Hewett, also served on the committee. Southwestern proponents were Charles Lummis and Byron Cummings. The AIA was responsible for Hewett's salary, and the legislature provided funding for the museum. The AIA never formalized a plan for covering the school's operating expenses, an omission that would generate endless problems for Hewett.[106] He also lectured around the country for the AIA, which not only enabled him to supplement his salary but also gave him an opportunity to extend his list of positive contacts. West of the Mississippi River, at least, Hewett embodied southwestern archaeology.[107]

Undaunted by the political complexity of his new position, Hewett firmed up the arrangements for the dual directorship and began to hire his staff. In the spring of 1909, Hewett asked Chap to join him in Santa Fe. Unwilling to abandon Springer, Chap agreed to an arrangement reminiscent of his schedule at Normal University. He would work for Springer part time. Then, with the understanding that he could specialize in projects in his field, Chap would work part time as the head of the museum's art department and secretary of the school. The combination suited Hewett, who was himself steadfast in his devotion to Springer.

A decade's worth of employment with Hewett and Springer had strengthened Chap's confidence, and he eagerly anticipated the opportunities ahead. Chap had reveled in the dedication and intelligence of archaeology's newest converts at the 1908 camp. Now he was ready to join them and make his own mark. He was perfectly positioned. The new job placed him at the heart of southwestern archaeology. To it, Chap brought a natural curiosity, years of artistic experience, and the conviction of his mentors, the prominent Springer and the charismatic Hewett.

CHAPTER 4

AWAKENINGS

Most of those who came to study, work on, and contribute to Hewett's programs
at Puyé . . . and the Rito de los Frijoles . . . were to become giants in the field of
American anthropology and also legends in their own lifetime. Some who were
the most brilliant tended also to be the most eccentric and interesting. One or
two, perhaps more, were a bit weird.

—MARJORIE LAMBERT, anthropologist

It was a remarkable time. Remarkable place. Remarkable people. Truly, considering
the caliber of those who were called to work with Hewett, it was as if magic itself
informed the early years of his school. Its managing committee was peopled with giants:
Alice Fletcher chaired the committee. William H. Holmes, artist and anthropologist—
and Chap's lifelong hero—served as the committee's vice-chairman.[1] In Santa Fe, Adolph
Bandelier, the legendary ethnohistorian who "discovered" Rito, became the school's head
of documentary history of the Southwest. Charles Lummis, promoter of the Southwest,
sat on both the school's managing committee and the museum's board of regents.

And yet the younger staff members, far from being intimidated, seemed to burn only
brighter. Besides Chap, the "enchanted valley" of the Rito nurtured Sylvanus Morley, Jess
Nusbaum, Alfred V. "Ted" Kidder, John P. Harrington, Maria and Julian Martinez, and
many others, providing them with the rich soil necessary to transform them into giants
in their own right.[2] Looking back, it is as if these men and women knew of their place in
history even as they sat around the evening campfires at Puyé and Rito. And yet, more
likely, Hewett's students and staff, ten to twenty years his junior, simply rejoiced in the
excitement of the new discoveries, the pleasure of each other's company, and the chance
to recognize their worth.

As head of the school's department of illustration, Chap joined the others in July
1909 at Puyé, where Morley, Nusbaum, and Kidder had labored in 1907. Chap remembered the site from his own brief visit in 1902 en route to Chaco Canyon. This time,

he worked alongside Hewett, Nusbaum, Morley, Harrington, and at least twenty Tewa Indians from San Ildefonso Pueblo, including Julian Martinez. First, they finished the excavation of South House and then began on the ruins of villages at the base of the cliff. In his annual report, Hewett emphasized the importance of the work, describing what they had found as a new class of southwestern architectural remains.[3]

At Puyé, they were visited by Fletcher and also played host to the first annual meeting of the museum's board of regents. After several weeks, Hewett and his staff moved their camp to Rito, where, during the excavation of two villages designated as the House of the Sun People and the House of the Snake People, they recovered a considerable amount for the museum.[4] In his report, Hewett, perhaps sensitive to the possibility of criticism after his experience with Tozzer in 1908, emphasized that the board backed his work and methods.[5]

Although his staff members were likely as proud of their work as Hewett was, their natural humor tended to flavor it with irreverence. Chap, Nusbaum, and Morley relished the chance to work with each other again, as they complemented each other's professional interests and delighted in a shared humor. "Morley, Chapman, and Nusbaum—what an excellent team!" remembered Barbara (Freire-Marreco) Aitken from those early years.[6] Nusbaum, who began working for Hewett in 1908, directed all fieldwork connected with the repair and preservation of the ruins. He was also head of photography and in charge of all alterations in the Palace of the Governors, the home of the new Museum of New Mexico.

Like Chap, Nusbaum's path to the school came by way of Las Vegas Normal University. Born on September 3, 1887, Nusbaum grew up in Greeley, Colorado (where Edgar and Cora Hewett had also lived in the 1890s). During his school years, Nusbaum worked with his father, Edward M. Nusbaum, in construction and in the summers learned photography. After attending Colorado State Normal School, where he specialized in manual arts and science, he accepted a position in 1907 as professor of sciences and the manual arts at Las Vegas Normal University. Like Chap, Nusbaum roamed the countryside around Las Vegas—except that Nusbaum's method involved an Excelsior motorcycle. (He broke the dirt road record in 1908, beating the time for passenger car travel by three hours from Denver to Las Vegas.[7]) Nusbaum certainly had his rebellious (or at least mischievous) streak, but his character was best expressed in his free-spirited camaraderie. It was hard to resist his candor and generous warmth. Nusbaum was well liked at the university, where its president, Dr. W. E. Garrison, told him that "never before have we had so much esprit de corps among the whole student body."[8] Nusbaum genuinely enjoyed teaching, but archeology proved an even greater attraction, as he discovered while assisting Hewett as photographer in 1908. Neil Judd, a member of the 1908 Utah expedition, remembered:

My summer was further rewarded by a first meeting with Jess Nusbaum. . . . Our annual permit was in the name of the School and, as was to be expected, Hewett came to inspect our diggings. But it was Nusbaum we saw first. With 25 pounds of camera and glass plates slung over one shoulder and deep sideburns he wore just to annoy the Director, Nausbaum [*sic*] was unique—6 feet 2 and lean as a Texan. What really set him apart, however, was his hat—a 15-cent straw from which some mule had eaten two-thirds of the brim.[9]

Sylvanus "Vay" Morley, the school's head of archaeology in Central America, probably had the most field experience of the younger staff members. Born in Chester, Pennsylvania, on June 7, 1883, Morley first trained as an engineer at the Pennsylvania Military Academy and then entered Harvard in 1904, where he studied under Putnam and Tozzer. Initially interested in Egyptian hieroglyphics, Morley turned to Mayan glyphs while at Harvard. In 1907, he not only demonstrated an unflagging nature during the Utah survey but also made his first trip to Mexico, where he visited many important Mayan sites including Uxmal, Mayapan, and Chichen Itzá. At Rito, the Tewa Indians called him "Little Hummingbird" (Kohe-'e) because of the way the short and nearsighted Morley "flitted diligently about," a name that was soon adopted by the others.[10]

Morley was also a good sport—even when sorely tested by his more devilish peers—as evidenced by an infamous practical joke played on him by Chap and Nusbaum that summer, a joke that Chap remembered later with much remorse. He never liked to hear Nusbaum tell of what they did.[11] According to Nusbaum, Morley was fascinated by the idea that the Maya of Mexico might be connected with the early Indians at Rito de los Frijoles. "He dreamed a lot and talked little while digging, so we began asking him questions and kidding him as he worked in fits and starts," remembered Nusbaum in *Tierra Dulce*.[12]

> Well, Vay began describing this thing and someone would ask him something about it, then Chap . . . would question him. Next thing we found Vay thought, should be a statuette of jade, a Tuxtla (one of the earliest possible contemporaneously dated objects), and he thought it would be about six inches high. Soon he had given us a complete description and we got Chap to help us and we carved pieces of cottonwood root, which people used to make Kachinas. The root is soft and has no grain so it cuts well and doesn't split.[13]

Ten years older than Nusbaum, Chap may well have wondered why he so readily acted the part of the younger brother by agreeing to color and create the fake Tuxtla. Yet he eagerly enlisted. Whenever he and Nusbaum were uncertain about an element, they would ask someone to talk with Morley, who would describe it in detail. When it was finished, they aged it by burying it in the horse corral. Meanwhile, Nusbaum, who was excavating next to Morley, had located a ventilator opening between rooms. From Nusbaum's point of view, the setting was perfect. He placed the faked Tuxtla in the corner, then packed it down with loose sand. The next day, Nusbaum busied himself, watching while Morley worked and talked about the parrot feathers that had been found earlier and his certainty that they had come from Maya country. "All of a sudden about 4 p.m. Vay exclaimed for all to hear, 'Allah! Allah! Allah!' and bumped his head to the ground repeating, 'Allah!'"[14]

As the rest of the crew arrived, Morley unearthed the statuette, cradled it in his arms, and then took it to camp to show it off. That night Morley talked about the discovery around the campfire, while the others listened. "There was not a peep out of any of us. Drs. Hewett and Springer were not in on our miserable deception."[15] By this time, Chap and Nusbaum, who were ashamed and sorry, agreed to confess. They went to Morley's tent before breakfast the following morning and made a clean breast of it. Later, they recounted that "Morley was livid with fury, exploding with a loud stream of profanity that could be heard all over camp and from one end of the canyon to the other. The air was blue with his curses."[16] Morley was in misery, saying, "Hey, you let me get up there and make a damned fool of myself before all those noted archaeologists and I don't know why I never questioned it, 'cause I knew it wasn't jade."[17] But he always admired the deceptive Tuxtla for its accuracy.

The third member of the school's staff, John P. Harrington, had also worked the summer before at Rito. Head of ethnology, Harrington's expertise was linguistics. He has been described as "a man driven by genius and so obsessed with a zeal for recording data that he . . . considered any activity which took him away from fieldwork with informants to be a waste of time."[18] Eccentric, reclusive, and intensely suspicious, Harrington became a legend in anthropological circles during his lifetime. According to Judd, when Hewett announced to the crew of Tewa Indians that Harrington wanted to learn their language, there was initially a surplus of Tewa volunteers. "But they didn't know Harrington. He was a master linguist and absolutely relentless in pursuit of a new word or a new interpretation for one heard before. After a couple of days he was able to converse with them in their own language and trapped his informants repeatedly in giving false information."[19]

Julian Martinez was one of the Tewa Indians whom Hewett had hired to help with the excavations on the Pajarito. It was his third summer with Hewett, as he had helped at Puyé in 1907 and at Rito in 1908, where he had been joined by his wife, Maria. Like many women from nearby San Ildefonso Pueblo, Maria Martinez made pottery for her household, primarily dishes and storage containers. As a child, Maria had learned the art of potterymaking, an ancient tradition, from her aunt. Maria's pottery had come to the notice of Hewett and another member of the excavation, J. P. "Jack" Adams, in the spring of 1908.* They saw Maria forming pottery during their visit to ask Julian about working again at Pajarito. After the tragedy of losing a child in 1907 with her husband away, Maria chose to camp at Rito with Julian during the summer of 1908.

At Rito, Julian's artistic skills had quickly come to be appreciated by Hewett and his staff. Adams had found a painting of a water snake in one of the caves and asked Julian to copy it. Maria remembered someone at camp had given Julian colored pencils.[20] Perhaps Chap, also part of that 1908 expedition, had produced those pencils for Julian as he had done in 1902 for Apie Begay. Certainly, he must have been curious about Julian's drawings. Although there is no evidence to indicate that their friendship was formed then, it seems likely that Chap's pleasure in art would have led to a meeting of minds with Julian and, perhaps, with Maria as well.

At the 1909 session, Chap may have been curious about the results of Maria's winter potterymaking. Possibly Chap saw the pot Hewett had purchased that spring. Maria had worked from potsherds gathered in 1908, trying to create a pot similar to the ancient ones. First she and Julian had searched together for fine sand to make the old-style pottery. When they found it, Maria used it to form five pots on which Julian painted designs. They were disappointed by two pots that blackened during firing, but the remaining pots clearly rivaled the ancient pots in craftsmanship and style. That summer, Maria chose to remain in the pueblo and continue her potterymaking so that it would be ready for Julian's designs during the winter months. But it is easy to imagine Chap talking with Julian at Rito about the pots and, especially, Julian's design work.

Each summer's day in the field must have produced a host of vivid images: Nusbaum joking with the crew while setting a ladder in place, Chap furtively coloring the faked Tuxtla, Harrington relentlessly questioning Julian or another San Ildefonso man about a new word, Morley expounding on his Mayan theory to anyone who cared to listen, and Hewett showing off the excavated ruins to a board member. These were

---

* Chap's comments about the reference to Adams in Alice Marriott's book *Maria: The Potter of San Ildefonso*: "No, Jack Adams was not KMC! Instead, a most likable fellow, perhaps 5 to 7 years younger than I. . . . He was from Greeley, Colo, and did surveying one summer . . . at Frijoles, 1910–11. . . . He had led a tough life but had the sweetest disposition of any one in our crew[,] . . . always offering to help . . . and keeping everyone in good humor. It made him a perfect natural with the Indians & no wonder Julian & Maria were fond of him for he helped them in many ways. Unlike me, he used to say, I'll eat anything that doesn't bite me first! In those days, I was off coffee, chili, beans, and lots of other foods. I never had a meal with them [Julian and Maria] and I never stayed over night with them. But I am happy to at least have had their respect" (AC2.157.1, KMC-SAR).

genuine treasures and doubtless worth many times the value of the archeological material unearthed that year.

At summer's end, the staff moved back to Santa Fe. Chap rented a large, square
front room in a house on lower San Francisco Street, eager to start his job as head of
the museum's department of illustration and happy not only about working again with
Hewett but also about being involved in a project so close to Springer's heart. Having
retired from his legal career after his illness in 1906, Springer devoted most of his time
to art and science. He had written Alice Fletcher of the museum's potential in August
1909, relaying his enthusiasm for the project, which embraced the museum-as-educator
philosophy of the burgeoning natural history field. "[The plans] are designed to make
of this museum something more than a mere storehouse for the relics of the prehistoric
races of the Southwest. It is to be, first of all, an educator, in which the student and
thoughtful visitor may find adequately presented the architecture, industries and life of
these ancient populations."[21] Chap was anxious to build that museum, both figuratively
and literally. He may have marveled at times that his childhood propensity for collecting
could now be pursued as a "grownup" occupation. As a member of the founding staff
of the museum, he and the others were charged with obtaining collections, books, and
equipment; excavating and studying the ancient ruins; preserving archaeological sites
in New Mexico; and publishing the investigations.[22] It was his and Dwight's own parlor
collection of God-stones, but on a much grander scale!

Chap counted on a similar enthusiasm from Hewett. In fact, Hewett's ideas about
the new museum, such as the notion of decorating rooms with murals to complement
the archeological collections, show a thoughtful consideration regarding the museum's potential. But early on it became clear that Hewett was much more energized
by the school and its charter for fieldwork—which was as broad as the continent—
than by the museum's potential for exhibits and study. The school's activities initially
focused on areas with regional archaeological societies: Missouri, Colorado, Utah,
and New Mexico.[23] But as early as 1908, Hewett had begun looking even farther afield,
stating that "it would seem that the fieldwork of the Institute within the limits of the
United States is now fairly well organized and some attention should be given in the
future to the related and higher cultures of Mexico and Central America."[24] That year,
Hewett secured $3,000 from the St. Louis Archaeology Society for explorations in
Central America.

Thus, only two weeks into his new position, Chap was gravely disappointed when
Hewett turned his attention away from the museum and to other projects. Chap had
assumed that his work would be to maintain and restore artifacts and prepare illustrations for reports. He expected that Hewett would supervise the alterations in the museum's portion of the Palace of the Governors. Instead, within ten days, Hewett announced

that he would be leaving for a several months' lecture tour for the AIA, the parent organization controlling the school. Hewett told them that Chap would serve as secretary and be in charge of the staff. He also ordered Nusbaum to complete necessary restorations and improvements in the Palace of the Governors and outlying buildings. Then, in a foreshadowing of things to come, Hewett told Chap that the renovations would probably require that he defer payment of some monthly bills, particularly those for water, light, and the telephone![25]

Some might have viewed Hewett's announcement as a promotion. But not Chap. His dreams were centered on art and archeology, dreams that seemed easily realizable when he had envisioned a museum run efficiently by Hewett. Without Hewett in Santa Fe, those dreams faded. Chap quickly grasped that running the museum primarily meant solving a growing number of problems. Possibly to make a point about his own priorities, Chap continued to work only part time at the museum. Afternoons, in his room on lower San Francisco Street, *at the window facing south, I managed to carry on my work for Mr. Springer, after my mornings at the Museum.*[26]

Despite his disappointment over Hewett's behavior, however, it is hard to imagine that Chap could have maintained a sour outlook for long. He was surrounded by friends who were always ready to laugh. Working at the museum that fall were Chap, Nusbaum, Morley—that excellent team!—Harrington, Carl G. Lotave (a muralist), Donizetta Wood (a part-time receptionist), and both Julian and Maria Martinez. The laughter embraced them all. Maria recalled a time when Julian tried to misinform linguist Harrington by giving the Tewa word for "Kiss me" when asked to name an object. According to Maria, the goodhearted teasing was the best part of being there.[27]

The primary task at the museum that fall was renovating its home—the Palace of the Governors—a task that fell to Nusbaum. The project was far from trivial. Even Nusbaum's sense of humor must often have been strained. The building had been built in 1610, occupied by the Pueblo Indians after the 1680 revolt, and then reoccupied by the Spanish in 1693. In 1846, Stephen W. Kearny of the U.S. Army took over the building when Santa Fe surrendered to the Americans during the war. At the time of the renovations, the governor's residence, the post office, and the historical society were still housed in it, despite its sad state of disrepair.

As part of the legislative agreement, the school had agreed to restore the ancient architecture of the building, preserving it as a monument to Spanish culture in the Southwest.[28] A consensus emerged as a result of Nusbaum's studies to preserve all surviving archaeological features and traditions that predated the American military occupation of August 1846, which had been progressively responsible for most subsequent modifications. Nusbaum noted the sorry condition of the building, including its hodgepodge of restoration styles and crumbling walls. Trash and manure reached well above the rear windowsills, the result of livestock having been stabled behind the building. It took twenty-one hundred small wagonloads to carry it away.[29]

At that time, Santa Fe was home to about five thousand people. Although the majority of the population was Hispanic, Santa Fe had yet to identify itself as the City Different, and the influx of Americans since 1846 had markedly changed the architecture. Adobe buildings now vied with Victorian facades, including the Palace of the Governors' "gingerbread" portal of the 1870s. The city had few pretensions and no formal plan for growth. Chap remembered the village as quiet and quaint, with unpaved streets that were sprinkled daily with water and stepping stones at the crossings around the plaza for passage in muddy weather. The old cottonwoods that leaned out over Palace Avenue shaded the wood vendors, who parked their wagons along the curb. *There their burros dozed while their owners loafed in the shade of the portal while awaiting buyers. Only rarely did an automobile chug-chug slowly around the Plaza, slowing down at the corners to avoid a broken spring or blowout, as it threaded between the stepping stones.*[30] Nusbaum maneuvered his motorcycle around the stones as well. He counted only five automobiles when he arrived in Santa Fe; his motorcycle brought the number of vehicles up to six.[31]

From September through December, Nusbaum supervised the installation of the heating plant in the main part of the Palace of the Governors, while the staff *walked or jumped over piles of dirt shoveled onto floors* that were *torn up for laying the pipes, and heaps of earth from the excavations lay beside each trench, some of it yielding sherds of various pottery wares.*[32] However, providing a steady hand over the renovations was only one of Nusbaum's tasks. He was also responsible for steadying the hand of Lotave, the muralist hired by Hewett. The vision for the murals, which were being financed privately by Springer, was to provide wall decorations for a series of rooms in the museum that would house artifacts from their respective excavations. "Each one of the principal culture centers is to be treated separately, so that their distinctive characters may be intelligently studied, and their relations to each other compared," Springer wrote Fletcher in August 1909. "For example, upon the walls [of the Puyé room] will be depicted, in an extensive series of large oil paintings, the surrounding landscape (in this place of great beauty), the Cliff in its original state, together with the suitable details of structures restored, and the life and ceremonials of the people."[33]

Initial plans called for two rooms, the Puyé room and the Rito de los Frijoles room. Lotave was hired to paint murals that would simulate the views seen when standing at the center of the sites. Hewett had met Lotave in 1909 during the exhibition of his murals in the Indian room of Denver's new Shirley Savoy Hotel. Hewett arranged for Lotave to travel to Santa Fe but, according to Nusbaum, the muralist was celebrating a little too much and did not appear. "In frustration Hewett called me early in August 1909 saying: 'Bring him down here if you have to rope and tie him.'"[34] When Lotave arrived, he began painting in the Puyé room, ending each day with a ritual of climbing a stepladder to survey his work. "[Lotave] was still drinking a good deal, and was pretty shaky, and I had to spend time steadying him. About 9 p.m. we would commence. It was quite a chore," Nusbaum recalled.[35]

Later, Nusbaum had to literally act on Hewett's injunction to "rope and tie" Lotave. Nusbaum recalled that Lotave "was making his colored sketches here [at Rito de los Frijoles] and his shaky mannerisms were growing worse. Whenever he got onto a high point anyplace and ha[d] to look down, it was very bad. I ended up roping him. I'd put a secure belt around his waist, then using two ropes, tied one to a tree or good stump and I remained holding the other to quiet his well-founded fear of falling off into the canyon."[36]

In autumn, amid the antics of Lotave and the wreckage of construction, Chap began his work. He set up the new department of illustration, whose primary task was to supply renderings of the school's work to Hewett and other staff for papers and presentations. In October, Chap prepared plans for a model of the South House at Puyé based on the study he had made of the ancient ruins over the summer. By midwinter, he had prepared a temporary exhibit in the museum's entrance hall, which, he wrote Hewett, "helped out a great deal in the explanation of Puye to the many visitors the past week."[37]

But Chap was also responsible for the museum's collection of artifacts and so assigned himself the task of pottery mending. Soon, puzzling over the designs on broken pottery pieces claimed as much of Chap's attention as the drawings. The sherds featured geometric and stylized life-form representations and had polychrome or black-on-white painted decorations. As an artist, Chap had reason enough to be enamored by brush strokes and repetitive patterns. But he knew that sherds could also illuminate ancient southwestern culture. As Rice details in *Pottery Analysis*, broken ceramic pieces have long captured the attention of anthropologists because pottery—humans' first synthetic material—lends itself so well to research. Although a whole pot is fragile, its broken pieces (sherds) are remarkably plentiful, durable, and also less compelling to treasure hunters than relics such as projectile points or jewels; thus they are more likely to be left at sites. Anthropologists also appreciate that during the creation of pottery, each successive step is captured in the final product.[38]

At the time of Chap's mending, archaeological studies of pottery were based primarily on the classification approach: pottery was grouped into classes of vessels or sherds representative of a particular culture at a particular time. Because clay's plasticity lends itself to different forms and decorations that are culturally specific and that change over time, archaeologists could observe new forms and decorations appearing and coexisting with older forms. Over time, the older forms diminished and died out. This waxing and waning of elements of style and form through time allowed pottery to be used as "index" artifacts, that is, as items that help to establish relative time sequences. According to Fowler, pottery seriation began in Egypt in the 1890s when Sir Flinders Petrie sorted pottery from various sites according to changes in shape, color, and painted designs. He calculated the frequency of these changes to chart the passage of time. George Reisner, also working in Egypt, used similar techniques, which he had passed on to Kidder during his graduate studies at Harvard.[39]

In the Southwest, researchers had begun collecting sherds as early as 1852. Some of them, who subscribed to Lewis Henry Morgan's 1877 theory, equated the appearance of pottery as a shift in southwestern culture from "upper savagery" to "lower barbarism." Bandelier recognized pottery as a marker of both culture and time, noting a marked resemblance among the decorations of pottery all over the Southwest.[40] Hewett, like Fewkes and others at the time, saw ceramics as cultural, but not chronological, indicators.[41]

As Chap washed and restored the pottery pieces gathered from the school's recent excavations, he began to see that they could be important in establishing cultural affiliations for the school and museum's archeological work. But it was the decorative motifs that evoked his wonder. He began to copy designs from the restored specimens and also from a large collection of sherds that he had picked up during the building renovations.[42] His interest was further aroused when, at Hewett's request, he created illustrations for a paper on Indian designs to be read by Morley during the holidays at the annual meeting of the AIA in St. Louis. *Preparation of that, and the interest shown at St. Louis led me to believe that there was a promising future in the study of decorative art.*[43]

A host of forces combined to awaken Chap to the possibilities of pursuing such study. Most compelling, the broken pottery pieces posed a puzzle that begged to be solved. The designs enticed him because of his own artistic inclinations, and his training promised him some authority in the field. Although, unlike Morley or Kidder, he was without a formal scientific education, his association with Springer's monographs had not only made him familiar with scientific classification but had perhaps also drawn him to it as a way of emulating his mentor. His participation in the school's summer fieldwork and acceptance by the others strengthened his credentials in archaeological study. Finally, Chap's interest may have been fueled by his acquaintance with the Martinezes.

Julian Martinez had joined the museum that fall as the building's janitor and was particularly curious about the ancient pots that were housed there. He copied designs for his own use and many times pored over pottery designs with Chap. Together, they looked at Chap's own drawings from the sherds along with the anthropological studies published in the Bureau of American Ethnology reports, which Kidder had mentioned to Chap.[44] At the same time, Maria and the children joined Julian at the museum, where luxuries such as running water, a cookstove, and electric lights left Maria with little housework to do. With time in abundance, Maria asked for clay from San Ildefonso. She began to make pottery during the evenings; later, Julian painted the designs.[45] Surrounded by ancient pots and contemporary artisans, Chap's new interest escalated.

Ironically, Chap's deepening interest in decorative art coincided with a profusion of administrative tasks. Nusbaum and Morley joined Hewett in Central America for field-work in December, adding to Chap's responsibilities at the museum.

All went well until early spring when Julian was called home to his pueblo at San Ildefonso for participati[o]n in the spring ceremonies of his pueblo. For two days we searched for a substitute and finally I gave up and took instruction from Julian for running the furnace and heater and served for 10 days as both acting Director and substitute janitor.

Not bad. The furnace and boiler room was in a building at the rear of the museum. I would arrive at 6 a.m., clean the flues, and get up steam, then hustle back the path to the museum. All the soot from the flues had fallen on the ground and to save tracking it inside, I would carry a big piece of cardboard and form a path before me.

Inside, I would prepare for sweeping floors of 4 rooms, by soaking old news-papers in water, and tearing it up into bits, and scatter it on floor, then sweep the damp mess before me. Often, there was a pounding and rattling of the front door before I was through. So I would sweep the mess under a case in a dark corner, hide the floor brush, and promptly at 9, open the front door and welcome the museum's group of impatient tourists.[46]

Besides janitor, Chap also briefly wore a doctor's hat that winter, rescuing the inde-fatigable Harrington from a bad case of food poisoning. During the winter months, Harrington was working steadily—obsessively, even—on Tewa linguistic material that he had gathered in 1908. As Chap later recounted, Harrington's eccentricities included cook-ing cornmeal in a large black iron kettle and then consuming it over several days' time. One Sunday night when Chap was checking the building, he saw a light in Harrington's studio. He found a very sick man, pale green in color, writing busily. When Chap asked what was wrong, Harrington pointed to the kettle. After Chap smelled it, he asked when Harrington had made it. "Oh, about four days ago," Harrington replied. Recognizing ptomaine poisoning, Chap suggested calling a doctor, but Harrington wanted none of it. So Chap purchased a bottle of peragoric medicine, some canned milk, and a large bottle of Horlick's malted milk tablets. He gave the medicine to Harrington, fixed some warm milk, and told him he'd check in the morning.

It was about 6:30 a.m. when I arrived. I was completely astounded to see a bright, cheerful J. P. hard at work, for I was sure he would not be up to much for several days, perhaps a week. I expressed my pleasure at seeing him so well. As I parted from him, I said, "Well, J. P., you won't forget to take your medicine and tablets will you?"

Whereupon he looked rather startled and then replied, "Oh, I already have. I took both bottles after you left last night."[47]

A tour guide, too, Chap escorted Mitchell Carroll, a member of the school's managing committee, to Puyé in March, where they slept in the caves and thoroughly explored the ruins and cliffs, which must have delighted them both.[48]

Artist, director, janitor, doctor, guide, anthropologist, curator. That first winter at the museum established an unfortunate pattern of varied duties that left Chap little time for his art or his research. Most frustrating to Chap were the administrative duties—usually, headaches—that he was forced to contend with in Hewett's absence. The fact that many grew out of Hewett's casual attitude toward finances only further exasperated Chap, who, following his father's example, kept meticulous accounts of his own transactions. For example, Hewett's capricious instructions in October to defer payment of some bills led to a midwinter crisis at the museum. Having waited several months for payment, the utilities company issued an ultimatum: pay in full within ten days or the facilities would be cut off. The incident ended with Nathan Jaffa, board treasurer, getting a loan from the bank. During a conference with Chap, Jaffa added, "If Hewett pulls another deal like that, I'll resign."[49]

Chap took a methodical approach to running the museum and school; Hewett, in contrast, tried to run them by being a consummate juggler. Besides his passions—the school's summer sessions on the Pajarito and the fieldwork in Central America—Hewett was responsible for lecture tours, museum collections, museum renovations, publishing, interactions with the AIA back east, interactions with New Mexico's legislature, and fund-raising. This last was a chronic struggle. Although the museum had an initial appropriation of $5,000 per year, Hewett had to negotiate for funds biennially through the legislature and also depended on the goodwill—and private funds—of Springer. Meanwhile the school had no permanent funding at all. Despite a newspaper report published soon after the school was established that assured Santa Fe citizens of a general endowment movement, in fact, Hewett was responsible for raising all of its money. Often, confronted with more ideas than funds, Hewett simply put one project at risk to save another.

As Chap left for Burlington, Iowa, to work with Springer in April, as was his custom, he must have wondered whether the congenial friendships and working relationships that Hewett promoted through the museum and school were worth the aggravation of Hewett's offhand methods of business. From Las Vegas, where Chap visited with his mother and sister, he wrote to Hewett, "I passed up my March salary and that for April 1–15 in order to help pay the Meininger bill." However, he also detailed his latest research finds to Hewett, knowing he had a friendly ear. "I finished a part of my series of pottery designs before leaving, particularly the birds," he reported, "and yesterday I spent the afternoon at the Normal looking over the old collection with renewed interest and where I had hoped to pick up four or five additional, I found 14, and the troublesome part of it is that very few serve as missing links in the chain of 30 I had built up in Santa Fe."[50] Later, he heard from Nusbaum that Hewett thought Chap was best qualified to research pottery design.[51]

Experiencing nearly equal amounts of support and frustration, Chap may have only hinted to Springer of his agitation over museum affairs and disappointment at how time for his work had eroded. Chap knew that the museum was close to Springer's heart and also that he maintained a loyal and enduring faith in Hewett. Although Hewett's nonchalance made Chap uneasy, it was not yet grievous enough to bring to Springer's attention.

At first I found it possible to attribute [Hewett's deviations] to hasty and ill-considered decisions made at a time when he had too many irons in the fire. In mentioning one such minor matter to Mr. Springer I had gone so far as to suggest that Dr. Hewett might save himself and those under him some annoyance if he would carry a little note book and jot down a memo of each promise or agreement at the time it was made.

That hurt Mr. Springer, for outstanding among his commendable traits was his unfailing loyalty toward the few in whom he placed his confidence, and among the favored few was Dr. Hewett. With this in mind, and remembering that I was pledged to continue with our cordial relations, I resolved that from there on I would try to keep such matters to myself.[52]

Chap likely highlighted the accomplishments of the museum that summer, talking to Springer of Nusbaum's near-miraculous work on the Palace of the Governors, Chap's collaborations with Harrington on the ethnology papers, Lotave's murals, Maria's potterymaking, and Chap and Julian's studies of pottery designs, while downplaying the unpaid bills and mounting headaches.

Perhaps Chap confided his mixed feelings to his brother during a summer visit in Chicago, where he stayed with Dwight and family. Or possibly he talked about the situation with his mother while visiting her and Vera in Las Vegas on his return trip.[53] Since their move to the Southwest in 1901, Mary Cordelia White and Vera had carved out a home for themselves in New Mexico, even with Chap's months-long absences from Las Vegas after 1905. His mother had found work at the Carnegie Library there and, after a brief marriage, Vera worked as secretary to the president at Normal University. *One way or another, we three pulled together, either Mother or Vera keeping house while the other was employed.*[54]

When Chap returned to Santa Fe, however, no ambiguous feelings tainted his enthusiasm for the summer fieldwork. Life in the outdoors, convivial friendships, an atmosphere of learning—these were the glue that mended any fissures in Chap's perspective. The 1910 session was particularly special, as Hewett had collaborated with Frederick Webb Hodge, recently appointed chief of the Bureau of Ethnology, to create an interdisciplinary study of the Upper Rio Grande Valley, which greatly impressed Chap.[55] The importance of the study masked the absence of Ivy League students at the session. Hewett's damaged relationships with eastern institutions—the result of Tozzer's criticism after 1908 as well as the animosity of Boas and others over the school location issue—had discouraged them from sending students to the field sessions. So Hewett turned instead to the public.[56] Hewett, Morley, Chap and Harrington lectured in Santa Fe, along with Hodge, George Grant McCurdy of Yale University, and Barbara Freire-Marreco of Oxford.[57]

Perhaps it was as Chap began his talk, struggling again with discomfort over public speaking, that his eyes lit on an attractive new visitor: Katherine "Kate" Muller. Twelve years younger than Chap—in her early twenties—Kate had an open gaze that was highlighted by sparkling eyes (a sparkle undiminished by her glasses), a brilliant smile, and an expression that forecast liveliness and daring.

Even if I had wished, I could not well have avoided meeting her, for Kate was attending the opening session of the museum's summer school of archaeology in the Palace of the Governors, and for weeks, wherever I turned, she was usually in the thick of it. Against the advice of her mother's old friends she sat at least an hour a day in the Plaza reading . . . , twirling her gay Japanese parasol, visiting with the old timers, and keeping up with the news from the younger fellows who passed.

One old dame cautioned her that her reputation was at stake—she should be sought, not tripped over.—"It just isn't done!" "Well," said Kate, "it's high time that someone made this dear old Plaza a meeting place for old friends. If I keep at it, maybe your girls will help."[58]

At last! A bright and original young woman, right in Santa Fe!

Kate's visit to the Southwest in 1910 was not her first. She had initially arrived in

Katherine "Kate" Muller, c. 1915. (Courtesy of School for Advanced Research Archives, AC02 753a.)

New Mexico in 1899, the same year as Chap. Then twelve years old, Kate had moved with her widowed mother and siblings for the health of Kate's older brother, Jack. The move brought improvement to Jack's health but a decline in their mother's. After her death from diphtheria, the Muller children—Kate, her older sister Allie, younger brother Joe, and Jack—were again uprooted and sent back east to live with relatives. There, Kate attended a convent school at Sharon Hill, where her Aunt Kate was the mother superior. Given later accounts of Kate's vibrant personality, it's hard not to imagine Kate brought to task by her aunt more than once for some mischief.

The convent school years were followed by two years at the Philadelphia Art School. But the Southwest—not the eastern seaboard—had captured Kate's imagination. Although advised against the trip by relatives, Kate traveled to Santa Fe for a summer holiday in 1910, obviously believing that advice against something was as good as a recommendation. She lived that summer at a boardinghouse run by two sisters, Flora Moore and Marion McQuarrie, in part of what is now Sena Plaza. Having seen a display of Chap's paintings at a teachers' convention in Santa Fe several years earlier, she took it on herself to make his acquaintance and volunteer her artistic talents in setting up museum exhibits.[59] Thus, Kate quickly developed an avid interest in the museum, and, clearly, an equally avid interest in one of its staff.[60]

Within a few weeks, however, Chap had to leave Santa Fe—reluctantly, perhaps—for Rito. Kate, remaining in Santa Fe, was no longer "in the thick of it" but possibly she inspired in him some very romantic notions. Meanwhile, Chap's passion for fieldwork and the host of interesting characters who attended the session proved a distraction. The school offered lectures, excavation work, walks with the instructors, and talks with the Pueblo Indians.[61] Also, as remembered by one of the summer program's staff, Neil Judd, there were several impromptu midnight concerts given by Lummis, who as one of the trustees, was entitled to the very best the camp offered:

> So he moved into a couple of caves just around the corner from ours, lit one of his big black Mexican cigars, and made himself at home. . . .
>
> More to the point, Lummis was one of those who believed, along with Edison and Steinmetz, that no man needed more than three hours' sleep. So he sat beside a small fire outside his cave and entertained members of the summer session with old Spanish and cowboy songs until 3:00 a.m. He knew every cowboy and Spanish song ever written but only one set of chords for the guitar.[62]

The August meeting at Rito of the school's managing committee was memorialized in a photo of all its members perched against the ladder leading to the Ceremonial Cave. Another photo taken that summer shows Hewett—known then as "El Toro"—and his remarkable staff, including Maud Woy, history teacher from Denver, and Freire-Marreco. The inclusion of women was notable, given the general lack of support for their participation in the field at that time, despite Fletcher's prominence.[63] Woy attended the 1910 session as a student, and Freire-Marreco was there to study the evolution of authority in American Indians. Marjorie Lambert, an anthropologist who worked with Hewett at the museum in the 1930s, noted that at a time when male archaeologists were sometimes resentful of women, she was grateful to Hewett for the opportunities: "He was a wonderful teacher and a good friend."[64]

When the group disbanded at the end of the summer, Chap chose to move into Lotave's studio at the museum. Lotave had left for New York after finishing the Puyé and Rito murals and three murals in the Palace of Governors, depicting Pueblo settlement, Spanish occupation of the Southwest, and the coming of the Americans. Although Lotave's artwork was much admired, his alcoholic binges had severely tested Hewett's and Springer's patience. They did not offer Lotave future work, even though historical painting remained important to them.

That fall, Hewett left almost immediately with Morley for Guatemala. Chap was again put in charge, but only Harrington, Wood, and the Martinezes remained in Santa Fe. Nusbaum, along with his father and Jack Adams, was working in Mesa Verde, Colorado, surveying and stabilizing Balcony House. Kate Muller, too, was absent, having left for Philadelphia, though possibly with a promise to return the following summer. Essentially on his own, Chap immersed himself in design studies, which he pursued after work hours. He mused on the evolution of design from realism to abstract art and back again:

> *Living in my studio room at the rear of the patio, I found it convenient at night to carry on my studies of Indian design, and in the course of a year had made an extensive series of drawings of design motifs and symbols from the pottery recovered from the excavations at Rito de los Frijoles.*
>
> *. . . As the study progressed, I found it possible in some instances to plot the mutations from one form to another. That led naturally to speculations as to which extreme of the series was the chicken and which the egg!*
>
> *The generally accepted theory among the archaeologists of those days was that every decorative or symbolic motif had developed extensively from a crude attempt at realism and that as decorative art progressed, the trend led to stylized forms scarcely recognizable as the end result of such an evolution.*
>
> *Lacking any evidence to the contrary, I found it easy to plot such a development with my material, and soon had my drawings arranged in a plausible sequence. I had gone even further with the experiment, in working over the material illustrated so lavishly by Holmes, Fewkes, and Hough and others in the Annual Reports of the Bureau of American Ethnology.*
>
> *At that time, to the best of my knowledge, the concept of a complete reversal of the supposed trend from realism to abstract had never been explored[.] . . . I had begun to probe its possibilities as early as 1910.*[65]

In these early studies, Chap used the design components to establish his sequence for an evolution of style. His studies built on the descriptive terminology that was emerging

Facing page: Kenneth M. Chapman (extreme left), with other staff and managing board of the School of American Archaeology. Charles F. Lummis, bottom of ladder; Frank Springer, second from ladder bottom; Santiago Naranjo, top of ladder. Photograph taken at the Ceremonial Cave in Rito de los Frijoles, now Bandelier National Monument, c. 1910. (Courtesy of Palace of the Governors [MNM/DCA], 42070.)

Edgar Lee Hewett—known as "El Toro"—and his remarkable staff at Rito de los Frijoles, c. 1910. Standing, left to right: W. W. Robbins, Donald Beauregard, John P. Harrington, F. W. Hodge, Edgar L. Hewett, Neil M. Judd, Maud Woy, Barbara Freire-Marreco. Seated, left to right: Sylvanus G. Morley, Kenneth M. Chapman, J. P. ("Jack") Adams, Jesse L. Nusbaum, Nathan Goldsmith, and Junius Henderson. (Courtesy of Palace of the Governors [MNM/DCA], 81919.)

with regard to pottery styles, employing common expressions such as "representational," "realistic," or "geometric."[66] Another vocabulary that Chap helped to establish referred to design components: "element," "motif," "configuration," "basic unit," "layout," and "structure." Chap's work concentrated largely on the first three: the element, which is the smallest self-contained design component; design motifs, which are fixed combinations of elements that form larger components, like the rain cloud; and design configuration, which refers to the way the decorative motifs are arranged to fill a space, such as the interiors of bowls.[67]

As Chap dug deeper into the mysteries of ancient Pueblo designs, his curiosity grew as did his devotion to the field. Designs drawn on cardboard crowded the walls of his studio as he happily set about tracing their evolution. At first, Chap seemed in no hurry to publish. Thorough to a fault, he may have been more conscientious than most about publishing before all data had been gathered and verified. In addition, he likely felt little pressure, secure in Hewett's assurance that he was best qualified to work in the field.

But his attitude was soon to change. In late fall, Ted Kidder and his wife, Madeleine, arrived in Santa Fe, planning a stay of several months. With Nusbaum and Morley out of state, Chap was particularly delighted to become reacquainted with Kidder, a close friend since 1908. Now the Austin Teaching Fellow at Harvard, Kidder had already published a paper for the school on the 1908 excavations at Cave Springs, Utah. In Santa Fe, he intended to prepare a study of Pueblo ceramic art. As Chap remembered it,

[The Kidders] called at my studio and were interested in my design sketches, mounted in groups and hung on a wall. Next day, Ted returned, by agreement, to do some sketching of designs from the restored pottery, and asked what plans I had for publication of my work. I told him that I had given no thought to such a possibility and that I would be happy to have them used in any way that would promote an interest in Indian art. I added that Dr. Hewett had seen them and later had told Jess Nusbaum that he thought I was best qualified to work in that field.

Ted then told me that he had received for himself the same assurance from Dr. Hewett in 1908 at the close of our summer's field work at the Frijoles camp, and that he had since then begun working on drawings and text for a paper that was then nearing completion. ("Pottery of the Pajarito Plateau and Adjacent Regions," 1913).

What a mixup! Naturally I was pleased to assure him of my cooperation in any way he might suggest and that day we agreed on a happy compromise. Ted would complete his work as a comparatively brief introductory paper on the Pajarito and

neighboring types, and I would continue mine as a more detailed study of the Pajarito wares only.

With that so amicably arranged, we settled down to many hours of work on the museum's collections, each selecting the designs best suited to his purposes.

That was the first instance I had encountered of Dr. Hewett's free and easy way of making and overlooking committments [sic], some of which were to lead to serious difficulties with his staff and with outsiders. Once in later years, I overheard Sylvanus Morley, in a controversy with the Director, in which he spat out, full force, "Dr. Hewett, your way is paved with broken promises!" As for Ted and myself, the experience only drew us closer.[68]

During early 1911, Chap and Kidder reviewed ceramics from the Harvey collection and studied the pottery at Pecos. Kidder, who was working on a detailed seriation of pottery types based on form and decoration for his dissertation, shared with Chap his understanding of pottery as indicators of time and cultural linkages, which he had absorbed during his fieldwork with Harvard's Reisner. The difference in the time they could devote to the projects, however, exacerbated some of Chap's earlier frustrations, despite the obvious pleasure he took in working with Kidder. In March 1911, Chap wrote to Hewett:

I do not want to begin on the series of Ananyu [sic] drawings until I have worked over my bird material in a thorough way, verifying every drawing in my series, numbering the piece or sherd from which it comes and packing the latter for future reference. Kidder has already had five times as much time for the work as I have found and my series of bird cards I largely based on rough sketches I made for comparison before I understood the subject. I know there are inaccuracies in the lot that would subject the whole series to suspicion if they were worked over by an outsider in their present state[.] . . . Kidder and I have checked up a few errors on each other, so far, and it is a great satisfaction to work together as little as we have been able to so far.[69]

The same tone likely found its way into letters to Springer. Ever the champion of Chap's artistic talent, Springer thought he saw a way to resolve Chap's frustration and, at the same time, promote his own interests in resurrecting historical painting at the museum. Springer was searching for a reliable artist to replace Lotave. In January 1911, Springer wrote to Hewett, "Do you know, I have been thinking of late that our man—at least for historical paintings—may after all be Chapman. In composition he is head and shoulders above the average artist. His natural ability, thoughtful habit, and scientific method of observation and study will furnish the foundation which we need."[70] Convinced that a year of oil painting instruction was all that Chap required, Springer proposed that Chap take classes when he finished work on the crinoid monograph. He pledged to support Chap during the classes, possibly as soon as the fall, and encouraged Hewett to think ahead to new staffing arrangements. "While we want Chapman permanently in the Museum, we must plan so as not to tie him down to the mere drudgery of details. I am sure he is capable of more than that, and I am going to make it my business to help him get to some of them."[71]

Although Springer's suggestion was a sincere effort to improve Chap's position at the museum, it ignored Chap's growing interest in Indian art and thus did not address his desire for adequate time for research or his need to publish. In contrast to Kidder's opportunities for publication through academic institutions, Chap's publishing expectations remained focused on Hewett, whose approach was to respond to periodic pressure by requesting articles at the last minute. "I hope I have not driven the entire staff into nervous prostration by the pressure for papers, reports, etc.," Hewett had written to Chap. "There are very special reasons for pushing our material to immediate publication."[72] Even so, funds were scarce, especially for costly graphics.

When Chap did finally break into print, it was through a national magazine, the result of an April 1911 meeting with Ellsworth Huntington, a journalist who was writing for *Harper's Monthly Magazine*. In the article, which was aimed at the general public, Huntington laid out Chap's "chicken and egg" theory, along with a general description of the Southwest's archaeological possibilities. Accompanying the article were Chap's drawings, which he had made that spring. The illustrations included one series of designs beginning with two realistic birds and developing into a rectangular symbol comprising four triangles and another set that illustrated a scrolllike design element mutating into a realistic bird. "Such studies as those of Mr. Chapman are not of value only or chiefly to the artist," Huntington wrote. "They belong to all who are interested in the study of the development of the human mind."[73] Significant for its national promotion of southwestern anthropologists, "Studies of the Primitive Mind" appeared in the January 1912 issue of *Harper's Monthly Magazine* and was condensed the same month for the *Literary Digest*.

Tantalized by the idea of pursuing pure research like Morley and Kidder did—especially when he contrasted that with the administrative difficulties he was asked to untangle—Chap felt the time had come to pursue more rewarding work. Also, he worried that Hewett's carelessness was seriously undermining the museum's reputation.

My disappointment had turned to actual resentment when I observed the erratic and even devious means [Hewett] was using to make amends for his dilatory ways.

Finally, having served through two years in various capacities as secretary, accoun-
tant, receptionist, and curator, interspersed with occasional emergency jobs as sub-
stitute janitor, not even the lure of a month or more of field work each summer
could have induced me to stay.

I was determined to look for some more rewarding activity in my own field
and with that in view I took the first opportunity to discuss the situation with
Mr. Springer who was then spending most of his time in his private museum at
Burlington. . . . But he took the situation philosophically, saying, "Dr. Hewett is
overworked; the Museum is a young and growing institution; I am sure that before
long he can begin to give it a better share of his attention. We must be patient and
help where we can."[74]

Springer recognized that Chap's patience had limits, however, and offered a partial
way out: Springer would employ Chap full time, receiving Chap's services as illustrator
for six months while essentially subsidizing Chap's own studies during the remainder.
Springer planned to work full time on his crinoid studies and wanted *renewed assurance*
that I would stand by him to the end. Accordingly we reached an agreement that was to
hold us closely as father and son until his death in 1927.[75]

Blinded, perhaps, by his affection for both Hewett and Chap, Springer seemed unable
to address directly the deepening rift between them. It was as if Springer expected that
an improvement in their relationship could be effected by the sheer force of his will.
Springer's vision for the museum included both Hewett and Chap, and he was unable to
replace this image with another. And so, even in the new arrangement, Chap promised
Springer that he would continue at the museum, if needed.

As part of the plan, Chap agreed to Springer's suggestion to study painting so that he
could serve as the museum's historical artist. Chap would take classes at the Art Students
League in New York—the very institution for which he had been putting away savings in
1898 in the hopes of full-time study. At that time, he anticipated meeting publishing contacts for book and magazine illustrations.[76] Now he made plans to attend the league for
Springer's purposes. During his year out east, Chap would work on the crinoid monograph with Springer at the National Museum of Natural History in Washington, DC,
where the crinoid collections were moving, and also take time to study pottery collections in the museums.

Even as Springer was providing assurances to Chap, however, a letter arrived in
Burlington that would embroil them both in one of Hewett's ill-considered stratagems.
In the letter, Hewett asked Chap to pack the collection of Pajaritan pottery at Las Vegas
Normal University on his return trip to Santa Fe for shipment to the museum. Chap
knew the collection well for he had not only been teaching there when Hewett had

acquired it but had also recently consulted the collection for his own purposes. *In his letter, which unfortunately I did not save, Dr. Hewett stated that the collection would be exhibited in a room at the Museum to be designated as the New Mexico Normal University Room, and furthermore, that in exchange, a collection of equal value and of more general interest for the Normal University's use would be prepared, delivered, and installed by the Museum.*[77]

Chap was very familiar with the material that the museum-school held in reserve and knew there was little to offer in exchange. However, he had heard that Hewett had hoped to acquire a valuable collection of prehistoric pottery from a trader at Houck, Arizona. When he mentioned this, however, Springer disclaimed any knowledge of such a purchase.[78]

Traveling back from Burlington to Las Vegas, Chap was besieged by doubts about the whole affair. Yet he dutifully packed the collection. *I . . . had just finished with the entire collection of more than thirty specimens and was labeling the barrels, when Dr. Roberts returned. On spying the empty case, he came to me at once. "Why, Chapman,"* he said, "[y]ou are taking the whole collection!" I showed him my instructions and he protested that that was not in accord with the written request that Mr. Springer had submitted to the Board.*[79]

Roberts agreed to let the shipment go, under protest, but made it clear that he would expect prompt action from the museum in providing a new collection before the beginning of the fall semester. *In reporting to Dr. Hewett next day, I told him of my predicament. . . . He dismissed my account of Dr. Roberts' contention . . . by saying, "Oh, he's nothing but an old trouble maker" and as for preparation of an exchange collection he asked, to my amazement, if we couldn't find something in our storage material that would serve the purpose! I told him that we had absolutely nothing in reserve worthy of exhibition. With a show of nonchalance that I was later to know too well, he dismissed the whole matter by saying, "Well, we must keep it in mind and be on the lookout for something."*[80]

The incident fortified Chap's belief that he was right to leave, but the 1911 summer session reminded him of all the reasons he had first chosen to stay. Always his favorite activity, the fieldwork that summer was made even more pleasing because of Kate Muller. She had returned to Santa Fe not only to attend the Santa Fe lectures but also the session at Rito de los Frijoles. According to Chap, Kate made the most of her time in the Southwest, free from Philadelphia's strict social conventions. She had an ample allowance from her grandfather's estate that let her give parties and take friends on mountain drives and on motor trips to Pueblo ceremonies.[81] That summer, she may have stayed at the inn near Rito, just opened by the Abbotts, as it was frequented by many at the session.[82] Lummis arrived with his son, Quimu, whom the Abbotts' granddaughter, Jane, remembered as very wild. Chap, however, was Jane's favorite because he never complained when she clambered around the ruins.[83]

As for Kate, the odd characters and richness of activity at camp would have suited her well, although there was the occasional mishap regarding her eyeglasses. *She was nearsighted, and . . . in camp had several most inconvenient experiences with broken glasses. I remember repairing her rimless glasses twice during the field session at Frijoles for use while replacements came from far-off Phila.*[84] Chap surely relished the opportunity to share Rito and all that it meant with Kate. He was also able to introduce Kate to Springer, when she received Hewett's permission to join a party of eight for explorations and excavations in the Jemez Valley. Perhaps that first meeting worried Chap a little, as he wondered whether the two would recognize in each other the qualities that Chap held so dear. Apparently, Kate's open and engaging manner met with Springer's approval, as his generous nature met with hers.

Although the school's summer sessions were to continue for several years more, the 1911 session seems to have marked the end of the initial exuberance and innocence that had characterized the fieldwork since 1908.[85] After the session, Hewett saw his first students ready to embark on challenging careers. Nusbaum and Judd both received appointments with the National Museum of Natural History. Morley's work in Central America was bringing him notice. Harrington was conducting ethnological research in Arizona. Chap was poised to resign from the school and travel east.

Hewett remained as director of the museum-school but was also looking toward new opportunities himself. When San Diego's Panama-California Exposition began to search for a director of exhibits, Lummis urged them to ask Hewett. Preparations for the exposition had begun in 1909 when citizens suggested that completion of the Panama Canal in 1915 would herald a bright future for San Diego. San Francisco had a similar idea and competed with San Diego over the exposition location. As a compromise, San Francisco hosted the World's Fair, while San Diego agreed to focus on exhibits from Latin American nations. The intent was to emphasize development of mankind, stressing the life of Mayan, Aztec, and southwestern Indian tribes.

Hewett's eagerness to pursue the San Diego project only strengthened Chap's belief that the museum was being neglected, while the Las Vegas mishap provided additional aggravation. In Milwaukee, he had been successful in "square dealing" by establishing discrete boundaries between his boss and himself when faced with disappointed clients. Chap now attempted to create clear distinctions between Hewett's obligations and his own. In the fall, Roberts visited the museum, but Chap told him frankly

that Dr. Hewett had shown no intention of meeting the obligation, and that from then on I would have no part in any such transactions. On his return to

Las Vegas, Dr. Roberts called on Mr. Springer and advised him of the situation. Mr. Springer wrote me next day to tell me of their conference, giving Dr. Roberts' account of our discussion, and adding that he trusted that I had been misquoted.

I replied at once that I seemed to have been quoted almost verbatim; that I could not go along with Dr. Hewett's methods and, further, that from then on I would do no more planning for the Museum's future, but would, of course, comply with any wishes he (Mr. Springer) might have in regard to my duties so long as he was contributing his time and funds toward its development.[86]

Chap's blunt words—especially for him—must have disturbed Springer. His plan, however, remained unchanged. He would provide the means of removing Chap from Hewett's employment, but Chap's ties to the museum could not be so easily severed. Springer's dedication to the museum and its goals meant that Chap would still be engaged there at Springer's request. To Chap, his resignation from Hewett's employment in November 1911 was a definite statement on his feelings about the museum's direction. Whether Hewett saw it that way, or simply attributed it to Springer's wishes, is hard to say. However, Chap's certainty that Springer would wish him to be associated again with the museum, conjoined with Chap's own temperament and the social conventions of the time, ensured that the relationship between Hewett and himself would remain civil.

Out east, however, many anthropologists who thought the school programs should be run more professionally felt no such compunction. Columbia University's Franz Boas struck out at Hewett's professional reputation in retaliation for disparaging statements that Hewett was said to have uttered.[87] The episode, which had begun a decade earlier, escalated with articles published in the *Santa Fe New Mexican*. While Hewett turned a blind eye and continued preparations for his marriage to Donizetta Wood, all of Santa Fe read about Boas's view of Hewett's work as unscientific and hasty.[88] Others also took the opportunity to voice their opinions. In February, Alfred Tozzer, who had disparaged Hewett's methods since the 1908 field session, wrote to Frederick Webb Hodge that he considered "Hewett's influence over the young men under him bad, his methods of work unscientific and too extended, his methods of scattering propaganda undignified, and his assumption of omnipotence unexampled."[89] Chap's memoirs do not comment on the brouhaha, but his own experiences with Hewett's methods must have given him some hope that perhaps Hewett would be brought to task. Meanwhile, Hewett's supporters rallied to his side, painting the episode as an instance of East Coast bullies vs. the West. The uproar soon subsided, but its remnants remained just below the surface where, like an archaeological cache, they would wait more than a decade to be exposed.

Hewett and Wood's wedding went off as planned. Because Wood had formerly been the receptionist, Hewett asked Chap whether Vera might consider working at the museum. Given Chap's disheartened attitude, it is curious, indeed, that Vera decided to leave Las Vegas Normal for the museum. Possibly, Chap had never divulged his discontent to his family—preferring to stress the positive aspects and keep close any unpleasantness—and chose to continue in that vein. Or maybe he encouraged Vera, hoping that her presence would benefit the museum. He may have actively discouraged her, but she had her own motives for wanting a move. At any rate, just as Chap was making preparations to leave the museum, he was partially securing his return by moving his mother, his sister, and Vera's daughter, Catherine, to Santa Fe, where *they were soon settled in the "old Catron adobe house," at the corner of Grant Avenue and Bower Street.*[90]

Chap's departure from Hewett's employment, then, would not mean a permanent absence from Santa Fe. His family's move provided some insurance that he could return to the people and the region that produced such engaging designs. The past two years had been rich in experiences—he had met distinctive personalities, developed close friendships, and become an integral part of the anthropological scene in the Southwest. They had reawakened his attachment to Indian artifacts and provided him the potential for establishing a name for himself, despite several obstacles. Now his new working arrangement gave Chap a way to distance himself from Hewett, enrich his artistic training, and reinforce his relationship with Springer. Unexpectedly, it had also reawakened a former dream of study at the Art Students League and a subsequent career in illustration. But cartoons were no longer high on Chap's list in 1912. Instead a priority was to search out pottery collections. Chap was prepared to follow a new muse.

CHAPTER 5

PASSIONS AND COMMITMENTS

Seagulls woke Chap now. By the summer of 1912, he had exchanged mountains for ocean. Where there had been burros dozing near adobe walls, now he witnessed a confusion of nets, tackle, and boats. Sunlight played on fields of waves instead of desert grasses. At home, the heart spoke of the land. Here, it told of the sea.

The surprise, however, was in the similarities between Santa Fe and Provincetown, Massachusetts, where Chap spent the summer. Both towns possessed a special light that drew artists. Charles Hawthorne, who founded the Provincetown artist colony in 1899, decided to establish his Cape Cod School of Art there after a visit in which he was captivated by the "jumble of color in the intense sunlight."[1] Provincetown was home to Portuguese-American fishing families, whose ancestors were sailors on eighteenth-century ships who chose to disembark and remain on the Cape. Hawthorne's portraits captured the essence of their community—much as artists would soon depict the Pueblo peoples' way of life. Known as Greenwich Village North, Provincetown fostered a bohemian community of artists and writers enticed by the light, the landscape, and the people. Chap's summer on the shore unexpectedly acquainted him with the type of artist society he would soon be mixing with in Santa Fe.

Hawthorne's school was Chap's first stop in carrying out Springer's plan to round out his art studies. On a friend's advice, Chap decided to attend a still-life course there after three months' work with Springer at the National Museum of Natural History, where they had collaborated on another of the paleontology monographs. Chap's Washington stay had been enlivened by the laughter of Nusbaum, who had been working at the museum since September, making piece molds and casts of archaeological materials for the upcoming Panama-California Exposition. Nusbaum visited Chap in New York, passing along in a letter to Hewett that Chap was well but didn't much care for the meals where he was staying—he took a pill after each and every one—and he was also going to have to get along without the dress suit that was expected of him. "Chap says that if he were living in N.Y. all the time he would do as the Romans do but as he was a roving artist, that he was not going to."[2] Chap then traveled to Provincetown because, according to Springer and Chap's arrangement, when the paleontology work was finished, the remaining months were his to fill. *I would leave Santa Fe in April, put in three months at*

Mr. Springer's work in Washington, and then have the balance of the year to myself. . . . I sentenced myself to hard work at the Art Students' League in New York and to painting in 1912, at Provincetown, under Hawthorne.[3]

Hawthorne's school, associated with the Art Students League, seemed an excellent choice. Artists flocked to Hawthorne, a naturalist painter who had studied with W. M. Chase at the league. Chap's decision to spend the summer months in outdoor sketching and painting seemed particularly wise, as his health always flourished when he could work outside. The port, and all its activity, must certainly have enthralled him, as would its summer climate and varied landscape. Some days, a heavy fog painted the country-side gray. Other times, sea breezes dispelled summer's heat and unveiled a glittering sea. Long walks surely beckoned, for hidden in the scenery were trails that led first through forests of stunted pines, beech, and oak and then onto rolling dunes.

Enjoying the pleasure of others, Chap may have made a friend or two among the students. And perhaps he felt a sense of release in being so far from snarled museum tasks. Yet by September, as he returned to the city for coursework at the league, he probably felt a nostalgic twinge at finding himself so far from Rito. Although no letters to or from his mother or Kate survive from this time, news from Kate, who was working at Jemez as an assistant to Hewett and Hodge, surely triggered memories of the Pajarito . . . and time with Kate. The two had managed a rendezvous in Philadelphia's Pennsylvania Station earlier in the summer during Chap's train trip up the eastern seaboard.[4] Although their physical selves had journeyed on to opposite landscapes—Kate, to spend the summer with the Boyle family in Santa Fe, and Chap, to his studies at the league's summer session in Provincetown—both must have sensed that their hearts traveled as one.

So, as Kate hiked among piñon in the Jemez mountains, Chap may have taken a turn around Central Park, musing on a problem in his life drawing class where he was study-ing under George Bridgman. Chap had known of the Art Students League by reputation since his early interest in art. Considered a radical institution, the league's philosophy embraced artistic creativity and a respect for those who devoted their lives to art. It had been founded in July 1875—nearly on Chap's birthday—when a group of students, dis-satisfied with the policies of New York's National Academy of Design, pinned a notice on the bulletin board at the academy to announce a meeting to form the league.[5] A particular grievance of the students against the academy had been the closing of its life drawing school for economic reasons.[6] Another was their being denied access to books on art and collections of artwork.[7]

In September 1875, the league opened its doors as the first independent art school in the country. The league's framework was completely different from the conservative principles of the Art Institute. The league allowed its instructors complete freedom. It did not prescribe course content nor did it make pronouncements about art. Instead, it endeavored to keep up with developments and ensure representation of differing points of view in contemporary culture. Initially, the league's teachers were the young artists who were then returning from study in Europe, proponents of the "modern" point of view.[8] Since then, many well-known artists, who shaped the course of art, have been instructors, lecturers, and students at the league. Some became better known as teachers, but all had solid reputations as artists. Ernest Blumenschein, a member of the Taos Art Colony, taught at the league during the 1911–12 school year. Georgia O'Keeffe attended classes there from 1907 to 1908. Jackson Pollock, Mark Rothko, and Roy Lichtenstein all studied at the league.

In electing to take a life drawing class with Bridgman in fall 1912, Chap had chosen to study with the master. Bridgman, author of several popular art instruction books, such as *Bridgman's Life Drawing*, was the originator of a drawing system known as constructive anatomy, which is still followed today. Bridgman believed that, for a drawn or painted figure to be lifelike and true, a thorough knowledge of the muscular system's movements and manipulations was essential. Given Chap's analytical tendencies, he must have enjoyed Bridgman's lectures on anatomy as a foundation for art.

Chap's classes with Bridgman were held in the American Fine Arts Society building at 215 West 57th Street, where the league had moved ten years earlier (and where it is still located today). Chap didn't just lock himself in at the league; he occasionally went out on the town, visiting with friends such as John Caskie, his close companion from St. Louis in the 1890s. He took the opportunity to socialize with Kidder as well as build relationships over lunch with members of the anthropological elite, such as Harvard professor Alfred Tozzer, whom Chap knew from Rito, and American Museum of Natural History staff member Herbert J. "Joe" Spinden. Since Tozzer and Spinden held no love for Hewett, it is intriguing to consider whether Chap's disaffection for Hewett's methods might have surfaced in such a conducive atmosphere.

Not too far from the American Fine Arts Society building, though, Chap found a particular spot in which he spent many pleasant New York evenings—the enormous reading room of the New York Public Library. The institution was the inspiration of Governor Samuel J. Tilden, who bequeathed much of his fortune in 1886 to establish and maintain a free library and reading room in New York City.[9] Over the next twenty-five years, as the site and its collections were readied, the New York Public Library joined forces with regional libraries, including thirty-nine Carnegie branches. When it opened its doors in May 1911, just about a year before Chap arrived, the library had seventy-five miles of shelves and more than one million books in its collections.

One million books! Selecting materials from such an immense collection must surely have been a thrill. Up until then, Chap's research had consisted primarily of field observations, from which he produced his drawings and notes. Comparative research was difficult. The museum in Santa Fe had only just created space for a library. Still, Chap noted, *the Museum provided only the scantiest material for my use.*[10] In New York, the anthropological and archaeological resources presumably offered Chap the first real opportunity to contrast his own findings with others in the field as well as consult classic sources on art and archaeology.

At the time, Chap was preoccupied with discovering the sources for the bird decorations on Pajaritan pottery. His research had led to professional relationships with both William Henry Holmes and Frederick Webb Hodge, distinguished members of the earlier generation of anthropologists. Discussions with Holmes that year motivated Chap to study the meander pattern (an angular design of bands within a border, often referred to as the "Greek key") and its derivations, which Holmes felt was the source of many Pajaritan decorations. Holmes was a member of the school's first managing committee and was then curator of the Smithsonian's National Museum and National Art Gallery. "Hoping to find this same development in Oriental Rugs in which the meander is so commonly used," Chap later wrote to his friend and mentor, Hodge of the Bureau of Ethnology. "I worked through some 30 volumes in the New York Public Library in addition to inspecting the collections in stores and museums. The results were very satisfactory. I have excellent examples showing the accidental origin of the 'bird' form and in addition, an example of the 'bird' form used independently as in the Pajaritan ware."[11] Well satisfied with the opportunities for research as well as with his art classes, Chap told Springer that he expected to remain in New York through the spring, where he would continue his regimen of classes by day and research by night. As midwinter's light shortened each day, however, Chap's resolve also began to dim.

> *Gradually my indoor work at the League by day, and at the Public Library by night, began to tell on me. Also I had neglected a swelling on the nape of my neck that had developed into a huge carbuncle. It required lancing and frequent treatments and dressings for many weeks. The whole procedure affected my work, so that I found myself longing for the sunshine of New Mexico. Mr. Springer approved my change of plan; I detoured to Washington, and after a few days work with him, was on my way home.*[12]

But if thoughts of home gave rise to dreams of long, uninterrupted hours in his studio, the reality gave Chap time only to ponder why, once again, he had been caught in the museum-school trap. At the January 3, 1913, meeting of the school's managing committee, held at the National Museum of Natural History, Hewett had declared that he would likely be called on to assume the duties of director of exhibits of the Panama-California Exposition and thus would not be able give full attention to the school.[13] In persuading his boards and other backers of the advantages of the new position, Hewett claimed that the tasks connected with the exposition would offer a wonderful opportunity to enlarge the school's activities, particularly in research, and to broaden the education and salary of the staff. He succeeded in convincing many on the board, although some members objected, believing that Hewett was already overextended. Hodge openly opposed the idea.[14] In a letter to Mitchell Carroll, AIA secretary, Hodge said that if Hewett were to take on the San Diego job, Hodge would terminate the joint School of American Archaeology–Bureau of Ethnology interdisciplinary study.[15] Regardless, the AIA approved Hewett's request, made Chap assistant director, and placed him in charge of the school.

Chap first heard of his "promotion" in Washington, where he had stopped briefly to work with Springer before returning to Santa Fe. Springer likely was pleased with himself for so quickly resolving the school's dilemma and perhaps especially for being able to act on his knowledge of Chap's availability. Chap, who never refused anything of Springer, nonetheless certainly suffered the news as a blow. Once again, he was being diverted from the work that claimed his heart. Once again, he would be involved in cleaning up Hewett's professional debris. Chap's loyalty to Springer demanded that he accept the assignment gracefully and put his own aspirations on hold. Yet in a letter to Hewett, who had apparently suggested that he and Chap spend a day together in Santa Fe to effect the transition, Chap's dismay is unmistakable.

My first intimation that I had been "framed up" came in your night letter of the 5th.

I learned the details later from Mr. Springer.

We are down to business at last, but he says he cannot get through with me here until Sunday at the very earliest. I am certainly out of touch with the institution after my long absence and doubt if you could have inducted me into office with a scant day's coaching, as you proposed.

I will look for instructions from you when I reach Santa Fe, and take up the acting directorship if you have left it in my hands. I presume the accounts will claim my attention first.[16]

Back in Santa Fe, Chap's prognosis of the situation did not improve. He could not move into his studio because Harrington refused to leave it until he received funds from Hewett. Chap himself was having trouble getting paid the salary that had been pledged to him at the January meeting. ("So I am putting in full time for the promise of $75 that I can't locate.")[17] And attending to the school's countless details (staffing, facilities, legislation) prevented him from pursuing his own work. "Having agreed to hold down the job,

I am still in it, but more dissatisfied with the situation than when I left last Spring."[18]

New Mexico itself, officially a state for nearly a year now, did not disappoint. Although Morley, Nusbaum, and painter Carlos Vierra were away—on an expedition in Central America—Santa Fe now offered the comfort of family. Even more satisfying, Kate was in New Mexico. Instead of returning to Philadelphia, she had stayed in town and was living with the Boyle family in their home on DeVargas Street. Now that Chap was back, Kate was ready to fill him in on the latest gossip, especially about a matter that spoke to her directly: architecture.

For centuries—from the 1600s through 1850—Santa Fe had remained relatively insulated with regard to architecture, satisfied with a style that the Spanish settlers had made nearly ubiquitous. Using adobe brick at the core, they had merged certain features of Indian Pueblo construction with Spanish colonial forms. Santa Fe residents began to introduce deviations from this style only after New Mexico became a U.S. territory, when the military's sawed lumber and fired brick tempted them to try out other architectural forms.

But the real blow to Santa Fe's traditional architecture came with the railroad. The new method of transport significantly lowered the cost of all building materials. Citizens with ambitions for Santa Fe perceived the Victorian style as progress.[19] An article in the *Santa Fe Daily New Mexican* on October 8, 1889, exemplified these citizens' attitude. Trying to promote Santa Fe, the paper slighted the adobe: "Occasionally, groves of cottonwoods with darker hues, and shade trees in the streets more completely each year hide the shapeless adobe houses that must give way to modern buildings."[20]

By 1910, the modern architectural trend in Santa Fe threatened to transform it into exactly what its opportunistic citizens had asked for—it was beginning to look like every other American town. At the same time, a small, but soon vocal, minority asserted a different vision. In March 1912, two months after New Mexico finally achieved statehood, Santa Fe held its first city planning meeting. Board members included city boosters such as H. H. Dorman (chairman of the planning commission and the chamber of commerce), Bronson Cutting (senator, owner of the *Santa Fe New Mexican*, and antagonist of Hewett's), and Santa Fe merchants James L. Seligman, Sam G. Cartwright, and Marcelino García. Governor Arthur Seligman had also appointed Hewett and Morley to the board. The purpose was to plan for a healthful, convenient, and attractive city and to preserve historic streets and properties."[21]

Morley's appointment to the board was significant because it placed him in a position of influence. Not surprising for an anthropologist, Morley was ardent about historic preservation. According to Nusbaum, "With the razing of each old historic building, or commencement of construction of a new California bungalow or other modern structure, Morley literally saw red, and become more vigorous and aggressive

Sylvanus "Vay" Morley. (Photograph by Jesse L. Nusbaum.
Courtesy of Palace of the Governors [MNM/DCA], 10313.)

in his public campaign to save 'The Old.' He talked to all who would listen; attempted
to persuade those who opposed; and probably talked Old Santa Fe in his sleep, for he
was so constituted."[22]

Morley also practiced what he preached. When he had arrived in Santa Fe in 1909,
he bought a somewhat battered adobe at the foot of Fort Marcy where he spent each
summer. Instead of tearing down the house or "modernizing" it, he repaired the main
structure, keeping its lovely portal with posts and corbels and replacing rotting vigas
with old carved beams. "I cannot remember where he found those, but I do remember
his joyous letter about their discovery and purchase," Kidder later recalled.[23]

Morley soon became the principal public spokesman for the city planning board,
promoting its Plan of 1912. Although originating within the nationwide City Beautiful
movement, Santa Fe's plan was innovative in that it merged the movement's emphasis
on order and refinement with the revival of a local style.[24] To promote this viewpoint,
a group of artists, writers, historians, archaeologists, conservative business leaders,
and citizens formed the "Old Santa Fe group," designating Morley as its leader. Morley
quickly grasped that the way to convince the new to keep the old was to frame the issue

in dollars. He stressed Santa Fe's potential for tourism, emphasizing that the city could acquire greater fame and more lasting prosperity by keeping famous and important buildings intact.[25]

Opposing progressives, however, were equally forceful in promoting a modern Santa Fe. Thus, the issue between those who wished to preserve and perpetuate the old and those who wanted to pursue modern trends soon became a matter of major citywide discussion and concern (foreshadowing the Indian art discussion that loomed in the city's future). In August, Morley presented a proposal to the planning board, asking it to sponsor an exhibition to educate the public about civic improvements. The exhibit, called "The New-Old Santa Fe Exhibition," opened in Santa Fe in November 1912.

Many at the museum, all supporters of "Old Santa Fe," helped with the exhibit. T. A. Hayden produced a large-scale topographical model of Santa Fe to help the public visualize the improvements. Carlos Vierra's wash drawings compared existing scenes with the same scenes after proposed developments. Nusbaum contributed photographs of early Santa Fe architecture and details. Jack Adams prepared measured drawings and scale models of historic buildings that merited preservation. Of special interest was a ten-foot scale model of the Palace of the Governors with its territorial facade replaced by a portal. The historical justification for adding the portal was made on the basis of Joseph de Urrutia's map, drawn before 1768 and stored in the British Museum, along with a corbel uncovered by Nusbaum in a previously walled up entryway. By the time that Chap returned to Santa Fe, the exhibit had served Morley's purposes perfectly. The public had attended in large numbers, impressed by what they saw.[26]

Although the 1912 plan never became legally binding, Morley's newly "educated" public thoroughly championed the idea of the Santa Fe style.[27] The episode had also shown the force that the anthropological/artistic community could bring to bear when united. Public enthusiasm for the Palace of the Governors' model during the exhibition also resulted in the legislature approving the addition of the portal. Before the exhibit, Hewett and others had told Nusbaum that he would have to give up the idea. As he later reported, however, "they reckoned without the public, who saw it and were strong for it and, by gosh, pressure was so great that money was allocated for me to go ahead and build it."[28]

Kate was one member of the public who had required no convincing. An art student who had by now participated for several years in the school, she identified with the New-Old Santa Fe movement and quickly put its philosophy into practice. Soon to be a renovator in her own right, she embarked on her first construction project when she moved into the eastern portion of the Boyles' large adobe house in 1913, repairing and remodeling it, at her own expense, in lieu of rent. A principal feature of her remodel was a full-sized portal with hand-hewn corbels that had been on display at the exhibition and that she purchased for the renovation.[29]

Coincidentally, architecture also became a primary focus for Chap, and this had the serendipitous effect of bringing Kate and Chap that much closer together. Almost as soon as he returned to Santa Fe, he was pleased to discover that he would be involved in plans for an extensive outdoor exhibit sponsored by the Santa Fe Railway company for the Panama-California Exposition. Herman Schweizer, of the railway's Albuquerque office, asked Chap to prepare detailed sketches for the exhibit from which a scale model would be made. Schweizer and Chap worked out a rough draft, and then Chap finished watercolor drawings in two views.[30] The watercolors were the basis for the plaster model created by Harvey Company architect Mary Jane Colter for the Painted Desert exhibit.[31] Colter was an avid proponent of structures that emphasized southwestern culture and featured native materials. Her architectural ideas are embodied in buildings such as Grand Canyon's Hopi House and La Posada in Winslow, Arizona. Intended to combine scientific, scenic, and artistic views, the Painted Desert exhibit featured Navajo hogans, kivas, and two pseudopueblos.[32] Positioned strategically on the "Isthmus," or midway section of the Panama-California Exposition, the exhibit became a main attraction.

Actual construction of the exhibit was entrusted to Nusbaum. "The Painted Desert is the greatest piece of landscaping, topographic, and geological reproduction ever made, and I do not think any man could have done it but you," wrote Springer.[33] During construction, the railway spared no expense. To add authenticity, the railroad freighted in building materials and plants from across the Southwest. The railroad also issued travel passes to twenty-eight San Ildefonso Pueblo families, including Maria and Julian Martinez. San Diego carpenters erected the wood-and-plaster superstructure, while the people from San Ildefonso constructed low adobe walls, beehive ovens, and chimney pots.

In California, Hewett watched over construction of the Painted Desert and other exhibits, and, at the same time, continued to keep tabs on the school's work through correspondence with Chap. Although Chap's letters never trespassed polite boundaries, his responses were tinged with impatience. In early February, Hewett provided budget information, which he encouraged Chap to have on hand to talk with legislators. Chap's reply detailed his daily tasks, including "my small [art] class of 6 or 8," which "doesn't leave me much time to trail legislators. Some of them have been in, and I have done my best, but it is out of my line."[34] In April, Hewett suggested that it would be a good plan for Kate Muller and Ruth Laughlin to canvass the town to encourage enrollment in the summer school.[35] Chap replied: "I had taken no action in regard to raising funds or getting an individual guarantee from the merchants for our coming summer school. Kate Muller, as you probably know, is now in California for an indefinite stay."[36] And the school's funding problems continued to inflame Chap's sense of propriety. In a May letter to Hewett concerning the accounts, Chap wrote: "If they are expected to wait for their money, I would want them to know that it is a matter in which I have taken no part."[37]

In late February, Chap wrote to Hodge to discuss ideas for revising the 1911 article on the Pajaritan pottery. In the new version, Chap hoped to incorporate his ideas on the meander that had come to him during his studies in New York. But, despite the optimism his letter exuded, his schedule remained too full to allow much time for his own research. He and Jack Adams surveyed the Pecos ruins for a modeled reconstruction of the pueblo and church, which Adams built for the Panama-California Exposition.[38] Otherwise, Chap's work with pottery seemed restricted to shipping it out of state. In early spring, Chap prepared a shipment of Jemez pottery for Charles Currelly, a member of the school's managing committee and Canada's Royal Ontario Museum of Archaeology. The pieces were sent in return for the Toronto Archaeological Society's contribution to the 1912 Jemez dig.[39] Nevertheless, Chap was beginning to voice his concerns about losing pottery specimens to out-of-state collectors. "Ruth Laughlin took us out to Tesuque this morning, where Professor Hill-Tout made some good purchases, one a fine large tinaja which I hate to see leave the country."[40]

Already overwhelmed by his museum tasks, summer brought an additional responsibility for Chap: jury duty in the U.S. district court. Swamped with preparations for the upcoming summer field session, Chap tried to postpone his obligation, but Judge William H. Pope personally asked him to serve. By attending to the museum early each morning and after leaving the courthouse, he successfully juggled both duties over the course of two weeks and thereby managed to please the judge. On the other hand, because *it was a paternity case, the court officials from reporter, down, slipped me by grape-vine their opinion that as a bachelor, I had no business listening in on such matters!*[41]

The plaintiff was a young woman who desired to establish rights for her illegitimate daughter so that the child could share in the inheritance of her natural father, now deceased. The case was filled with twists and turns, including a dispute over whether evidence had been tampered with, specifically whether a particular letter had carried a one- or two-cent stamp. The question spurred Chap to invent a method by which the question could be resolved to the jury's satisfaction. Despite his long days, he arranged to perform a test at home one evening. *From the museum and my home file, I salvaged a few dozen cancelled stamps of several denominations, soaked them off, and dried them. Then I began examining the back of each stamp with a magnifying glass and was thrilled to find that I had hit on something!*[42]

During the printing process of that time, each sheet of stamps was laid down, face up, on other sheets before the ink on the sheets beneath was dry. As a result, the back of each sheet generally held a few flecks of color from the undried sheet beneath it. By turning the stamps face down, Chap found that he could identify over three-fourths of them by the flecks on their backs, green for the one-cent and red for the two-cent ones. So, next morning, primed with this information, he explained his findings to the jury's foreman. The judge subsequently sent the envelope to the post office in Washington, asking for a report, and later, the case was resolved in favor of the plaintiff. (The official U.S. Postal Service report did not figure in the case's conclusion, but its subsequent arrival confirmed the court's decision.)[43]

Although Chap was clearly stimulated by the judicial puzzle, the addition of that duty to his already demanding schedule may have cemented his wish to again quit the museum. He still yearned to study Pueblo decorative art full time or, at least, manage a half-time arrangement between his own studies and Springer's work. In June 1913, when Hewett asked about plans for the fall, Chap told him that he wanted to leave by September. At first, Hewett considered asking Kidder, who was writing his dissertation, to replace Chap, but then wrote that the "affairs of the institution are not in shape for a new man to take hold of. As I see it now, it is a matter of five or six months more of patient plodding along under the difficulties that have beset us in the past, because of lack of funds, and then in December of this year when the new appropriation begins to run, a general clearing of the sky."[44] He assured Chap that he would be completely paid up by the first of September.

With a lightened spirit occasioned by the knowledge that the museum "sentence" would soon be up, Chap enjoyed the companionship of Morley and Nusbaum, who were back in Santa Fe. They brought their good humor as well as a bit of chaos. Well able to imagine the scene, Hewett had written to Chap from San Diego, "When Morley gets back I want you to have the frankest kind of a talk with him about his work. Our rooms back there have become altogether too public. . . . I know it will be agreeable to you, and I think it will to all the boys, to close out absolutely that continual visiting to which all are so much subjected during working hours. The waste of time is enormous. I hope you will apply the rule pretty rigidly to every department. It will all be easy until Jess gets back. You may then have to take some extreme measures."[45]

Although responsible and dependable within their professions, Morley, Nusbaum, and Chap could not help but bring a lightheartedness to nearly every situation. The events of a story told to Marjorie Lambert by Chap during the 1950s, which she titled "The Strange Disappearance of Sylvanus G. Morley," may well have occurred during that summer of 1913. In her retelling, Chapman, Nusbaum, and Morley were traveling to Albuquerque to meet a dignitary. At that time, the road between Santa Fe and Albuquerque was hair raising under the best of circumstances, especially the hairpin turns at La Bajada. Neither Chap nor Morley could drive, so it was up to the very daring and skillful Nusbaum to man the wheel. "Driving with Jesse was never restful," Lambert remembered Chap saying, "and this trip was no exception."

The three were in an open touring car, well past its prime. As Chap recalled, he sat in front, with Morley behind. There were huge boulders on the road that had rolled down during an earlier storm. "But these were only a greater challenge to the intrepid driver who maneuvered the old car in and out of each dangerous area," Chap said. During the trip, Morley had been talking nonstop, in his usual way, until the car began to bounce him from side to side and up and down,

whereupon his verbiage became punctuated with streams of profanity. At one especially bad place, Jesse couldn't avoid hitting a deep pothole. "It was either doing this or go over the cliff," said Chap.

Finally, Nusbaum got the old car down to the bottom of La Bajada Hill. It was at this point that Chapman turned toward the back seat to see why Morley hadn't answered a question he had asked. To his horror and amazement, the seat was empty.

There was nothing else to do but to turn around and labor back up the grade in search of Vay Morley. "Needless to say, we were very concerned," Chap said.

They were about a third of the way up when the radiator began to pour steam out through the hood of the car, "But through the steam we could see in the distance a small and somewhat battered Morley limping along, and we could hear his outpouring of blasphemy in both English and colorful Spanish."[46]

Apparently, when Jesse hit the pothole, Morley had been thrown from the car and then fallen over the edge of the narrow road. According to Chap, Morley's pride was hurt worse than his small, light body. And, fortunately, he didn't hold a grudge. "But when Vay told of this adventure, he could sure curse Jesse."[47]

If the adventure did take place that summer, Morley, Nusbaum, and Chap may well have been on their way to collect a guest lecturer for the school's summer session. Several lecturers had been invited, despite the school's continuing financial difficulties. "We have not been able to make the Summer School self-supporting as yet and consequently, are not able to offer much in the way of inducements, unless the opportunity for a pleasant outing may be so considered," Hewett had written to Lewis B. Paton, when asking for his participation.[48] The 1913 session featured one week at Rito, where Chap directed some excavation work, and another week at Quarai, near Mountainair, New Mexico. At Quarai, they excavated the ruins of one of the early Franciscan missions in the area.[49] In addition, the school sponsored demonstrations of potterymaking on the Palace of the Governors' patio by San Ildefonso potters, as it had done the previous summer. Maria and Julian had moved back to the pueblo by this time but came to town to participate in the event. Hewett had written Chap that he could not guarantee wages, but "we will give them a good place to live and work, and every possible facility for selling their wares."[50] Chap was asked to speak with other members of the pueblo, who also promised to come, although Chap noted that the men could not leave their crops without a guarantee of wages.[51]

In September, Chap escaped his museum responsibilities when Paul Walter took over as acting director, while Hewett continued as director of exhibits for the Panama-California Exposition. Originally from Bethlehem, Pennsylvania, Walter had come to Santa Fe in 1899 to work as editorial writer for the *Santa Fe New Mexican*. Early on, he established friendships with Springer, Hewett, and McFie through the archaeological society, and throughout his tenure at the *New Mexican*, Walter's promotion of the museum's work was sincere and unflagging.[52]

Forced to sell the *New Mexican* to Bronson Cutting in 1912, Walter moved briefly to California. But he soon returned to Santa Fe, this time to work for Hewett at the museum. Besides serving as secretary—and acting director when Hewett was in San Diego—Walter also edited *El Palacio*, which published its first issue in November 1913. The result of a $10,000 bequest from Abby White of Boston, *El Palacio* was officially the publication of the New Mexico Archaeological Society and, under Walter's direction, soon had a wide public readership.[53] Like the AIA's *Art and Archaeology*, the journal integrated aesthetics and science—and during the first decade of its existence it also included a sort of Santa Fe social column about the doings of the staff and artists. Each issue was a virtual "salon," feeding the intellect as well as providing tidbits of local who's who. *El Palacio* also provided insurance that those whose work might not gain publication elsewhere would see their work in print through the house press.

Freed from the demands of the acting directorship and encouraged by the possibility of publishing opportunities, Chap took the winter to work on pottery research. By then, Chap was well aware that along with Springer's generous support came uncertainty over any research schedule. As obstacles to his own studies mounted during these years, Chap often reevaluated his situation, particularly after he began to appreciate the professional prospects that his friends enjoyed. Yet in his memoirs, Chap always rationalized his decision to remain, declaring loyalty to Springer and his dependence on New Mexico's climate as his reasons.

That winter, however, he was determined to make the best of an opportunity for research and devoted his time to preparing his paper, begun in 1909. In line with his and Kidder's earlier agreement, Chap's study focused solely on Pajarito pottery. Had it been published during this period, it would have been the first paper on Pajaritan pottery (Kidder's dissertation of the region's pottery was not published until late 1914) and would have included over four hundred black-and-white drawings. As Chap noted in a 1927 letter to Hewett, the study represented "a contribution on the development of

Kate and Chap, c. 1915. (Courtesy of School for Advanced Research Archives, AC02 n109 and AC02 n106.)

Pueblo art fully justifying the amount of work I put in it." But prospects of its publication "grew more and more dim," with Walter admitting that *El Palacio* lacked funds for illustrations, and eventually Chap's work was superseded by that of Kidder (1915) and Jeançon (1923).[54]

At the time, however, Chap believed that his study would soon be published. And why not be optimistic? He was in love. The growing affection between Chap and Kate was intensified by their shared interests, such as the architectural contest Morley had persuaded the chamber of commerce to sponsor. Prizes were offered for the best design of a Santa Fe residence not to exceed $3,500 in cost.[55] It is easy to imagine Kate and Chap's enthusiastic deliberations over architectural possibilities, which Chap then transformed into several drawings. And what delight when one of Chap's designs won first prize! According to Nusbaum, the "beautiful proportions and perfect balance of the doorway and adjacent wall spaces, including the water spouts, were the features which won for this design the first prize."[56] (Second, third, and fourth prizes went to Carlos Vierra; another of Chap's designs won an honorable mention.[57])

Love and art. From September through April, as Chap happily edited his paper in his museum studio or discussed architectural designs with Kate, he enjoyed an exhilarating tonic of both. Other artists were also beginning to sense a future in Santa Fe. Gerald Cassidy, a lithographer from New York, and his wife, Ina, a writer, frequently visited Santa Fe as they considered a permanent move. Sheldon Parsons, a painter, had settled in Santa Fe for his health earlier that year. And in a nearby studio, an old acquaintance, Donald Beauregard, was beginning work on a series of murals about St. Francis, which Hewett and Springer had commissioned. Chap knew the Utah-born Beauregard from the 1909–10 Pajarito excavations. After that, Beauregard had traveled to Europe to study art, with an allowance from Springer, in preparation for painting the murals, which were to be hung in the New Mexico building at the Panama-California Exposition.

Beauregard arrived in Santa Fe in September 1913 after illness forced him to leave Europe. He thought of returning to Utah for "the care that only a mother can give" but instead came to Santa Fe, bringing along his sketches for an allegorical series depicting the life of Santa Fe's patron saint and European influence in the New World.[58] He painted until late February 1914, when illness again began to interfere with his work. In March, when his condition worsened, he traveled to Denver for an examination, telling Chap that he expected to return within two weeks.[59]

Beauregard's optimism was not justified, however, as the exam revealed stomach cancer. Two months later, Beauregard passed away in his family's home. Without Beauregard, Hewett and Springer had to consider whether to continue the project. In reviewing the mural studies, Hewett was impressed with their scope and depth, assuring Springer that the idea had been a sound one. But finding a replacement would be difficult.

Before his death, faced with the problem of the unfinished murals for the Panama-California Exposition, Beauregard had recommended that Sheldon Parsons complete the work. Hewett, however, felt that Parsons lacked certain artistic strengths that the project required. (An additional concern was that Parsons, recovering from tuberculosis, was physically weak; having lost one artist to illness, Hewett was surely not about to risk another.) In a letter to Springer, Hewett wondered whether, instead of Parsons, Vierra and Chap might together finish the murals. Vierra, the first artist to move to Santa Fe, had assisted Nusbaum with the restoration of the Palace of the Governors and recently been hired by Hewett to paint murals for the Panama-California Exposition. Thus, while Chap readied himself in the spring for his trip east to work on the monographs, Springer was writing to Hewett with new plans for Chap:

> It would suit me <u>infinitely</u> better if Chapman could do the work and if he feels enough confidence in himself to undertake it. I am prepared to give him the opportunity for all the necessary special study to that end. Beauregard was very much impressed with Chap's handling of color as shown by the sketches he has done during the past couple of years and he told me that by all means Chapman should go on with oil. If he and Vierra could do it as team work that would be the next best thing, but if Chap can handle it alone, I should prefer it. This can all be subject to future conference, but as Chap will be here soon I will have a heart-to-heart talk with him with a view to deciding what the real possibilities or limitations are. To have the work finished by some of <u>our own men</u> will be fine. (emphasis in the original)[60]

Springer broached the subject while Chap was in Washington, DC. He not only suggested that Chap take on the project but again offered to pay for art studies that would supplement Chap's knowledge and skills. Confident in Chap's abilities but faced with a tightened time schedule (the exposition was due to open in January 1915), Springer proposed to Hewett that they prepare the murals for display in Santa Fe. "My thought now is to give up all idea of finishing them for the Exposition . . . and let Chapman try it, perhaps with assistance of Vierra. Chap is with me here and as soon as he finishes some odds and ends for me (perhaps 10 days now), he is going to New York to see what arrangements he can make for special studies in this line."[61]

Saying yes to the mural commission could not have been simple for Chap. For one, he had watched the center panel of the triptych, *The Renunciation of Santa Clara*, take shape under Beauregard's hand, and Chap may have felt uneasy about usurping the creative work of another, regardless of the circumstances. He also knew his limitations. He had no experience with oils and very little with landscapes. The summer of additional art studies would also place him out east, far from Kate. Finally, his research into the questions provoked by the Pajaritan pottery would suffer.

On the other hand, it was clear that the murals were important to Springer and, as always, Chap was loath to either assert his own vision or hinder any longing of his mentor's. Besides, work on the murals would not only satisfy Springer but also ensure that Chap's position at the museum would be that of an artist, not an administrator. Thus, Chap found himself, once again, in New York for art studies, though this time he summered in the Catskills at Woodstock, where he attended John Carlson's landscape class.

Carlson, only a year older than Chap, was a highly influential teacher of landscape painting whose book, *Elementary Principles of Landscape Painting*, has served as a bible for generations of artists. Carlson was known for the harmonious color schemes of his landscapes and his delicate glazing technique. As a teacher, Carlson's philosophy was to present the student with "certain common sense ideas of procedure, without stifling the enthusiasm that is to carry him on."[62] The school itself was favorably reviewed by an artist who pointed with "peculiar pleasure" to the work done at the Art Students League's Woodstock school as a step in the right direction. "They have achieved a summer school founded on the common sense basis of concrete knowledge instead of the precariously fascinating stilts of feeling and inspiration."[63]

Given his artistic and analytical aptitude, Chap would have savored Carlson's approach as well as the opportunity to work again out of doors. Hewett hoped that Chap would find time to return to Santa Fe for fieldwork, but Chap chose instead to take another life class at the league in New York City with Bridgman. Since Chap's purpose in these art studies was to prepare for completing the murals, he was particularly pleased that Bridgman himself pointed to Chap's potential. *Bridgman, just before I left in 1914, picked me as one of three (one was Norman Rockwell!) whom he thought might qualify for a position then open with a firm of mural decorators.*[64]

Chap's successes at the league, however, did not diminish his dedication to pottery. Between sessions, he traveled to Philadelphia to view a museum collection. (One wonders whether Kate, also, may have been visiting at the time.) And he continued to take advantage of New York's resources. *The two years were not a total loss. I could not forget my studies of Indian design and I had spent most of my weekends in museums, by day, and nights in research at the New York Public Library. What a wonderful place to work! I often thought of it later when I tried to snatch time here and there for my studies in Santa Fe.*[65]

In October, Chap began his journey back to the Southwest, first stopping to visit with Springer, who was still corresponding with Hewett regarding the final plan for the murals. In July, Hewett had told Springer, "The New Mexico building [for the Panama-California Exposition] is finished and the result is beyond what I anticipated. It is a wonderfully pleasing structure in every respect; the exterior is striking and in perfect harmony with the Exposition plan. . . . The chapel is a gem, but the empty niches, all beautifully finished and framed, in which our cherished St. Francis plan was to be worked out, give one a feeling of pretty deep sadness."[66] Now Springer wrote Hewett that, with regard to the mural commission, Chap "looks upon it with more confidence than when I spoke to him first about it. The season in the East has done him a lot of good and he is beginning to get a grasp of things more firmly than before. What he needs now is practice, and I intend to see that he has the opportunity for this uninterrupted."[67]

As Chap traveled back to Santa Fe, he was rewarded this time with a trip in which he could dwell at length on the increasing bounty of his life as he neared forty. His research in New York had strengthened his ideas about the origins of the designs on the Pajaritan ware, and through that, he was developing professional relationships outside Santa Fe. His recent art studies had expanded his artistic skills, increasing his confidence in taking on the mural commission. And he was traveling home to Kate. She had her own studio at the museum now, where she taught as well as participated in art conferences and lectures.[68] Partners in art, Chap and Kate were also looking forward to a more intimate tie: they were to be married in September 1915.

Except for Kate, however, Santa Fe was nearly devoid of intimate friends. Morley had left in late summer to take a position with the Carnegie Institute. Nusbaum and Vierra were in San Diego, working on the Painted Desert exhibit and the Mayan murals, respectively. Maria and Julian Martinez were in San Diego as well, as was Vera, who had gone there to recuperate from an apparently grave illness. In an arrangement typical of Springer's generosity and concern for Chap's future, Springer had written to Hewett that because of Vera's illness, "I shall probably have to help her, which I should feel like doing in order to obviate worry to Chapman and interruptions of his work, which I am very anxious he should keep up steady, now that he has got into the swing of it again. I feel that this is a crucial time with him, to find out whether he is going to be able for larger things. So I wish to do what is necessary to take care of his family, but in Vera's case I shall prefer not to do it directly, at present. The idea would be, if it seems best for her to go to San Diego, to arrange some work for her there under you—which I would pay for through you."[69]

Springer's solicitude on Vera's behalf and a plenitude of projects kept Chap from worry. Almost as soon as he returned, he began busily preparing his paintings for a December art show in the museum, creating a set of bird designs to be displayed at the Panama-California Exposition, and looking ahead to publication of his design research. He also began the mural work.

At the time, Chap's artwork was already on display in the museum—two watercolors hung in the Pajaritan room, while the Rito room held one of the Ceremonial Cave. Springer requested that Chap prepare his New York artwork for exhibition at the museum, however, so that he would have something tangible to show for his present status as mural artist.[70] According to a newspaper report, Chap's work in the mid-December show made "a most beautiful art exhibit" that included "splendid landscape studies. The pictures have atmosphere, the skies are well done and the drawing is finished, lacking the crudeness of the impressionists."[71] The following month, Chap's paintings were part of a larger museum art exhibit that also featured works by members of the now legendary Taos Society of Artists. While waiting for Vierra's return to Santa Fe so that they could divide up the mural work, Chap honed his painting skills. An oil portrait, owned by Chap's son, Frank, of a Mexican man has a note on the reverse side in his father's handwriting that identifies it as "my first try at portrait painting [in oils], after a summer I had spent at the Art Students League's Landscape School [which was] my first experience with oil painting. I dragged in my model from the Plaza and finished the job at one sitting. This I did as practice for cooperating with Carlos Vierra in finishing Beauregard's St. Francis murals."[72]

Did Chap feel at ease or anxious about working in an artistic partnership with Vierra? They had long been friendly—shared interests and the proximity of his plaza studio meant that Vierra was known to the museum staff well before 1912, when he officially began work there. However, Chap may have fretted about comparisons between Vierra's experience with mural painting and his own. Vierra was also renowned for truly artistic photographs (though he wrote his sister that he made "funny photos of ugly people").[73] Born in Moss Landing, near Monterey, California, on October 3, 1876, Vierra was the son of Portuguese immigrants from the Azores. He had hoped to be a marine painter (his father had been a sailor) and studied art in San Francisco. However, as with Chap, lung problems encouraged Vierra to settle in the Southwest in 1904.

A slight, handsome man, Vierra was popular in Santa Fe. All the townspeople counted on his traveling to Bernalillo each autumn—when he would traverse the infamous single-lane road down La Bajada Hill in a huge open Packard touring car—to purchase grapes for wine.[74] Along with Morley, Vierra became a dynamic force in promoting the Santa Fe style. In 1915, Vierra had just completed the murals for Hewett, which hung in the exposition's California building and depicted scenes from the Mayan country that the school had explored under Hewett and Morley. Vierra's viewing of the sites firsthand in early 1914 contributed to their excellence, and visitors to the exposition exclaimed over them.[75]

So possibly Chap felt some concern at being compared to Vierra. He often responded to uncertainty with anxiety, which occasionally surfaced as stomach problems. But for this venture, he seems to have looked forward to the prospect of painting, having been buoyed by Bridgman's recommendation as well as by assurances from Kate. Springer was satisfied with the plan of Chap and Vierra completing the murals as a team and informed Hewett that they were "perfectly willing to work together, and to do it as well as they can with the sole idea of carrying out Beauregard's ideas, and not of obscuring them or minimizing them for their own glory, as many an outside artist would be inclined to do."[76]

As Chap and Vierra considered how best to transform Beauregard's sketches into wall-sized murals, Springer was ensuring them a home. When the project was first conceived, the murals were expected to be displayed in the Palace of the Governors (after being shown in San Diego). But, at Springer's behest, the winter session of the New Mexico legislature now authorized construction of a fine arts building. The need for a new building had long been a topic of discussion between Springer and Hewett, who had done their best to encourage the arts in the limited space of the museum. In October, Springer had written to Hewett that "I suppose you are to spend some time in Santa Fe this winter & it may be that we shall meet there, as I intend to put in a little time with the Legislature (confidential, I don't wish it mentioned, but want to manage the matter in my own way & without any display). . . . [T]hey all assured me that if I would come personally and explain these matters they felt sure the Senate would stand for anything the State can reasonably afford."77 Springer's influence resulted not only in the state authorizing funds but also in legislating his building preference. The 1915 legislation approved "the construction of a building which shall be substantially a replica of the building known as the 'New Mexico Building.'"78 Apparently, if the murals could not be finished in time to hang in San Diego, then the building would simply come to the murals!

The murals, however, did not replace Pueblo pottery in Chap's life. As the Panama-California Exposition was about to open, he was asked by Hewett to exhibit the results of his design research. Chap prepared drawings (with the assistance of Kate) of bird forms from southwestern Indian pottery decoration with comparable examples of birds from worldwide sources.79 The drawings remained on display for two years. At that time, publications on Pueblo pottery were scarce. Although the Smithsonian had printed the illustrated pottery descriptions of James Stevenson in the mid-1880s, there had been little systematic exploration of Southwest artifacts.80 The works of Bandelier and Cushing broke scholarly ground in the early 1900s, while the Bureau of American Ethnology published illustrated annual reports containing the work of Holmes, Fewkes, and Walter Hough. Essentially, though, the field of Southwest pottery studies was wide open for any enterprising researcher. Chap submitted an article based on the exhibit to *Art and Archaeology*, which was published in December 1916.

He enjoyed professional support that summer from Kidder and Nusbaum, who were in New Mexico working at Pecos. Kidder, who had completed his doctorate at Harvard, was leading an archaeological investigation there sponsored by Phillips Academy in Massachusetts. Earlier in the year, the ruins had been deeded to the Museum of New Mexico, which, in turn, granted permission to the academy to excavate the site. As part of its permission, the regents stipulated that the mission church be repaired, and Nusbaum had been appointed to manage the work.

Since Kidder's last extended visit to New Mexico in 1910, when he and Chap had amicably divided up research, Kidder had profited by extensive fieldwork and publishing opportunities. Kidder's *Pottery of the Pajarito Plateau*, which was soon to be published, emphasized stratigraphic and typological techniques that he had practiced during his studies in Greece and Rome with Reisner. Now Kidder was in New Mexico to test these theories.

Kidder had recommended the Pecos site to his sponsoring organization based on his and Chap's discoveries there in 1910, when they had both been struck by the variety of types represented at the site. In 1915, Kidder was pioneering a new, more precise, and more purely chronological method of dating and felt certain that if stratified remains for creating a chronological record could be found anywhere, it would be at Pecos.[81] Ultimately, the work begun that summer resulted in a groundbreaking synthesis of southwestern archaeology by Kidder, which set the pattern for subsequent studies throughout the field.[82]

Although Chap did not officially participate in fieldwork, he and Kidder would have spent time at the site as well as many hours comparing pottery notes. Chap, nearly forty, still harbored expectations that his treatise on Pajaritan pottery, which he had completed the previous spring, would be published. He and Kidder shared a particular enthusiasm for the excavated ceramics and what they revealed about the people who made them. In fact, their good-natured teasing over whether this or that abstract motif was actually a bird had resulted in clever cartoon lampoons of each other. Gaiety must have enveloped Santa Fe's cool summer evenings, whenever Kate and Chap socialized with the Kidders, Nusbaums, and Morleys. Kate was still living at the Boyles' residence, which, as noted by the *Santa Fe New Mexican*, was "one of the attractions of Santa Fe, and in it many notable persons have been entertained by the hostess with the charming hospitality so well known to the social circles of the capital."[83] It is easy to imagine the eight of them sharing stories far into the night.

Chap and Kate had opportunities to do their own fieldwork when they accompanied Springer on a September expedition to the caves at Rito. The group included Carlos Vierra and his wife, Ada, Santiago Naranjo (governor of Santa Clara Pueblo), Myrtle Boyle, and Eleanor Johnson. Because Chap had earlier found evidence of cave paintings, reinforced by later discoveries of Vierra, the expedition was organized to reexamine the cliff dwellings, many of which were inaccessible except by ladders and could not be satisfactorily studied without artificial light. The group examined two hundred cave dwellings, and Chap, Vierra, and Kate made over one hundred copies of the prehistoric drawings they found on their walls. Chap agreed to present the discoveries at a science meeting in November and write about them for publication in *El Palacio*'s December issue.

As if September's schedule were not crowded enough, Chap decided to squeeze in a trip to California between the cave expedition and his and Kate's wedding. *I attended the two expositions in California, at San Francisco and at San Diego, and then returned in*

ample time for the big event of the year, my marriage with Katherine A. Muller.[84] Ample?
Chap returned to Santa Fe two days before his wedding date! However, he came home not
to a blushing bride-to-be but a feverish one. The Monday wedding had to be postponed
so that Kate could recover from a bout of blood poisoning. But with health restored, on
the morning of Thursday, September 30, 1915, Kate and Chap exchanged their vows in
St. Francis Cathedral. This time the ceremony was delayed only slightly as Chap, Springer,
and other friends waited for the ever-spontaneous Kate.

> I was living at that time in Mrs. Boyle's apartment which had never had a real
> bathroom—the tub was in the kitchen and had a cover which let down to make
> a table. In my excitement in preparing for the wedding I had forgotten to lock
> the kitchen door when I got into the tub, and just then I heard the grocery boy
> coming in with all the supplies for the wedding. I quickly pulled down the lid
> and he put the supplies on top of it! I was a little late for the wedding, but every-
> one expected that.[85]

Kate and Chap's wedding was unusually felicitous, according to a headline in the
Santa Fe New Mexican. "It may be truly said," the newspaper wrote, "that no event of
this kind has ever called forth more sincere and heartfelt good wishes from the people
of Santa Fe than those which will follow Mr. and Mrs. Chapman upon their wedding
journey."[86] Kate and Chap explored caves at Puyé and Santa Clara on their honeymoon
(where they discovered more pictographs, though not as many as at the Rito caves) and
traveled to Chimayo, *sketching, photographing and exploring the country for miles about,
in four weeks of perfect autumn weather.*[87]

With true love at his side, Chap's life could be defined as one of abundance. In nearly
every respect, he was fully engaged. His own family lived nearby, and now he had, in
Kate, a friend, a fellow artist, and a wife. He lived in a town that respected his contributions and style. He continued to maintain the loving patronage of his friend and mentor,
Springer. And, to cap his happiness, his work demanded the full breadth of his skills and
inclinations. Poised at the crossroads of art and ethnology, Chap found himself absorbed
in work—art shows, mural painting, pictographs, and pottery research—that demanded
from him what he was most willing to give: the eye of an artist.

CHAPTER 6

Establishing An Identity

C hap angles his long limbs and crouches in the shadow of a pueblo adobe. Inhaling the pungent fragrance of burning piñon, he studies timeless symbols on coiled clay. A promising anthropologist with established friendships among potters, he respects the slow evolution that characterizes their traditions. He remembers last year's strolls through clamorous urban canyons on the East Coast. There, in an art museum by day, he had scrutinized Rembrandt's earthy palette, Van Gogh's signature strokes, Picasso's improbable anatomy. As a developing artist who might well exhibit there, he pondered the place of conservatism amid snowballing modernism. But by dusk, hunched over a library table, a private muse had beckoned his interest elsewhere. Now Chap is committed to wife and work in Santa Fe. As his fingertips trace an abstract design, he contemplates the compelling riddle that will shape his life: how can I best express what moves me? Or, as a Pueblo potter might ask, how is the clay telling me to form the pot?

Chap turned forty on July 13, 1915. The advent of middle age precipitated a vocational reckoning:

> I had regained my health in New Mexico, and experience had taught me not to risk leaving the Southwest. I had married and had bought and developed a desirable residence property. Mr. Springer by then had made his settlement with me and though he thought he might do without my further services, I still stood in readiness to take up his work again in any emergency. And I had also to consider Mr. Springer's deep interest in the Museum and the possibility of helping in its further development in ways that would please him.[1]

This inwardly reflective artist had professional decisions to make as he and Kate began a family. Should he strengthen his fine art ability with Springer's help? Extend his museum administration? Pursue his belief that there was a "promising future in the study of decorative art?"[2] Or continue with the haphazard amalgamation of all three that characterized his record with Hewett's institution?

As an artist, Chap had much to recommend him. He was a highly skilled illustrator, and his breathtaking work for Springer's volumes was innovative. He was comfortable with a variety of media. In addition to early pen-and-ink drawings, he had executed watercolor and gouache paintings to sell to tourists in Las Vegas and to the railroad. His Twitchell illustrations were watercolors, showcasing his light, almost ethereal, technique. His recent studies in oils were successful, his instructors finding promise in his talent. He felt ready to test the learning that Springer had sponsored.

Springer was all but Chap's patron, investing in the younger man's promise as an illustrator and muralist. Springer was prepared to carry him under the aegis of Hewett's organization, or independently, or both. At the same time, the sprouting Santa Fe Art Colony was enlivening the local scene, and Chap made friends among them. The hours he had devoted to the study of art history had helped clarify his own aesthetics, taste, and philosophy of art. Yet despite powerful influences that were pushing him in the direction of a fine art career, Chap was about to make a pivotal decision to reject easel and smock. At the "tender" age of forty, Chap began forging an identity so unique that it would set him apart from art, ethnology, and archaeology, yet allow him to retain a lasting name in each.

His honeymoon over, he returned to the varied duties that constituted his midlife conundrum: handling administrative/curatorial responsibilities in Hewett's absence, completing the Beauregard murals, assisting with the planning and construction of the new Museum of Fine Arts, and finding time to research and publish his studies. Although Paul Walter reported that for the first time in its history the museum ended 1915 with all of its debts paid, there was still no money for the printing process that Chap's illustrated work required.[3] Yet this news did not deter Chap from undertaking research in the field whenever possible. In early December, a wonderful opportunity presented itself. Chap and anthropologist Nels Nelson of the American Museum of Natural History made a reconnaissance of the Taos region, where they located a number of mounds, and visited Puyé on their return. The trip cemented Chap's friendship with a member of an academic circle larger than Hewett's.

Back in Santa Fe, Chap's mural commission and related duties for the new museum demanded an artist's eye and imagination. During the winter of 1915–16, Chap and Vierra finally began work on the murals. They had a deadline: the murals would be placed in the new museum's St. Francis Auditorium, and construction was to begin in the spring. Springer's guarantee of matching funds assured that the estimated $60,000 for the structure was attainable. The board of regents had chosen a site on the corner of Palace Avenue and Lincoln, across from the Palace of the Governors. The site was occupied by an old barracks building, whose commercial tenants paid rent to the Santa Fe city schools, which owned the land. The deeding over of the site was contested by school board president Colonel Jose D. Sena. By year's end, the promoters of the new museum struck a compromise and the land changed hands. Springer turned over $30,000 in private funds and on April 12, 1916, demolition commenced.[4]

The auditorium murals, as envisioned by Beauregard, would be made of six oversized paintings: three triptychs and three single panels. The canvases, which still grace St. Francis Auditorium, are each over 8 feet tall. The triptych's center panels are 5½ feet wide; the sides nearly 3½ feet wide. The two artists divided the work to suit their talents, Chap being the stronger in figures and Vierra the stronger in color. *Vierra and I had cooperated in other projects and we were agreed that we would hold as closely as possible to Beauregard's theme.*[5] Beauregard had completed only the center panel of the triptych, *The Renunciation of Santa Clara,* before his untimely death. Chap agreed to finish the two side panels and, in addition, paint the *Apotheosis of St. Francis* triptych and *Conversion of St. Francis (see plate 21).* Vierra worked on *Vision of Columbus at La Rábida, Building of the Missions of New Mexico,* and the triptych *Preaching to the Mayas and the Aztecs.*

Chap painted in his small courtyard studio, and Vierra set up another for himself, but neither space well accommodated the work. In order to stand his panels upright, Chap propped them under a skylight that had an undesirable exposure. For an objective assessment of color values, both artists had to place their panels sideways. To gain perspective on the work in progress, they took them outside in good weather. Chap was faithfully transforming Beauregard's sketches, changing very little, and conscientiously avoiding imposing his own technique. Vierra, on the other hand, took greater liberties.[6] He brought exuberance to the murals, using an impressionistic technique that was free and broad.[7] In his *Vision of Columbus at La Rábida* he even included a self-portrait of himself as the great Genoan.[8]

A welcome critic and supporter of this effort was Jess Nusbaum, who returned to Santa Fe after his feat in bringing the San Diego Exposition to life. He worked first on the Palace of the Governors' patio and, by the spring of 1915, had "transformed the ruinous Placita, or Patio, into a thing of beauty," according to Springer. "That you were a 'crackerjack' we always accepted on the authority of Lummis. Now we know it ourselves, and . . . we are prepared to see any kind of miracle wrought by you any time you may take a notion."[9] Nusbaum was prepared to execute such a miracle, for he had agreed to manage construction of the new museum. The creative services of Rapp and Rapp were again engaged, following the success of the exposition's New Mexico building. Using it as a prototype, and incorporating eclectic architectural elements from mission churches and pueblos, Rapp and Rapp created a building that exemplified the stylistic ideals advanced by the 1912 New-Old Santa Fe movement. Anthropologist and writer Oliver La Farge's later response was tepid, though he admitted that the building was beneficial in developing modern Santa Fe style.[10] Most viewers admired it, however, as noted in the *New Mexican*: "The New Mexico museum is so entirely different, so completely in a class by itself, and is in itself such an artistic achievement that no comparison can be made."[11]

As Nusbaum orchestrated construction, Chap made time to join Springer on another expedition to Rito de los Frijoles, accompanied by Carlos Vierra, Eleanor Johnson, Cecily Myrtle Boyle, and Kate—who was expecting a baby in October! Together, the group explored over four hundred dwellings, taking photographs of cave drawings by flashlight (of which they later made almost two hundred reproductions), and making plaster casts of figures that had been worked into Rito canyon walls.[12] On return, Chap was drafted to design furniture for the upstairs reception room of the museum women's board and pews for the St. Francis Auditorium as well as assigned other timely tasks. The site of the new museum had seen both Native American and Spanish settlement, so Chap supervised the recovery of artifacts unearthed during excavation, organized and exhibited this collection, and redesigned a corner of the building with the approval of the architects. In his off-hours, he prepared for the birth of his and Kate's first child, but even that flowed back to the museum. Within days of Frank Springer Chapman's birth on October 14, 1916, the Palace of the Governors' reception room was the site of a brief exhibit of two pieces of "Indian design" furniture. These "unique and exquisite pieces" moved one reporter to wax exuberant, remarking that:

> the marvel of it is its simplicity and the quaintness that it unites with beauty. One piece is a crib placed quite high above the floor. Upon the creamy white background and placed in red and black [is] the ancient symbolism found on the old Ildefonso pottery. On the long sides are two plumed serpents, tails intertwined and above them the rain clouds and thunder birds, symbols of the blessings of the gods. The ends are ornamented with the rain cloud or inverted pyramids and the forked lightning or avanyu symbols. The rain altar or kiva steps are used as places for handle holds. The other piece is a "hope chest" with the ancient butterfly symbol, wrought in black and red with charming effectiveness. To view these substantial and yet delicately made pieces . . . certainly is to get a glimpse of possibilities for local craftsmanship and industry that should eventually give employment to many hands.[13]

Before the infant named for Chap's beloved mentor was brought home, Chap had his hands full. During Kate's two-week postpartum confinement, a domestic transition forced him to delay sending birth announcements. He wrote Hodge, "I have been so rushed . . . with moving to my mother's house and consolidating the junk of two households into one. . . . All the parties concerned are prospering. Morley offered, on receipt

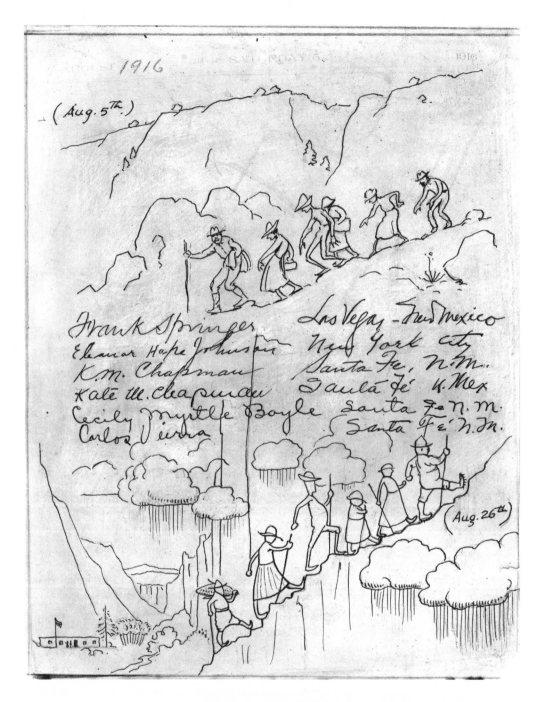

Cartoon of 1916 Springer expedition to Rito de los Frijoles; apparently the weary crew heading into the canyon (top, by Kenneth M. Chapman) was rejuvenated by the three-week expedition (bottom, by Carlos Vierra). (Courtesy of School for Advanced Research Archives, AC02 773b.)

of particulars, to case the kid's Maya horoscope. We have sent him the required data and are anxiously awaiting the dope."[14] Once settled in his auspicious crib, Frank hopefully gave his father many nights of unbroken slumber; with Hewett's acceptance of a paid position in San Diego, Chap needed his rest. For now, his fifty-fifty arrangement with Springer and the museum was over. Springer retained use of the museum office/studio that he shared with Chap when he was in town and required it; aside from his occasional need of Chap's time, it was understood that Chap would otherwise devote himself fully to the museum. While Hewett converted the exposition's remains into a permanent science of man exhibit in San Diego, Chap often took on the daily running of the museum. Hewett first designated him associate director, then assigned him curator status and made Paul Walter the associate director. These switches appeared whim driven:

Judging by my own experiences I would say that [Hewett's] decisions in regard to changes in the titles and duties of his staff were seldom arrived at through conferences with those affected.

Instead, they seemed to have been made as he approached Santa Fe after his long absences. Knowing his pattern of procrastination I had soon reached the conclusion that he deferred until the last minute and then grabbed his answers out of the air.[15]

Despite Hewett's absences and the U.S. entry into World War I in April 1917, plans to open the Museum of Fine Arts in the fall remained unchanged. Santa Fe regarded the opening as a gesture of confidence in the future and as a consolidation of "many threads of southwestern culture."[16] Even before the dedication, the new museum became a community center. The Red Cross and Naval Nurse Corps met there almost daily in early November, "and the hum of their industry" was "heard from one end to the other."[17] In the hectic preparations for the dedication, Chap found himself attending to an unexpected crisis on behalf of Springer. While vacationing at Rito, Springer had brought the introductory chapters of his *Crinoidea Flexibilia* monograph for a final prepublication reading. But other matters caused him to ignore the manuscript and then, preoccupied with something else, he lost it. Chap had no recollection of the package as Springer described it but dutifully searched high and low for a week. When his "toilsome" hunt turned up no sign of the one-hundred-page manuscript, Springer "finally gave up all hope of finding it and returned to Washington, faced with the ghastly necessity of rewriting a work that had claimed a good share of his attention for the past fifteen years! His letters of that period tell of the great difficulty he found in making headway with it, but finally, as he again got the subject in hand, he held uncomplainingly to his task."[18]

Chapman (left) at his easel on the Palace of the Governors' patio
with Carlos Vierra (to his right) and Sheldon Parsons (far right).
(Photograph by Wesley Bradfield. Courtesy of Palace of the
Governors [MNM/DCA], 13324.)

Three days of festivities opened the museum. At the November 24, 1917, dedication, over two thousand people (more than a quarter of the population!) had gathered,
according to news reports, though only half were able to enter the auditorium, and
many hundreds left without even attempting to gain entrance to the building.[19] Chap's
artwork was everywhere in evidence: his murals adorned the auditorium, his wood-
work enriched both the auditorium and the reception room, and his paintings hung in
the opening exhibition. The exhibition was the first of Hewett's "open-door" exhibits, a
democratic form of art exhibiting that Oliver La Farge noted brought shows that were
"sometimes startling, sometimes laughable, sometimes fine."[20] Simply put, the open-
door policy meant that the museum's walls were available to anyone who applied for
space; it was merely a matter of waiting one's turn. Santa Fe thus blossomed into a vigorous art center. At that first exhibition, Chap's paintings hung alongside those of Taos
artists Oscar Berninghaus, Ernest Blumenschein, E. Irving Couse, W. Herbert Dunton,

E. Martin Hennings, Victor Higgins, Bert Phillips, Joseph Sharp, and Walter Ufer. Santa Fe artists represented in the opening exhibit were Henry Balink, George Bellows, Paul Burlin, Gerald Cassidy, William Penhallow Henderson, Robert Henri, Leon Kroll, Ralph Myers, Arthur F. Musgrave, Sheldon Parsons, Julius Rolshoven, Eva Springer, Theodor Van Soelen, Carlos Vierra, and, of course, Chap.

Where had all these Santa Fe artists come from? When Vierra and Chap began work on the murals, the only other local artist was Parsons. Cassidy and his wife, Ina Sizer Cassidy, had bought a home in Santa Fe in 1915, but after Cassidy completed his San Diego exposition work, they decided to spend time in New York City, leaving Parsons and his daughter, Sara, to housesit. By the museum's opening, however, more than fifteen artists were residing in Santa Fe or spending summers there. Some of them, like Parsons, had originally arrived seeking health. Henderson, for example, relocated in 1916 because his wife, author Alice Corbin Henderson, needed to recuperate at Sunmount Sanitarium.

Many came because Santa Fe had been promoted to them as a source of inspiration. The town charms and country vistas of Santa Fe were the subjects of national publicity. *Art and Archaeology*, the museum's newly established *El Palacio*, and popular magazines touted the romance of the City Different. The Atchison, Topeka, and Santa Fe Railway conducted its own tourism campaign with calendars and posters utilizing art acquired from Chap and others. For visual artists, this small community in the foothills of the Sangre de Cristo Mountains mixed topographical textures with an earthy palette in an inverted bowl of light. The area held two other compelling elements: the Pueblo people and their geometric villages and weaving, basketry, and pottery arts, and Hispanic ethnicity with its design and color influences. Finally, both Santa Fe and Taos offered affordable economies for struggling artists.

The San Diego exposition had also given the attending public a peek at a New Mexico that was represented as unique, exotic, and accessible. Hewett had recruited artists, including Robert Henri, who was one of the leaders—along with John Sloan—of the New York independents who rebelled against the academies and jury systems of the day. Hewett's open-door policy was a golden opportunity for these and other artists seeking to establish themselves. At his invitation, Henri spent the summer of 1916 in Santa Fe. He liked what he saw and returned in 1917 with Burlin, Bellows, and Kroll.[21] After the museum's opening, Henri wrote to a friend that

the new museum is a wonder. With the influence of Dr. Hewett and the excellent men about him, Santa Fe can become a rare spot in all the world. . . . Most museums are glum and morose temples looking homesick for the skies and associations of their native lands—Greek, most likely. The museum here looks

as though it were a precious child of the Santa Fe sky and the Santa Fe mountains. It has its parents' complexion. It seems warmly at home as if it has always
been here. Without any need of the treasures of art which are to go into it, it is
a treasure of art in itself, art of this time and this place, of people and related to
all the past.[22]

Though Chapman has been identified as a pioneer, founder, and leader of the Santa
Fe Art Colony, there is no evidence in his memoirs or articles that he even identified
himself as a member of it.[23] Despite the artistic pleasure of the Museum of Fine Arts
projects, including his lovely 1916 watercolor of the new building and other proposed
structures (see plate 1), the newcomers who inspired each other failed to motivate him to
develop as an artist. As curator, he hung scores of Santa Fe/Taos shows. He displayed his
own art in at least seven art museum exhibits from 1914 to 1921, but his work manifested
ambivalence—he moved back and forth between producing subject paintings (primarily landscapes) and meticulously executed examples of pottery design in which he was
increasingly steeped (culminating in the so-called butterfly designs in the eighth annual
exhibit in 1921).

The idea of working with pottery had clearly superseded his dream of making it as
an illustrator. The clay had revealed the shape it was to take. After 1915, Chap solidified
his intention to devote his career to serving Indian art. Later, he would look back on the
midlife bend in his career path without regret, humbly believing that "his work of preserving and exhibiting the art of the Indians would be a more lasting contribution than
anything he could have done with his own art."[24]

Around this time, the landscape of U.S. archaeology in general, and the Southwest
in particular, underwent significant changes. While Hewett's attention was fractured
between two states, the American Museum's Huntington Southwest Survey (1912–17)
brought new scientific blood to the Galisteo Basin south of Santa Fe, in the person of
anthropologist Nels Nelson, with whom Chap had traveled in late 1915. Nelson was
now making innovative headway in the chronological archaeology of the Southwest
by applying stratigraphic analysis to excavated layers of potsherds; during the same
period, Hewett's summer field schools began to focus less on Southwest archaeology,
though they still catalyzed enrollees' imaginations.[25] Hewett's protégés Kidder and
Morley had moved on to more scientific circles and had advanced far in their careers;
they were in the vanguard of those developing an archaeology that was of relevance
to anthropology.[26]

Chap must have perceived that Nelson and Kidder, to name but two friends, were
outstripping Hewett intellectually. In later years, he reflected on El Toro's demand for
absolute loyalty from "the boys" at the museum, and how Hewett "stormed whenever

any of them deviated from broad and proven generalities to explore new ideas—no matter how constructive and enlightening they might prove."²⁷ In his own case, however, absolute loyalty to Springer kept him virtually hostage to Hewett, a man less interested in research advances than in promoting his charismatic vision of how the study of vanished American races could lead to a better future for humankind. To avoid association with Hewett's lackluster academic reputation, Chap had to establish his intellectual turf with resources at hand and without his boss's backing. Either that, or flounder in midcareer limbo.

Chap's work on Indian art at this time reflects his professional environment. His initial view of Pueblo ceramics had come through the archaeological lens afforded by his early years with Hewett. Chap, like his peers, pondered the problems posed by archaeology and anthropology. "Who were the ancestors of modern Pueblo people? When and where did they establish their settlements? How long did they stay in one place, and why did they eventually move elsewhere? What explains the Pueblo Indians' gradual consolidation into larger and larger settlements? Were they influenced by other cultures, and did they influence neighboring groups?"²⁸ Chap understood his work as addressing these issues. As an artist, however, he puzzled over additional questions, questions raised by the arts and crafts movement and his own schooling.²⁹ He responded to other mysteries, treasuring the pots and sherds as objets d'art requiring careful preservation. His undated jottings (possibly c. 1920–30) on Indian art open with the universal question, "What is art?" and he responds, "Art is that beauty which the imagination has created and which makes in the observer an emotion of pleasure similar to that of the creator. Art is the making or doing of anything that gives pleasure. Primitive art is that produced by people in a stage of development & culture where every individual does each thing for himself."³⁰ The nameless artists who had fashioned and adorned pots and sherds spoke to Chap's own heart.

Among his scientific colleagues, Chap thus had a special vantage point as he pondered artistic arcana. What was the decorator thinking or feeling when applying this crosshatch or dot? How would a pot's shape inspire the application of a certain figure? How did realism and abstraction interrelate? How might one potter have influenced another? What was the creative lure for an individual who conformed to tradition? Timeless debate would have shaped his queries. Are there global criteria with which any piece of art may be judged to be better or worse than a similar piece? Who determines artistic taste, and how? Studying the evolution of design drove him; he wrote that it afforded "an opportunity to present graphically the divergence of both the individual and the community and the effect of the individual in moulding [sic] the expression of the community. While in linguistics only the results of these divergences are to be had, the study of decorative art is not limited to such results for we can also present the steps by which these divergences were reached. Thus we can note not only the trend of a community but of the individual."[31] Anthropologist Bernstein recognized Chap's overwhelming interest in the universals of art and their development. "Chapman was a design analyst seeking to discover the way in which designs were universally constructed, in turn, providing evidence of evolving styles that could be tracked spatially, despite modifications. He was specifically interested in discovering a sequence of pottery designs that showed how increasingly complex constructions were rendered by the judicious adding of lines."[32]

Chap's first substantive contribution in this area was a January 1916 article in *El Palacio* titled "Graphic Art of the Cave Dwellers." It was extracted from his November 1915 presentation to the New Mexico Association for Science in Albuquerque following the Springer expedition to the Pajarito caves. The article explores the connection between textile and pottery design, a connection first examined by William H. Holmes in 1888.[33] The idea that geometric pottery designs mimicked the woven patterns on baskets complemented Chap's 1910 exploration of pottery design as evolving from abstraction to realism. Few examples of fragile textiles survived over the centuries, so Chap details the important discovery of textile patterns scratched on the smoke-blackened plastering of the cave walls at Rito. He includes an inventory of the numbers and types of figures and a brief analysis of the differences between realism and symbolism and then returns to the connections between pictograph patterns and textile design, concluding with an enthusiastic critique of the free, sweeping lines of many of the figures. To Chap, these lines represented a stage analogous to those seen in the cave drawings in southern France, a departure from the geometries of basketry.

He softened that evaluation in a second address on the cave pictographs, this time to a December 1916 meeting of the AIA. This lecture was printed, with some alterations, as a freestanding paper of the School of American Archaeology and is a more developed treatment of the pictographs themselves.[34] Chap also mentions that before the cave drawings were available for study, pottery had been the chief source of information about the graphic arts of the ancients. He comments on how the cave art, in addition to pottery, will further knowledge of the relationship between the bygone Pajaritans and the modern Pueblos. The same month, Chap's article "The Evolution of the Bird in Decorative Art," which described the symbols on Pueblo pottery in the context of worldwide decorative art, appeared in *Art and Archaeology*. The article ran alongside pieces on American anthropological subjects by Hewett, Holmes, Lummis, Fletcher, Harrington, and Walter. In 1917, *Conservatism in the Evolution of Decorative Art* was published by the school; this paper also drew on his New York research where he had begun to trace the widespread use of symbols over time and geography. In Pueblo pottery, examples of geometric designs that persist as decorative motifs over centuries showed that "holding to the use of old motives . . . has at least counterbalanced the varying tendencies of [influence from] outlying groups."[35] In time, Chap would use this argument to buttress his conviction of the value in studying post-Spanish pottery.

When he began publishing, Chap received inconsistent support from Hewett, who now seemed to betray earlier assurances that there would always be opportunity to continue his work.[36] The encouragement Chap most cherished during this time came from Dr. Hartley B. Alexander, head of philosophy at the University of Nebraska, member of the school's managing board, and lecturer on Indian culture. In his frequent visits to Santa Fe, he checked on Chap's progress, exhorting him to privately seek other publishers since the work was his to market. He also assured Chap that he would put in a word with Hewett.[37] Nothing came of either approach. When Chap looked back upon the years from 1915 to 1925, he would bemoan his enmeshment with the museum at a time he was chafing to get on with his research. Using the pages of *El Palacio* and *Art and Archaeology*, however, he gradually established his credibility, so he held on. "In those ten years . . . through my own efforts I had gained recognition for my published articles on Indian arts and saw a bright future in that field."[38]

Neither his growing zeal for pottery studies nor his association with artists, however, insulated Chap from the administrative tasks that continued to pile up during Hewett's absences. One of Hewett's ideas for expansion included a vision of the school as an institution with its own buildings and permanent faculty in Santa Fe that would sponsor fieldwork and publish research on both Americas.[39] In 1917, the school, with permission from the AIA, changed its name to School of American Research and incorporated under New Mexico law, both to indicate its expanded activities and, optimistically, to permit its legal acceptance of property as an endowment. Springer drew up all the necessary documents, including House Bill No. 177. Notably, with regard to the permit to accept property, the privilege was expanded to include not only the granting of museum property rent free to the school but all property "now or hereafter belonging to the Museum of New Mexico."[40] While theoretically enhancing Hewett's agenda, the incorporation further complicated an already problematic institutional arrangement, putting greater demands on his overextended leadership.

Hewett's charisma was a two-edged sword, affecting Chap, Nusbaum, Morley, Kidder, and Wesley Bradfield (first hired by Hewett to assist with Southwest ethnology exhibits and collections for the Panama-California Exposition[41]). Chap privately documented their frustrations. In Chauvenet's interpretation, the success Hewett enjoyed in San Diego not only made him more ambitious but also made his management style more authoritative.[42] El Toro was now downright overbearing according to Chap, who had noted a puzzling shift in Hewett's personality for some time following the death of his first wife.[43] *The Director was spending two-thirds of his time away from New Mexico, in teaching and lecturing, in archaeological work outside the United States, and in attempts to build up a chain of museums in Arizona and southern California, under the management of the School.*[44] *The museum, he observed, was at a standstill, there were no funds for purchase of the fast disappearing arts of the Southwestern Indians, needed for my studies, and I found it necessary at times to give up my own projects for secretarial and curatorial work, including at times the entire management of the Museum. Mr. Springer deplored the situation but urged me to hang on, with the belief that conditions would soon right themselves.*[45]

Chap was particularly troubled by Hewett's mixed messages. On the one hand, the director promoted Chap's research and encouraged him to publish. On the other, Hewett seemed unable to generate financial support for publishing, especially during the last two years of World War I, when resources were nationally scarce.

> *Paul Walter's frank admission that El Palacio could not provide funds for illustrations, and Dr. Hewett's repeated defense of his procrastination—that the Bureau of Ethnology had a back log of manuscripts of the past 20 years awaiting publication—that the School must raise funds for publishing its own material—all this left me in the doldrums.*[46]

While giving Hewett just due for his contributions in defining Southwest culture and protecting excavation sites, Chap fumed over Hewett's stubborn and incorrect analyses of "salt" glazes and obsessed over Hewett's dislike of the accepted archaeological term "black-on-white pottery" and subsequent declaration that there is no white Pueblo pottery, ancient or modern. (In response, Chap's tendency toward precision ran amok. To bolster his position, he referred to *Webster's International Dictionary* for the definition of "white" and its compound uses, finding no less than seven hundred of them filling fourteen columns on pages 2915–20. Likewise for "black"!) Chap attempted to reason with Hewett when his statements were questionable, *but he would not concede that my factual evidence was worth considering.*[47] Marjorie Lambert verified the difficulty of going head to head with El Toro. "A strong-willed man he was, with an excellent legal mind. One seldom came out the winner when arguing with him."[48]

It was apparently easier for Hewett to overlook mounting tension. He could not conceive of the price Chap paid for corking up frustration. Hewett was a justly proud man who consistently looked ahead. As he industriously applied himself to his growing enterprises, his ego enabled him to get past the hard feelings and stinging reviews that it sometimes provoked. He must have been baffled at outbursts such as Morley's "shrill" accusation some years earlier that Hewett's way was "paved with broken promises."[49]

For scientists like Harvard's Alfred M. Tozzer, who accompanied El Toro and protégés at Rito, Hewett's amalgamation of personality, ambition, and unorthodox or even sloppy archaeology was intolerable, and he did not hesitate to publicly excoriate Hewett. Over time, other critics of Hewett's personality and field methods, such as Franz Boas and Roland Dixon, echoed Tozzer's criticisms. They derided Hewett's scientific work, which failed to incorporate chronology and was clouded by his expressive nature. They disparaged Hewett's emphasis on museum collections, which valued the artistic and spectacular over context.[50] The decline in his professional status seems not to have overly troubled Hewett. His supporters focused on his other strengths: innovative field schools and influence in the shaping of other archaeologists' careers.

While Chap's commitments to the Southwest, his research, and Springer kept him inextricably involved with the museum-school, his friends quietly distanced themselves by gradually moving on to pastures green with full-time professional positions unconnected to their early mentor's academic regionalism.[51] There is no question of the original love and admiration that they and Chap bore the idealistic and ambitious Hewett, who truly launched and protected Southwest archaeology. Indeed, Hewett was one of the two angels who made Chap's transplant to New Mexico not just a possibility but a joy. The tarnishing of that love, however, receives disproportionate space and energy in Chap's memoirs and papers. His grievances take on redundancies characteristic of one who feels powerless to change miserable circumstances. To Chap's credit, his private writings comprised the sole container of his unhappiness. He maintained confidentiality because of his personality, loyalty, and scruples—professional traits that would eventually be recognized and rewarded by philanthropist John D. Rockefeller Jr. It took inordinate provocation and evidence of wrongdoing for the protégé to overcome his innate reluctance to tell tales out of school, even to Springer. In later years, Frank Chapman could not recall his father ever contaminating family life with his disgruntlements, and if Chap spoke about it with Kate, Frank didn't know. He felt that his father's style was to suffer in silence.

In the summer of 1918, Chap experienced another misery, this time having unwittingly been the agent of pain to his cherished Springer. In preparing Springer's camp outfit for his annual vacation that summer, Chap discovered the missing *Flexibilia* manuscript that he had unsuccessfully searched for during the weeks before the new museum opened. It was tucked away in a large envelope in Springer's box of camp equipment. Chap was in agony as he realized that he could have saved Springer from the past year's arduous task of rewriting.

I have known remorse, but never such as I suffered for the next two days until I could tell him of my part in the lamentable affair. I begged him to make as vigorous comment on the subject as the situation seemed to demand and I knew well his capability in that direction. Instead, he took it calmly, and, after what seemed an age of reflection, said simply; "Well it's of no use to us now; I have spent the best part of the past year re-writing it." And then, opening the envelope and finding something else within it, he added "By George! At least we have saved some good sheet music."[52]

In a happy closing note to the story, Springer called on Chap a month later and thanked him for a blessing in disguise. After comparing the two manuscripts, Springer realized that his rewrite was so superior that publishing the original would have been a mistake.

Relieved of his sense of shame, Chap could only marvel at such unconditional friendship. In fact, friends, family life, and Santa Fe society often reaffirmed his blessings. Chap enjoyed a warm and stable home life: Frank was a toddler; a sibling was expected in the spring. His mother was a loving addition to his life in New Mexico. An artist herself, she must have delighted in Santa Fe's newcomers. Chap also felt cherished and revitalized by an independent wife who was making her own architectural name. In 1917, Chap took time off to work with Kate on their home at 615 Acequia Madre, which then sat on six acres that included an orchard with fruit trees. Kate had an excellent reputation as a remodeler around Santa Fe and was pretty well sought after, according to her son, Frank. "She liked [her houses] to come as close to the original construction as she could get it and still have it be livable with a leak-proof roof."[53]

Their social life was vigorous. Chap and Kate were members of the Third Year Book Club, which gathered "for social purposes as well as for the serious discussion of world events, community welfare and the fostering of art and science."[54] At home, Kate's dinner parties were noteworthy both for their tasty discourse and her inattention to the prosaic details of getting dinner on—word was, if invited to the Chapmans, eat a bit beforehand and prepare for a late supper. The conversation must have been irresistible for the guests to have developed such good-natured tolerance. Anecdotes confirm that the hostess herself became so immersed in the discussion, no doubt illuminating it with her own gaiety, that Chap would have to gently draw her attention to the hour and everyone's appetites. On one particularly notorious occasion, she simply could not locate the roast she had planned to serve. While history leaves no record of what she fed their company, the increasingly odiferous haunch revealed its presence a day later, in a bureau drawer!

Chap and Kate's social group not only indulged in what one contemporary termed the "essential recreations" of visiting, talking, and partying, but also in civic-minded and politically forceful activities.[55] A Santa Fe visit from writer Mary Austin in November

1918 resulted in her offering to help assist the Santa Fe Women's Club establish a permanent community theater similar to one she had helped found in Carmel, California. Kate, several months pregnant, did not take an active part in its first theatrical event, but Chap joined in, chairing the stage construction committee that included Vierra and newcomer Gustave Baumann. Parsons chaired the scenic committee, with members Warren Rollins and Henderson. During the next two and a half months, the newly formed Community Theater put together a four-part production of plays and songs in Spanish and English. Some members, disturbed at the facetious manner in which the staff was developing the program, confronted Austin about their lack of dignity. "Who ever heard of a dignified infant," she countered. "I am delighted to see this youngster to whom I seem to be elected godmother, kick up its heels."[56]

Santa Fe found itself host to more pageants that year. After World War I, Santa Fe chose to revive Fiesta. This annual celebration, originally a religious observance, had begun in the 1700s as a remembrance of the Spanish reconquest. In 1911 and for a few years after, Santa Fe held a more civic-oriented celebration, DeVargas Days, around the Fourth of July. For the 1919 revival, Twitchell served as the official director, and the school had almost complete responsibility. Hewett was behind the historic pageantry, which he hoped would enhance his scholarly reputation.[57] Although popular support for historic pageants was waning, Hewett remained attached to them because of their success at the San Diego exposition. He arranged a reenactment of DeVargas's 1692 reconquest of the city. Indian dancing was also featured as it had been at San Diego's Painted Desert exhibit, thus exposing new audiences to Pueblo cultures and reinforcing the cultural climate that extolled Native American values.[58]

About this time, Chap and Kate were enjoying their enlarged family—Helen was born on March 11, 1919—and Chap was strengthening his commitment to Indian art by his association with relative newcomers to the area. Rose Dougan had built a summer residence and workmen's quarters at the foot of Tsankawi mesa in 1917, living there with Vera von Blumenthal.[59] Von Blumenthal, a Russian woman, had developed a successful project in prerevolutionary Russia to improve the quality and increase the sale of lace produced in peasant villages. The women hoped to duplicate that success by establishing an Indian craft center, inviting museum staffers Chap, Bradfield, and then curator Olive Wilson to act as advisory committee. By mid-1919, the well-intentioned duo was disappointed, for they found that their summer-only contact with a few San Ildefonso potters was not producing the desired effect. Feeling that more contact and supervision was needed, they approached Hewett, suggesting that the school take over the struggling program and offered initial funding of $200 for the first year. Hewett accepted, and appointed Chap and Bradfield to work out a better organization with the women. They hit on a formula:

1. Ask potters to submit pieces to Chap or Brad before offering them for sale elsewhere.
2. Have each potter set her price for each piece.
3. Select one or more outstanding pieces, if any, and explain their merits (form, finish, decoration, etc.).
4. Add at least 25 percent to the potter's price for such pieces and promise higher prices for further improvement.
5. Explain that the museum would sell them at a sufficient markup to cover the school's administrative expenses. (This part of the formula was eventually dropped due to anticipated conflict of interest with tax-paying retailers who would object to sales competition from a publicly supported institution.)

They felt the third point was necessary because in many potters' experience, time spent in refining their work did not pay; generally, their pots were sold by the wagonload.

After a bumpy but productive start, Chap and Brad took over the fledgling program. The greater part of the seed money, which turned out to be the only funding for the work, was used to buy pottery before the 1920 tourist season opened. While some was sold at cost to visiting museum officials, Wilson sold most of it at profit to tourists that summer.

As fall deepened, neither Chap nor Brad could be spared for fieldwork, even if the coming winter road hazards had permitted travel to the pueblos. Because the potters rarely came in their farm wagons during winter months, a decision was made to halt further project development until spring. An unexpected problem occurred when Julian and Maria turned up with a wagonload of pots.

They were the last we would have picked for our experiment, for they were accomplished crafts workers who might resent our suggestions toward improvement of their wares. However, we knew that they were forced to limit the time expended on each piece, for they had learned that the dealers would not pay higher prices for a more finished product. So, in hopes of finding one or two more outstanding pieces in the lot, we decided to test our plan. It worked wonders!

We set aside four unusually well formed and finished pieces and asked their prices. Then we commended them for their attractive qualities, and paid 25% more than they had asked. That concluded, we told them of our plan and promised even more, for others in their next lot, if they showed further improvement.

Considerable time elapsed before we found an opportunity to extend our contacts, and it so happened that another San Ildefonso potter, Tonita Roybal, was the next to benefit by the system. I met her near the Museum, as she was returning

Tonita Roybal of San Ildefonso Pueblo, c. 1909–16. (Courtesy of
Palace of the Governors [MNM/DCA], 42330.)

from a house to house tour of several blocks, carrying two pieces of her pottery, and
discouraged over her inability to sell them. One water jar showed promise, so after
praising it, in Brad's absence, I raised her price by 50 percent and asked her to give
even more time and thought to her next lot. Tonita had inherited the Black-on-red
style from her mother, so I advised her to specialize with that. The result was that
within a few months, she was finding a ready sale at three times the price of her
former work.[60]

Although word spread rapidly within San Ildefonso, Chap and Bradfield had to rely
on chance meetings with potters from San Juan and Tesuque to promote what Chap
drolly termed their "missionary work," which resulted in a slight improvement in their
technique. Contact with more remote potters would wait a few more years until the first
Indian Fair, but an important turning point had occurred in Chap's work with pottery.
This venture was his first in identifying to their makers pots that he considered of high
caliber and generating a market strategy for them that included higher profits. As for
Chap's sensitivity that the Martinezes might resent suggestion, Maria was something of

a born trader, and though shy about being observed while throwing a pot, she welcomed Anglo advice to improve her sales.[61]

Julian, meanwhile, succeeded with a sales innovation of his own. Around 1919, he developed and perfected what brought him and Maria their greatest fame: the black-on-black wares. In the version promoted by Marriott, the discovery was partly the result of Julian's own curiosity, and partly an artifact of having to use sheep dung for firing when cow and horse dung was scarce.[62] Prior to firing, Julian had simply decorated a pot that Maria had already polished, painting the designs on with the same slip. Maria was concerned about losing a saleable item, but she indulged Julian. The sheep dung produced the "best smoke yet"; when the vessel finally emerged from the ashes Julian, ever the trickster, enjoyed a good laugh. The Santa Fe retailer who came out to pick up a load of plain black pottery asked the couple about their technique, but they told him that since no one else at San Ildefonso knew about it, they would be laughed at if the secret got out. The shopkeeper dropped the subject and set off to Santa Fe to see how the unusual pot would sell.[63] Recognition came swiftly. While Chap's new intervention was generating gorgeous traditional pots, the power of sales catalyzed innovation, a process that Chap entirely approved as long as the design merits of the pots were not compromised. As for Maria, the technique was a boon on an artistic level. She was learning the designs from Julian, but not having to balance the color scheme simplified production, making it much easier.[64]

In Santa Fe, vibrant scientists and artists shared space, ideas, politics, and social life. As the population of artists increased, they tended to cluster in one of two neighborhoods. The traditionalists were closer to the plaza, along lower Canyon Road and Acequia Madre—the Chapmans' neighborhood. The modernists occupied homes up on old Telephone Road, renamed Camino del Monte Sol at the urging of Alice Corbin Henderson, after she and her family moved there in 1917. Neighbor and artist Frank Applegate also made land available along Camino del Monte Sol for the construction of small adobes by other artists. In the late teens and early twenties, they were joined by "los cinco pintores" (modernists Jozef Bakos, Fremont Ellis, Walter Mruk, Willard Nash, and Will Shuster—the "five little nuts in five adobe huts"[65]), who contributed to the amusement of the town as earnest would-be architects of structures that sometimes toppled in the midst of construction.

Hewett's total science of man included the contribution of art. "The artists who are painting here are just as truly researchers as are the scientists. . . . In truth, anthropologists, with a few conspicuous exceptions, have done scant justice to the Indian culture. . . . It is through the artists and poets and scientists combined that this remarkable race is at last being truthfully represented."[66] Shuster, in a 1940 interview, presented the Museum of Fine Arts scene from the artist's view:

Now let us go down in the basement. There's Sam Huddleson presiding over a carpenter shop where Joe Bakos and Fremont Ellis and several other artists are busy making frames and crating their paintings. For those who didn't have the know-how there was a good old Sam ready to lend a helping hand or a bit of advice. . . .

Look over there in this other basement cavern. There is an etching press and there are the budding etchers Willard Nash, Fred Monhoff, Will Shuster and others, working hours on end, sweating and swearing over their plates and proofs. And Nordfelt and Co. chipping in with their own acid criticism and advice. . . .

There's Wes Bradfield the Museum photographer and a thorough archaeologist. Something tall and Lincoln-like about Brad. He did practically all the copying for the artists at a modest fee and if one was sufficiently skillful the well-equipped dark room facilities were made available to the artists to do their own work with much good advice thrown in. . . .

. . . Upstairs Sheldon Parsons is hanging a new show, we take a look-see and then go across Lincoln avenue to the patio of the Palace. Yes sir, that's right; there are four studios here, available for a time to newcomers until they get settled. George Bellows worked here, Robert Henri, John Sloan, Randall Davey, Willard Nash, Warren Rollins, Julius Rolshoven, Paul Burlin, Andrew Dasburg, on and on goes the list. A great roster of painters.[67]

Pueblo painters also held studio space at the museum. Among Chap's students were San Ildefonso artists; by 1915, he believed several would benefit from studio experience. At his urging, Hewett assigned studios to Awa Tsireh and Crescencio Martinez, among others.[68] Aspiring painters from other pueblos who joined them worked in a style characterized by the use of flat outline and color without modeling or the use of perspective. Fred Kabotie from Hopi and Ma-Pe-Wi from Zia emerged as outstanding young artists.

Hewett's generously offering studio space in the Palace of the Governors afforded a stimulating work environment for incoming artists, but not enough of it. Chap and Kate profited from the demand for more work sites when they purchased the Methodist church on San Francisco street in the spring of 1919 and converted it to studio space—called Chapel Studio—that they rented out to artists. Over twenty-four years, this structure housed the creative endeavors of at least a dozen artists and writers, among them Baumann, Cassidy, Rollins, and Davey. Chap always found the artists to be "reasonable and reliable tenants. During all those years not one rubber check passed hands. On the contrary, rentals were often had far in advance."[69]

As a new decade approached, some of the representational artists in Santa Fe echoed the seventy-five-year-old heritage of pioneer western artists like Thomas Moran and Frederick Remington, who recorded or mythologized what was uniquely American when the wilderness was pristine, the cowboy romantic, and the Indian not entirely threatened by genocide or assimilation. Others were innovators with a different message. After the 1913 Armory Show in New York, an avant-garde wave had roiled the Western art world. Restless American artists and writers, exposed to the European modernists, questioned more traditional aesthetics. Many were bothered by the alienation besetting an increasingly industrialized and metropolitan society.[70]

In Santa Fe, both groups consciously incorporated Native elements into their art. The more conservative realists depicted their sometimes sentimental perceptions of Indian life, a culture that to many seemed precariously near extinction. The modernists integrated symbols, geometries, and rhythmic patterns of Pueblo design and ceremony into their expressionism or abstraction.[71] Members of both groups upheld Native spirituality as an antidote to accelerating materialism.

Some art colonists, rebelling against European standards, were seeking a uniquely American aesthetic and in Native culture they hit pay dirt. Modernist Marsden Hartley published several essays beginning in 1918 in which he defended the genius of Native expression, including in such forms as dance and the visual arts. His 1920 essay argues for Indian art *as art*: "I want merely, then, esthetic recognition in full of the contribution of the redman as artist, as one of the finest artists of time . . . and master among masters of the art of symbolic gesture."[72] Likewise, modernist painter Paul Burlin was captivated with the art of the Pueblo potter: "Why was a bowl decorated in this abstract fashion? By contrast all other picture-making seemed like story telling trivia. These disturbing factors—none of which had anything to do with 'representation' were the vague beginnings of an esthetic credo."[73] A circa-1919 publicity photo of newlywed Taos artists Victor Higgins and Sara Parsons jointly holding a black-on-black pot is hand captioned, "We will build our new Home around THIS."[74]

In this respect, the intersection of Chap and the art colony was a meeting of minds. Chap's research, writing, and lectures were at the forefront of a shift in Anglo attitudes toward indigenous art. During the first two decades of the twentieth century, museums presented Native utilitarian and sacred objects as cultural relics, classified in orderly Anglo fashion by region and history. Interpretation of symbols aside, little effort was made to educate the general public on the aesthetics of what they beheld. Identifying and preserving indigenous culture prior to that time fell to archaeologists, anthropologists, museums, and a few rarely accessible private collections. But the times were changing. Hewett's forceful conviction of all that Native peoples had to offer, especially that which had endured since prehistoric times, carried persuasive weight among his devotees and the public who attended his lectures. The inclusion of San Ildefonsans Maria and Julian Martinez, among others, at the San Diego exposition where they demonstrated their pottery had resulted in increased public appreciation of their living heritage. Maria and Julian's pots already had a small local market; tourists either bought the pots through a Santa Fe retailer or at the pueblo itself despite the inconvenience of traveling there.

Chap's writings during this period reflected and reinforced this shift in attitude about Native art. His expertise in Native pottery and his friendships with the potters made him an eloquent cultural broker between Anglo and Native worlds.[75] In late 1920, two years after Hartley's first essay had been published, Chap gave a brief but impassioned talk to the Women's Club in Tucumcari, New Mexico. He pointed out that the young United States, filled with transplants, had borrowed heavily from classic European art while the activities of nation building had forced "our creative activity . . . into a practical groove."

> Perhaps it is first of all, this battle with . . . the live problems of our own that has kept us from a better understanding of the art of the American Indian.
>
> No race has ever made a greater use of symbolism. In his art we find it, freed from all the unessentials, and reflecting clearly the mental characteristics of the race.
>
> We feel that the life of the Indian is in close harmony with all nature about him, and we find in his art a simple and sincere expression of this relation. And since art is a part of his daily life, we find his symbolic ideas, reduced to pure design, which he has adapted to the decoration of everything he makes or uses. . . . No field of art history has had so little recognition.[76]

Blending insights from both art and anthropology, Chap's position reflected three professional influences. First, the idea that modern peoples could gain by learning how their ancient counterparts had approached humanity's universal problems was a notion embraced by Springer and promoted by Hewett, whose own "increasing interest in art was as a logical outcome of his view of both the humanistic roots of archaeology and its relevance to issues of [Southwest] identity."[77] Second, the conviction of Chap's fellow art colonists about Indian *art* added contemporary reinforcement. Third, the collecting, conserving, and cataloguing activities of museums paralleled Chap's systematic approach to pottery designs and his increasing need to preserve and raise awareness about Native art, particularly the Pueblo ceramic art with which he was most familiar.

Between 1915 and 1920, Chap's vocabulary includes words and phrases that reflect classical Anglo aesthetics and dance around his formative ideas of Native visual expression: "craft," "art," "primitive art," "arts and crafts," "decorative art," "abstract decoration," "aboriginal American art," "geometric art," "masterpieces of other cultures," for example. Their interchangeability in his writing and speaking lends an uncharacteristic sense of imprecision or indecisiveness, but in fact reflects his coming of age with respect to his own body of work. When the sentiments of his art colony contemporaries and his own artistic sensibilities were added to anthropological and art movement influences, it was inevitable that Pueblo pottery would provide Kenneth Chapman with an intellectual niche that he was uniquely qualified to fill.

Chap was now gaining recognition as a living data bank, rewarding his time spent on research. His name began appearing in the press in Santa Fe and elsewhere in connection with his work on Indian art. In a 1918 letter, ethnologist Jesse Walter Fewkes had commended Chap for his ongoing work on the morphology of the bird design and requested his help in distinguishing feather symbols.[78] From this period on, Chap's collected papers are sprinkled throughout with grateful correspondence from students, collectors, and professional colleagues with whom he shared his knowledge, resources, and gentle wit. His mission was getting the attention it deserved, and his sterling character the recognition. Adelaide Chamberlin wrote to art colony devotee and pottery enthusiast Eva Fenyes, "Mr. Chapman was always clever, and moreover, always generous and helpful with his ability. I have watched his work with great interest."[79] With all this reinforcement, he still needed a graceful way to bring Springer on board with his true calling, since he could see no other way to disentangle himself from museum duties and enmeshment in the Springer-Hewett-Chapman triangle.

Jess Nusbaum, on the other hand, found a ticket out with a position at the Heye Museum in New York in 1917. Chap lost the company of one of his staunchest allies—and certainly the most mischievous. For Nusbaum, the sadness of parting was eased when Frederick Webb Hodge also joined the Heye Museum soon after; he and Nusbaum developed a lifelong friendship that naturally included Chap. However, Nusbaum brought hard feelings toward Hewett east with him. While working for Hewett, he had repeatedly submitted expenses incurred in his duties of photography, rehabilitation of the Palace of the Governors, work on the San Diego exposition, and various expeditions and repairs for which he was not reimbursed. During Hewett's absences, he had occasionally been forced to draw upon personal savings to pay vendors he was authorized to engage. Whenever Hewett returned, Nusbaum renewed his request for payment only to be told the bills were long past due or of lower priority than other pressing bills. Then Hewett would slip Nusbaum's current copies into his bulging briefcase and leave again. By 1917, Nusbaum was owed $1,577.90.

Nusbaum and Chap both had a filial relationship with Springer, enhanced for Nusbaum by his friendships with Springer's sons, Ed and Wallace. Chap had urged him to go over Hewett's head, but Nusbaum stuck to organizational protocol. Chap had even contemplated conspiring on Nusbaum's behalf, a side of him that Nusbaum seemed to bring out.

> *In considering such a deal as Nusbaum's, I did give considerable thought to the possibility of getting some action from Dr. Hewett without word of it reaching Mr. Springer. Two different courses came to mind, but neither seemed feasible.*
>
> *First, I might have faced Dr. Hewett with my knowledge of his unfair treatment of Jess. But very likely he would have advised Mr. Springer of my unfriendly attitude.*
>
> *The second course would have been to ask one of the members of the Museum's Board if they were acquainted with the deal, and if so, why they had done nothing to correct it. But such a move on my part would very likely be brought at once to Mr. Springer's attention, as President of the Board, and I would have violated the pledge I had given him.*[80]

While in New York, Nusbaum enlisted to fight in World War I, which pushed him to take action. No longer obligated by museum-school procedure, he decided at last to bypass Hewett. In May 1918, he wrote to Springer that he was getting his papers in order before shipping out for France and needed money for life insurance. He enclosed copies of his bills, and it appears from Chap's marginal notes that Nusbaum gave him a copy of the letter to edit. Nusbaum enumerated repeated futile efforts and Hewett's various reasons for not making good, calling it "the only sore spot that I have ever held against the Museum[.] . . . I am tired unto death with the uselessness of it all."[81] When he left for the front, his letter followed Springer through forwarding addresses, finally catching up with him in his Rito camp where he had no checkbook. Months later Springer responded by sending a check for $200, care of Nusbaum's father, and wrote Jess, "I shall bring up the matters of which we have written in due course, and hope to see them properly adjusted—but of course cannot give any guess as to when it will reach the stage of payment."[82] Springer seems not to have pursued it at the time, and it would return ultimately in more troublesome form.

Chap's allegiance to Springer—and growing impatience with Hewett—was tested around 1919 when Hewett came to Santa Fe and offered Chap a full-time position with the West Coast museum. Hewett was not only directing the new San Diego museum but also heading a new anthropology department at the state teachers college in San Diego, hence living there part of the year. He needed proven staff in California. With what Chap perceived as a plan to lure him out there, El Toro gave a glowing sales pitch. *He urged me to take part in it, and showed his annoyance with my determination to stick with Mr. Springer's work. It was then that I first told him that nothing could drag me away from my adopted state of New Mexico and that I was more concerned with the development of the Museum than with his School's widely scattered projects.*[83]

In no uncertain terms, Chap discounted participation in Hewett's promotional work beyond Santa Fe. Perhaps this surge of autonomy caught Hewett off guard, or Chap inadvertently revealed animosity. The two wills rammed. Hewett blundered into another approach that Chap interpreted in the most offensive light. El Toro eventually backed off, but it delivered a lasting blow to Hewett's credibility in Chap's eyes. *I was shocked when he said that I was wasting my time with Mr. Springer's work for there were wonderful opportunities in California. He was for doublecrossing his best friend. Fortunately I could remind him that while attending the San Diego and San Francisco Expositions I had encountered a fog that left me with a severe cold and a vow that I would never return to California.*[84]

The hostility that surfaced during that interview was subsequently submerged beneath the professional cordiality to which both men had been brought up and were accustomed. However, neither would escape what sociologist Kenneth Dauber described as a pattern of alienation between Hewett and his male protégés.[85] The estrangement had simply been deferred.

Thus the period in Chap's life from 1915 to 1920 was a five-year stretch during which he married, began a family, settled on a career direction—and still found himself the employee of a man who had given him the source of his recently chosen life's work and now was its greatest obstacle. It coincides with the time during which the childless Hewett watched the first young men he had nurtured come of age and leave, using what he had taught them as a springboard for undertaking research and forming associations that increasingly conflicted with his own interests and style. Uneasily positioned between his two mentors, Chap was the only remnant of that beloved and exhilarating Pajarito group. Dependent on one, disillusioned with the other, how was he to assert what he inwardly claimed? The confrontation with Hewett gave him the impetus he needed. As his forty-fifth birthday approached, he took stock:

> *I was dissatisfied with Dr. Hewett's neglect of opportunities and with his make-shift switching of staff members between Santa Fe and San Diego—in emergencies that made it necessary for me to take charge of the Art Museum, and other odd jobs.*
>
> *In reviewing my ten years with the Museum it became quite clear that my concern for Mr. Springer's interests had led me to waste much of my time in the position of a "jack of all trades" and that it was time for a showdown.*[86]

In early 1920, Chap informed Springer that his work with pottery design held great potential and offered to do any museum work Springer might prefer provided Chap could have half time to pursue his own studies. Springer agreed to approach Hewett. Chap showed unusual muscle by issuing a concurrent ultimatum to Hewett. Either let him devote half of his salaried time to his own studies or he would leave to resume commercial art in Denver (where he had connections with muralist Allen True). Between Springer's influence and his assertiveness, he got what he wanted. *I was amused, a few days later when Dr. Hewett came in to tell me of a plan he had been considering for some time, that would allow me half-time for my own studies!*[87]

Chap had solved the dilemma of how to convert Springer's former enthusiasm for his art into an approved arrangement that would support his mission, for which he was just gaining recognition. It temporarily buoyed him up. It was a bit of a Faustian pact, however. The adult artist who at last knew that he wanted to put his talent at the service of a culture not his own did so at a price: he was still stuck with Hewett.

CHAPTER 7

PROMISING DIRECTIONS

Jazz. Flappers. Bootleg. The 1920s iconoclasm energizes Santa Fe, but it's a weary Chap who emerges from the museum. Pausing on the top stair, he shrugs off the day's confrontation with Hewett and recalls that he must pick up a new toothbrush. The plaza is bedazzled with late afternoon gold. Long diagonal shadows inspire an idea. He fishes a folded envelope from a pocket. Sketching a design as he wends his way toward the drugstore on San Francisco Street, he instead finds himself inside the grocer's. Muddled, he tucks the drawing away, covers the error with a food purchase, and walks back toward the old Palace of the Governors where the portico swallows his absurdly lanky silhouette. He assumes an easy stride when he turns up Acequia Madre. A neighbor waves, and the murmur of the Mother Ditch eases his spirit. Pausing outside his home, Chap mentally appraises a recent cornice repair. The toothbrush will keep for another day, as will his dissatisfaction and design. Around town, the twenties are starting to roar. He opens the door into Kate's bracing warmth and kisses young Frank and baby Helen.

After World War I, the Versailles diplomats reconfigured international lines. The American social map was also redrawn: immigrants established themselves, the wealthy erected mansions, and Americans got down to expansionist business. Santa Fe was a boisterous microcosm of the national boom. Its influx of artists, writers, and independently wealthy liberals began tipping the political scales, posing competition to the Old Guard. Tourism soared, rebels flouted prohibition, Anglos championed Indians. The art colony acted as a burner, keeping the heat on simmering social chemistry among ethnic groups. Santa Fe crested into an intercultural heyday, an appropriate era for the launching of Chap's independence from Hewett.

Amid all of it, Chap's outward stability was an assumed anchor for those who knew him. If he was dispirited, he didn't let it show. Take a typical month in the early twenties: quirky artists squabbling; museum staff barely scraping by on their salaries; Lansing Bloom acting less as assistant to Hewett and more as dictator in his absence; the new La Fonda Hotel attracting large numbers of visitors while Wes Bradfield scoffs at the "many comical renditions of Santa Fe Style in it. [But] Chap is the same old scout; who would expect Chap to change anyway[?]"[1]

If Chap appeared predictably stable, it was because he strove to cultivate detachment when butting heads with El Toro: *In my nearly forty years before entering Museum work in S.F. my varied experiences with thwarted plans had made me well aware that minor frustrations must be accepted as the bitter with the sweet. And from them I learned to view each incident without undue emotion, and to plot my own path over or around it.*[2] But he tempered stoicism with wit. His letters to the newspaper during this period reveal quirks of life, Santa Fe, and himself. The term "fruiterers" in a news item out of London sparked him to comment on the

> increasing number of articles that have come to masquerade as real food during the past twenty-five years. . . . What I allude to in particular are the tiny pink radishes, and other little shiny and bright-colored vegetable mistakes that women love to serve on or in salads. . . . All such trinkets ought to be classed as Arts and Crafts goods, along with the painted wooden beads and enameled jewelry.
>
> Lettuce was all right when we kept it where it belonged, but nowadays it is too much in the limelight. Refreshing though it may be, it isn't a real food. Rightly speaking, it is only a packing material.
>
> Yours nutritiously, Gastro Nomic[3]

Similarly, he lampooned himself by recounting a good-natured contest with Kate. He submitted a pseudonymous column describing how he had inadvertently wandered into Kaune's grocery when he meant to purchase a toothbrush at Zook's drugstore. Mindful of "Uncle" Ralph Twitchell's ability to name in order every business around the plaza, he chided himself:

> I was bowled over by the performance, but on my way home I said to myself, "It's all in keeping your mind on it! I know that Zook's is east of Kaune's, and it's only because my mind is usually working on something really important that I make such breaks. I'll bet I know the location of everything around the Plaza."

At home, he tested himself on a blank diagram. "Friend Wife" teasingly asked if it was a new system for mah-jongg. He replied yes, but said he didn't know if he should call it Mah Fe or Santa Jongg, and confessed his earlier mistake. Kate declared this would never happen to her, provided she was alone (conversation was as much her distraction as musing was Chap's). She accepted his challenge to the game. Comparing results, Chap found several discrepancies between their respective versions. He was sure he had her! Pocketing the two, he told her he would confirm the victor next day. And so he did. On his way to work he stole a few moments' direct observation in the plaza.

What a pity it is that we Santa Feans don't take a little time each day to sit in the
Plaza. What a restful place it is on a large, handsome, blonde morning in May,
and won't it be great when all the store fronts are done over in Santa Fe Style like
Julius Gans' building?

Then with a jerk I remembered why I was there. Triumphantly I unfolded
the diagrams and—Friend Wife was right! Can you do it?

SUNSHINE ROW[4]

Chap's humor offered symptomatic relief, but the same old scout still faced the same
old issues. To ease the deeper ache, Chap leaned on the alliances he had formed with old
friends and new, among them a growing number of Pueblo potters. When Frank occasionally accompanied his dad to the pueblos, he was enfolded into their communality.
As he recalled:

Since we had no automobile in the family in those days, it was rather rare that
somebody who had an automobile and wanted to go out there [to the pueblos]
would take me along, just a young brat who didn't have much real reason to be
going . . . but I got in a few visits with them. Maria and Julian . . . knew that I was
Dad's son, so I was welcomed into the house, and I listened to some of the chatter that was going on between my Dad and them. The same was true with some
of the other pueblos, and I got to know a few of these Indians. Santiago Naranjo,
of Santa Clara, who was the cacique, the old timer, the one who . . . taught the
younger people in the pueblo what the stories were, carrying the myths of the
ages down to the next age. He was the one who, when informed of my birth and
the circumstances surrounding it, named me Oku, which meant Turtle. . . . That
name was spread around the pueblos, because of Dad's, how should I say, his
acceptance by those Indians as a person who was interested in them, not just
as curiosities or something the way so many of the people treated the Indians.
He knew he was working with them and for them, so that name that I got was
transported to all the pueblos eventually. Kind of funny, the way that works, isn't
it? But that was my name.[5]

Genuine relationships with Pueblo artists also kept Chap's professional battery
charged. He walked an interesting line with the potters. His sketches gave them access
to the prehistoric and historic design vocabulary unique to their own pueblos, and Chap
encouraged their use, thus reinforcing a traditional conservatism. Yet he also encouraged experimentation and artistic innovation. This comfortable dualism marked his recommendation that they try working in media besides clay. For example, a 1920 Santa Fe

Julian and Maria Martinez of San Ildefonso Pueblo on the Palace of the Governors' patio, c. 1912. (Photograph by Jesse L. Nusbaum. Courtesy of Palace of the Governors [MNM/DCA], 40814.)

Arts Club exhibit of thirty drawings by San Ildefonso artists grew out of his suggestion that they record their traditional ceremonies but via nontraditional forms of art.[6]

Above all, Chap was sensitive to the norms of Pueblo social culture. Because talent or fortune might distinguish a potter, making it uncomfortable for her and her pueblo, Chap's tact and empathy helped strike a balance, as many have noted.[7] He accommodated Pueblo rhythms of life, their planting and harvesting and their ceremonies, and accepted unexpected interruptions. He refrained from gushing over new work. Instinctively, Chap's own temperament—reserved with a ready wit—matched the manner in which Indians guarded their culture. They typically demonstrated a justifiable wariness, often delivered with dry humor, and a reserved, unflinching politeness that could frequently convey the unstated message, "Go away closer," according to author Coe. "But generally welcome are those persons who take time to learn Indian feelings and preferences, who do not press indelicate questions . . . and who, most of all, carefully sustain respect as well as interest when they are vouchsafed a glimpse into the Indian spiritual world which is as mysteriously rewarding as it is difficult to enter."[8] Maria's niece Carmelita Dunlap recalled the "tall and skinny" Chap as "a nice man, kind and everything. He was respectful, and always wore a white hat."[9] Maria's daughter-in-law Santana described him as "a very, very good man" who would stand around and quietly watch the potters at work; the understanding between Maria and Chap was based on "not a lot of words or writing."[10]

In the summer of 1920, the Museum of Fine Arts exhibited seventeen pieces of Maria's pottery, including some of the new black-on-black ware. As Maria and Julian's happy accident acquired technical sophistication, its modernist appeal reinforced sales. Chap quickly drafted notices to be included with sold pieces, warning buyers that the wares weren't fired at sufficiently high temperatures for waterproofing, but the pieces moved quickly despite diminished utility. Maria's relative affluence started to threaten her pueblo's infrastructure, which already suffered from an internal government/religious rift, so Chap understood Maria and Julian's decision to equalize matters by sharing their discovery with fellow potters. Then, in 1920, a dialogue with Maria got his attention:

I have acquired considerable information in pottery design from the women of San Ildefonso, and on one occasion while showing Maria Martinez some of the designs I had copied from the collection at the Normal University, I told her that a certain bilaterally balanced design was called "butterfly" by the woman from whom Dr. Hewett had bought the olla in 1896. Maria did not agree with this and pointed out its component parts of mountain, clouds, leaves, seeds, seed-pod, etc. On her next visit to the Museum, however, she told me she had shown the design to the oldest potters who discussed its meaning among themselves. They agreed that her interpretation of the elements of the design was correct, but that because the design appeared to "open out like a butterfly" it might have been given that name.

"I see," I said to Maria[.] "What the old lady was trying to tell Dr. Hewett, was that it was what we could call a butterfly arrangement." Then, without realizing what would be involved, I added, "If I learn all the kinds of leaves, and seeds, and clouds that you use, do you think I could put them together and make other kinds of the 'butterfly'?" Maria had the right reply to that. "Why, Mr. Chap," she said, "[y]ou ought to do better than we can, because you have been taking all our old pottery

away from us and making pictures of it, and then sending it away, and we can't remember any of the old designs." That gave me food for considerable thought.[11]

He noted the increasing need to safeguard pots as well as their designs. Then, intrigued by Maria's plaintive comment, he indulged in obsessive design tinkering. He listed the most commonly used San Ildefonso elements and began combining them in "butterfly" arrangements. For weeks at odd moments, wherever he happened to be, he covered backs of envelopes, margins of magazines, and papers until he had over 150 permutations. He reproduced almost 100 of them in black-and-red on ten-inch cards that he mounted on large exhibition boards. He never forgot Maria's reaction:

Briefly, she was amazed at the endless variety—she was excited over a few, she approved of many others without comment, and she picked the one I had purposely included in hopes of getting a rise out of the San Ildefonsos. It was "no bueno" she said, not good San Ildefonso, not even permissible in any pueblo.

I learned how easy it is for them to hand out adverse criticism and how hard it is to tell why a thing is good. And as for endless variety; it can be hopelessly bewildering. No pueblo potter ever seeks deliberately to produce it. Instead, she reaches her ideal of a concept often by years of gradual change, without remembering all its steps. From there on she experiments with minor changes, one at a time and perhaps months apart. Only rarely can she save an example. But to be confronted with a hundred of them—that would never happen. After 15 minutes, Maria had to be going—she must buy flour, she must collect her family; it was a long way home by wagon.

I learned much by listening to the comments of other potters. The collection [of my own butterfly designs] was exhibited, in several states and used in lectures, and once used in almost undecipherable miniature cuts in School Arts Magazine *without my permission. Otherwise it has never been published. And to this day, those who remember it, forget that the designs were created by an Americano, a mere white man. They give all the credit to the potters themselves. I should be happier if that were so.*[12]

He realized that he had inadvertently corrupted that which he sought to respect, exacerbating his private dilemma of how to preserve the authenticity of each pueblo.[13]

To get his family life in comfortable order, Chap asked for a three-month leave in early 1920 to work on his home and the Chapel Studio. Springer approved the request. Meanwhile, the vigorous Hewett had been spending his time not only directing the new San Diego museum but also instituting an archaeological society there. He had, in addition, taken a winter teaching position at San Diego State College and was continuing to spearhead new excavations and projects. Chap's efforts in managing the resulting organizational flotsam in Santa Fe resulted in further complications among himself, Hewett, and Springer.

By his own declaration, Chap was thoroughly disillusioned. Since approving Chap's fifty-fifty split between museum work and his own studies, Hewett had requested a written job description in preparation for 1921 programs and budget. Chap produced a two-page document that began by addressing two museum loose ends.[14] One was a collective staff effort to complete the Sun House project. The other was the need to complete the cataloguing and labeling of collections so as to remedy the slipshod way its specimens were being tracked, identified, and classified. He pointed out that if everyone pitched in here as well the cataloguing could be finished efficiently. As it turned out, he was setting himself up to be bushwhacked by El Toro. The ambush was indirectly the result of Rose Dougan's previewing, at curator Bertha Van Stone's suggestion, Hewett's exhibit of his private Navajo silver collection. Among the items was a bracelet Dougan had specifically donated to the museum! Rather than confront Hewett, Dougan entrusted her outrage to Chap, enlisting his aid to rectify the situation. Such sideways channeling of grievances typifies the dysfunctional museum-school system, as does Chap's evident relish at the ensuing encounter:

> *When she left I went to Dr. Hewett's office and found him in conference with Mr. Springer. It was the first occasion in many years in which I had found the two together—too good an opportunity to pass up. Dr. Hewett asked what was on my mind, and I gave it to him and then added that after ten years of marking time, his Museum had not even as good a system as it started with, the first week it opened. There was no catalog of specimens, nor a record of their source. I asked him what chance it had of receiving gifts if others like Rose Dougan found what a mess we were in and spread it around Santa Fe.*
>
> *My little talk backfired for next day Dr. Hewett called me to his office and directed me to get at the cataloging of the Museum's collections and to stay with it to the finish.[15]*

Hewett thus turned Chap's own proposal against him, thwarting his desire to involve the staff in the project. Chap went at it with his usual thoroughness, but his resentment escalated over the huge work detour. It rekindled his disgruntlement over Hewett's slapdash procedures, including his taking personal custody of Dougan's donation. The chore gave him a passive-aggressive way to impose his own boundary between the museum and the school and symbolically between himself and Hewett. Chap reasoned that all specimens were museum property, since artifacts had been acquired during state-funded museum expeditions, and donors never specified the school as beneficiary. Believing he held the higher ethical ground (justified by his understanding of public museum fiscal procedures), he deliberately labeled objects as museum property alone. This system was maintained until his tenure ended, when Hewett finally discovered what he had done.[16]

Chap's moral hackles were raised again by another ownership incident close on the heels of the first. This situation was to trouble him well into his old age and involved Hewett's sleight-of-hand with the Pajaritan pottery collection that had been loaned, under protest, to the museum in 1911 by Las Vegas Normal University. In 1920, Hewett learned that Neil Judd of the National Museum intended to survey and excavate a Chaco Canyon site. Hewett felt triply threatened by the news. First, Judd's association with the National Museum aligned him with eastern anthropologists, who had already questioned Hewett's science; since Hewett lagged in adopting stratigraphy and dendrochronology (tree-ring dating), Judd might be breaking more than literal ground in Hewett's bailiwick. Second, not only was Judd the nephew of Byron Cummings and a member of the 1909 Pajarito field session, but his backers included former Hewett protégés Kidder, Morley, and Earl Morris. This alliance among those whose careers Hewett had nurtured underscored the growing professional rift between him and "his boys." Finally, Chaco Canyon represented Hewett's initial success as an anthropologist; he had led the fight to investigate the activities of Richard Wetherill and the 1896–97 Hyde Expedition in Chaco Canyon.[17] Hewett abruptly decided to act on his own nearly expired site permit and excavate Chetro Ketl in Chaco, a project long delayed by involvements elsewhere.

Hewett had cooperative arrangements with five institutions under which they financially sponsored a museum-school dig. Any resulting collection of artifacts would then be divided, with one-third to one-half allocated to Hewett's organization. The 1896 Hyde Expedition's discovery of over one hundred pottery bowls and a 1,214-piece turquoise mosaic at Pueblo Bonito in Chaco was well known among anthropologists. Hewett now wired Charles T. Currelly, director of the Royal Ontario Museum, one of the five supporting institutions, intimating archaeological treasure similar to the earlier finds; Currelly pledged $4,000 and tapped one of his own patrons, who quickly wired $1,000 to the school. Receipt of this advance was acknowledged by Paul Walter as both treasurer of the school and secretary of the museum, writing on First National Bank stationery—where he was an officer—illustrating the confused institutional boundaries that bothered Chap. Excavations ran from midsummer into October; Chap arrived for two weeks in late September to help with mapping, sketching, and other odd jobs.

The results of the excavations thus far had been most disappointing; for all the rooms then uncovered had proved to be practically sterile. Only two or three restorable bowls had turned up, and not one bit of turquoise such as had been recovered many years before in amazing quantities at the ruins of Pueblo Bonito, less than a mile distant.

Mrs. Hewett was in camp at the time, and the most distinctive impression of my visit was of her anxiety over the poor showing. She repeated to me, time and again, "I don't know what Dr. Currelly will say when he learns how disappointing it has been. Dr. Hewett assured him that there would be some rich digging, and you know practically nothing has come out so far. Dr. Currelly put up the money for this year's work and I am sure he is expecting a good haul."[18]

A month before the close of the dig, Hewett wrote Currelly requesting the balance of $3,000. A cautionary hedge was embedded in his rosy report: "I can not yet say how prolific this first season will be in museum material, but the scientific results will, I can assure you, be fully up to our expectations."[19] He went on to promise that an article on the dig would be published, a commitment that was subsequently fulfilled in *Art and Archaeology*. But when Currelly finally arrived to claim his share of the nonexistent booty, Hewett scrambled to appease him. Back in town, Chap discovered the two inspecting a number of pots spread out on the lawn. Chap was appalled as he recognized what was happening:

In my ten years' experience at the Museum, there had been several such instances of Dr. Hewett's rash and unfulfilled promises, but I had not foreseen the outcome of this one. . . . The Museum's storage collections yielded but little to satisfy such a connoisseur as Dr. Currelly, so, as a last resort, the Director was forced to bring out of storage the collection of Pajaritan pottery . . . [originally obtained] as a loan from the New Mexico Normal University . . . under circumstances that would seem incredible in this day and age, but which are attested by documents now in my possession. . . .

Dr. Currelly had made a tentative selection of a few dozen pieces, and was still at it. Dr. Hewett came to meet me, and as often before in such situations, said quite casually, "Chap, Dr. Currelly is picking out some of our [sic] Pajaritan pottery for his museum. If you want to make any sketches or photographs of it, you had better get at it at once."

Knowing Dr. Currelly as I did, I am confident that he accepted the Pajaritan collection merely as security for his advance of $1000, hoping to exchange it for more attractive material from some future excavation.[20]

Chap now became preoccupied with Hewett's freewheeling ways with specimens, and Hewett's callousness further estranged him. He drafted several recommendations for the board of regents, presumably undelivered, in which he suggested that all sales, exchanges, gifts, and discards of material be approved by the board, which was ignorant of the director's modus operandi. Chap's own scruples about such matters would serve him well in years to come.

If the mild-mannered Chap seethed over mishandled collections, Hewett's unpaid bills must have driven him wild. Chapman was, throughout his life, a painstaking accountant, so Hewett's questionable use of fiscal cunning to cover shortfalls or avoid reimbursing staff invoices particularly bothered Chap. His memoirs detail two specific episodes: the first concerning Hewett's offhanded fund-raising and the second reporting Hewett's mishandling of Nusbaum's accounts.

When Hewett had become director in 1909, he had gone on public record saying that the founding of the School of American Archaeology was the beginning of a general endowment movement. Chap was sure that back then Hewett would have discussed endowment prospects with him, had there been any; even if he had received assurances of funds, they never materialized, so all along the director had compensated with other monies, including his own and the museum's. Furthermore, since he had apparently neglected or botched his exclusive responsibility to raise money for the school, therefore failing to tend to business at home, Chap felt that he had no right to expand his institutions out of state. Chap could excuse Hewett for not soliciting local funds, which would cast doubt on his claim that the AIA and the school would seek endowments large enough to generate income that would match or exceed the state's annual appropriations. *But there was no reason why he should not have taken advantage of his travel from coast to coast to ask the members of the Institute's branch societies, for introductions to possible donors in their communities.*[21] As Judge McFie once remarked to Chap, "They say Hewett is a wonderful promoter, but he never cleans up."[22]

Hewett could and did elicit excavation funding from his support network, but his staff suffered with salaries dependent on state funding. Hewett's San Diego enterprises competed for his fund-raising attention, and salaries there were also low. Chap recorded that lack of pension plans added insult to capricious job assignments, and that although offering fieldwork treks in lieu of paid vacations was okay for employees, it was hard on families. Some personnel supplemented meager pay with outside resources while others were simply willing to make sacrifices, but those with families needed a dependable cost-of-living wage. Chap's salary from the museum fluctuated over the years as did his salary from his arrangements with Springer. He and Kate had shared means, but salaries like his curator's $125 per month were hardly sufficient for others.

Hewett encouraged staff to supplement with publication and outside work, even as he maintained a fiscal juggling act that never seemed to raise red flags with his board or the legislature. Chauvenet states that staff members suspected Hewett of covering up how much the state museum carried school expenses.[23] During one of his absences, Chap and Bradfield successfully lobbied with the state for the largest budget to date. On Hewett's return, he reversed this accomplishment by asking for a reduction, persuading legislators that the school greatly benefited the museum. Why he did so is a mystery; salaries would be hard hit by the cut. Springer, trusting Hewett's accounts, continued to supplement from his own pockets as necessary. Because Chap was aware of this, he was galled that Hewett consistently gave the impression that shortfalls were the state's doing. He once overheard a school board member remark to a visitor that *the School could have made much better progress with the Museum "if the State legislature were not so niggardly with its appropriations."*[24] Chap privately compiled statistics on several other state museums. He calculated a per capita allocation of public funds using population, assessed valuation, and annual budgets. He found that New Mexico's appropriation was eight to nine times that of Colorado and more than twenty times that of New York! Of course, no one ever complained about being the recipient of Springer's largesse, but it led to problems and resentments when Nusbaum's outstanding claims suddenly resurfaced.

Nusbaum returned to New York after his military service and in 1920 married Aileen O'Bryan, taking on responsibility for Deric, her son by a previous marriage. In 1921, Aileen became severely ill. The hospital bills mounted. Pressed for cash, Nusbaum resubmitted his accounts directly to Springer who now intervened as he should have done in 1918. He came at once to Santa Fe and sought Chap out. "Why, Chap," he said, "What does this mean? It's a bolt out of the blue. Our Board has never heard of this. Why, a great part of the account is now outlawed. I must call a meeting of the Board, but not a word of this must leak out—it would wreck the Museum!" Chap was determined to dispense long-overdue justice.

> *I could no longer hold back what I had known from the beginning. I said, "Mr. Springer, do you mean that in all the years of your annual meetings, Dr. Hewett has never submitted an account of bills payable?" "Absolutely not," he replied. I then outlined the whole deal, and assured him that no one who knew Jess, and his meticulous accounting as I did, could ever doubt the validity of his claims. Mr. Springer not only agreed with me, but also (as I learned later), had shown his confidence in Jess by sending him a check for $500 to tide him over until the Board could take action.*
>
> *Within an hour after Mr. Springer had left, Dr. Hewett came to see me, and said, "I understand that Jess Nusbaum has turned over to Mr. Springer some*

accounts he has had kicking around here for years. Chap, you know how careless, and how undependable he was with everything. His shop was always in a mess. Jess Nusbaum! Why the only reason we ever held onto him was that we felt sorry for him!" . . .

"No, Dr. Hewett," I said, "I can't go along with you in that. As for his shop, during all those early years it was a run-way, a gathering place for everyone who wanted to use it, whether he was in or out. . . . But more to the point, whenever as secretary I had occasion to consult Jess regarding any account that concerned his work he would go to an iron bound trunk in his photographic department, and pick out the item from his orderly files. And furthermore, if the Board wishes a statement from me regarding this long standing mixup, I will tell them exactly what I have told you, and more, for I feel that Jess deserves a square deal."[25]

Chap hoped this would force Hewett to back down, but the next day he found himself in even deeper. Springer had scheduled a special board meeting for that afternoon. He had a luncheon engagement before the meeting that he thought might delay him a bit, so he handed Chap a package of Nusbaum's accounts and asked him to deliver it to him in person at the meeting. That he asked Chap to serve as errand boy is puzzling; nonetheless, Chap took the package in promptly at 2 p.m. He found several of the board members conferring with Hewett, but no Springer. He turned to leave when Hewett asked, "What is it, Chap?" Chap explained that he had a delivery, and Hewett replied, "Oh, Mr. Springer should be here any minute. Just leave it on my desk and I will see that he gets it." Chap complied. Knowing Hewett's tricks, was Chap being stupidly obedient? Or was he laying a trap for Hewett?

Later that afternoon, Mr. Springer appeared and asked, "What went wrong? Didn't I ask you to hand me that package?" I told him exactly what had happened and his only comment was "Well he didn't give it to me."

On his next visit a few days later, I told Mr. Springer that I had no wish to pry into such affairs, but since I had had a part in the recent unpleasantness, I would be greatly relieved if he would at least assure me that the package had been returned to him. He deliberated for a moment and then said, "Yes,—I got it back." I knew from experience, that that ended any discussion of the matter.[26]

Chap's interpretation implies that Springer never got the papers, and it seems Chap was right. On a sheet later summarizing Nusbaum's total submitted bills, Hewett noted, "Unauthorized accounts and fraudulent claims presented by J. L. Nusbaum to Mr. Frank Springer. They were never seen by the Director or Regents of the Museum. E. L. H."[27]

The discrepancy between Nusbaum's version of repeatedly submitting his claims and Hewett's denial of ever seeing them is extraordinary. Hewett's final, bitter record was written from San Diego:

> These claims presented by J. L. Nusbaum to Mr. Springer, and which I suppose were personally paid by Mr. Springer, represent a portion of Nusbaum's unauthorized expenditures while with the School and Museum. He represents that he could not get us ["me" scratched out] to act upon them. The fact is, most of them were never shown to me. He continually exceeded his authorizations, was repeatedly admonished about it, but never heeded. His offenses of this kind would have brought summary discharge in any strictly administered institutions. Recognition of his unusual ability and good intentions, together with a deep personal interest in his career from early boyhood, constrained us to overlook this grave fault. It should be noted in this connection that in his employment with the Normal University at Las Vegas, the Fred Harvey Museum at Albuquerque and the Museum of the American Indian in New York, his relations with the administrative officers were unsatisfactory. [signed] Edgar L. Hewett
>
> Since writing the above memorandum I have gone into these claims with great care, hoping to find some justification. There is none. They represent lawless expenditures in the name of the institution that was giving him his opportunities, kept from my knowledge for fear I would discharge him, and a large amount of personal unregulated extravagance. He was always harassed by debts, even when getting a good salary. On leaving San Diego, after a long period of exceptionally good wages, his personal effects were attached to pay his hotel bills. Doubtless when leaving for the war he was swamped with debts and made this appeal to the sympathies of Mr. Springer. I have heard that Mr. Springer sent him $1000. He never presented the claims, nor mentioned them to me. He knew Nusbaum's irregularities well, and in his great kindness always helped him. E. L. H.[28]

Chap's account of the episode contains a copy of Hewett's early lavish praise of Nusbaum, contradicting his later indictment. If Hewett tried to diminish Springer's esteem of Nusbaum, it had no effect. Springer's further correspondence with Nusbaum, who was like a brother to Springer's adult children, is lovingly paternal. Nusbaum's intimacy with Springer's son Wallace allowed him to confront with brotherly concern that son's alarming aimlessness, and Springer was grateful. While the truth of the incident lies somewhere between Chap's and Hewett's versions, the outrage in Nusbaum's

1918 letter, Chap's memoirs, and Hewett's memos shows the pain of poorly severed bonds between El Toro and nearly all his protégés. In May, with Aileen recovered, Nusbaum's financial problems were eased when he was appointed superintendent of Mesa Verde—the outdoorsman's dream come true. But Chap's nightmare worsened, since his obvious alliance with Nusbaum poisoned what little cordiality was left between Hewett and himself. *Following the Nusbaum incident I found myself in disfavor with the Director. . . . From then on I was not entrusted with items or information such as those regarding the School's expected endowment, that had been passed on to the more favored members of his staff.*[29]

The Nusbaum incident aside, Hewett's general control over information flow served his directorship. The board accepted his word on matters without seeking objective validation, and Chap's principles prevented him from going over Hewett's head to volunteer corrective information. Walter once referred to him as a "benevolent despot."[30] Chap went further:

> *Everything considered, in the course of a few years he had become not merely the Director of the School, he had become literally the School itself! For he had not only control of his hand picked staff, but, by withholding in his annual reports to the Executive Committee, such items as the few I have recorded[,] . . . he was assured of their unanimous approval, year after year.*
>
> *In all that period from 1909 to 1929 I was never consulted by one member of the Board regarding School or Museum matters. In fact I had never even met some of them. But that gave me no concern, for I felt that I could not cope with such a rarified atmosphere.*[31]

However, Chap acquired inside data through unidentified confidantes and behind-the-scenes observation. At least one fellow staff member kept Chap clued in. Springer also still confided in him. He sought Chap's opinion of Hewett's plan to employ Polish anthropologist Maria Antoinette Czaplicka, who had recently completed well-reviewed ethnological work in Siberia. Chap could not bite his tongue. Having pent up his rancor for so long, he was now on a roll: *I told him that . . . considering the language difficulty involved, I doubted that the results would pay for the extra expenses of bringing a foreigner into the southwestern field. Then since he had asked for it, I took the opportunity to add that in my opinion Dr. Hewett's scheme was apparently due to his unfortunate lack of contacts with competent women ethnologists who had received most of their training at Columbia, under Boas, his arch-enemy.*[32]

This venomous jab, with its implication that Hewett's scholarship was considered dubious by the Boas camp, probably led to a final, tacit agreement that Hewett's doings were now a taboo subject between Chap and Springer—a sad pass between two old friends caught in a such a web. The remark also reveals Chap's awareness of Hewett's professional vulnerability, since increasing sophistication in the field was cementing divisions between national and regional interests. Hewett had few sympathizers beyond AIA members, but Chap was consolidating personal and professional relationships with ranking American peers. He was friend and ally of Nusbaum, Kidder, Morley, and Judd. He enjoyed professional camaraderie with Alfred Tozzer and Joe Spinden. His friendship was deepening with Hodge, now director of the National Museum of the American Indian in New York. The two had been corresponding since Hodge mentored Chap during his meander research back east; concurrently, Hodge had a longstanding gripe with Hewett that was instigated by Hewett's turning his back on their shared vision of a Pajaritan field school and instead committing himself more fully to the San Diego museum. From 1921 on, Chap was on the lookout for good black awanyu pots of Maria's for Hodge, and his communication reflects the kinds of personal tidbits he likely shared with Hodge on a regular basis:

> I have been working . . . down at the church studio ever since you left, & the pottery had to be left to our carpenter, who was at the Chaco when you were here[.] . . . I put in all my time getting [Gustave] Baumann settled in the church studio. I had great luck until yesterday when I hammered a finger & will carry a souvenir blood blister for a couple of weeks to remind me of my past 6 weeks activities. There is still a little finishing to be done, but that can wait until I return from Albuquerque . . . for the annual 3 days hen party: the NM Educational Association meeting, of which our NM Science Association is a part.
>
> I get a 3 days' rest & hope to be in shape, then, to get down to business in my studio.[33]

With regard to Hewett, Chap tried to swallow his irritation, but his agitation manifested itself in occasional stomach ailments. In the rare moments when Hewett consulted Chap, their differences surfaced. Hewett asked Chap's thoughts on his plan to excavate the untouched north house at Puyé. Chap offered his best reasons for leaving it undisturbed: *First, to give visitors [an] idea of an unexcavated ruin and, second, to be saved for decades, if possible, to enable future archaeologists to record features that we would have overlooked.*[34] His agenda was to focus on the dwindling supply of historic Pueblo pots in which Hewett had little, if any, interest. More important, his comment suggests his awareness of Hewett's reputation for inept scholarship and excavation methodology. Hewett and Chap returned to their corners at the end of this round, and El Toro proceeded as he wished.

In 1921, *Art and Archaeology* published Chap's account of the Chetro Ketl pottery finds in "What the Potsherds Tell," an article that Chap, later in life, placed on his list of recommended articles. It described the archaeological importance of pottery and conveyed Chap's fascination: "Potsherds tell of many things: of clays and tempering materials, or slips and pigments. They record every process in their making and every variety in form. They show the individual touch of their makers; the crude work of inexperienced hands or of hands grown old and infirm, as well as the deft touch of expert potters who sang as they moulded and painted, even as the Pueblo women of today. They record the creative instinct."[35] Meanwhile, Chap was chafing to get at his survey:

> I soon found it advisable to increase the scope of the study to include an account of the development of each craft through nearly four centuries following the impact of the Spanish under Coronado in 1540.
>
> The archaeologists, beginning in the 1870's had spurned the post-Spanish period in the belief that the material culture of the pueblo Indians was strongly influenced after 1540 by Spanish contacts. With the exception of Dr. A. V. Kidder, and Dr. N. C. Nelson who had done some exploratory digging in the Tewa and Tano areas, no one had given the pueblo ruins of this period any serious study, particularly by means of stratigraphic tests.
>
> I therefore proposed to Dr. Kidder, then engaged in his excavations at the ruined pueblo of Pecos, that I work back from modern times with the view of meeting the archaeologists half way.[36]

Chap's decision to focus on historic pottery filled an important niche. The gap between the prehistoric people (e.g., the Anasazi, whose culture appeared to vanish) and the modern Pueblo peoples has perplexed archaeologists for nearly two centuries. With regard to pottery, it was difficult, for example, to see a connection between a fifteenth-century pot excavated from Puyé and a contemporary piece made across the road at Santa Clara Pueblo.[37] Chap recognized the urgency of such work. As Maria had pointed out, post-Hispanic pottery was now scarce, owing to numerous factors. The Pueblos had been decimated by disease and had lost land rights and suffered famine. They had less mobility now, and trade among postconquest Indian peoples had declined as result. Utilitarian pottery had been replaced by manufactured wares after U.S. occupation and the railroad's arrival, and the Pueblos were inclined to keep what remained close to home (away from Spanish and Anglo eyes), where they would use the pieces until they broke. The Pueblos now also spent more time producing "degraded" or inferior pots for tourists, and finally, an untold number of older pots had found their way into scientific and commercial collections.[38] Chap's mission fired the imagination of his young midwestern

Chapman taking photos of pottery designs on the Palace of the Governors' patio. (Courtesy of School for Advanced Research Archives, AC02 820c.)

nephew John Sheffield Chapman, who recalled "Uncle Bud" describing his quest for a missing link that would unite the archaeology of the prehistoric Southwest with the post-Hispanic work of the late nineteenth century. Though John was a youngster at the time, it made a lifelong impression.[39]

Chap's goal was to document the particular design styles from potterymaking pueblos, which he hoped would lend credence to his belief that a distinct style had evolved in each. Chap proposed that Hewett authorize a decorative art survey, a formalization of what he had been trying to accomplish for several years. "I am more firmly convinced than before that the need of concentrating on this work is more urgent than any museum work which has interfered with it during the past year, and that I should resume at once my work of making photographs, drawings, and notes of native handicraft that is fast disappearing."[40] He was undaunted by the arduousness of assembling a database of pottery designs, a process that Bunzel called laborious and time consuming, "as any archaeologist will agree."[41]

Chap also reiterated his belief that his research ought to be published; Hewett repeated that lack of money for printing illustrations was the reason why the school procrastinated in publishing his articles.[42] Lack of funds also meant limited access to the pueblos (aside from Bradfield's sporadic jaunts there) so town resources would be crucial, including paid informants. Chap began photographing all the pottery in local shops and the historical society's collection, which contained excellent groups of Zia, Acoma, and Zuni ware, but only a few mediocre specimens from Tewa, and nothing from Cochiti or Santo Domingo. This imbalance bothered him, so on his rare visits to those pueblos he recorded a body of designs for future publication. He created beautiful mounted panels for display at the museum and use in talks at clubs, classes, and Indian schools. In the summer of 1921, they were exhibited as far away as Salt Lake City.

During this time, museum personnel came and went and remaining staff took on new duties. Paul Walter left his position in 1920 to take up banking, though he continued devoting editorial time to *El Palacio*. Archaeologists Bloom and Bradfield assumed various administrative and curatorial positions. Currelly invited Bradfield to train for his new responsibilities at the Royal Ontario Museum, so Hewett approved his two-month leave in the spring of 1922. Bradfield wrote Nusbaum, "I sure need the raise in salary; perhaps the coming trip to Toronto will help out some; that will quiet H's remarks to others that I have never been anywhere, and have never had any 'training.'"[43] Sam Huddleson covered carpentry, maintenance, and the logistics associated with exhibits. Parsons, appointed director for the thriving Museum of Fine Arts in 1920, supported artistic experimentation, though he was a traditionalist in his own work. His frequent granting of museum wall space to modernists gradually became a point of contention in Santa Fe, as some felt he gave them an unfair advantage; art patrons squawked, for instance, over an exhibit of B. J. O. Nordfeldt's work. Hewett, in San Diego, worried that state allocations were in jeopardy, so in early 1922 he released Parsons and redistributed his tasks. In April, he designated Chap curator of art (later retitled associate in art). Chap, like Parsons, was seen as able to work with high-strung personalities; unlike Parsons, he was not known as a proponent of modernism. Chap was not pleased at the prospect of dealing with artists' egos. He and Kate had a place amid the roiling eddies of the town's social whitewater, and he knew well how wild the ride could be.

Santa Fe was a colorful stage for artists' lifestyles. It contained microneighborhoods where many colonists resided in adobe "urban compounds." Such were the modernists on Camino del Monte Sol who inserted their bon vivant into Santa Fe conventions. They flaunted prohibition, eluding apprehension by moving their madcap bootleg bashes from residence to residence, one step ahead of the law. Many women artists and writers sported geometrically bobbed hair and dressed in velvet blouses and Indian jewelry, a unique regional costume. Some of the wealthy single women who arrived in Santa Fe, like artist Dorothy Stewart or the White sisters, Amelia Elizabeth and Martha, became benefactresses to the colony's pet causes and entertained modernist and traditionalist alike. Writer Mary Austin and her friend Mabel Dodge Luhan, whose libertine salons and raucous arguments with her Indian (and fourth!) husband were a Taos soap opera, became forces to be reckoned with in both art colonies. The black sheep of East Coast society families, often homosexuals, found haven in a town where the flamboyant poet Witter Bynner lived with his lover and secretary Willard "Spud" Johnson—before Mabel enticed Spud to her Taos compound. Spud delivered biting social commentary via the *Laughing Horse*, a Taos paper—conservatives and stodges beware!

Gradually, longtime supporters of Hewett, such as politicians and businessmen, gave their influence to the art colony and its bedfellow Senator Bronson Cutting, who commanded the favor of many Spanish descendants and was Hewett's political foe. Cutting, owner of the *Santa Fe New Mexican*, was abetted by his editor, Dana Johnson, who sympathized with the artists and literati. The colonists began to dominate society with the help of the press. Many were dedicated nonconformists seeking radical artistic expression, sexual emancipation, or narcissistic fame, and this element lent an air of license to the town and notoriety to the Museum of Fine Arts. Santa Fe absorbed and accommodated them, relishing the diversion as long as the colonists paid their bills, were productive citizens, and did not publicly stray too far from conventional relationship norms. Kate was at ease in company that bridged the reverent and the irreverent; Chap, ever inherently diplomatic and conventional, seemed a safe and pragmatic replacement for Parsons.

If Chap was relatively boring in Santa Fe society, a glimpse at his brother Dwight's family during this period is a study in contrasts. Though Chap was the soul of respectability by art colony standards, his sister-in-law on Chicago's North Shore looked askance at their casually provincial Southwest kin. Dwight had married Ethel Carpenter in South Bend, Indiana, and they eventually settled in the more affluent Chicago suburb of Wilmette. As recalled by their son John, Uncle Bud's visits to their Wilmette home were rare and provocative. Dwight would receive a surprise phone call at work: "Hello, Chap. Chap here. I'm in Chicago." After a stunned pause, Dwight would invite him to come home for dinner, to which Kenneth would respond, "Why, I'd love to." Dwight's call to Ethel would send her into a tizzy. While Dwight picked up "Bud," she would scrap whatever ordinary menu she had planned and scramble to prepare a fine roast for the surprise guest. Later she would privately give Dwight an earful. By John's account, Ethel had social aspirations, hence her criticism of such inconsiderate behavior.

Worse still, in Ethel's eyes, was Chap's outrageous wife, who did not accompany him on these trips but whose growing architectural business in Santa Fe lent her an exaggerated bohemian reputation back east. In Ethel's world, Kate's tardy dinners would have been deemed offensive, while her plays and poems would have associated her with those suspiciously libertine Santa Fe females. John's mother thus frowned on that mysterious aunt, what with her unladylike clambering up and down ladders in men's work duds—generally a serviceable pair of jodhpurs. Local legend has it that one afternoon Kate arrived at La Fonda in her usual professional garb. She and her friends had a regular table for tea, but the maître d' asked that she leave because of her attire. The following day, the entire group came in trousers, and the management capitulated. Ethel was probably unaware that La Fonda was the only Harvey hotel that did not require men to wear a coat and tie in the dining room, simply because it was not realistic to expect the artists to comply. So when tales of Kate's spunk made their way to the Wilmette dining room, perhaps relayed with a twinkling eye by Bud himself, Ethel's final word to Dwight was always a rebuking "That Kate!"

Chap may have been bemused by his Illinois relatives' mores, but he was not an unruly artist himself. He did not want to assume authority over them either; after all, these were people with whom he and Kate intersected socially. Hewett's naming him curator, and assigning him Parsons's multiple responsibilities to boot, thus nettled him. In April 1922, he wrote Hewett to protest, implying that he would quit over the hours robbed from his survey. El Toro's response to "My dear Chap" began solicitously enough:

> I have had little time to think over the problems you present but can give you my first impressions now and we will discuss the matters when I get to Santa Fe, in about three weeks.
>
> . . . There was no thought of piling this all upon you. [Parsons] did a good deal for the photographic department and that, of course, should go to Bradfield. . . . There is no reason why the management of the studios should be turned over to you. . . . It can be handled from the Museum office better than any other way. Attention to visiting artists and people of note is a part of the duties of every member of the staff. It should never be made the peculiar province of any one.

Then, as if Hewett's patience were thinning, he shifted his tone and launched into a parental lecture:

> This brings the work that rather naturally falls to you down to the one thing, management of the Gallery. Systematic handling of this can certainly reduce it far beyond the requirement of half time which you apprehend. In the first place, the physical part of it, the actual hanging and taking down of pictures, should all go to Sam and his aide, you simply telling them what to do. Dealing with the artists, deciding what to hang and where, and when, can take much

or little time depending upon the method you adopt. Discussion with a good many Art Museum directors and with the New Mexico group of artists in the Nordfeldt case last fall, brought out the practically unanimous expression that what [Victor] Higgins calls the "steam roller method" is the only satisfactory one, that in the long run the artists themselves can see its superiority. You can take it entirely in your own hands, or you can protect yourself with a hanging committee of which you will be chairman. . . . Make all your decisions at the studio where the work is received, turn it over to Sam with directions to hang, and then retire to your own den. I certainly should not give more than thirty minutes a day to handling that business . . . or one hour if you think more is essential, and post that on the street door of the studio, making it clear that you do not discuss Gallery matters at any other time.

Finally, Hewett went for the jugular:

Suppose we try it out on some such plan for a while and if we find it won't work then we will face the problem of relieving you of everything except your research work. I do not know that you have any reason to hope for such a condition unless you can attain . . . [financial independence]. Even so, you probably would find, as has almost everyone who has been so situated, that some institutional connection was desirable and if it came to that I doubt if any institution in the country could give you a larger proportion of your time for research than we can. . . . It is a question to be seriously considered, however, whether or not one gains in the long run by cutting loose from all activities other than one's own narrow line of investigation. Personally, I am inclined to think that one's mind is made and kept a better instrument if under the daily requirement of meeting some situations and making prompt decisions outside of its own favorite rut[.] . . . I would recommend that you go ahead on approximately the lines I have suggested.[44]

"Favorite rut." There it was, like shaming a child into compliance. Defeated, Chap took on the curatorship, attending to his survey when possible. There were diversions: his 1922 *Art and Archaeology* article, "Life Forms in Pueblo Pottery Decoration," allowed him to detail the continuous use of symbolism from prehistoric pots through post-Spanish pottery. "It is surprising indeed to find them still a decorative element in modern Pueblo art," he wrote.[45] In July, he accompanied Hewett on a trip into southern Chihuahua, where Hewett wanted to research the Tarahumara Indians and where the prehistoric Casas Grandes pottery was of benefit to Chap. Other expeditions were also turned to advantage, such as the October trip south that same year with Bloom and Bradfield to make a preliminary study of Mimbres ware.

By hook and crook, Chap managed to amass over seven hundred pictures of specimens, nearly half of them from San Ildefonso as production increased and the market for black-on-black ware brought potters into town. Though potters made fewer polychrome wares at San Ildefonso, Chap continued to share design resources, such as the photos of old pots that he showed Tonita Roybal. If it were in his power, he desired to foster a renaissance in historic designs, which would serve the interests of potters and their art as he understood them. The larger problem of conserving the legacy of a culture and people that were not his own presented a challenge. Did he bridge the culture gap by referencing his formative experiences as an art student? There are clues that he did. At the Art Institute of Chicago, his ABC's in fine art were derived from Euro/American culture; artistry was honed by the discipline of producing countless sketches of anatomy elements from plaster casts, paintings of still life arrangements, and copies of masterpieces. Though his schooling there was brief, he was at an impressionable age when the importance of observation, of repetitive drawing practice, and of delving into his cultural treasures were drilled into him, shaping his understanding of what it meant to be an artist.

This foundation seems to have informed how he set about gently guiding potters to their disappearing legacy, allowing them to build on it, while trying to avoid cross-cultural influence as much as possible. By the early 1920s, Chap had amassed hundreds of Pueblo design masterpieces for the potters to observe, copy, practice, vary, and improve as they would within their own tradition. Rounding up a collection of pots was the desideratum, but that still lay ahead. Chap had made a good start by placing their design heritage in their hands and generating informed demand for their works. He was able to gather accurate data on each of twenty-three pueblos. He uncovered the history of potting in each one as well as charted its decline and learned how many women were currently throwing pots, the quality of available clays, and the importance of pottery as an economic resource. He provided an evaluation of its quality using his standards. Many of his colleagues viewed the pottery situation as deplorable. Chap concluded otherwise, demonstrating that more production occurred than was considered market worthy.

Meanwhile, a proposal in the spring of 1922 by Rose Dougan offered new hope for creating a market for Pueblo wares. *El Palacio* published a March announcement that Dougan would donate $85 as prize money for the best Indian arts to be exhibited during the September Fiesta. This competitive element redefined the usual display and sale of Indian arts and crafts. The article predicted that Dougan's strategy would grow in importance with each succeeding year. The May issue publicized a list of monetary prizes for the best pottery, crafts, Indian students' reproductions of designs, and drawings or watercolors of Indian ceremonies and occupations. This list reflected not only Dougan's values and Chap's agenda for preserving authenticity but also the growing enthusiasm of modernist artists over the "discovery" of Indian painting.

The time was ripe for the success of private strategies to educate Anglo consumers on fine authentic Indian art and boost direct-to-consumer markets for it. Twenty years earlier, Bureau of Indian Affairs commissioner Jones had supported Native arts and crafts by encouraging the use of traditional standards, materials, and techniques. Changing leadership, uneven implementation of government certification initiatives, and World War I resulted in diminishing federal interest and the failure of Jones's plan, but meanwhile an economic momentum had been established. By 1920, sales in Indian products had reached a reported national high of almost $2,000.

In Santa Fe, the Dougan–von Blumenthal initiative had made local gains. Chap, Bradfield, and Bertha Van Stone now oversaw museum sales of acceptable pottery. Kidder noted that the "museum bought many good pieces, and Mr. Chapman, who from the beginning had been a leading spirit in the attempt at rehabilitating the art, himself purchased large amounts of pottery, never refusing a creditable piece, never accepting a bad one."[46] Burgeoning tourism was such that by the end of August 1922 the museum alone sold over $900 worth of ceramics. That venture was doomed, however. The market value of pottery was stabilizing in the Indians' favor, aided commercially by former staff member Olive Wilson who had opened a Santa Fe teashop with a sideline of fairly priced Pueblo products for which she took a small commission. Local tax-paying dealers, resenting competition, began protesting the state-supported museum's sales. Chap had foreseen their complaints. By way of phasing out museum pottery sales but still keeping Indian art alive there, he recruited Pueblo artisans for ongoing summer demonstrations on the patio. This was soon commandeered by Twitchell,

> who really is the moving spirit in most of these things. . . . Twitchell happened along one day, stood around for a while, and finally said to Chap, "You can't handle this; turn it over to me." Chap told him he was pleased to do so, and in less than a week Twitchell was headed for Washington to obtain support for his Indian Fair. It was held in the Armory and it was surprising what they had on exhibition. The Indian Department in Washington took a big interest and exhibits were sent from nearly all corners of the country, many of them very fine.[47]

Encouraged, Dougan enlarged her original offer. She put forward a $1,000 bond, the interest to be used as prize money then and in the future. The chamber of commerce supplemented these funds. Judges were enlisted for dance events and displays.

The first Indian Fair, forerunner to Indian Market, held in the armory building in Santa Fe, New Mexico, 1922. (Courtesy of Palace of the Governors [MNM/DCA], 1501.)

The exhibition of pots, baskets, beadwork, silver, embroidery, and weaving represented not only the Pueblos but also other nations including Sioux, Ute, Apache (Jicarillo and Mescalero), and Navajo. Entry requirements were strict: works must be of traditional materials and methods, and the designs had to be specific to each pueblo or nation. Thus, Indian Fair was one of the first occasions in which Chap made concrete his own theories about each pueblo creating decoration specific to their culture. The design criteria also reflect a strong emphasis on pottery decoration as opposed to form. As one of three judges who would ensure that objects met the established criteria, Chap was forced to consider what "traditional" meant. It implied designs, materials, or methods that had been handed down within a pueblo or other nation. The potters' culture guided his thinking. While the precise Euro/American term "tradition" might not exist within their language, Pueblo artists embraced the concept of *doing things right*. "We don't have a word for tradition," Pueblo dignitary Gabrielita Nave explained during the mid-1980s, "but we do have words for 'old-timey' and 'done in the right way,' because these are important to us."[48]

Chap's objectives for the fair were to (1) encourage Indian arts and crafts; (2) revive old arts, preserving each pueblo's characteristics; (3) create markets for all Indian products, products that would be priced reasonably and fairly; and (4) guarantee Indian authenticity and fair business practices from retailers in return. All arts were represented, but pottery dominated. The three-day fair opened September 4, breaking economic ground that precipitated a minor clash between Chap and Hewett.

> *Shortly before the opening hour, Dr. Hewett, who had been giving the displays a hurried inspection came to me and said, "Chap, some of the pottery prices are getting out of hand. Tonita Roybal has an ordinary size bowl priced at $12.00! You ought to do something about it." I reminded Dr. Hewett that the San Ildefonso potters had come a long way since he gave them their first encouragement, and that they knew a lot more about selling than any of us. Then I asked, "Do you know any better way for them to find what the buyers will pay?" He had no ready answer.*
>
> *I had admired the bowl, a little gem, and within a half hour after the doors were opened, I took the first opportunity to listen for comments on it, but was delighted to find that its price tag had already been marked "SOLD." That meant that the price, plus the Fair's ten percent handling charge, came to a total of $13.20.*[49]

The three-day fair was promptly lauded in the news:

> Talk of decadence of Indian arts and crafts has rather disappeared since the opening of the First Annual Southwest Indian Fair in connection with the Santa Fe Fiesta this year. . . . Their art is unique[.] . . . [I]t is a genius for decoration unequaled by any nation of people, inherent and inherited. . . . It would be civilization's misfortune if they and their works should be lost to us. . . . It is with great satisfaction that we observe this great movement[,] . . . eliminating carefully all that which is not truly Indian and fostering and encouraging that which is the real thing.[50]

Many labeled the fair a "revival" in Indian arts, a term used in the late 1890s when ethnologist Jesse Fewkes earned a reputation for promoting a pottery "revival" in the Hopi pueblo of Hano through his interactions with the artist Nampeyo. In 1923, Fewkes (now chief of the Bureau of Ethnology) congratulated Chap for "setting before the Indians the art of their ancestors as an incentive to do the best that is in them in that line."

> [Nampeyo] was a true artist and her mission was to get my permission to copy some of the beautiful conventional symbols of the ancient Hopi. She asked for

paper and pencil and with her mate she made drawings of the most striking examples of ancient Hopi art revealed by our excavations. On my return to Hopi country the following year I found she had made a great many copies of Sikyatki ware to sell to visitors, and on subsequent visits she was employed by [Fred] Harvey to make more. In fact she never went back to the old Tewa symbols with which she decorated her pottery before 1895. Nampeyo was a true artist; she not only recognized the superiority of the work of the ancients, but likewise adapted it and created new designs following the lines of the ancients, and much of the pottery we now find on sale from Los Angeles to Santa Fe may practically be called the creation of Nampeyo.[51]

Thus Fewkes credited Nampeyo with revitalizing Hopi ware. In the same way, neither Maria Martinez nor any potter needed an Anglo to tell her how to make good authentic pottery. All who saw Maria and Julian's pots acknowledged their artistry. They both had a natural curiosity about decorative ware. They were also eager to obtain prehistoric and historic designs because so many of the pueblos' best pots were now in remote collections, as Maria had ruefully reminded Chap. He could not pilfer national museums and restore pots to the pueblos. But he hoped to compile for them an accessible, comprehensive visual vocabulary.

Indian Fair was an ideal opportunity to form a collaboration with the potters—Maria, Tonita Roybal, Lufina Baca, and others—that would serve to bring together pots from each pueblo and at the same time convert exceptional pottery into an economic advantage. Potters may not have verbalized such an idea, but they understood that for pragmatic reasons they needed an endorsement from the dominant Anglo culture to help establish a market for valued Indian art. Assuredly, many Pueblo potters were initially reluctant to risk investing time and energy in good pots for sale, because they had learned to rely on minimal income from travelers who were easily satisfied with imitative raingods. Chap's genius in combating this trend incorporated a missing element: education of Anglos.

Chap had spent hundreds of hours mending pots and classifying potsherds. The experience had given him insight into the difference between a good pot and an exceptional one. The potters' own artistic standards provided them with the same. Chap believed he could help make Indian art standards so clear that Anglo markets would distinguish an exceptional pot from a merely good one. In discerning, establishing, and fulfilling this unique role for himself, Chap was blessed: Maria and Julian were his greatest allies in creating demand for well-made pottery.[52] Many would later call this partnership, which Chap, Maria, and the other potters forged in the early 1920s, a "revival" of Indian arts. More to the point, it was a movement to stimulate sophisticated taste in Anglos.[53] All the ingredients were in place: Pueblo potters who took pride in their art and were open to innovation; a local society of influential artists, writers, and wealthy liberals; and an abundance of southwestern tourists who were eager for a remembrance of their contact with an ancient culture.

While the initial Dougan–von Blumenthal commitment and the Indian Fair flowered into economic advantage for the potters, it also set the precedent that Anglo artists, Chap in particular, would determine the criteria of excellence or taste in decorated pottery. The fair even influenced which style a potter might use, similar to the way Chap had influenced Tonita Roybal when he encouraged her to pursue the black-on-red ware. Such intervention as this was a logical consequence of the perception that Indian art had so devolved that it "inspired both revulsion and paternalism in whites, as well as nostalgic idealization of traditional Indian life."[54] Well-intended Anglo manipulation of product and marketplace has long fueled academic debate, the direction of which depends on the winds of social awareness and political correctness at any given time. In Chap's day, Santa Fe's cross-cultural breeze was stirred by two distinct sources of social conscience: the preservationists and the integrationists. Both grappled with what was in the Indians' best interest. In Paul Horgan's words:

> It was a question which agitated many people in Santa Fe, where partisanships were swift to come on any issue, and violent in their sway, and shrill of claim. Champions of the Indian in his tribal integrity [preservationists] complained that if he became a manufacturer of curios, he would soon be a lost soul among his own kind. Others [integrationists] replied that he would be better served if he had a chance to earn a little money to raise his standard of living into closer conformity with that of the white Americans. The reply to this was that before the white Americans did so much about the Indian they would do well to purify the values of their own society.[55]

The preservationists included many art colonists who were convinced that the Indians' purchase of commercial metal or ceramic housewares and production of tourist trinkets represented a devolution, even extinction, of aboriginal American art. The promotion of "excellence" by this circle of newcomers can be interpreted as self-aggrandizing. Dauber points out that as arbiters of connoisseurship, the art colonists elevated their social status by unconsciously exploiting Indian art; they appropriated it to establish an authoritative niche for themselves, as arbiters of taste.[56] In fact, the artistic and literary subgroup generated a powerful political bloc around Indian-related and other issues, an unprecedented accomplishment for a patchwork of socialites, artists, writers, and assorted eccentrics. Chap's familiarity with traditional pottery design served the aims of these preservationists nicely. On the other hand, his encouragement of artistic experimentation generated pots with modern appeal, enhancing the work of integrationists like Dougan in their economic strategy for viable sales. Chap's commitment to Pueblo art benefited both Anglo factions as well as Pueblo potters and their descendants.

Chap's independence of purpose transcended alliances. His scientific colleagues believed that they were gathering a permanent record of tribal societies that would soon be assimilated by material progress. For Chap, Native art was, as is all art, a living phenomenon. He neither glorified the Indian way of life nor romanticized the Old West. Rather, Chap approached his single-minded interest pragmatically more than sentimentally. He was hardwired for tenacity in collecting and classifying; he was guided by aesthetics, an intuition of the anchoring value of a cultural heritage, and a concern over the inaccessibility of pottery specimens. As today's artists and academicians (both Native and Anglo) debate the merits of the scientists, teachers, and patrons who have intervened in Native art, their only real criticism of Chap's design legacy concerns his penchant for the meticulous. His reproductions of ancient designs reflect his disciplined hand, executed in ink and paint on paper or board; he eliminated irregularities created by yucca brushes on curved, hand-thrown surfaces. Potters who have since copied his legacy have a technical precision not found on historic ware—hence the irony of "authentic" elements subtly "improved" by Chap's artistic style.

For both preservationists and integrationists, the fair was a triumph. It had established success in reinforcing the Indians' art heritage and also in educating Anglo buyers. The institutional affiliation granted the work legitimacy not attached to selling through curio dealers as well as a more lucrative venue. The first annual Indian Fair exposed Pueblo artists to inspiring works from their own communities, but the Anglo style of recognition (the incentive of cash prizes and potential sales for individuals) was awkward for the communally minded potters. Awards went to Lufina Baca of Santa Clara and Tonita Roybal, but Maria won the most, a whopping $23! Sensitive to how this inequity would set her apart, Maria made it clear to Chap that she wanted no more prize money until other potters from her pueblo had earned monetary awards.

Accommodating Maria's wishes was difficult, given the Anglo belief that art is more valuable if done by an outstanding artist. And the Anglos believed that the Indians' pottery would become even more valuable if the potters would sign the wares. To the potters, though, signing wares was nonsense; each artisan's unique design work was recognizable within a pueblo, no matter how subtle the differences. Anglo influence prevailed, through the persuasion of Chap and Chester Faris, superintendent of the Santa Fe Indian School. According to Spivey, Maria began regularly signing her pottery in 1923, and by 1925 the custom was well established by Maria, Tonita Roybal, and others. It was probably Chap who suggested that Julian's name be added to the pots he painted.[57] Faris felt it was important to keep the signatures familiar to the audience, and recommended that "Maria" or "Marie" be used rather than the various spellings of her Tewa name, Poveka. For her part, she found a way consistent with her culture to utilize the value of her name. She signed pots not exclusively her own but which others had shaped, polished, or painted and on which she added some finishing.

When it came to acknowledging the fair's success, Hewett lacked Maria's generous humility. Though attached to the school-run fiesta, the fair had autonomy: a separate organizational committee, outside financial assistance, and break-even gate admissions. Who should get credit for this remarkable achievement? Chap acknowledged Dougan as the prime mover. Wallace Springer identified Twitchell as the man who put Chap's patio exhibit on the national map. Clearly, many people could rightly "sign the pot." However, a mere month after Fiesta ended, Hewett stepped forward. His director's report and a subsequent *El Palacio* article implied that the fair was a proprietary feather in the school's cap. He lauded the school's role in the art revival and market generation. He boasted that the exhibition had resulted in the formation of certain organizations within the school itself to foster Indian arts and crafts. Coming from a man who routinely failed to fund Chap's work or collect pots and who arbitrarily dispersed prized pots, such posturing must have irked Chap. He may have turned to his simpatico colleagues for consolation. Even two years later, when Dougan's and Twitchell's names had slipped through the cracks while the fair's renown grew, Chap received a Denver news clipping from his friend Allen True, with a penciled note at the top, "Perhaps you have seen this?" It said of Chap, "It was this quiet, but effective archaeologist, that first suggested the Southwestern Indian fair."[58]

The success of the fair gave Chap hope for the future of potterymaking. But he continued to mull over Maria's point that since he had helped take all their old pottery away they couldn't remember the designs. "For the first time I realized what we had been doing to our Indian friends."[59] Motivated by a desire to place historic pottery in professional hands rather than see it lugged off by amateurs, he had assisted out-of-state museums in acquisitions. *This I had considered a worthwhile activity for it insured good care and use of rare specimens where they could be available for study.*[60] Study by whom? How many Pueblo people would ever visit Toronto or tour San Diego? In hindsight, he regretted his role in implementing Hewett's directives. His remorse over the fate of the Normal University collection was still fresh. To guarantee authenticity in Indian art, it would take more than designs on cardboard or published in articles.

Something—perhaps Hewett's spurious claim of the school's role—pushed him to new resolve. He needed a way to collect and preserve the fine old wares where they could be studied by the potters, though a purchase fund was unimaginable. According to Chap, it was Hewett's refusal to acquire historic and contemporary pottery "that led me in 1920 to break away from archaeology and to begin a study of the surviving arts of the Southwestern tribes."[61] Later, he came to believe his persistent devotion to that dreamed-of survey led to the fulfillment of his true desire. Following the fair, an autumn dinner party resulted in a venture that would rely on Chap's wide knowledge and connections to establish a permanent collection of indigenous art.

CHAPTER 8

POTTERY AND POLITICS

Autumn evenings in Santa Fe are delicious reminders of how New Mexico enchants: while sunlight fades on purple asters and golden aspens, a hint of winter slips into the air. Inside, a fire has been set, so the scent of piñon accompanies anyone who strolls along winding lanes past adobe homes. On such an evening in 1922, Santa Fe perhaps cast her spell over an intimate dinner gathering. When party chitchat turned to Indian pots, the result was an enduring movement to honor and safeguard Indian art.

As legend holds, writer Elizabeth Shepley Sergeant hosted the dinner party. She and her guests exemplified Santa Fe's new cultural guise: Sergeant, who was dividing her time between Tesuque, New Mexico, and New York City, was a relative newcomer to Santa Fe. She was also a friend of Amelia Elizabeth White (known as Elizabeth) from Bryn Mawr and a member of the American Indian Defense Association.[1] Dr. Harry Mera had just permanently moved to Santa Fe but could be considered "old" Santa Fe because of his series of visits over the years. He was a district official with the county health office and an amateur archaeologist, who was "for twenty years a student of Indian crafts and unusually well informed on pottery."[2] An unidentified artist and poet completed the group.[3] At some point, the diners' conversation centered on the degradation of Pueblo pottery, a trend toward cultural and spiritual compromise in their eyes. They probably bemoaned tourists who reinforced trinket production, decrying the loss of historic pottery through damage and scattered collections.

> The hostess complained because a servant had broken a fine old Zuni olla. Dr. Mera said that perhaps it could be put together again, so she gave the broken olla to him. . . . Dr. Mera showed the olla to Dr. Chapman, and while talking to him asked if something couldn't be done to save the good material before it all disappeared; that Mera had room in his house to store the things collected. That was when the idea of the [Pueblo Pottery Fund] came to them, and a little group was formed, to save the crafts for the Indians, themselves.[4]

This new group included Mera, Sergeant, and Chap, who was asked to help organize their efforts. They were soon joined by Wesley Bradfield. Motivated by "the need of prompt and vigorous action in order to save the arts of the Southwestern tribes for future generations of craftsmen" they dubbed themselves the Pueblo Pottery Fund.[5] Mera became chairman and Chap curator. They were literally "midwives attending the birth of the Fund," midwives who, "having brought it into this world, . . . continued to tend it with vigilance, brains, and persuasive determination."[6] The mended olla was the first catalogued item in what was intended to be an aggregate of about fifteen pots from each pueblo. The fund was significant in that, unlike at other institutional collections, artistic merit was the acceptance criterion. It was the founders' intention to make accessible to potters the finest available examples from their own ancestry. As the number of pots grew, so did the cultures represented; the collection eventually included wares from pueblos in which the art of potterymaking had declined substantially or was virtually nonexistent.[7]

The pots were to be inspirational models. Though archaeological evidence pointed to a dynamic history of adaptation, the founders turned to the past because they were more concerned with what they and a host of scientists believed was the deterioration of a great indigenous culture through outside contact.[8] According to anthropologist Bernstein, "This step was viewed neither as the introduction of foreign designs nor as a scheme for economic gain; rather, it would allow Pueblo culture to return to its former high level of civilization."[9] As a matter of conscience, the fund's members felt bound to intervene. They found willing and eager collaborators among the potters.

The logistics of the infant organization unfolded organically. Initially, each fund member personally donated one or more pots to form a nucleus for the collection. The founders then leaned on friends, who in turn solicited contributions from every part of the country. Additional support came from trader James MacMillan whose Spanish and Indian Trading Company had the cream of the pottery business. The fund also worked with another prominent dealer, James L. Seligman, and Herman Schweizer of the Fred Harvey Company, who could be counted on giving them first refusal. Purchase decisions were easy. Chap and Mera could hold a street corner meeting and decide virtually anything.[10] As he had promised to do, Mera housed the collection. Chap privately sent residents and tourists alike to view it, resulting in individual contributions of as much as $100 toward the purchase of specimens. The fund soon held twenty pieces.

Chap spoke of his early fund work as simply a "most gratifying diversion." It was much more. Here at last was the chance to collect actual pots, not simply photos or cards with reproduced designs. If the pots still existed and were wisely chosen, the resulting collection would represent the design standards for each pueblo. Chap discovered that there were indeed good historic pots yet to be had at the pueblos and that the prices were reasonable, given what dealers charged for comparable material from other cultures.[11]

His subsequent actions suggest this promising endeavor was more than a satisfying pas-
time. Nearly fifty years old, he was galvanized into very non-Chap behavior. He exercised
uncharacteristic outreach, practically strong-arming potential donors and improvising
fund-raising tactics that he would draw on again in the next decade. He broadened the
fund's economic base by recruiting local shopkeepers and traders, offering them silk-
screened fund member identification cards for multipurpose publicity:

> These little placards were to be displayed in the show windows of the dealers to
> indicate, in a mild sort of way, that the dealer . . . might be likely to have a stock
> of very nice Indian material for sale.
>
> It was hoped that the dealer would demand better quality from the Indian,
> benefiting the Indian with better prices, that the dealer could charge more and
> thus make more profit and the buyer would benefit by having an article which
> was much more satisfying in the long run. This worked to some extent![12]

The seed planted at Sergeant's dinner party took root. Chap carved out extra hours
to capitalize on local interest in Indian art on the fund's behalf. The timing was most
opportune. Since the arrival of the railroad, the social order of local Republican elites
had gradually destabilized. The tourist influx and the settling of art colonists resulted in
"new groups with a stake in a revised image of what was central and what was peripheral
to the region."[13] The pots that occupied so much of Chap's life suddenly took on political significance for Santa Fe Anglos. Overlapping the fair and the fund's launch, Chap
and Kate became involved in the newcomer-driven movement to defeat the Bursum
Bill in Washington.

On July 20, 1922, Senator Holm O. Bursum (R-NM) had introduced a bill to settle
the claims of non-Indian residents on Pueblo lands. The measure had the support of
Secretary of the Interior Albert B. Fall, a past senator (R-NM, later praised by Hewett's
board for his support of the Indian Fair). The bill was designed to sort out the jumble of
Spanish, Mexican, and United States land grants affecting 60,000 of the 340,000 acres
to which Pueblos held title. Any non-Pueblo who had "peaceable possession" backed
by land grant would be deemed full owner; trespassers could purchase their tracts following a favorable judgment in court. This action was intended to curry the favor of the
Hispanic citizenry, who comprised many of the affected settlers. The Bursum Bill also
provided that internal Pueblo disputes were to be settled in federal courts rather than
under Indian jurisdiction, thus jeopardizing Pueblo cultural autonomy. A measure that
would have passed a few years earlier now met unanticipated resistance as Santa Fe writers and artists raised a national alarm.

Defeating the measure depended on two factors: nationwide awareness of Native art and its economic potential for Indians and the influential personal networks of the art colonists.

With regard to the first, Indian artists were now gaining a wider audience (and therefore the value of their cultures was becoming more widely appreciated) thanks to New York exhibits of the self-taught Pueblo watercolorists who had been encouraged by Hewett, Chap, William Penhallow Henderson, and others. The works of Julian and Crescencio Martinez, Alfonso Roybal (Awa Tsireh), Fred Kabotie, and others set style precedents that would dominate Indian painting for nearly fifty years. Anglo modernists incorporated Pueblo motifs in their work. Exhibit catalogues and art reviews popularized the vitality of "red" culture. This growing consciousness circled back to Santa Fe, where the ready availability of Native ceramics drew tourists in such numbers as to make the Pueblo Indians both a local economic asset and an ascendant factor in regional identity, over Anglos and Hispanics.[14] The desire and energy around preserving Pueblo culture through efforts such as Indian Fair and the new Pueblo Pottery Fund resembled the will catalyzed by the New-Old Santa Fe architectural movement but from a newer base with wider repercussions.

The second factor, networks, resulted in political strength. Chap and Kate became members of the fledgling New Mexico Association on Indian Affairs (NMAIA), founded by writers Alice Corbin Henderson, Elizabeth Sergeant, Mary Austin, and writer/socialite Mabel Dodge Luhan to oppose the bill. Kate's friend Margaret McKittrick chaired the group. They were soon joined by Elizabeth White, whose father was an owner of the *New York Evening Post*. They capitalized on prominent connections, especially in the General Federation of Women's Clubs, to raise the hue and cry. In New York City, the Eastern Association on Indian Affairs (EAIA) was established, and shortly afterward in Chicago the American Indian Defense Association was born. At least seventeen Pueblo leaders, backed fully by the Pueblo people, worked ceaselessly on the campaign; many joined the lecture circuit to publicize violations of Pueblo rights and the disaster that would ensue should the Bursum Bill succeed.[15] In Santa Fe, the distinction between the land issue and the Pueblo art revival movement was blurred; the local reformers used the Pueblo Pottery Fund to draw attention to the economic value and welfare of the Pueblo Indians, overshadowing the concerns of Republican politicians and pushing rural Hispanics into the background.[16] Within days of the 1922 fair, the *New Mexican* jumped on the bandwagon. It touted the "great movement underway to re-energize the creative arts of the Pueblos," and exhorted, "They cannot develop their ancient arts and crafts for the delight and education of the world unless they can continue their communal existence."[17]

Pro-Pueblo propaganda began appearing in the national press, and a flood of outraged correspondence poured into Washington. In New Mexico, the newfound clout of the artists, writers, and patrons surprised and disturbed the Santa Fe Old Guard who had viewed them as a harmless aggregate of eccentrics and as a tourist attraction. By year's end, the Bursum Bill was effectively moribund. The NMAIA, having lost its raison d'être, might have disbanded except that then the specter of drought and disease at the pueblos caught their attention. In January 1923, Lansing Bloom and Chap motored to Santo Domingo to check out rumors of destitution there. Other affected pueblos were San Ildefonso, Tesuque, and Santa Clara. Their overlapping needs—economic, political, social, and cultural—generated multiple commitments for Chap and the anthropologists and artists who now took on social reform as well as art preservation. The NMAIA and the Pueblo Pottery Fund shared membership as well as agendas. The former, which raised relief monies by, for example, putting on plays, focused on the material welfare of the Indians, but an ongoing passion of its members was the promotion of Native art, especially pottery, as viable economic alternatives to farming. While the reformers' agenda was narrowly focused, at another level their concerted activities engendered for them an identity as a dominant new group in Santa Fe.[18]

During this time, Chap continued to make use of whatever speaking and publishing opportunities the museum afforded, but his work for the fund provided additional data to enrich his hypotheses. In 1923 he delivered his paper "The Pottery Decorations of Santo Domingo and Cochiti Pueblos" at the New Mexico Association for Science in Las Vegas, New Mexico. In it, he argued that post-Spanish pottery "shows little or no trace of European influence, either in form or decoration" and also described how to distinguish between good and bad pottery. The summary published the following year in *El Palacio* disseminated his belief to a wider audience.[19] Later, Chap modified his argument, noting, for example, that in fact the addition in pottery decoration of the flower symbol was a result of Spanish influence.[20] Contemporary experts observe that vessel form also changed as Pueblos regrouped after the Spanish invasion and trading among Indians came to a halt.[21] Chap's assertion, however, was intended to establish post-Spanish pottery as a continuous element of traditional art among the southwestern Indians. Even today, the making, form, and decoration of pottery is much the same as it was in prehistoric times, having weathered changes wrought not only by Spanish guns and traders' dollars but even Chap's own zeal in encouraging the resurrection of traditional styles and motifs.

In the spring of 1923, Hewett was arranging for an eight-month sabbatical in the Middle East, to begin in August. Springer tapped Chap once again for full-time illustration services for another one of his publications, so Chap was given a hiatus from museum work that lasted about eighteen months. Meanwhile, planning got underway for the second annual Indian Fair. Chap served on the committee, chaired by John D.

DeHuff, superintendent of the Santa Fe Indian School. (Since 1918, John's wife, Elizabeth, had taken an active role encouraging young Pueblo watercolorists who attended classes there.) Starting months ahead, they decided to hold the fair in the armory from September 3 to 7 so that it would partly coincide with Fiesta, which would end on September 5. A month before the fair, the Hewetts embarked on their journey. Despite the fair committee's efforts, the entries were not up to par. In Chap's estimation, he had lost a number of Pueblo contacts while he was away working for Springer, and he believed that adversely affected the caliber of fair participation. DeHuff was more optimistic, declaring that the fair showed that the trend had been halted wherein Indians had been laying aside their arts and handicrafts.

Partly to address the problem of getting Chap out to the pueblos, Rose Dougan intended to put up $1,000 for an Indian art education fund. It was also a step in her plan to win Bureau of Indian Affairs funding to teach Indian art in Indian schools and use Indian Service workers to encourage Pueblo crafts. Although Charles H. Burke, the commissioner of the bureau, favored assimilation of Native Americans over preserving Native culture, Dougan's model gained his endorsement. She advanced $200 to Chap for three months' fieldwork doing art supervision in the Indian schools during the 1923–24 winter.

However, Chap's commitments to Springer's crinoid project limited his availability, and $200 was inadequate for the fieldwork as conceived. He therefore used the seed money to assemble photographs and designs, sending them to field supervisors to distribute among the boarding and day schools. This method at least educated pupils, especially girls, on each pueblo's designs and improved their fair entries. As the design revival progressed, Chap was still dealing with the confusion of roles among the museum-school, the fund, and the NMAIA. By December 1923, McKittrick felt that the NMAIA could relax its Washington campaign and initiate a program for the betterment of Pueblo arts and crafts. She invited Chap to join a planning committee. Chap preferred to unlink arts and crafts from the NMAIA; during the anti-Bursum Bill campaign, the group had aroused some antipathy. He was relieved when McKittrick backed off of Indian art, having come to the realization that NMAIA committee members were already overextended. The NMAIA ended up confining itself to national politics and local relief efforts and intruded only sporadically into Chap's arena thereafter.

As 1923 drew to a close, the Chapmans' Yuletide was enhanced by the visit of muralist Allen True and his wife. They stayed at the Chapel Studio, while True worked on Indian themes for a Denver National Bank mural. The holiday must have rippled with gaiety. Perhaps Chap and True talked shop, discussing both Springer's illustrations and True's concept.

The 1924 New Year came and went. A winter modernist exhibit at the museum provided a town diversion from the February doldrums and an occasion for Chap to muse on modern art. By now, the art colony had gelled into subgroups based not only on mutually beneficial marketing strategies but also on philosophy and style of art. Revolutionaries, traditionalists, postimpressionists—descriptive titles shifted over time. The Museum of Fine Arts continued to sponsor all and sundry. As if still smarting from the 1922 public outcry that resulted in Parsons losing his curatorship, *El Palacio* defended its policy of giving free space to art that reflected cultural progress. If a particular school seemed to dominate a particular exhibit, "it is merely an evidence of an exuberance which no one will condemn, but on the contrary will sincerely welcome."[22] Chap himself defended experimentation even if it resulted in something at odds with his personal aesthetics. His humor and economic savvy quickly surfaced as lines were drawn and the furor over the February exhibit hit the press.

The works of modernists Bakos, Applegate, Dasburg, Mruk, and Nordfeldt filled several alcoves at the art museum. The paintings were interpretations of Southwest themes, the palettes relatively neutral by art colony standards. *El Palacio* reported that this important and praiseworthy display of art manifested earnest expressions of the artists' response to their environment. The article described press reaction as wide ranging and animated. In fact, the *New Mexican* concluded its own review with sarcasm: "There are no jokes in this exhibit. All of the pictures are painted by men who have learned to draw and who know how to mix colors."[23] Spud Johnson issued a rejoinder, asserting that "there are very precious few who would be capable of writing intelligently about the pictures."[24] The gauntlet was thrown.

Chap and a group of cohorts hastily mounted a concurrent "self-expressionist" exhibit in a nearby alcove. Contributors included Chap, Mera, Bradfield, Halseth, Huddleson, and E. Dana Johnson. Letters to the *New Mexican* poured in, signed by the likes of Cockatoo, Cockamingo, Para Queet, Another Parrot, Bughouse, Titmouse, and the Airedale Pup. Flamingo was first into the good-natured fray, opening with "Coronado, we are here! Hail to Halseth, Brad and Chapman! The Banana Bearers of the Expressionists and to their followers hail!" A travesty critic extolling travesty art, Flamingo noted, "Chapman's splitting headache pattern is an excellent piece of work, possibly the effect of too many cracks in pot mending."[25]

A week of riotous commentary flew by before Local Color (Chap's pseudonym) got into the act.[26] In his piece, Chap defended the modernists:

Maybe there is something to their system and maybe it is all bunk; I don't pretend to know, but anyway no one can say that those fellows haven't been looking around the Southwest. I was sizing up some of their landscapes when a squarish built man stepped in beside me. I soon discovered that he had some squarish built ideas that he handed out rough-sawed. . . . "Say, what are they drivin' at, anyway?" he asked[.] "Do you get it?"

"I'm afraid I don't altogether," I confessed. "They have got me guessing too, but I like the stuff for a change because it isn't real. I spend eight hours a day wrangling facts, and when I get through with a week of it, I want to dust off my Sunday imaginator and take it out for an airing. No, I don't claim to know why artists want to take such liberties with the truth, but anyway, you must admit when they made these flights of fancy, they took their jump-off from the Southwest." "Well, for all of me," said the squarish built man, "they can take a jump off the rim of the Grand Canyon!" And with that he made square-toed tracks for the door.

What's the use of arguing with a man like that? Maybe I am too strong for this "Made in New Mexico" stuff, but I look at it this way: it's a business proposition. Our cattle and sheep and wool and copper and a lot of our other products don't advertise us much. They go out of the state in the rough, and when they finally reach the consumer he doesn't know whether they came from New Mexico or South America, and he doesn't care. . . . So I say, "Let's add every style of 'Made in New Mexico' art to the list." . . . What if we don't understand half of it ourselves. Let's encourage the artists to show it here, and to send it out of the state, on a chance that somebody will. As for understanding, I don't claim to understand a New Mexico goat, but if the fellow that eats him, back in Chicago, thinks he's good mutton, que le hace?[27]

Though he did not specify Pueblo art in his letter, the idea of promoting products indigenous to the state reflects his awareness of economic possibilities for Pueblo art as well.

The self-expressionist show evoked a sheet of scrawlings revealing that Chap had ideas about the future of his own Anglo-European heritage in addition to ideas about Indian art. Chap's afterthoughts on the exhibit included a sketch of a hypothetical picture frame with random curves, angles, and points. His scrawled notes foreshadowed modern museum architecture by suggesting that abstract art be exhibited in equally radical buildings. He mused that such art is not served by conventional frames,

> to say nothing of the rectangular requirements of doorways and other details. The rectangular frame of them adds to the subservience by further rectangular details and even realistic details . . . within vertical walls and level floors and the rectangular meeting of the two. . . .

An art gallery itself is in theory a frame for a work of art. Therefore a conventional rectangular frame is superfluous and incongruous when used to delimit the nonconformist exhibits of a work of modern art for it only apes the rigid limitations of architecture rather than conforming with or even fortifying the painting itself.

One difficulty is the lack of imagination in the use of rectangular forms for the flat surfaces for [paintings]. Thus we have the spectacle of modern art thumbing its nose at conventional rectangular architecture, while subserviently bowing to its limitations. . . .

As my first experiment in such an innovation I made a lop-sided pentagonal frame, and then cut my painting to fit it. When my fellow artists saw it, they asked, "How shall we hang it?" I suggested that they provide a hook on the wall, then toss the opus at it, and let chance decide how it should hang.[28]

The self-expressionist episode, which took place four months before Chap finished Springer's illustrations and resumed his art curatorship, illustrates the versatility of a man dedicated to cultural conservation and also able to champion artistic innovation—albeit playfully in this case.

In March 1924, Hewett's sabbatical ended, and he returned to Santa Fe briefly before heading to San Diego in April. Disappointingly, Dougan's program had not produced the results necessary to secure Bureau of Indian Affairs funding, and *El Palacio* reported that an endowment of $25,000 was being sought for the fair. Serendipitously, Springer received an inquiry from Anna Burdick of the Federal Board for Vocational Education. She wrote on behalf of Boston philanthropist and former board member James P. Munroe, who had heard McKittrick speak during her NMAIA fund-raising tour. Munroe was interested in the idea of improving tribal economic status by reviving Indian art. Springer directed Chap to write back, so he seized the chance to request funding for Dougan and himself. Chap opened with a review of the 1923 fair, which outwardly appeared bigger and better than the previous year's event, though insiders knew they had lost ground.

For a general gain over last year, there should be some personal contact with the adult workers in the various crafts. If my engagement with Mr. Springer should terminate by June 1st, I would still have time for some effective field work among the Pueblos, and the results would be sure to appear in the 1924 fair. . . .

Without this field work the fair will continue, of course. . . . But the purpose for which it was founded will be defeated as long as the Indians have no one to tell them what it means.[29]

Chap then described a plan that reveals how much he pondered the problem of how to reach Indians scattered throughout a wide territory. Solving the problem would involve strategic use of existing bureaucracies. Museum staff would tutor a competent art teacher who would make the rounds of Indian boarding and day schools, coordinating Indian art courses. Field-workers would be trained to engage the cooperation of Indian Service agents in the revival, adaptation, improvement, and marketing of artists' wares. It would be more cost effective to produce wood or linoleum block prints of Chap's "vast fund of decorative art" than for Chap to continue doing this work by hand. These designs could even be published in better editions and sold nationally to help the project pay for itself. Chap was sure that degreed applicants would abound once positions were funded. A combination of museum staff, a school arts and crafts teacher, and a part-time field-worker would begin to put a system in place that would gain the approval of the Bureau of Indian Affairs and the support of donors.

He concluded with an astute analysis of the entire situation. The NMAIA and EAIA had overlapping plans for material Pueblo improvements. Though more occupied with legislative concerns, McKittrick was still invested in supporting Indian art education. "This would seem to be a most favorable opportunity to ask for their friendly assistance in a work they could not well handle directly without much needless expense." He pointed out that regional ethnicity was great for the tourist trade and had helped found a direct pottery market but that state monies were inadequate to finance art education in the pueblos. He promised Munroe that A. V. Kidder, Alfred Tozzer, and Joe Spinden would heartily endorse his work. "Everything considered, we have made a most remarkable record in the past ten years."[30]

Unfortunately, Chap had to add a dismal postscript. Dougan's stock dividends had suddenly dried up. There was no start-up program for Munroe to help fund, and Chap's expectation of paid fieldwork was dashed, though the museum made a show of encouraging the work. On the strength of that encouragement, Chap took two weeks to visit Isleta, Laguna, Acomita, and Zuni. He shared his discouragement with his friend, Hodge:

I did manage to furnish a good series of drawings and photographs for Zuni & Laguna, which have brought good results. But then funds gave out (though available for other purposes less urgent in my opinion) and so I simply quit. We did not even get results in our next Indian Fair, as Supt. Bauman held the Zuni exhibit for Gallup alone, and the Laguna teacher failed to send her exhibit in.... It may look as if I am indifferent to the needs of the Pueblo Schools, but there is enough grief here without stirring up more, when there is no backing.[31]

So Chap limped along, making brief autumn treks to the pueblos during those years (one chilly expedition from Gallup to Zuni involved hitching a ride on a mail truck in eight inches of snow). These were multipurpose collecting jaunts for the fair, the fund, and even the museum—or so Chap believed until Hewett again misled him. Hewett delegated the task of buying good specimens "for us" with about $75 he said was available for that purpose to Chap. Chap took him at his word and purchased thirty good pots. He felt duped when Hewett shipped the best of it to the National Museum of Mexico, hoping that the gift would facilitate permission to excavate in that country. Chap was not surprised when the scheme failed, but he was bitter that he had again unwittingly helped expatriate pottery.

Chap began leaning on Roscoe Rice, an Indian Service field agent, whose job was collecting Pueblo statistics for annual reports. Rice's fume-belching, stripped-down Model T occasionally transported pottery from the outlying areas to Santa Fe for Indian Fair and, after 1925, for the fund. In Chap's opinion, it was the best cooperation the fund ever had from an Indian Service employee.

During the years between 1922 and 1925, as Chap's photographic pottery record and the fund's collection bloomed, he continued to act as a design clearinghouse for the potters. Julian himself had amassed prehistoric and historic motifs that were not only San Ildefonso, but also Zuni, Zia, and Acoma. Maria was capable of earning $200 per month, though she limited her sales to half of that in order to avoid offending anyone within the pueblo.

As Chap continued his research and collecting, others also contributed to knowledge of Pueblo pottery. Anthropologist Carl Guthe, museum staffer Odd Halseth, and ethnologist Ruth Bunzel each pursued his or her specific area of interest. Bunzel particularly relied on Chap's assistance in her intimate study of the potters of San Ildefonso. Though each scholar worked independently of the others, they shared resources and mutual respect.

Hewett was due to return to Santa Fe in mid-June. Meanwhile the fund collection was outgrowing Mera's home.[32] Chap, still in Springer's employ, approached Bradfield, acting director/curator in El Toro's absence, and together they arranged for the fund's pottery to be housed on shelves in an unused area of the art museum's basement. In return, the Pueblo Pottery Fund would permit Bradfield to use the collection as an added museum attraction but without reference to its origin or ownership. To avoid any chance of Hewett's disapproval, Bradfield stipulated in writing that the fund's members would not divert visitors' attention to the collection and would limit their soliciting of memberships and contributions to contacts made outside the museum. Photographing or copying of the specimens was to be permitted only with the written approval of the fund.

When Hewett learned of the agreement, he made a derogatory comment that was relayed to Chap by an unnamed staff ally. "Let the boys play with it for a while and then, as usual, when they grow tired of it we will sweep it in."[33]

In early May, ceramicist Frank Applegate, a noted fund supporter, joined Chap and Mera for an evening presentation at the museum on the preservation of pottery and its decoration. The event, which culminated in an audience viewing of the collection, was reported in the *New Mexican*. It was a departure from the terms of the agreement, as it probably resulted in new fund subscribers. But then, Hewett was in California, and Bradfield was Chap's buddy and a fund champion.

Applegate had another pet passion besides Hopi ceramics: Spanish santos, or woodcarvings of saints. He and Mary Austin, another fund backer, had a great interest in preserving Spanish colonial arts and crafts, such as furniture and tinwork. Given the promising resuscitation of Indian art and the fund's financial health, they persuaded the fund's directors to consider enlarging its scope. In 1924, the committee tentatively adopted the Indian and Spanish Crafts Fund as its name, and letterhead stationery was printed. This undertaking catalyzed a period of self-definition for Chap and the other founders. They realized that standards were suffering not just in pottery but also in silver, textiles, and other Indian arts. Thought was given to obtaining specimens of these as they became available, which made more sense than integrating the Austin/ Applegate interests, but it would take time to draft a precise charter and to recruit a representative board.

While the fund's internal activity percolated, life crawled along at the museum. The year had seen a drought and a recession. Museum appropriations were in shortfall as state tax revenues suffered. Hewett was challenged to meet payroll. Though under scrutiny by the AIA for relying on local patrons for school monies instead of securing endowments, Hewett still had the support of R. V. D. Magoffin, a professor of classics and AIA president. Before leaving on his sabbatical in 1923, Hewett had arranged a speaking tour for Magoffin, who was to address the regional archaeological societies throughout "Hewett territory" on the AIA's behalf.[34] However, Magoffin's trip brought unexpected results for Hewett. After he returned east, Magoffin chastised Hewett for his financial shortsightedness and with considerable roughness wrote, "I hope you will not mind my expressing my admiration for the way you are able to bring forward so many good reasons for not doing any of the things I suggest. . . . Los Angeles has gone entirely to pieces, San Diego has practically dropped away to nothing, and the Santa Fe society you rather like to hold as your personal property."[35] Still, Magoffin divulged to Hewett the AIA plans for reorganization, which included broadening its popular base and approaching the Rockefeller Foundation. A Rockefeller endowment not only would enrich the school but also would enable Hewett to launch a grand network of

Southwest and Latin American archaeological institutions. Magoffin told Hewett that the AIA was pursuing an amount of no less than $1 million, and Hewett would have a chance to pitch his dream to John D. Rockefeller Jr.

In 1924, Rockefeller was touring the West with his three oldest sons, John III, Nelson, and Laurance, partly on vacation but also in pursuit of his own vision of educational museums at national parks and other sites. Just as he would soon support the restoration of colonial Williamsburg, a restoration that would turn it into a hands-on learning environment, he was intrigued by the idea of a space that would integrate Native culture, geology, and botany into an educational experience. Rockefeller was accompanied by R. C. Corwin. Corwin was a physician with Rockefeller's Colorado mining interests who also had ties to Hewett and Jess Nusbaum. He served on the museum's board of regents and enjoyed a rewarding friendship with Nusbaum. En route to Santa Fe, the Rockefeller party arrived in Mancos, Colorado, on July 3 where they were met by Nusbaum, who escorted them into Mesa Verde.[36] Rockefeller was captivated by the Nusbaums and their imaginative custodianship. The party visited still unexplored ruins, had a steak-fry, enjoyed an Indian pageant directed by Aileen, and talked about preserving the wilderness and its peoples, finding common ground in the ideal of housing archaeological, historical, and ethnological collections in authentically restored buildings. The Nusbaums did not approach the philanthropist with an alms bowl in hand, which Rockefeller appreciated. Rather, an affinity of spirit moved Rockefeller to commit to supporting Nusbaum's Park Service work and led to the forming of a personal friendship.

Knowing that Rockefeller's next stop was Santa Fe, Nusbaum seized the opportunity to expound on the possibilities awaiting him. It is easy to picture the energetic Jess Nusbaum waxing eloquent, the campfire adding sparkle to his eyes as he described the plaza, his transformation of the Palace of the Governors, the political achievement of the art colony's "Old Santa Fe Style," and his construction of the Museum of Fine Arts modeled after Pueblo missions. He would have described prospects that only such a multicultural and historic location could have fulfilled. On that June night, surrounded by the spirits of those who inhabited Mesa Verde a thousand years earlier, Nusbaum was a free-spirited Kokopelli sowing utopian ground with exciting ideas. Might he unconsciously have added a few seeds of revenge? This was the same person whose spontaneous complicity with Chap, more than a decade earlier, resulted in Chap's pangs of conscience over the mischievous artifact they had planted to "prove" Sylvanus Morley's theories. Did Nusbaum know, through the professional rumor mill or maybe even from Chap, that the AIA was courting the Rockefeller Foundation on Hewett's behalf? A grudge can run deep, and the desire to help a friend or avenge a wrong may lead one to cloak old feelings with rational assessments and noble intentions. Someone as bright and intuitive as Nusbaum would have recognized quickly that Hewett's institutions and management style might be incompatible with Rockefeller's intentions, so perhaps he dropped hints (though Rockefeller, a keen judge of character and ethics, was difficult to manipulate and therefore would no doubt have come to be suspicious of Hewett on his own). By the visit's end, Nusbaum had won Rockefeller's trust and respect and learned of his interest in museums.

Meanwhile, energy in Santa Fe crested over the much-anticipated guest. Corwin was to introduce Rockefeller to Hewett, whose timely return from San Diego would afford him the opportunity to show off his Santa Fe enterprises. The tour would serve as a prelude to revealing his grand plan. Chap, nearing completion of his term with Springer, as yet had no formal duties at the museum apart from occasional consultation. When that great June day arrived, Hewett was in a dither, as he was barely home when he received a telegram that Corwin and Rockefeller would arrive that morning. He called Chap at 7 a.m., asking him to come to his office immediately on an important matter. Chap needed breakfast and replied that he would be there in an hour. When he arrived, Hewett explained that he had found the museum in "great disorder" and urgently needed Chap to "take charge and straighten things out." Chap realized he would save time by handling it himself.

> So I pitched in as I had done before and gave the whole establishment a good going over, from end to end, finishing in the patio of the Art Museum by pulling weeds, and trimming vines and lawn with my pocket knife and office scissors!
>
> There was only one interruption when Dr. Hewett asked me to select some of my mounted drawings of Pueblo pottery designs and to place them in his office. Later I stood aside in a hallway of the Old Palace as he came through with Mr. Rockefeller and his party. That was to be my only glimpse of the distinguished visitor.[37]

Chap spent the afternoon on Springer's work in his studio. Hewett hunted him down to invite him to tea at five in Rockefeller's honor at the art museum. Kate was off for an afternoon motor trip, and Chap felt that the social demands that would be placed on him without her there would be too high a price to pay for the privilege of shaking Rockefeller's hand. He looked forward to leaving work on time and spending an hour with Frank and Helen in the orchard with the family's turkeys and their lively broods. Just as he was leaving, however, he learned that an art dealer had arrived with two hundred Balinese batiks he hoped to loan the museum, and he had only a small window of time. Chap resigned himself to the negotiation, selected some, and handled the business details.

That finished, I placed the batiks in storage, had just returned to the front desk and was again ready to leave when Dr. Corwin came downstairs from the tea party and, spying me, called out, "Chapman, where have you been? Please come upstairs.—Mr. Rockefeller is interested in your furniture and would like to ask you about it." So up we went by the rear stairway and into the hum of a typical Museum tea. "Where is Mr. Rockefeller's party?" he shouted. One of the ladies said they had just left the room. We made our way through the crowd to the Beauregard gallery and down the front stairs. Then, just as we neared the front door we heard the roar of motors as the guests left for Bishop's Lodge![38]

When Kate returned home that evening, she admitted to disappointment that he could not satisfy her curiosity about Rockefeller. Chap's debriefing of another improvised museum day was lighthearted, but the day held more far-reaching consequences than he imagined. Nusbaum recorded that after the tour, Rockefeller picked up on Nusbaum's suggestions and now envisioned a Santa Fe project that would include providing new exhibition buildings for all collections, rehabilitating the old Palace of the Governors with historic furnishings, and combining all local libraries (museum, school, city, and state) into one well-equipped institution to better serve all interests. He discussed these ideas with Hewett, acknowledging "that New Mexico, with small population [*sic*] could not do more than it was doing—therefore he would appreciate receiving a report on the cost of carrying out such a program of proposals as he made and would give such a report very careful consideration."[39] This request indicated significant Rockefeller interest in Hewett's plans. Because the AIA had been courting the foundation for an endowment for the Santa Fe school as well as its other institutes in Rome and Athens, possibly Rockefeller asked Hewett to draft a report in connection with its proposal. More likely, though, he was less interested in the international archaeology network than in his own enthusiasm for museum and park programs in the West. The philanthropist fiercely protected his privacy, but it was common knowledge that he and his trusted aides personally examined the merits of each case and the personalities involved. A personal request for a report was to be treated most seriously.

After Rockefeller left, Hewett seemed to gloat. He had already purchased a three-hundred-acre tract on the north side of Santa Fe, anticipating expansion. Making mysterious prophecies about the soon-to-be-homeless pottery in the basement, he warned Chap to brace himself for a change in museum circumstances that would warrant each collection having its own space, strictly for its own purposes, including the school's pottery collection.

It cost Chap some inner peace to ignore the bait, but at least he knew that, come what may, he had the lasting friendship of Springer, Hodge, Kidder, Bradfield, and Nusbaum and the professional esteem of numerous others. Around this time he received a gener-ous token of Twitchell's affection. Many years earlier, Bandelier had presented Twitchell with several little terra cotta heads from his personal collection of artifacts. During his residence in Las Vegas, New Mexico, however, these objects "gradually disappeared through the efforts of my friends who were inclined to pick up souvenirs in my library regardless of the fact that the things they carried off were of personal value me. I gave the one remaining to K. M. Chapman, who prizes it very highly."[40]

At the end of June, Chap wrapped up Springer's work, returning full time to a catch-all curatorship at the art museum and continuing to pursue fund donations and mem-berships. The chamber of commerce hoped to establish a fund of $25,000 to cover Fiesta and Indian Fair, but by late June it was clear that was a pipe dream. Desperate, the cham-ber turned to Hewett, who accepted responsibility for the September events under the banner of the school. Hewett then met with an artist committee to plan a Painters of the Southwest exhibit for the Fiesta. The Taos Society's traveling exhibition was already scheduled as a separate Santa Fe group show in late August. Gus Baumann proposed that for the duration of the fair, the Taos show be part of the Fiesta exhibit. The commit-tee approved this; a Taos representative agreed, pending society acquiescence. The next two months brought stress as museum-school staff had to organize the art show and the fair along with the usual Fiesta spectacles. Chap, pressed into service as chairman of the hanging committee, questioned Hewett about mingling the Taos group with the Fiesta display. Hewett said he would attend to it, made a trip to Taos, and then reported to Chap that the proposal was satisfactory. Chap received the society paintings on August 20 and added them to the Painters of the Southwest show, which included at least two paintings by each of eighty artists. He recruited volunteers to assemble the large exhibition catalog he developed.

The fair, now called the Southwest Indian Fair and Arts and Crafts Exhibition, was again mounted in conjunction with Fiesta. Chap felt it was an improvement over the 1923 effort. Per Hewett's agenda, it was emphasized that Pueblo dancers, singers, and drama-tists should draw on their traditions and religion. In his passion to educate the public on ancient life, Hewett had no trouble telling Indians how to be Indians. The pageantry he valued was a symptom of his increasing alienation from the art colonists, who found his Fiesta too backward looking. Inspired by an idea from Kate, Witter Bynner and Dolly Sloan organized a counterpoint called Pasatiempo, essentially a satire of Hewett's event.[41] A parade of bohemians in flamboyant Santa Fe fashions included a two-story effigy of Old Man Fate, or "Zozobra." Pasatiempo ended with a Zozobra bonfire, a legacy that continues today.

Upstarts though they were, the artists' commercial value was obvious. They themselves, not just their work, were a tourist draw. Their realty investments also contributed to Santa Fe's economic health. A nosy reporter totted up some figures and found newsworthy "the so-called 'newcomers,' including the artists, writers and others who have featured [in] the growth of this city in the past decade or so. Some idea of their estimated economic value to the city is also pertinent and will doubt-less be informative to many people who are not familiar with this growth." The long and gossipy article mentioned Kate and Kenneth who "have lived here many years, own considerable real estate improved and unimproved, some one [*sic*] suggests invest-ment may be $25,000." As reported, the collective worth of artists Chapman, Vierra, Nordfeldt, Baumann, Henderson, Parsons, Raymond Jonson, Balink, Davey, Rollins, Sloan, Applegate, Nash, Bakos, Shuster, Ellis, Mruk, Dasburg, Olive Rush, and Cassidy totaled $144,000. The writer concluded, "All these build in the community archi-tectural style. The artists and writers probably give more widespread publicity than any other class."[42]

In October, Chap caught flak from the Taos Society. Secretary E. Irving Couse com-plained that one of Walter Ufer's paintings had been omitted from the Taos Society grouping. Couse warned that unless their rules were complied with, Santa Fe would be removed from the circuit. Chap responded with a review of the circumstances, point-ing to Hewett's claim that the society had agreed to permit paintings by society artists to be hung without exclusive society identity. The summer having taken its toll, he then washed his hands of the job.

> I presume that, as usual, Dr. Hewett will wait until next summer to call another meeting of the artists. Judging by the growing success of the free-for-all Fiesta exhibitions year after year, I feel safe in assuming that they will favor a con-tinuance of the non-society plans. Dr. Hewett will be in San Diego, care of the San Diego Museum, until January 1st, and if you must have an agreement soon in regard to the plan of the next Fiesta exhibition, it will be necessary to write him direct.
>
> I shall be out of the Art Curatorship from now on, and Mrs. Van Stone will take charge.[43]

Throughout the 1924–25 winter, the NMAIA and other organizations maintained relief efforts at the Pueblos, as drought had prevailed all year. In the spring, San Ildefonso's material resources improved along with the weather. A new bridge gave tourists greater access to the pueblo, so Maria opened a shop at her house, a boon since she was expecting a baby. She encouraged others to open shop and consolidated a cot-tage industry, paying others for work on pots she signed. Production stepped up. Maria shared her economic edge by purchasing bulk canned and dry goods then selling them at cost to those not directly involved in pottery. Chap was concerned that the tourists visiting the pueblos to buy on-site pottery would have negative cultural repercussions:

> It is discouraging to find the independence and self respect that we have been trying to build up among our Indian friends, battered down by the hordes of tourists who over-run the reservations and villages with no understanding or regard for what they are destroying. . . . [This] should be brought to the attention of everyone who is interested in preserving what we can do for the American Art of the future.[44]

On the other hand, Maria's creative approach preserved dignity and made good economic sense, as Chap also recognized. His pottery-buying treks acquainted him with Pueblo difficulties that his programs couldn't solve. In an apparent effort to help, he wrote to several purveyors that year in search of untanned deer hides to provide to Indian craftsmen at cost, but it was a drop in the bucket.[45] He wrote of his personal helplessness in the face of pleas from Acoma potters:

> *"Why don't you bring us things to trade instead of paying us money? You can buy everything cheap in Albuquerque and pay us with sugar and coffee, and lots of other things we need. That way we could save money. Do you know what they ask for sugar at the trading stores in Old and New Laguna, and Cubero? Twenty cents a pound, and everything else the same high prices. It costs us too much to go to Albuquerque every time we need something. But we know how low the prices are there."*
>
> *I could figure out no way to help them. First, I was under obligation to the traders, who were most cooperative in providing storage for my pottery and other things, and in saving cartons for packing. Then too I have no way of delivering a stock of goods on my trips to Acoma for I have no car, and depended on train and bus for travel to Laguna. . . . I tried to think of some way the potters could cooperate among themselves by sending one of their number to Albuquerque to do the buying for them. But they always point out objections. At that time not one car or truck was owned at Acoma and the Government's local agent for Acoma did not dare interfere with the business of the traders—indeed the agent at that time, Roscoe Rice, was in business "on the side," with his family conducting a little store and post office at nearby Cubero.*
>
> *In all those years the Model T. Ford was the principal means of travel, and there were little filling stations and repair shops springing along the unpaved highway (now 66) from Albuquerque to California. I once met two Acoma youths on*

the trail up to the Pueblo and had a long talk with them. They had learned the auto mechanic trade at the Albuquerque Indian School, but could find no employment along the highway. "Why can't the government help us start a place of our own?" No doubt the answer was that the Government Indian Service could provide jobs only for the few employees at Indian Agencies and Schools, but they were forbidden to put their trainees into business in competition with tax-paying whites.[46]

Chap plugged away at his museum, committee, and fund-raising work. He hoped that the fund's collection would help him fill in the missing pottery link. "I have done very little on the prehistoric pottery since Mr. Bradfield took charge of the field work a few years ago. Instead I have felt it of greater importance to concentrate on the post-Spanish [pottery] while we can save what little is left. The inclosed account of our Pueblo Pottery fund will show the necessity for our activity of the past three years," he wrote in early 1925 to a Chicago patron.[47] In a related area, Elsie Loudon sent gratifying word that his encouragement had paid off in her revival and promotion of Pueblo embroidery. Building on his success, she had presented a proposal to Commissioner Burke and Secretary Work in Washington for supporting embroidery that was modeled on his for pottery. She was thrilled at having landed a salaried Indian Service appointment, including a car and a grant. She asked Chap to arrange a fair embroidery booth.

Such good news was offset by anxieties. The stoicism he tried to cultivate belied digestive ailments severe enough to warrant medical attention. Springer, convalescing at his daughter Ada's home in Philadelphia from his own cardiac problems, was so concerned that by June he felt compelled to intervene, interpreting Chap's gastric distress as stress driven. He wrote Hewett, "He has a stomach and intestinal condition that imperatively calls for considerable rest treatment—one of those things that can develop into a serious disability. A repetition this summer of the kind of work he had to do last year . . . might result in great damage. . . . I would propose to assume his salary for a couple of months, during which he could do some work for me, which he can manage at his house without interfering with his necessary rest periods."[48] He asked that Hewett find someone to cover Chap's work. Hewett dared not complain while Chap was under Springer's aegis.

Why the recurrence of Chap's digestive ailments at this time? True, the coming summer was going to be hectic at the museum and with organizing the fair, but that was not the sole problem. As the fund took shape in fulfillment of his desire, he was also participating in strategizing ways to establish a facility solely for that organization. Was he conflicted over working for the museum while forging a competing organization? Or was a profound need for autonomy gnawing at his guts? Reading between the lines of his memoirs suggests that chronic discontent was as much a source of gastric bedevilment as his summer strains.

Whatever work Chap then did for Springer, it gave him space and sufficient energy well into autumn to network with potters on behalf of himself, the fair, the fund, and even his friends. Still on the lookout for a fine pot for Hodge, he sent descriptions of various pots by Maria and suggested considering Tonita Roybal's red ware with black decorations by her husband Juan Cruz. One of her pots had won first prize at the highly successful 1925 fair.

Working part time for Springer also allowed Chap to ponder the fund's most pressing matter: defining its mission and how to fulfill it. The fund's founders were focused on revitalizing Pueblo pottery, but they also knew that their goals were interwoven with a complex and evolving political, social, and economic matrix in Santa Fe. Chap's aim was the most single minded and consistent. Other trustees had interests that were economically broader (e.g., Pueblo welfare), more romanticized (e.g., a longing for a mythical past), or tangential (e.g., Spanish folk art). It would take careful thought to formulate a few well-targeted objectives and gain group agreement.

A significant decision was now made to incorporate and rename it the Indian Arts Fund (IAF). Chap insisted on keeping the word "fund" in the title, arguing that it was an excellent talking point. The members elected to include pottery, basketry, textiles, and silver—and to jettison Spanish arts and crafts. Austin and Applegate would remain on the corporate board of trustees but also branch off on their own.[49] The work of delineating the IAF charter began in earnest, and the founders recruited a coast-to-coast, politically comprehensive board of trustees that included activists and artists, male and female alike. Some members represented traders' interests; some commanded social power. The addition of luminaries in anthropology added professional and scientific identity. Altogether there would be thirty members. The executive committee would be chaired by Mera, trader MacMillan would serve as secretary, and Chap would be treasurer.[50] Their common bond was Indian art, but it was a child of its time—no Indians were included, an unacceptable breach in today's world. And while varied representation seemed like a good idea, it could result in myopic self-interest obstructing consensus.

The articles of incorporation were signed on September 11, 1925, by Chap, Mera, Applegate, Dasburg, and attorney Francis C. Wilson, but the incorporation itself was not officially announced until October. Chap conscientiously intended to balance his respective museum and IAF commitments, but potential conflict of interest lurked. Chap wrote Hodge that his hope of finding Hodge a pot had been realized and that his dream had been, too. Hodge, now director of the National Museum of the American Indian, was a key connection—and Nusbaum's intimate friend as well. It was to Hodge that Chap spoke openly on the matter. Chap assured Hodge that despite the lack of its own building, the IAF faced no other obstacles to acquiring good material while it was still available. Chap stipulated that the IAF did not wish to duplicate or rival existing organizations but rather intended to fulfill its mission by cooperating with U.S. museums. In asking Hodge (a charter Pueblo Pottery Fund member) to now become an IAF trustee, Chap opened his heart:

> Dr. Hewett, naturally, felt that our organization is superfluous, and that we ought to be working for our Museum. I believe that I can maintain my loyalty to both, and that I am right in insisting that until the Museum & School have a more definite policy in regard to the disposition of such unit collections as ours, we cannot consistently make the Museum our depository while assuring donors that their contributions will remain in Santa Fe. I don't believe the Museum has spent $1000 on post-Spanish material, of all sorts in its 15 years existence.
>
> . . . We are simply pledged to build up and maintain a collection of Southwest Indian Arts, for exhibition and use in Santa Fe, for the public, for students and for the Indians themselves. . . . I feel that the personnel of the board is a guarantee that the affairs of the Fund will be administered in full accord with the accepted code of Museum ethics.[51]

The fledgling IAF, having secured a national board and come up with a plan, was maturing. Its incorporation was announced in a four-page bulletin printed on expensive paper—witness to its wealthy sponsors. It is noteworthy that the relatively conservative founders invited the notorious *Laughing Horse* editor, Spud Johnson, to wield his pen in their service. He lauded the IAF's mission to return to the Indians the work of their ancestors and its goal of encouraging them to set even better standards in their modern art, which would inevitably help solve Pueblo economic problems. Then the provocateur took over:

> There is, by now, a Pottery collection that is beginning to be the envy of local and of national museums. But where is it? It is in that same dark corner shelf-space in the cellar of the state museum where sits in reconstructed state the original old Zuni bowl that belonged to Elizabeth Sergeant.
>
> Who sees it? Nobody except the members of the organization. (This is almost literally true in that practically everyone is a member who is sufficiently interested to even hunt up the dark corner in which the invaluable collection is at present stored.) It is perfectly obvious what the present need of the society is: a building—therefore money. . . .

Plate 1. *New Art Museum, Santa Fe—South Front*, by Kenneth M. Chapman, 1916. Watercolor, 11 ⅝ x 28 ½ inches. Collection of the New Mexico Museum of Art. Museum acquisition, before 1918.

THE CONVERSION OF ST. FRANCIS

Facing page: Plate 2. *Conversion of St. Francis*, 1917. Mural, designed by Donald Beauregard and painted by Kenneth M. Chapman, for St. Francis Auditorium, Santa Fe, New Mexico. Collection of the New Mexico Museum of Art, gift of the Honorable Frank Springer, 1917.

Plate 4. Silkscreen, by Kenneth M. Chapman, undated. (Courtesy of John Sheffield Chapman.)

Plate 3. Cowkid, an example of Chapman's novelty cards, c. 1906. (Courtesy of John Sheffield Chapman.)

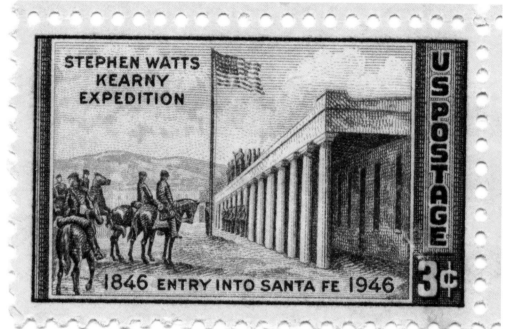

Plate 5. Chapman's drawing, which appeared on a 1946 Centennial U.S. postage stamp, of General Stephen W. Kearny's 1846 entry into Santa Fe, New Mexico. Chapman originally created the illustration for Ralph E. Twitchell's *The History of the Military Occupation of the Territory of New Mexico from 1846 to 1851* (1909). (Courtesy of Janet Chapman.)

Facing page:
Plate 6. Gouache painting, by
Kenneth M. Chapman, 1903.
(Courtesy of Karen Barrie.)

639   SANTO DOMINGO
2639/12   Food Bowl   7½" x 13"   used   1926-57
1971-350

Light with black decoration on interior and exterior, red and
orange underbody

Purchased from O.S.Halseth - 1926   neg.roll 53

Plate 7a. Detail from accession book for pottery by Kenneth M. Chapman for IAF catalog number 639, Santo Domingo bowl. (Courtesy of School for Advanced Research Archives, AC01.67.639.)

Plate 7b. Interior of Santo Domingo bowl (IAF.639), artist unknown, c. 1900. (Photograph by Addison Doty. Courtesy of School for Advanced Research catalog number IAF.639.)

Plate 7c. Exterior of Santo Domingo bowl (IAF.639), artist unknown, c. 1900. (Photograph by Addison Doty. Courtesy of School for Advanced Research, catalog number IAF.639, exterior.)

ZUÑI   used   Acc.1923-3
Water Jar   11" x 14½"   broken and repaired

White with thin brown and red decoration, brown underbody

Gift of Elizabeth S. Sergeant - 1923

500⁵⁵
(174)

neg.roll 33

neck

same as top, reversed

body

Plate 8a. Detail from accession book for pottery by Kenneth M. Chapman for IAF catalog number 9, Zuni water jar. (Courtesy of School for Advanced Research Archives, Ac01.65.9.)

Plate 8b. Zuni water jar (IAF.9), artist unknown, c. 1880–90. (Photograph by Addison Doty. Courtesy of School for Advanced Research Archives, catalog number IAF.9.)

1166
3166/12

SAN ILDEFONSO
Storage Jar   15½" x 19"   unused

Light with black and red decoration, red underbody

Purchased from Maria Martinez of San Ildefonso - 1928
Made by her in 1926   neg. roll 36

Plate 9a. Detail from accession book for pottery by Kenneth M. Chapman for IAF catalog number 1166, San Ildefonso storage jar. (Courtesy of School for Advanced Research Archives, IAF.1166.)

Plate 9b. San Ildefonso storage jar (IAF.1166) by Julian and Maria Martinez, 1926. (Photograph by Addison Doty. Courtesy of School for Advanced Research catalog number IAF.1166.)

. . . [I]t seems time to ask assistance not only for the roof that is necessary to cover the collections, but to explain that such a building will not only be a museum, but a school for students who wish to study Southwestern Indian Arts at their source, as well as for Indians who may care to know their forefathers' surpassing skill in form and decoration, who may want to carry on the old tradition. . . .

The building, when it becomes a reality, will be unique. There will be no other museum of its kind in America either in purpose or activity. It will not only provide the proper kind of display for the proper kind of material, but it will contain laboratories in which the old clays and pigments, the old dyes and fabrics will be tested and studied, looking toward the future of Indian Arts as well as towards the past.[52]

Spud was clearly well informed regarding IAF purpose and resources. When the document reached Hewett, perhaps he merely snorted, unaware that IAF membership held a potential trump card in the form of the person whose outstanding accounts he had once refused to honor. But now its agenda—including its wish to erect another museum building—was identified irrevocably in print. Recognizing that Spud had waved a red flag in El Toro's face, Chap may well have experienced gastric distress.

The executive committee had distilled the number of IAF objectives down to two: to revive Indian arts and crafts by providing Native artists with access to fine specimens and to educate all people of America on the value of its only indigenous art. What Indian Fair had begun was now carried into the IAF. Chap chose a relatively narrow array of pots, both old and new, that he deemed the finest examples of ancestral design (see plates 7, 8, 9). There is no evidence that Chap asked directly for any potter's opinion about what to include in the collection. However, the potters never seem to have questioned Chap's judgment, implying acquiescence, and Chap educated his Anglo cohorts about the standards of evaluation he used. As ethically as possible, the IAF supported either replication of the designs or innovation that incorporated traditional elements. Chap recognized that problems could arise from cultural paternalism and strove to avoid the kind of patronage that would force artists into a particular cultural groove.[53]

The mutually advantageous reciprocity between Pueblo potters and Anglo patrons began to reverse the tourist-driven trend toward cheap souvenirs.[54] The "fine" pots, imbued with "improved" artistry, deeper meaning, and greater value, benefited the potters economically; being authorities on excellence and arbiters of taste benefited the Anglo newcomers by providing them with greater social identity and stature. As author Dauber points out, this arrangement would have been disturbing if it had simply been the product of a dominant culture interested in hierarchy for its own sake, but at the core of the IAF was "the idea that cultural essences can be identified, and that they have value."[55] For instance, crucial to the founders' mission was holding the collection in the environment that cradled its origins, although they acknowledged that that meant potters would have to overcome many obstacles relating to transportation, weather, and seasonal obligations to see the actual pots. The observation about the obstacles bears Chap's stamp—Maria's poignant complaint clearly still echoed in him.

Chap hoped to charter the IAF in such a way as to avoid Hewett's mistakes. To preclude conflicts of interest, Chap worked cooperatively, within professional boundaries, with rival interests, an approach that contrasted with Hewett's style of enmeshing as many interests as possible. But Chap was increasingly a servant of two masters, which began to take its toll. His health problems escalated well into November, constituting what Springer termed a breakdown. Only Springer's patronage allowed Chap to maintain IAF involvement, of which Springer presumably approved. Probably because of Springer's heart condition, both Chap and Hewett kept him ignorant of the true complexities and politics of the situation. Hewett realized his own grasp on the situation was slipping. He was nearing his sixtieth birthday and only recently recovered from broken bones he sustained in the Middle East the previous winter. He began arranging to spend more time in Santa Fe. He sent Bradfield to San Diego to oversee operations there in his absence. In late October, he informed Springer that Chap's health had improved and he wanted his time back. The news pleased Springer, but he disappointed Hewett:

> While supposed to be in my service, he could not entirely cut loose from matters downtown where he was so much needed, with the result that he tried to do too many things at once—which was evidently the chief cause of his breakdown. I have been carrying his salary during his illness in order to relieve him of anxiety about that, and shall continue to do so for a while. . . . If he gets in shape to work regularly, and can keep at it without interruption—which he has not been able to do during the 4 months I have been carrying him, I think he could finish most of what he has on hand for me in a month's time. But I am expecting it to take longer, as I have urged him to take things easy, as his Dr. advises. Until he is quite recovered, I shall take care of him, but otherwise I should not expect the work for me to continue much beyond January 1.[56]

Chap thus had a chance to catch his emotional breath and improve his health. Springer also regained enough strength that winter to finalize his crinoid work. On New Year's 1926, Chap returned to a fifty-fifty arrangement with Springer and the museum. The next month he journeyed with Lansing Bloom to Jornada del Muerto to collect surface finds, and his account was published in *El Palacio* the following month.[57] Kate

Chapman with his mother, Mary Cordelia White Chapman, and his daughter, Helen, c. 1925. (Courtesy of School for Advanced Research Archives, AC02 754 1f.)

continued her architectural pursuits and during this period helped old and new friends locate desirable property. One repeat summer visitor, Margretta Stewart Dietrich, had become enchanted with Santa Fe. Dietrich, her husband (Senator Charles Dietrich of Nebraska), and sister (Dorothy Stewart) had first visited in 1921, when Margretta lectured for the League of Women Voters. Known to intimates by her childhood name "Sister Piggy," Margretta loved the arts and had seen the Pueblos' plight after the drought. When she decided to purchase a residence in 1925, Kate located the home she bought at 519 Canyon Road. In 1926, Kate attended to its restoration and expansion, identifying in the process Benita, a fireplace builder from Tesuque Pueblo, who was the only person who could correct the building's smoking fireplace. Margretta's new home also meant that her sister, Dorothy, would make more visits to Santa Fe. An artist and illustrator—and soon-to-be-notorious Santa Fe character—Dorothy was fascinated by other cultures. She and Kate recognized each other as soul mates, and their friendship flourished.

Kate's skills were constantly in demand, though the form her payments took was occasionally surprising; for one job, she received a Chinese bowl and plates in lieu of her fee. While Kate worked, Frank and Helen attended nearby Catron School, and Chap also looked after them when he worked from home. Throughout their lives, Frank and Helen called their mother by her first name, which may seem less than maternal. However, Kate shared their delights and tended their illnesses, handling Frank's broken arm with aplomb. Her sweet poems reveal how much she doted upon them and how she graced family life with a happy tempo:

Helen Rides the Singlefooter

Helen rides her Eppie horse
Up and down Delgado Road:
All along Delgado Road,
Rides the single-steppie horse—
Fatherly old Eppie horse—
    Taking care of Helen.

"Listen, Kate, to Eppie feet
Making all that beating sound;
Hear the music on the ground
From his single-steppie feet!
I love the noise of Eppie feet
    Making songs for Helen."

> May she ride her Eppie horse
> Blythely through her baby-hood.
> Through her grown-up-lady-hood
> May the feet of Eppie horse—
> Gallant single-steppie horse—
> Magic rhythms always beat
> > In the heart of Helen.

Frank recalled that neither parent worried excessively, for a child's life in the Acequia Madre neighborhood was friendly and secure; Frank and Helen roamed freely up and down the Mother Ditch. According to Marjorie Lambert, Chap loved to tell the story about Frank's first view of the "mighty Mississippi" during a trip east together. The train had a long enough stop in Iowa that passengers could disembark and stretch their legs. "The conductor came out and he said, 'Well, sonny, are you enjoying the walk?' And Frank said, 'Yes, sir, I am.' And he said, 'Well, what do you think of the mighty Mississippi? Is this your first view?' 'Yes,' he said, 'but I live on the banks of the Acequia Madre in Santa Fe, New Mexico.'"[58]

At the time, nearby Canyon Road was not the gallery district that it is today but residential, with only two general stores. On Garcia Street, residents included Anglos and Hispanics. Frank recalled there were at least a dozen bilingual kids who got along pretty well. Calling to mind several friendly fights, he said their orchard was a favorite play spot, because apples made handy weapons.[59] Frank joined the Boy Scouts and enjoyed camping in Tesuque Canyon; his scoutmaster was a prominent Englishman, Benjamin Talbot Hyde, for whom Santa Fe's Hyde Park is named.

In April 1926, Springer finished his work and returned Chap to full-time museum status. While Chap settled into quiet desperation, Kate became involved in a new controversy that polarized Santa Feans. This time the substance was Santa Fe's cultural identity. Again the newcomers prevailed. The Texas Federation of Women's Clubs had chosen a site near the Sunmount Sanitarium for a permanent cluster of buildings where educational programs modeled on upstate New York's Chatauquas would be offered. If successful, it could bring as many as three thousand people to the town each summer. Hewett and the Old Guard, including the chamber of commerce, favored the center with its potential economic advantages, but somehow their collective fiscal intentions were poorly translated. Mary Austin organized a group calling itself the Old Santa Fe Association to protest an educational model that was perceived as an unwelcome import from New York State.[60] The art colony exercised its clout again, with Kate and Dorothy Stewart joining in. The dispute continued into the summer, with the Old Santa Fe Association gaining an upper hand in press and publicity. With shared impishness,

Kate and Dorothy quietly purchased strategic acreage at the proposed site. Ultimately the federation backed down, but the city's split confirmed for Hewett's antagonists that he was more promoter than scientist.[61] Kate now held land that would appreciate, a boon to the Chapmans.

While that situation percolated, a more welcome venture came to Santa Fe: the Indian Detours of the Fred Harvey Company, the Disney of its day. The Harvey Company had bought the La Fonda Hotel as well as the Koshare Tours, a Pueblo sightseeing business developed by Erna Fergusson and Ethel Hickey in 1921.[62] The Harvey Company established La Fonda as headquarters for the Indian Detours and hired Fergusson to supervise its staff of specially trained and costumed female couriers, who would educate carloads of tourists and address their questions knowledgeably. The Harvey connection with the Santa Fe Railroad meant ample promotion. The famous Harvey Girls in prim black and white uniforms were the hotel service staff. The gift shops were stocked with fine Indian art thanks to experienced buyers, and the Pueblo tours completed an exotic yet gracious experience. The company worked out a deal with Hewett by which Chap and other museum staff would train couriers and provide evening lectures to Harvey tourists. Four-week courses for the couriers were designed to teach them Southwest essentials. Over the next few years, Chap taught his own areas (archaeology, ethnology, Indian arts and crafts, pottery, map study, and pictographs) as did Frank Applegate (Spanish arts), John Gaw Meem (architecture), Alice C. Henderson (writers of the Southwest), and Jesse Nusbaum (Mesa Verde).

The first training course began April 19. Naturally, Chap's pupils received meticulously detailed material. He expected them to know Pueblo population statistics, food, culture, inventions, architecture, caste and rank, linguistic classifications, government, Southwest history since 1539, and geology! Chap administered thorough tests that included such questions as

1. What are the facts concerning the decline of the population at Pecos Pueblo?
2. Discuss the conflicts of Apache Canyon dated March 26 & 28, 1862.
3. What has been the effect of building railroads upon New Mexico?
4. In what period were the boundaries of New Mexico fixed?
5. Why do people come to the Southwest? What are they interested in and what do they want to know?
6. Give in one or two pages what you will tell about the Pueblo Indians of New Mexico, having in mind a proper balance between their origin, history, customs and a dozen other necessary and interesting details.[63]

Frank and Helen also participated, indirectly, in the Indian Detours. They often played in the water of the Acequia Madre, where tourists, catching sight of the children as they rode by in their touring cars, "got a big kick out of it."[64]

At the museum, with Bradfield gone and Hewett not yet back from teaching in San Diego, Chap had to carry out routine administrative duties as curator and acting director during the summer. He exercised his creativity preparing drawings and notes on the meander, or Greek key, design motif for Bradfield's classroom use at the state college in San Diego. His work there was as endlessly repetitive as the design. Then a new opportunity for Chap to teach his beloved Indian art presented itself. James F. Zimmerman, farsighted president of the University of New Mexico in Albuquerque, was establishing a department of anthropology that would initially concentrate on Southwest archaeology and ethnology. Zimmerman asked Hewett to chair the department, which would share the school's resources. Though arrangements were still pending, Chap was chosen to teach a two-week summer class in Indian art, the first course to be offered by the new department. His services were initially contributed by the museum; later he was paid directly for his time. Chap's association with the University of New Mexico was the beginning of a mutually satisfying relationship between Chap and Zimmerman that lasted until the latter's death in 1944. The professorship was flexible to accommodate Chap's needs and eventually included summer courses at Jemez, semester courses that met one day per week, and night courses. The extra income was welcome, but more gratifying was the reception he received. His students loved and admired him.

Chap's reputation as an expert in Indian arts had greatly expanded since he had first chosen to follow his heart. His assertiveness about the importance of his studies helped foster his autonomy. His forays into independence led him to develop the Indian Fair, establish partnerships with potters, and accept a teaching position at the University of New Mexico. He had also reinforced his contacts in the national field through friendships with Nusbaum (Mesa Verde), Kidder (Carnegie Institute), and Hodge (National Museum of the American Indian). The Springer-Hewett-Chapman web still held him, but he was finally differentiating himself; his work had useful local purpose for both preservationists and integrationists as they tried to help Pueblo peoples in their respective ways. His unremitting passion for Pueblo pottery had found an outlet in the IAF, independent of the museum. The dream of giving the collection a home of its own would beget the chance of a lifetime.

CHAPTER 9

CHAPMAN AND ROCKEFELLER

In late May [1926], during Dr. Hewett's absence, I received word, indirectly, that Mr. and Mrs. Rockefeller were planning a visit to Santa Fe and that they had been advised to meet me at the Museum. . . . I assumed, naturally, that he had been favorably impressed with the picture of the combined School of American Research and the Museum of New Mexico as presented by Dr. Hewett [in 1924], and that his principal objective was to share his enjoyment of it with Mrs. Rockefeller.

Thus in meeting them I had two matters to consider. First, that I would be representing Dr. Hewett in his absence—an awkward situation, for in recent years our relations had been far from cordial; he had not taken me into his confidence and I knew little of his often shifting plans for the institutions. And second, above all else, that I should not divert the attention of Museum guests to the work of the Indian Arts Fund.

On the morning of June 10th [1926] Mr. R's secretary called me from Bishop's Lodge, to inform me that the party would visit the Museum at 1:30 p.m. and that Mr. R. wished to meet me.

Dr. Hewett was in San Diego, where he was finishing his course in Anthropology, at the Teachers College, and he was not expected to return within a week.

Both Museum buildings were in considerable disorder, and I realized that the janitor would have his hands full with his routine work. So, in the absence of anyone who could assume any responsibility I rolled up my sleeves and spent the whole morning putting things in order. The basement in particular was in a deplorable state, and I expected that Mr. R. would wish to show his party the printing plant and archaeological laboratory in the basement, which I understood he had inspected on his prior visit in 1924. I gave this part of the building as much time as possible and then managed to get a half hours rest at my studio before 1:30.

The party arrived much later and spent not more than an hour and a half in both buildings.

I found Mr. R. keenly interested in the permanent collection of paintings in the Art Museum, while Mrs. R. gave much more time to the current exhibition, which included the work of a group of local artists with decided modern tendencies. In

1924, Mr. R. had asked to meet me, when he found that I had designed the fur-niture for the Women's Reception Room. I was detained by Museum business at the time and did not arrive at the reception given for him until after he had left. I found him again much interested in the furniture and the possibilities of its use in that type of interior.

Returning to the main floor, I told them that there were several departments in the basement which I would be glad to show them if they had time for it. I had in mind particularly the photographic department, printing office, and archaeologi-cal laboratory and storage. Here Mrs. R. said "That reminds me. I was told that there is a wonderful exhibit of old pottery in the basement. May we see it?" I led them directly to the Indian Arts Fund collection and there they spent fully a third of their time. Following is an outline of Mr. R's inquiry in regard to the Fund.

R. "How is it conducted? How do you get your funds?"

C. "It is an organization distinct from the Museum and School. We are car-rying on this work because those institutions have had neither the means nor the interest in the work. We are incorporated and we solicit funds in amounts from $5.00 up. Five dollars pays for an annual membership but we try to get more than that, by every known means short of sand bagging our victims."

R. "Why is such an important collection here? Hasn't the Museum a better place to exhibit it?"

C. "No, every available bit of space is used for other purposes. But we are thankful for as good a place as this until we are assured of a permanent museum installation."

R. "Isn't there any room for the Museum to expand?"

C. "No. The last available corner of our lot is now being built upon to provide a carpenter's shop and packing room and the basement space now occupied by them will be needed by other departments."

R. "But, if the Museum could expand, this is the first thing you would put on exhibition isn't it?"

C. "I am afraid not. I could name a number of things that have been given precedence in the past, and several more that would probably be given first consideration."

R. "I'd like to ask, what would be considered of more importance than this col-lection. Tell me one thing."

C. "Well, we would be content here with the assurance that we could use this basement room for the next few years. But we were told only a few months ago that it could be needed as soon as plans mature for the expansion of the printing department."

R. *"Printing department! What's that for? Do you mean to say they have a printing office here in the Museum?"*

C. *"Yes. I thought Dr. Hewett showed you through our basement two years ago."*

R. *"But why do they need a printing office in the building? That could just as well be a mile away from the Plaza. What do they need of more room?"*

C. *"Dr. Hewett says we are to do a great deal of the Institute's printing, in the near future."*

R. *"Tell me something else that you think would come ahead of this."*

(by this time we were upstairs and leaving the East Gallery.)

C. *"Well, I'll take the first thing that comes to my mind. Look at the space given to Modern Art, both on this floor and that above. As I told you, the new carpenter shop and storage rooms at the rear will make room for more storage for pictures in the basement. The Drama League would have made permanent use of our pottery basement for property storage, if they had not found our Auditorium unsuited to their needs as a little theater. I feel that these things, and others, have been given too much attention. I leave it to you whether it is worth while."*

R. *"If you leave it to me, I would say that this Modern Art is over done."*

(Then, on the way across the street, in the rain, to the Old Palace.)

[R.] *"Can't the Museum get any more ground to the north of the Art Museum? It seems to me that was pointed out to me when I was here before."*

C. *"It would be hard to get it now. None of it is on the market. But most of the property north of the Old Palace can be had."*

R. *"Now I remember they pointed that out, too. What are those buildings?"*

C. *"The Elks Club, Elks Theatre and the Armory."*

R. *"They look like pretty good buildings, don't they? Any ground back of them?"*

C. *"Only a narrow strip. There is some desirable ground beyond them, but they are in the way."*

Here we caught up with the others of his party and entered the Old Palace. They showed no particular interest until they reached the pottery room in the Historical Society's section. Here they enthused over the exhibit and were especially interested in the installation of 5 floor cases of Arts Fund pottery. They were out of the building within a few minutes, saying that they had other engagements.

I offered to take them to the Cliff dwellings but Mr. R. said he regretted that they could not take the time, as their schedule had been cut down from four to only two days about Santa Fe, and that they had a pretty full program for the *following day. He thanked me and said he owed our meeting to Jess Nusbaum who had written him, and that he was very glad I had been on hand.*

Friday, June 11th.

I was notified at 10:00 a.m. that Mr. R's schedule had been re-arranged and that he wished me to come out to the Lodge at 1:30 and go with them to San Ildefonso.

When his party had been seated in other cars, he asked me to get between himself and Mrs. R. and when we had started, said "Now we have you where you can't escape, and I want to continue the discussion of some things we brought up yesterday." For the entire time, both going and returning to Santa Fe, he bored in, and would allow nothing to divert him from the subject.

Only once, when we were settling ourselves, after hitting a rut on the Jacona road, Mrs. R. "took the reins" and said, "Now John, it's my turn. I just want to ask one question. Mr. Chapman, are you married?"

"Well," said Mr. R. "Now that we are off our subject, suppose you tell us something about yourself."

I made it snappy, with a little account of my relations with Mr. Springer as a prime reason for having held on so long with the Museum.

That out of the way, he dug in again, and must have been considerably disappointed with my reaction, for I didn't know what he knew of the situation and as a Museum employe [sic], I felt that it was my duty to put the institution in the best possible light. But before we reached Santa Fe, he said, "Now that I have the Museum's situation pretty well in mind, tell me some more about the Fund."

Here was my lead. I said, "Now that we are acquainted, I want to ask you if you realize what an uncomfortable position you had me in yesterday, when I found you both so much interested in the Fund's work. Our status at the Museum is very uncertain, and, as a Museum employe, I don't feel that I can divert the attention of Museum visitors to the work of the Fund, which is a thorn in the flesh of the Director."

"Oh, that's all right," said Mrs. R., "[d]on't you worry about that. I asked to see it, and I asked because I was urged before we left home. But I don't need any further urging. We are both very much interested in it."

(This is the result of good team work, which—I wrote Mr. Springer—is aiming high and is still getting results. We have word through our higher ups that the R's are only awaiting the consideration of the reports before determining what to do for the Fund.)

By this time we were entering Santa Fe, and I could not go into the Funds [sic] work in detail. We were passing the High School, when he said, "All right for the

Fund. It needs help and I will be writing you about that within a few days. But something else I want you to do for me. I want you to prepare a statement for me, in regard to all we have covered this afternoon. I asked Dr. Hewett to prepare one for the Museum, two years ago. He didn't do it, or at least, I never saw it. You can make this confidential if you prefer. Or if you think best, you can talk it over with Dr. Hewett and ask him to submit one. If you two can get together, all right, submit a compromise report too. But in any case remember that I want yours substantially as you outlined the situation to me today. Let it include the Fund if you think best. If not give me a separate report on that. I expect to be back in New York early in September, and would be glad to have them then."

Mr. Rockefeller made it clear that his interest was a personal one and that all correspondence should be directed to his private office.

He remarked again on Jess' thoughtfulness in suggesting our meeting.[1]

John D. Rockefeller left that day for Mesa Verde, but the Rockefeller-Chapman encounter, which began with local concerns, quickly ballooned to include broader interests. Leaders in American anthropology with varied agendas would soon capitalize on it, to the detriment of Hewett.

Chapman, reserved and studious, was to be an important player in the drama. The IAF collection held great appeal for Rockefeller, and it linked Chap with women who had Abby Rockefeller's ear. His friendship with Nusbaum and Kidder would prove influential as the Rockefeller project drew players from around the country. Significantly, Chap's ethics served Rockefeller's philanthropic values. Chap and Kate's Old Santa Fe Association membership also allied Chap with Hewett's consistent local opponents: Senator Bronson Cutting, who could affect state funding, and Dana Johnson, editor of the *Santa Fe New Mexican*, who frequently wielded his pen against Hewett. Finally, no love was lost between Chap and El Toro. Springer's advocacy had constrained Chap to remain in his employ, but Chap had joined the ranks of those disenchanted protégés who had enjoyed the best of Hewett's mentoring and endured the worst of his meddling.

For his part, John D. Rockefeller Jr. had both wide-ranging intellectual curiosity and the ability to track business details. He relied on expert advice from men of trusted character. Because his wealth kept him in the public eye, his greatest protection against scandal was his personal moral fiber. He expected the same of those whose help he received and of those who benefited from his largesse. His relationship with Nusbaum had deepened, and it was Nusbaum who now set in motion a ball for Chap to carry.

Hewett's absence during Rockefeller's visit suggests that he was confident of control over his institutions. He perhaps overlooked the alliance among Nusbaum, Kidder, and

Chap. Hewett had long been the major figure in southwestern archaeology. Nevertheless, his stature had slipped, and his record in securing sustainable funding was disappointing. His contacts within the AIA were pursuing a Rockefeller Foundation grant to support all three of its schools. Chap hypothesized that Hewett's colleagues, while leading him to think they were working on the school's behalf, were actually courting Rockefeller on behalf of their self-interests. However, it gave Hewett a rationale to shirk his development responsibilities.[2]

> *In my opinion Dr. Hewett's part in the fiasco was not merely neglect, but rather his deliberate ignoring of Mr. Rockefeller's request, on his first visit to Santa Fe in 1924, for a report on the School-Museum combination. Knowing Dr. Hewett as I had for a quarter century, and of his scorn for the easy living of rich men's sons, I believe he felt that Mr. Rockefeller was presumptuous in requesting for himself, information that was to be prepared for submission to the Foundation. The delay of over two years must have been unique in Mr. Rockefeller's experience. He was most emphatic in discussing it with me at the time of his second visit in 1926, for he said: "You may not realize this, Mr. Chapman, but I keep close watch of everything that goes on in my office, and I am positive that no such papers have been received."[3]*

When Rockefeller arrived at the Nusbaums' center, they must have all reviewed the Santa Fe tour with shared enthusiasm. Nusbaum sent Chap a prophetic epistle:

> I sent a personal letter to Mr. R. telling him of my great admiration for you, of the work that you had accomplished and were doing notwithstanding the difficulties placed in your way, that you were the salt of the earth, modest to the nth. degree, and that I knew of no one who could so capably show him and his wife and party the various points of interest in and about Santa Fe, and do it quietly and without a fan fare of trumpets and receptions etc.
> . . . He also went very fully with me first into the Santa Fe situation, told me of his ideas and plans and wanted my advice. . . . He also told me I believe that he had made certain pledges to you for carrying on your Indian Arts work, that H. was of the opinion that this work could well wait on other developments . . . to which I gave him a most decided no—saying it was a case of now or never. . . . He talked over the whole matter with Aileen and our views in nearly all matters coincide absolutely, and I am sure that . . . your ideas and mine would conform on most points. He told me you were to prepare a full report for him on the situation. He also said that he never received any report from Dr. H. in

response to his request of two years ago, and did not understand it. Your ears should be burning yet over what I told him of you and your work and how you had manned the guns thru thick and thin and held body and soul together when everything seemed ready to crash.

Both he and Mrs. Rockefeller thanked me for putting them in touch with you as they said that you had made their visit there so worth while—and this from me Chap—Once a friend, always a friend and more . . . when he knows your sincerity and purpose. . . . He always selects as his representative in any deal of this kind, someone of keen business ability, who has studied out the problems, knows the lay of the land, is not involved in various different lines of endeavor—in other words, one who has a singleness of purpose and a definite idea to work out—and the one that he takes the matter up with as far as I know is the one he will see thru to completion. From what he said of you, which was most complimentary, you are the one of his choice, and altho he said nothing against Dr. Hewett, he did say . . . that no institution could well survive and progress that was not directed by a person who devoted his whole energy to it at all times.

. . . The best thing is to work absolutely in the darkness—come to brass tacks with Dr. H.—let him take one side or the other and stick to his last—he will be opposed I know because the whole matter is coming thru you. . . . The thing to do now is to have your talk with Hewett, get him to come out flatfooted on the proposition, either for or against—I fear it will be against—but it will bring him out into the open where we want him. . . . Mr. R. will insist on one single head for the whole development, in other words a combining of both structures, new and old, about a great court where heating etc. can be carried on economically. . . . He doesn't want a mass of organizations to deal with—with their conflicting aims desires and prejudices to contend with that will prevent the best ultimate development. . . .

We will probably both lose the friendship of Hewett before we are thru . . . but he was extended the chance and did not accept or comply—we have always done more for him than he paid us for and it means too much for Santa Fe and the state to stop now no matter where he stands. It might be appreciated by Mr. Springer if you would drop him a line there on Chap as he stood so loyally by for so long now and contributed so much to the cause. . . . Give my best to Kate and the children.[4]

Nusbaum set Chap up beautifully. He coached Chap on what Rockefeller wanted to see in his report. Knowing his friend well, he tried to ease Chap's misgivings over the rage and hurt El Toro was sure to feel, with assurances that Hewett could only blame himself.[5]

Before Rockefeller left Santa Fe, he had sent a note to Chap on June 12, pledging $2,500 on Chap's call to assist the IAF. It was the first of four pledges until the Laboratory of Anthropology was funded in 1929 and the collection housed there. Chap's accountability for these monies proved his trustworthy acumen to Rockefeller, an impression reinforced by Chap's careful budgeting so as not to affect market prices. Well aware of how Santa Fe gossip traveled, Chap deposited the funds in an Albuquerque bank. "Not even my associates in the Indian Art Fund knew of the amount, and I made small payments to local dealers on account, as if it was the best I could do."[6]

With the IAF now provided for, there was the requested report to draft. Chap was in a painful quandary. Whatever resentment he bore Hewett, he wanted to be fair. Rockefeller left him free to maintain confidentiality or not, indicating he would welcome a museum/IAF compromise plan. In conscience, Chap had no choice but to confer with Hewett as Nusbaum urged, though he withheld Rockefeller's request of a separate IAF report:

> *I had planned to give Dr. Hewett, 1) Mr. Rockefeller's message concerning his request of 1924 for information on the School and Museum, and, 2) to advise him of Mr. Rockefeller's particular interest in the <u>Museum</u>. This I had expected to lead to a more general account of our discussions of the various possibilities of museum expansion, but I had not foreseen the complications that were to arise at our first meeting, which lasted less than an hour.*
>
> *Dr. Hewett expressed great surprise at Mr. Rockefeller's statement, saying, "Why, this is a most serious matter. I have no recollection of such a request. Mr. Rockefeller must be mistaken. I must take time to consider it. I will give it further thought tonight and will call you tomorrow." He then disclosed the details of a prospective grant of one million dollars to the Archaeological Institute. . . . Further, he assured me that the grant would soon be in hand for, at the invitation of "one of the Rockefeller organizations" the Institute was preparing a comprehensive statement, toward which he had contributed a report on the School.*
>
> *Apparently Dr. Hewett believed that Mr. Rockefeller had been at least aware of the negotiations; that his previous visit in 1924 had given him a favorable impression of the situation in Santa Fe, and that his recent visit accompanied by Mrs. Rockefeller was further confirmation of his interest in the <u>School</u>.*
>
> *In our second conference . . . Dr. Hewett began with an obviously well-planned statement. . . . He said he was positive that [Rockefeller's request] had not come to him, and suggested that Mr. Rockefeller might have asked Dr. Corwin for such a report. "But, Dr. Hewett," I protested, "you have told me that for several years*

Dr. Corwin had been promising to bring Mr. Rockefeller on a visit to the Museum. If the request had come to him, would he not have told you at once?"

Dr. Hewett had no answer for that. . . .

. . . Dr. Hewett repeated his emphasis on the School and insisted that any attempt to promote separately the Museum's interests would be misunderstood by the Archaeological Institute, and would jeopardize its anticipated grant. Continuing, he said:

"Take that sum of $30,000 raised by Mr. Springer, in 1916, to match the legislature's first appropriation for the Art Museum, let me remind you—that was paid to the School and not to the Museum." "Yes," I replied, "but were not the contributors interested primarily in doing something for the State?" "Not at all," he said[.] "The majority of Mr. Springer's group were from outside the state—many from the East. Look it up for yourself in the 'Organic Acts.' That will straighten you out." I knew that I was right. . . .

I tried to tell Dr. Hewett that Mr. Rockefeller's interest in the Museum was distinctly personal. I knew his scorn of "pigmy minds" [sic] and was not surprised when he broke out with, "You don't know what you're talking about. Mr. Rockefeller does nothing like this on his own account. Oh, maybe in little, inconsequential amounts, but important matters such as ours he leaves to the Foundation or his other agencies. Ask anyone who knows!"

"Dr. Hewett," I replied, "I am sorry to disagree with you, but I am convinced that I know more about this than you do. I remember distinctly that Mr. Rockefeller directed me to communicate with him through his personal office. But to make certain that I had not misunderstood him I have consulted the World Almanac of the past four years. There I found benefactions, listed separately by foundations and individuals, and I assure you that Mr. Rockefeller's have been anything but trivial."

. . . [T]hen, like a head-master dealing with an unruly pupil, he asserted his authority and brought our conference to an abrupt close, by saying, "Well, we have had enough of this. There is only one way to settle the whole matter: To go back to the beginning, when I found that I couldn't return in time to meet Mr. Rockefeller I advised him that you would represent me. All right, in my absence you were asked to submit a report on the School and Museum. But naturally that should come from the proper source—the Director, and therefore I will attend to that myself."

At that point I took over and held my ground to the end. "You say that you advised Mr. Rockefeller that I would meet him. If that is so you should have notified me of the appointment. Instead, I was caught with only a few hours'

John D. Rockefeller Jr. (left) and Edgar Lee Hewett, 1924.
(Courtesy of Palace of the Governors (MNM/DCA), 7361.)

notice and . . . pitched in as a janitor and spent the entire morning cleaning up the place.

"Two years ago I did the same thing for you. You had just returned from San Diego and learned that Dr. Corwin and Mr. Rockefeller were to arrive within a few hours. You may remember that you called me that morning at seven o'clock and asked me to come to your office at once. Though I was not then on your staff, I complied as promptly as possible. There you told me of your predicament, the Museum was in great disorder and you asked me to take charge.

"On that occasion I did not have an opportunity to meet Mr. Rockefeller. But this time he had been advised to consult me. He has asked me for a report on the general museum situation in Santa Fe, in which the School is not primarily involved. I have agreed to prepare it, and I intend to do so. I know very well what this means, and if you feel that it ends my usefulness on your staff I shall be glad to hand you my resignation at any time."

Apparently Dr. Hewett feared Mr. Springer's displeasure, for I continued with the Museum until the latter's death in 1927.[7] (emphasis in the original)

Chap followed through with his two reports. Rockefeller's dissatisfaction over Hewett's neglected submission had left a deep impression on Chap, so he kept Rockefeller apprised of his progress. After reviewing his drafts with Jess, Chap assured Rockefeller that he and Nusbaum were of like mind, but that finishing the reports must wait for the close of Indian Fair.

Meanwhile, Hewett drafted a report on the school, outlining its character and its research and discussing its museum and educational work. He emphasized his vision of archaeology in Latin America. He proposed plans for the acquisition of properties adjacent to the Museum of Fine Arts and the Palace of the Governors, which could be got for a moderate price if he acted soon. He requested $250,000 for land purchase, $50,000 each for five new buildings, and $500,000 to invest, its income to cover maintenance. Hewett, having inadvertently alienated Rockefeller two years earlier, was now requesting $1 million!

Chap kept Springer informed of the situation, and the twenty-year-old dynamics of the triangle intensified. Springer sought to keep unity. When Hewett asked Springer to review his draft, Springer approved it but urged Hewett to allow Chap to submit his own per Rockefeller's invitation. He wisely pointed out that if a man of Rockefeller's stature expressed a wish, it would be best to honor it.[8]

Hewett had agreed to give a copy of his report to Chap but waited until four days before his August 24 trip to New York, just as Chap was leaving for Gallup. There was no time for discussion; Chap told him that it was a fine report from the school's standpoint, but it did not cover the matters Rockefeller was particularly interested in. He would therefore submit his report. Ignoring Springer's advice, Hewett insisted otherwise. It must have troubled Chap to report to Springer, given the elder man's failing health:

> I told him that I found his recommendations so evenly balanced that it would be hard to explain the stress laid upon the subject of Indian Arts if it were included in his report, and that . . . I would first have to get the approval of the Fund. I believe I made it clear that I felt that inadvisable but that I would gladly see what could be done about it if he wished. He did not ask for it and so the subject was dropped. . . .
>
> Mr. Rockefeller told me that he hoped my suggestions in regard to a compromise of the various interests would lead to results and asked me to go into that phase in detail. I learned from Jess while at the Mesa Verde that he favors the Fund's work even if it has to go on its own. Dr. Hewett has told me flatly, in the past that there can be no compromise whereby the Fund can have control of its collections quarters maintenance within the Museum and I look for no compromise so long as he speaks for the Museum. In talking with him Saturday I was led again to expressing in a few words, my views in regard to the whole situation, as I have done at rare intervals in the past. I might better have left it unsaid and I have vowed to let it be my last. . . . I see nothing in his report that gives the Museum a better show than it has had in the past. Expansion under the present system would only add to our complications.
>
> I have held on all these years hoping that I could do something to further your interests in the Museum, for I believe you have held it above such projects as a "laboratory for Psychological Research" in San Diego and a dozen others that turn up as I look over the Annual Reports of the School!
>
> A Director of the <u>Museum</u>, on the job, with his heart and mind in Museum work, could have worked wonders here, and it isn't too late to make a start, as we of the Fund have proven to our satisfaction. I hope you will approve of my report. The Director insists that one coming from this end will jeopardize the Institute's project[.] . . . I believe I can do him and the institution a service by suggesting some means by which they can be brought together.
>
> Dr. Hewett intimated that . . . I would be presuming in carrying out Mr. R.'s request, but please remember that Mr. R. had planned to meet me as I learned more definitely from Jess.
>
> I have written him that my report is under way, and to back down now would throw this whole project under a cloud.[9] (emphasis in the original)

Hewett sent his statement to Rockefeller on September 8. His cover letter expressed urgency over acquiring land and beginning construction, and confidence that he could attract additional patrons. Rockefeller had left for Europe for several weeks. It fell to Thomas B. Appleget, one of his secretaries, to maintain correspondence and steer decisions; this was a powerful position, one that he would occupy throughout the coming drama. Chap hoped that Nusbaum would stop in Santa Fe before heading east. If so, Nusbaum would then be able to fill Hodge in on the latest developments, including the growth of IAF's collection, now up to 750 pots and "still going strong."[10]

Chap mailed his two documents on October 5: (1) a plan to integrate the school, museum, and IAF that included information on less expensive properties on the town outskirts, and (2) a report on the IAF, in the event that interinstitutional collaboration proved unfeasible, that described plans for a new research/exhibition building away from the plaza. Chap's accompanying letter was candid. He was pessimistic about cooperation, noting Hewett's unfinished projects and chronic absences:

> I hope the Nusbaums have made it clear to you that I have never been lured by an executive position. I have hung on at the Museum all these years, first, to see Mr. Springer's work through, and, second, hoping for a chance to finish some of my own. The first is now completed and I am now trying to renew my acquaintance with my Indian Art.
>
> If my suggestions lead to developments in which my experience and interest will be of value, you can count on my help in any way that will not involve a greater sacrifice of my own work than I have made in the past. As I told you last June, I feel that after seventeen years, I have earned the right to see it through.
>
> . . . I want to assure you, Mr. Rockefeller, that the preparation of these reports has been a most interesting and profitable experience to me, and I want to thank you for having given me the opportunity to go into the matter.[11]

Hewett's plan and Chap's first report were similar in many ways. Both proposed a cooperative arrangement that included the historical society, the museum, and the school. Hewett emphasized his intercontinental vision, while Chap focused more on local needs, as exemplified by the IAF. Chap had done his level best to represent the advantages of Hewett's projected institutional integration while at the same time suggesting the need for greater administrative boundaries. In putting together his IAF report, he had had Nusbaum's inside tips on Rockefeller's desires. Besides Nusbaum and Kidder, Chap had another ally in Morley. With covert input from friends whose issues with Hewett were a common denominator, Chap defended his integrity when he wrote Hodge, "Morley worked with me on the [second plan] and has picked it as the winner. I have done my damdest [*sic*] on the first and will have a clear conscience if it loses out."[12] With no secure future, he was rapidly burning his bridges with Hewett.

While waiting for a response, Chap kept Springer posted. "Routine museum work keeps me plodding along without much chance to get at my own. I have just finished a paper and drawings for the coming meeting of the New Mexico Association for Science. The subject, 'Stone wall construction in ancient Pueblos' is new to me but I thought I ought to be making a noise like a Curator of Archaeology from now on," he wrote in late October.[13] "All the family are well. Kate is finishing another house which promises to be her last for the year. I have had to finish off my summer vacation with a few afternoons at home getting things ship shape for winter."[14]

During October, Rockefeller and Hewett were both abroad. Rockefeller's organization now set to work. Appleget contacted Hermon Bumpus for consultation. Bumpus was a trusted acquaintance of Rockefeller's through Brown University. He had also served as a member of the school's managing committee in 1909. Philosophically, Bumpus embraced tourism enthusiastically. He responded to the burgeoning numbers of travelers to the shrinking western wilderness and its heritage with expansive ideas of outdoor exhibits and dioramas to help Americans understand themselves. Like Rockefeller, he favored "trailside museums" that embraced archaeology, anthropology, ethnology, and geology. By the time Appleget tapped him, he was a key member of the American Association of Museums.[15] The association was active in promoting such projects at the national parks and had even gained backing from the Laura Spelman Rockefeller Memorial Fund. Coincidentally, in 1926, the American Association of Museums' outdoor education committee had recommended to the Spelman Rockefeller Memorial Fund the establishment of an archaeological museum and laboratory in the Pueblo region.

It appears that Bumpus first mentioned this idea to John D. Rockefeller Jr. when asked his opinion about (1) the possible merger of Santa Fe museum organizations and (2) the IAF.[16] Bumpus's vision harmonized well with Nusbaum's and Rockefeller's. In November, Bumpus wrote Appleget, damning Hewett's efforts with faint praise. He held that the museum, located in an ethnically rich historic area with an art colony to boot, could always count on the tourist trade, whereas the school showed poorly when compared to its sister institutions overseas. He pointed out that it failed to draw serious students and that other authorities in archaeology, namely the Boas camp, had a poor perception of its scientific caliber. (Their evaluation reflected the striving of a relatively young science, American anthropology, for national professionalism and status, sometimes at the expense of local and original talents such as Hewett.) Bumpus's appraisal was sufficient for Appleget to draft a November 16 letter to Hewett, rejecting further consideration of his proposal. Hewett was down but not out.

Chap reached out to Kidder for advice. Kidder represented the "new archaeology," particularly through his advancement of stratigraphy as a method of establishing chronology, as Nels Nelson had done. Having achieved prominence in the anthropological world, he was active with anthropologists from other institutions through his position with the National Research Council.[17] Though he was based in Andover, Massachusetts, he focused on the Southwest in his work. He still felt a forceful connection to it and to Chap—he was a wholehearted member of the IAF board. As he happened to be excavating at Pecos at the time, Chap was able to meet and confer with him. Kidder was deeply interested in Rockefeller's tender of immediate IAF support. He surprised Chap by sharing that for several years he had mulled over a plan to establish a permanent Southwest headquarters for anthropological research, a sort of laboratory, to provide graduate field training and research facilities for visiting and resident anthropologists.

> *"Obviously," said Ted, "with due respect to Dr. Hewett for his early and most timely activities in rousing interest in, and protection for, archaeological remains, he would not fit into the present picture where modern ideas of research would be devised and tested."*
>
> *Therefore, for such an independent institution, he believed that Mr. Rockefeller's interest might be the solution, for the Indian Arts Fund with its prestige in preserving and promoting Indian Arts would fit well into such an enterprise. I then offered him an opportunity to present its possibilities at a meeting of the Fund. His plan was unanimously approved by the Fund's Board.[18]*

The IAF endorsement amounted to a green light for Kidder. Later that fall, he and the executive committee of the anthropology and psychology division of the National Research Council proposed a Southwest field school modeled on the Marine Biological Laboratory at Woods Hole, Massachusetts. It would capitalize on what Chap had told him. Kidder's November 20 letter to Chap confirmed that he had seen his reports, courtesy of Nusbaum. In his opinion, Rockefeller would not back a cooperative plan, but it would be grand if he supported the IAF. He assured Chap of his desire to be of help, and clearly he was well placed to provide such help.

Chap sought counsel from Bradfield, his sympathizer in San Diego. Brad's angst over Hewett's whims (including the whim that had resulted in his current assignment, where he greatly missed New Mexico) paralleled Chap's, forming a basis for commiseration and collusion. Chap sent a registered letter via an agreed-on mail arrangement that would bypass the secretary's desk. Based on Chap's description of his and Hewett's reports, Brad replied that Hewett's would lack credence. If necessary, he intimated, Chap might fight "out of court" by blowing the whistle on Hewett's favoritism toward the school and

Jesse L. Nusbaum at Painted Desert Exhibit, San Diego, California, c. 1915. (Courtesy of Palace of the Governors [MNM/DCA], 60487.)

AIA. "H. said to me that he had the ideal arrangement in Santa Fe as the Board never asked questions and their meetings were mere forms." Knowing of Chap's reticence with Springer, Brad urged, "Stick to your guns with Mr. Springer. Keep on being frank with him and tell him enough times so the repetition will count. He would never look at anything that criticized H. at one time you know." He asked Chap for copies of his and Hewett's reports, reminding him to use an alternate address "so Miss A. will not know even any frequency of letters."[19]

On December 1, the Nusbaums traveled from Washington to New York to meet with Rockefeller and Appleget. Appleget's subsequent memo cautions that because Hewett's vision was aimed elsewhere, he should not gain a controlling interest in Chap's work if Rockefeller's investment was to be protected. The next day, Appleget formally invited Bumpus into the process, charging him to meet with interested parties in the Northeast and in Santa Fe and to report back to Rockefeller with his assessment and recommendation. He would publicly represent the American Association of Museums while discreetly acting as Rockefeller's agent.

After the meeting with Rockefeller, Jess sent a triumphant encoded night wire to Chap:

WASHINGTON DC DEC 4 1926

EL TORO FELL IN CROWDING FENCE. YOUR BIG HORSE HIGHLY COMMENDED. INTERESTS HAVE SELECTED TRAINED MAN TO THOROUGHLY STUDY SITUATION. YOUR PET COLT WILL RECEIVE SEPARATE CONSIDERATION IF BIG HORSE FAILS. HAD MOST INTERESTING CONFERENCE. MUMS THE WORD. JUST RETURNED. LEAVE MONDAY WRITING FULLY.[20]

Springer urged Chap to maintain amity between the museum and the IAF, but this was no longer tenable. Rockefeller's organization was sensitive to the potential for the outright expression of antipathy between Hewett and Chap. To prepare Bumpus for his investigative work, Appleget sent him "a little confidential information":

In the first place, Dr. Hewitt [*sic*] and Mr. Chapman are not in very sympathetic accord. Dr. Hewitt's emphasis is, apparently, on archaeological and ethnological studies involving both Americas and, if possible, even the Orient, at the cost, we believe, of any development of studying collections in the immediate Southwest. Mr. Chapman, on the other hand, is vitally interested in the region in which he is working and is anxious to make an adequate study and presentation of the Indian culture, both pre-Spanish and post-Spanish, of the New Mexico area.

. . . Mr. Rockefeller has . . . indicated an interest to them both. Chapman went to some pains to prepare two plans, both of which are enclosed. . . . Dr. Hewitt simply sent him a general statement of needs and program. As far as a general presentation was concerned, it seemed wise to decline the request from Dr. Hewitt. Mr. Rockefeller now wants to go into the suggestions which Mr. Chapman made and has indicated a willingness to do what seems best. Actually, there is very little difference in the two plans presented by Messrs. Hewitt and Chapman.[21]

Appleget specified that Chap's plan called for taking the museum out from under the school's control and subsuming cooperating bodies under an umbrella organization; it also proposed an autonomous facility for local material (the IAF collection).

While Hewett would enlarge and remodel existing buildings, Chap proposed new buildings in the quadrangle devoted to museum activities. During the December strategy
session among himself, Rockefeller, and Bumpus, they opted to plan along Bumpus's
line of a comprehensive Southwest anthropological laboratory. Rockefeller then notified Chap of Bumpus's upcoming visit, informing him that Bumpus had already
proposed a scenario similar to what he and Chap had discussed, backed by leading
authorities in the field; in light of Hewett's and Chap's reports, Santa Fe was a likely
site. The situation was encouraging, he wrote, asking that Chap trust the wisdom and
judgment of his deputy.

Though mention of the IAF was conspicuously absent, Chap was to find that Bumpus
was, indeed, sympathetic and a consummate diplomat. Before the old year rang out, Chap
received a note from Bumpus: "Through a strange series of coincidences, I have recently
met several of your friends and feel that I shall arrive somewhat acquainted with at least
a few of the problems. Mr. Rockefeller has handed me your report—I might say excellent
report—and I am most anxious to have a real visit with you and see if we cannot work
out something that will be a real boost for the archaeology of the Southwest. . . . While in
Washington I was fortunate in meeting Nusbaum, Kidder, Morley, Morris, Judd; in N. Y.
Wissler; here in Brookline, Guernsey & Spinden. I have also seen Riggs & Heggeman."[22]
Strange coincidences? Chance is rarely so kind. Bumpus must have orchestrated them,
possibly with the help of a confederate or two.

Nusbaum continued to work the system on Chap's behalf. Naturally, all parties
were practicing their best gamesmanship as confidential information was sleuthed out
and exchanged. Manners cloaked motives; innocent curiosity camouflaged sly prob-
ing; poker faces belied calculated self-interest. Nusbaum was on the closest terms with
Hodge, the friend he called Téluli, so Hodge had the inside story.[23] After Hewett called
on him, Hodge wrote Chap that he had feigned ignorance as El Toro explained his hope
for expansion, "not leaking a hint of what Jess had told me of Mr. R's visit to Santa Fe
and of the part you have played in the scheme. Hewett mentioned nothing of this."[24]
Since Chap had already declared to Hodge his effort to represent Hewett fairly, what
did Hodge mean by "scheme"? Primary synonyms for this word, according to *Roget's
Super Thesaurus*, include: "plan," "plot," "stratagem," "ploy," "machination," "intrigue,"
"conspiracy," and "maneuver." The letter holds no other clues to what Hodge meant
by "the part you have played in the scheme," but the comment insinuates that Hodge
believed Chap to be capable of intrigue with close friends, provided that the end was
justified. These friends would know of Chap's passion, talent, and discontent and how
to persuasively preempt qualms of conscience, like those that surfaced whenever Chap
remembered his and Nusbaum's prank with the faked Tuxtla, at Morley's expense. But
this alliance was not the product of youthful hijinks. Chap's digestive ailments may

have been a signal of the apprehension he felt about his role in the "scheme." Hodge, on the other hand, clearly relished his part in the drama. Hewett had enjoined him to secrecy—and Hodge readily told all to Chap, for whom there was no turning back.

As for Hewett, word arrived from Appleget as if it were a holiday gift. As capable of machination as the rest, Appleget framed Bumpus's proposal as an American Association of Museums initiative, informing Hewett that in the light of this development his report would be reconsidered. All bets were on; Appleget was keeping options open.

Before Bumpus arrived in Santa Fe, word was out in the anthropology network that something big was afoot in Pueblo country. Information was sniffed out, alliances formed or renewed. Hewett, back from Europe, took some time back east to recruit support for his resurrected proposal. Like Hodge, Kidder played dumb when Hewett came calling. He reported to Chap on January 10, "I have seen the Director twice recently,—once before and once after his visit to New York. I do not know whether he learned the details of the project which you submitted to Mr. Rockefeller. On the occasion of his first visit, I told him that I thought you had submitted a project. He did not appear to be greatly concerned by this, and I think that if he comes a cropper it will be due to an under-estimation of the opposition which has developed in Santa Fe. He has, for example, no conception of the strength of the people who are behind the pottery fund."[25] Hewett could not have been unaware of his fading academic status. Even his AIA sympathizers did not carry enough weight to match what he was now up against. Chap relayed Kidder's letter to Hodge, remarking, "[Kidder] thinks he underestimates the Fund's strength, but I believe his attitude indicates self-hypnotism."[26] Hewett was awake to the threat if Chap gained Bumpus's ear. In the same letter, Chap told Hodge that the director tried to induce him to leave town by offering a three-month leave and heavy support to take his monograph work (and his family!) to southern Arizona. Chap tried to break it gently that he was expected to meet with Bumpus and would stay in Santa Fe.

Springer was now chronically ill with heart disease. Chap, ignoring Bradfield's advice to confront Springer with the facts, softened his correspondence and avoided mentioning the mounting crisis. In January, he wrote Springer to congratulate him on the publication of the *American Silurian Crinoids*, which had just come out. "Altogether it is a great achievement, and I am so proud that I was able to rally so soon after my knockout and see my humble part of the work through. Your generous acknowledgement of it is just the finishing touch."[27] He chatted on about family matters, sharing that while Kate and the children were away for an extended vacation in Dragoon, Arizona, he grabbed the chance to paint and repair the house before the De Huffs arrived for two months' use of it.[28] When they took occupancy, he moved into the little black house, the household nickname for a tarpaper outbuilding on the adjoining lot, rehabbing it as well. He expected to catch up on neglected work at the museum. Having focused on odds and ends that had claimed his time for so long, Chap wanted to keep things shipshape in the event that a new curator was hired whom he would need to teach the ropes. He discussed his relationship with Hewett only in terms of numbers:

> Dr. Hewett has asked me to prepare a schedule of my proposed activities for the legislative appropriations committee, and is now considering my first draft of it. I feel that it is useless to . . . talk of a 100% appropriation of my time for my own work, and that the committee will be more favorably impressed with about a 70–30 division, the 30% being for the inevitable activities which I cannot sidestep.[29]

Bumpus arrived on February 1, 1927, and stationed himself in Chap's studio at the museum for three weeks where, according to Chap, he seemed intent on promoting his project for a Southwest research laboratory/museum. Hewett had returned as well, and the inevitable conferences and social gatherings afforded Bumpus access to key persons. Because Hewett was due in San Diego in mid-February, he spent as much time as possible with Bumpus, choreographing meetings with board members and politicians. The two collaborated in preparing a lengthy report addressed to the outdoor education committee of the American Association of Museums, dated February 11, which the school typeset and Bumpus distributed. It described the concerned institutions and organizations and their interrelationships and made a recommendation to the committee that in view of their own, Hewett's, and Chap's applications to Rockefeller, all parties submit an integrated, cooperative plan for the establishment of an archaeological laboratory and museum at Santa Fe. The essential points of the plan echo Hewett's proposal to Rockefeller, especially noting the importance of expediently acquiring property for an expanded complex. The report promises that both Hewett and Chap were pledged to the best interest of all concerned and to making such compromises as would serve that end. That same day, Chap wrote to Rockefeller, glowing about his agent:

> I presume that you have heard from Dr. Bumpus of the splendid progress he has made since his arrival, a week ago.
>
> I can't tell you how encouraging his presence has been and as for his delightful personality, and that of Mrs. Bumpus, the privilege of knowing them has already repaid me for the digging I did on those two reports.
>
> Dr. Bumpus has preferred to finish his business first with Dr. Hewett, who leaves tomorrow, and then will meet with the executive committee of our Fund. The difficulties I had felt, even up to the day of his arrival, are already

disappearing under his tactful handling and I am now confident that there will be a complete agreement when he has prepared his recommendations.[30]

Hewett departed, confident that he had Bumpus's full support, and so it appeared. Untimely floods delayed getting mail out, but Hewett was finally able to write Appleget and press for immediate funds to buy his desired land. Chap and Bumpus now spent most of their time projecting plans for a new institution. Herbert Maier, executive agent for the outdoor museums project and an architectural draftsman, arrived and was given the use of a museum studio. There were frequent conferences among the three as they created alternatives to Hewett's blueprint. Bumpus vigorously engineered results:

> *Within a week, after one of our mid-morning sprints around the block to the north of the Old Palace, ostensibly to "get the feel of it," Dr. Bumpus . . . finally said, "Well, Chap, what do you think of . . . the problem of fitting into part of a city block, all that we are planning, and can get if we go at it right. What's the sense of squeezing everything into the center of town. This is the dirtiest town of its size I've ever been in. Soft-coal smoke belching out of smoke stacks and chimneys[;] . . . my linen is blacker here than in Pittsburgh! Then, another thing, what about parking space? It is already a problem. What will it be like in another ten or twenty years? I've been in museum work over <u>fifty</u> years and it doesn't seem more than ten. Look ahead!— before long you'll see not only bus-loads of tourists but whole fleets of busses, plying between our National Parks. . . . Have you thought of a site further out for your Indian Arts Fund?" "Yes," I said, "and we have one promised as a gift." "Let's see it," said Dr. Bumpus, and we taxied out to Mary Austin's place on the Camino del Monte Sol. "Not bad," he said, "when you get here, but you need a wider street, and acres of parking space!"*
>
> *Dr. and Mrs. Bumpus were in constant demand at teas, dinners, and other get-togethers. He kept hammering at his project—land, land, land!—until finally he was invited by Francis C. Wilson and the Misses White, to view sites within their DeVargas Development Company's property. Within a few days they arranged to provide a large tract, which, with gifts of adjoining lands donated by Bronson Cutting and Knaebel provided a total of over fifty acres for the new institution.[31]*

(emphasis in the original)

The land donation, aided by lawyer Francis C. Wilson, gave partial direction to the outcome. But this wasn't the only thing that swayed Bumpus in favor of Chap's proposal; it was also Hewett himself. Bumpus had discerned an aspect of Hewett's modus operandi with which Chap was all too familiar but had been too loyal and discreet to reveal. Rockefeller's deputy, whose personality made him a natural at building trust and eliciting facts, soon ascertained the long-standing problems of Hewett's directorship. He opened his mind to Appleget in a handwritten letter of February 15, 1927:

> In his zeal to get things done and, perhaps, in his desire to keep things in his own hands, Dr. H. has constructed a veritable web of connections which may prove dangerous entanglements. As Director of the "School" (his *real* interest) he has induced the Legislature to found the "State Museum" of which he becomes the Director and the Regents (largely his associates in the "School") are the legal controlling body. The <u>State</u>, most generously, appropriates $25,000 annually for the maintenance of the Museum, but this, as a matter of fact, is used very largely to pay the salaries of the staff of the <u>School</u>. I consider this most unwise, not to use another adjective. In the meantime the collections that have come to the State museum (the archaeological finds, which in certain cases have resulted from excavations made at the expense of the State) are officially accredited <u>not</u> to the State museum but are announced, to the parent "Institute," as belonging to the "School." The Legislature, in the meantime, is told how wonderfully the State museum is growing. A case in point: At the urgency of the Legislature, the priceless documents covering the Spanish Mexican & Territorial periods were turned over to the State by the Federal Government. For want of a better place and perhaps through the activity of the Regents, these have been placed in a semi-fireproof closet in the Art Museum. The Director has definitely informed me that these are the <u>property</u> of the "<u>School</u>," indeed they were so included in "our report" but I have taken the liberty, after conferring with others, to mention them where they belong. . . . [T]here are many more [examples] of minor importance which lead me to fear that at some time there will be a "blow up." It was not, however, until I found Dr. H. disinclined to allow the State to retain possession of the Armory . . . that I realized what was really going on. . . .
>
> Concerning the name: "<u>School of Research</u>." There is no school in the proper sense of the word, no school room, records, laboratory, faculty, students—or pay roll. There is little research and no atmosphere of research and the "boss" is away interested in things in San Diego.[32]

Seen through the moral filter of the Rockefeller organization, Hewett was increasingly unappealing. Bumpus could not recommend any plan that would involve Rockefeller in the affairs of the school. The school might be all right as a neighbor, "but

I should hate to marry into the family," he wrote.[33] He contrived a protective duplicity. He advised Appleget to wire him (Bumpus) thus: "Would think it wiser to defer action until you have received some comprehensive plan. Thomas B. Appleget."[34] After Bumpus received the wire to himself that he had dictated, he relayed its content to Hewett on February 19. Bumpus thus orchestrated the Rockefeller rejection of Hewett's request in a way that kept him in Hewett's good graces. For safety's sake, he admonished Hewett that he expected continued cooperation and goodwill from all parties. Ironically, Bumpus's letter was on its way as Hewett, unaware of the stall tactic, again mailed Appleget on the urgent property purchase.

By this time, Chap must have begun to fret about Hewett rallying his AIA allies. He need not have been overly concerned; as Kidder knew only too well, eastern institutions and their leaders had long surpassed Hewett on his own turf.[35] Kidder responded to Chap's anxiety from this perspective. He played to their shared ambivalence about their old mentor—Kidder, like Nusbaum, knew Chap's scruples. He reminded Chap (as Nusbaum had done) that Hewett was now his own worst enemy. He closed with a firm statement that there was no longer room for past sentiment. They would always honor El Toro and desire to save his pride, but if Hewett provoked a showdown, he would only lose.

> If Dr. Bumpus is still there and seems to be discouraged over the outlook for cooperation, please tell him that I am morally certain that if the general plan is being jeopardized by Hewitt's [sic] attitude, the whole question can be fought out in the Institute with, I am sure, perfect certainty of success. The whole business is too big to be blocked by the wrongheadedness of one man. I owe so much to Dr. Hewitt, both for my early opportunities for work in the Southwest and for his thoroughly cordial attitude which made the Pecos excavations possible, that I should intensely dislike to have to take part in such a fight; but . . . Hewitt has changed too much since his early days as an archaeologist to allow personal feelings to deter me.
>
> Please give my best to Mrs. Chap and the Chapitos, and be sure and let me know if I can do anything.[36]

Though they exchanged such confidentialities privately, all parties outwardly professed harmony of purpose. Perhaps Appleget persisted in his charade as a means of ensuring Hewett's continued cooperation or as a way of retaining his goodwill should the outcome not be in his favor. He wrote Hewett, praising him for his collaboration and accord at this stage of brainstorms and deliberations. Privately, though, he had already notified Rockefeller, "Dr. Hewett has his good points. He is, within his limitations, a useful man. Among scientists, however, he is without much reputation. Unfortunately he is unable to sacrifice his own work and plans for any larger good and unable to realize that the development of this new enterprise in Santa Fe will supplement and not compete with his own projects. . . . If matters come to an open break, we are convinced that Dr. Hewett can harm no one but himself."[37] A terse summary note attached to Nusbaum's version of these events perhaps says it better: "Dr. Hewett's primadonna attitudes afraid of his age and slipping authority—he destroyed the wish of Mr. R. to help the Museum and property in town area."[38]

By March 1927, Bumpus was back in New York. On the eighth, he met with Rockefeller and Appleget to terminate his relationship as Rockefeller's agent (now he would solely represent the American Association of Museums) and to outline a Santa Fe archaeological and ethnological center with a national significance. Rockefeller expressed an interest and a willingness to "gamble" $4,000 to option eight acres of property through Francis Wilson.[39]

With tension between Chap and Hewett mounting, going in to work must have been abysmal for Chap. He applied for a month's leave of absence to join Kate and the children in Dragoon, suggesting that he could bring museum work with him, but Hewett now insisted that he stay and concentrate on his curatorial work—not that there was much to do these days. In March, Chap summarized matters in a sociable letter to Hartley Alexander at the University of Nebraska. He reported that Bumpus had "cinched" the fifty acres near Sunmount.

> The "R" deal is coming on. . . . In addition to a fine letter from R. I am told by Nusbaum who was there in December that R. said that not one report in a hundred comes to them so well prepared. . . . Dr. B. is in New York organizing a committee of Museum and University men to devise plans for a Research Laboratory in which our Fund will have a part, Dr. Hewett evidently saw the handwriting on the wall, for he has agreed to cooperate in every way though still trying to get some R. money to buy the Elks Club for the School.[40]

Perhaps to make visible his support of Indian art, Hewett encouraged Chap to dust off his half dozen papers and prepare them for *El Palacio*. Working on them kept Chap occupied while his professional fate was in the balance. He drafted a letter to Hewett expressing irritation with earlier lack of support for publishing his Pueblo pottery monograph, having long since missed a 1914 window when his design research would have made a more significant contribution. By 1927, other work including Kidder's had eclipsed it, so Chap saw no point in publishing it without modification in the light of new finds. In early March, *Art and Archaeology* invited Chap to submit an article on

San Ildefonso pottery. Chap felt this had little purpose since San Ildefonso had gotten more than its share of limelight—a large study, for example, had been published by Carl Guthe in 1925. Instead, Chap proposed that the journal promote the results of the IAF's cumulative efforts: "I feel that the potters of the other pueblos should have due recognition for maintaining the good old standards of their craft. . . . The inclosed bulletin of our Indian Arts Fund and a few photographs give only a hint of the variety of wares produced in the ten pueblos where the art is still alive. I believe that a paper on the pottery of these . . . would serve a very good purpose at this time."[41] Chap made his case. Both *Art and Archaeology* and *El Palacio* published the resulting "Post-Spanish Pueblo Pottery."

Chap, along with Mera, continued to acquire pottery for the IAF, pursuing the task with a dedication that Chap likened to a squirrel gathering nuts. Privately, they both had moments of doubt about how the IAF would fit in Bumpus's endeavor, which now had taken on a life of its own. In fact, Bumpus told Chap in so many words that drawing attention to the IAF to the distraction of the grand scheme would upset the applecart. Chap pondered whether he should contact Rockefeller to make sure Bumpus wasn't distorting their original vision, thought better of it, and instead turned to Kidder who promised that IAF interests were safe.

Bumpus was actively networking with anthropologists in Washington, DC, Chicago, Cambridge, and New York. His proposed membership of a board of directors for a Southwest anthropological laboratory included Kidder, who already conceived of a Woods Hole type of laboratory. Bumpus estimated total costs of $200,000 for construction and $40,000 in annual operating costs. He waxed enthusiastic in a March 21 letter to Rockefeller, but four days later he advised Appleget to apply the brakes. News of a proposed museum in Pasadena that would be well funded, and a fresh Hewett demand that Bumpus meet with him and a committee chosen by him, indicated a need to wait. Meanwhile, Bumpus considered how to structure project funding. Rockefeller policy was to provide seed money to launch and sustain a program for a calculated period, with the expectation of eventual self-sufficiency, so Bumpus specified to Appleget that a contribution should initiate but not maintain the museum and laboratory.[42] He was confident, based on the Woods Hole experience, that ongoing support for the Southwest facility would easily generate itself. Kidder, on the other hand, would hold out in favor of an endowment, since he felt it was demeaning to expect men of science to raise their own funds.

Chap could not have predicted, even with Nusbaum's private correspondence, that the Rockefellers' visit less than a year ago would have precipitated plans for a new anthropological institute in Santa Fe. Some days he felt bolstered by Bumpus's and Kidder's assurances. He could envision the IAF collection on magnificent display, available to

Pueblo artists, as part of a facility whose primary focus aligned with his own interest in regional Native art and anthropology. He imagined being able to pursue his studies in an atmosphere of respect and support. Other days, he reverted to doubt, imagining the collection as an afterthought, housed in a darkened extra room. By spring of 1927, professional interests from New York to Los Angeles were looking at New Mexico's capital for the birth of a new enterprise, backed by Rockefeller wealth. Chap and the IAF's futures hung in the balance. All they could do was wait.

CHAPTER 10

THE FOUNDING OF THE
LABORATORY OF ANTHROPOLOGY

In the basement of the Museum of Fine Arts, Chap pauses before a low shelf of San Ildefonso pottery. He is searching for a particular pot to show Tonita Roybal when she visits later that day. He has to hunch over to look at each pot, but no matter. He is happiest when surrounded by the bold designs of the IAF collection. He occasionally brings potters and townsfolk into the basement but often lingers here alone, as if in an exquisite garden. When he spots the sought-for vessel, he has to push aside one of Maria and Julian's smaller black-on-black feather design pots to reach it. It is about nine inches tall and twelve inches wide, with a ridge in its neck intended to support a lid. Chap is intrigued by this older black-on-red vessel, which is covered in intricate triangular designs. It is new to the collection; other new pots sit with it on the now crowded shelf. Although Chap is pleased that the shelves are packed with important pots, many newly acquired with Rockefeller money, he regrets that they still remain cramped and hidden here. But here they will stay, until Rockefeller approves a plan for a new home—a plan that now attracts the attention of national anthropologists.

While Chap tended to the IAF collection, several institutional interests were symbolically colliding in the persons of Bumpus, Hewett, and Kidder. Bumpus represented the American Association of Museums' desire to establish centers that would translate social science into educational field centers for the public; he also filtered strategic information about the Santa Fe situation to Appleget and Rockefeller. Hewett stood for regional archaeology, the preservation of specific sites and artifacts, and a visionary "science of man." He and Ralph V. D. Magoffin, AIA president, now teamed up to convince Rockefeller that he should fund the AIA to increase its prominence and affirm Hewett's twenty-plus years of southwestern experience by enlarging his Santa Fe school. Harvard-educated Kidder, associated with the National Research Council and the Carnegie Institute, exemplified the desire of academic anthropologists to create systematic research and training methods and thus consolidate both a scientific and a national professional identity; a handful in this camp viewed Hewett with outright scorn. By the spring of 1927, Kidder found himself the principal negotiator for

Alfred V. Kidder, c. 1920. (Courtesy of Palace of the Governors [MNM/DCA], 7599.)

the eastern establishment: the first Pecos Conference and his stratigraphic research in the Southwest had made him a visible leader in "modern" archaeology. His long-term relationships with Chap and Hewett, his extended interest in the Southwest, and his diplomatic talents recommended him for the arduous task of creating a single melody from the cacophony of anthropological voices.

Chap's interests were the most parochial of all and therefore the simplest to protect. He was dedicated to his own studies and to custodianship of the IAF pottery, a quiet mission that had merited Rockefeller's personal assistance. The possibility of foundation sponsorship for a more encompassing venture now cast the IAF in a new light.

Rockefeller philanthropy held a powerful lure, and competition for it brought out the best and worst of each person. It is worth understanding Chap's place among the interests jockeying for favor and how his qualities drew new friends to him at this important time. He preferred to assume a background role but creating and funding a home for his "pet colt" precipitated a manic period for allies and foes alike and therefore thrust him into the limelight with them all. Throughout, his integrity remained constant, the challenges serving only to strengthen his commitment to his mission.

In April 1927, Kidder met with several persons in Washington to wrangle over core principles of the new organization. He entrusted his frustrations to Chap:

> I am in a state of complete nervous and physical collapse, following two days of more or less acrimonious sessions with Hewett, Bumpus, et al.
>
> Wednesday morning at the Cosmos Club reminded one of the lobby of a convention hall. Hewett was buzzing with Hrdlicka and Magoffin in corners; Bumpus with Hodge and Holmes in other corners. We met at two—the executive committee of the Museums Association, the members of Hewett's board who could be in Washington, the President of the Archaeological Institute, Dr. Magoffin, and certain innocent bystanders like Judd and myself. Hewett opened the meeting by recounting the history and achievements of the School, and then voiced his alarm . . . lest the establishment of the new institution serve to discourage legislative appropriations. Bumpus countered this. . . . Dr. Magoffin then uprose and . . . stated that he . . . regarded with alarm and disapproval the foundation in Santa Fe of an organization exactly paralleling in its aims the Institute's School of American Research. . . . [T]he discussion then degenerated into a sort of dog fight, which led nowhere but which eventually resulted in the appointment of a small conference group to attempt to get together on fundamentals. This group consisted of Bumpus, Hewett, Judd and myself; and we put in yesterday afternoon drawing up a declaration of principles, which is very sugary. . . .
>
> . . . Hewett has really had his back put up by statements made in Santa Fe which have come to his ears, that the new Laboratory will serve to mop up and sweep out the School. Knowing as I do the state of public opinion in Santa Fe, I can readily believe that such statements may have been made by some of the more radical of his opponents, but I most sincerely trust that they may be halted and that people like yourself and Mera will do everything that you can to stop them, and to spread the feeling that the older institutions are to be treated with every consideration. . . . I can hardly emphasize this too strongly, because I feel that the Institute has some ground for alarm, and if loose talk in Santa Fe or

elsewhere gets their backs up they are, of course, in a position to make things very uncomfortable for the proponents of the Laboratory.[1]

By early May, Bumpus felt he had an understanding with Magoffin, such that Hewett would not interfere. Hewett was not easily restrained. He suspected Bumpus of rallying opinion against him, especially in Santa Fe, and confronted him. Bumpus warned Chap about Hewett's increasing acrimony. Their letters reveal their mutual trust:

Dear "Chap":

I have refrained from writing you heretofore because I sensed from the beginning that my relations with Dr. Hewett might blow up at any moment—as they have—and I wished to be entirely free from the charge that I had entered his camp in disguise and fomented discord etc. Then too, I did not want you to suffer because of my misdeeds. Now that the explosion has come . . . I shall try to keep you posted in regards to events at this end and hope you will be willing to write freely in regard to affairs in Santa Fe.[2]

My dear Dr. Bumpus,

. . . I had a little taste of the controversy in an interview with the Director lasting over two hours, just before he left for the fight, which served to help me realize what you have been up against. It would have come up, even if there had been no Association cloud on his horizon, and once driven to it, I discussed plainly some matters that I have not brought up for fifteen years. I got nowhere, except that I believe I made it clear that I have had no hint of an offer from the Association, but that I do not feel bound to end my days with the Museum if I see a better chance to further my own work.

I feel that I am working in the interests of my own institution and the State, in helping in any way that does not interfere with my Museum work.[3]

On May 11, Appleget gave Bumpus authorization to propose, under the American Association of Museums' umbrella, a new anthropological institute in Santa Fe. Appleget stressed the organization of a proactive board to demonstrate, in his words, a "going concern," as Rockefeller would only consider a request from an operational body.[4] Also, Bumpus's proposal should clarify commonalities among his, Chapman, and Hewett's plans and the impact the institute would have on local institutions. Finally, other potential financial support for the infant organization should be identified, which would not only fulfill the expectation of future fiscal autonomy but also serve as a yardstick for its objective merit.

Bumpus turned to Kidder who, as chairman of the National Research Council's division of anthropology and psychology, was positioned to call a national meeting. Kidder could utilize Bumpus's proposal to fulfill his own dream of a Southwest graduate field training facility. The meeting's purpose would be to constitute a board to support a proposal from the outdoor committee of the American Association of Museums for a museum and laboratory of anthropology in Santa Fe and to prepare a request for funding. The board would be freestanding, representing its own interests. The meeting was called for June 6, 1927, at the Yale Club in New York City.

Bumpus wryly asked Appleget to clarify the phrase "a going concern": "In your opinion is a Ford fresh from the factory but with an empty gas tank a *going* concern? I imagine it is *going*, if you push it. Which shall be revised—the phrase or the Ford?" He diplomatically postcripted: "It is not expected that Chapman, & some others at a distance, will attend but we thought it would be good business to have them feel that they were invited and could consider themselves as possible 'founders.'"[5]

Meeting invitations were sent to major U.S. anthropological institutions. Among their representatives were some, like Boas, who had long harbored a grudge against Hewett. An impressive collection of minds was assembled, representative of the past, present, and future direction of professional American anthropology.[6] The meeting culminated in a motion by Boas, which passed unanimously:

> That the representatives of the institutions present at this meeting consider the establishment at Santa Fe of an institution for the purposes of research education and graduate instruction in the field as highly desirable, and constitute themselves an organizing committee for promoting this object. At the same time they pledge themselves to attempt to secure the cooperation of the institutions which they represent.

An executive committee was appointed, of which Kidder was named chair and Chapman (in absentia) secretary.[7] When Chap finally received the minutes and other enclosures, he and Harry Mera studied them together, concerned about implications for the IAF. Mera interpreted that it had no standing, but Chap was more optimistic. As far as Chap was concerned, things were starting to look up on many counts. Two of his articles had just been published—"Chance Forms Derived from the Meander," a brief discussion of his 1914 studies, appeared in *El Palacio* and "Post-Spanish Pueblo Pottery" was published in both *El Palacio* and *Art and Archaeology*. The latter recognized pottery from pueblos other than San Ildefonso and included illustrations of pottery from each, underscoring the need for preservation. "The coming of the Spaniards brought great changes in Pueblo land. . . . But pottery-making, always a domestic art of the women, survived the shock and has flourished since in more than half of the twenty-five pueblos as they exist today. A distinct type of ware was finally developed in each, but just how early these marked differences began to show themselves is yet to be determined. There is but little of this early post-Spanish pottery left to tell its story."[8]

Chap and Kate's social life was also regenerative. Santa Fe's artists and Pueblo culture amplified the bond among Dietrich, Stewart, and the Chapmans. The community theater also offered plenty of creative outlets. In June, Chap's good cheer was reflected in a rare gem of his own, dramatized at the Fred Harvey's Indian Detours staff party. A note from Taos Society's founder Joseph Sharp implies that the skit may have been Chap's brilliant roast of the Taos Society of Artists in the form of an Indian creation myth (appendix A). Sharp reported that he had enjoyed Chap's creation immensely: "Please accept my sincere thanks for the credit & boost you gave me in the very clever skit read at the Courrier [sic] dinner last night. Fine lot of girls! Our women folks had to eat at home alone or with the dog!"[9]

Only Springer's failing heart marred Chap's good spirits. Chap had to tuck away his concern as Kidder arrived in July to incorporate the new institution. Incorporation would achieve two ends: it would reinforce the "going concern" and establish the laboratory and museum as an institutional (if still hypothetical) New Mexico presence, thus making it more difficult for Hewett to obstruct. Francis Wilson drew up incorporation papers, and Kidder began circulating them to executive committee members for signatures. He continued to meet with Chap to draft tentative building plans and discuss how the new enterprise would function.

In the mission statement, Kidder described the proposed organization as having four broad aims: (1) to promote anthropological research, (2) to provide public education, (3) to offer graduate field instruction, and (4) to attend to the welfare of the Native races. Kidder's agenda could be found in the first and third; Bumpus's interests were represented by the second. IAF interests were subsumed under the fourth. He estimated a budget of $200,000 for initial construction and $40,000 per annum to cover salaries, maintenance, and research. "The museum should be planned and developed in view of an eventual consolidation with the departments of Archaeology and Ethnology of the State Museum and Historical Society. With this eventuality in mind the museum should be planned as one unit of a larger building designed to house a comprehensive display of the Archaeology and Ethnology of the Southwest."[10] It's no wonder Hewett's back was up.

Chap's expertise in Indian art studies and his intimate involvement with the Rockefeller proposal brought up the question of whether he would consider serving as director, should all go as planned. Acknowledging the honor, Chap made it clear that he preferred to concentrate on those tasks that he had been forced to sideline these many years. He wanted a fresh start—no more competing administrative responsibilities!

Kidder summarized for Rockefeller the progression that resulted in the proposed museum and laboratory of anthropology. He explained how the committee had adapted Chapman's second plan (a building to house the IAF collection, provide Indian art research facilities, and foster Native arts). Chap's proposed approach to research, acquisitions, and Native welfare was so sound that all concerned (Bumpus, committee members, etc.) felt it should serve as the basis for the new laboratory/museum. The executive committee had entered into agreement only with the IAF, whose aims were perceived, or opportunistically construed, to be identical with theirs. Chap must have allayed Mera's concerns, since Kidder reported that "[the IAF] has pledged its continued cooperation in furthering with the Museum-Laboratory a joint program of research."[11] By agreement, the IAF would continue its fund-raising provided it was assured of ample facilities for the display and use of its collections and assured that the collections would be put on public display.

Kidder and Chap were now piggybacking on each other's career successes to establish themselves on their former mentor's turf at the risk of a cold war. It was only a matter of time before El Toro guessed that Nusbaum was also involved—had, in fact, masterminded Rockefeller's meeting with Chap. In Nusbaum's mind, Hewett's overbearing pride was his own undoing. Like a controlling father, the director refused to foster his protégés' success, even attempting to belittle, manipulate, or thwart them, in a pattern of gradual alienation that many of his male associates endured.[12] Chap's correspondence with Kidder, Bradfield, and Nusbaum indicates that their fellowship—and complicity—deepened as a result of such treatment. Nusbaum's unpaid museum accounts made his pain singular, but he was not alone: "Morley, Kidder, Chapman, Judd, Morris to mention only a few. . . . He cant [sic] see a man who has ever been with him advance independently."[13] How did Hewett account for his "boys" turning on him? What reprisals might he concoct? Planting the new laboratory in Hewett's backyard was asking for trouble, and Chap knew it.

The day after incorporation, Kidder convened the 1927 Pecos Conference, which must have been a welcome break after a month of paperwork and secrecy. He had invited a number of archaeologists and anthropologists with an interest in the Southwest to "camp with him and Madeleine, and talk over a number of issues."[14] Two of those were the methods that should be used to accumulate and present data and the need to develop a standardized nomenclature for artifacts, decorative motifs, and periods of culture. A major accomplishment of the conference was the Pecos Classification, a series of eight relative time periods, loosely based on house forms and pottery types.[15] Chap, exhilarated at being one of over twenty-five contributors, dashed off a letter to Bradfield, noting the increasing importance of stratigraphy. "The Conference was a great success, though the Director may submit a minority report on that. . . . Notice I am Curator of Archaeology & Ethnology, on the new stationery. I can't keep track, but will save a sheet for future reference. Have a lot of cataloguing to get at now the rush is over."[16] He added that the laboratory project was proceeding quietly but satisfactorily.

After the conference, Hewett returned to San Diego. Chap's letter, he claimed, was in plain sight "where I could conveniently find it."[17] Was this Bradfield's surprising oversight or the product of a suspicious Hewett snooping? Either way, Hewett stored a copy as evidence of Chap's disloyalty.

After Pecos, Chap immediately became immersed in Indian Fair. Though Hewett dropped Fiesta as a museum-school program, Chap was active in the fair as judge, buyer, and promoter. Dietrich chaired the new volunteer management committee that included Chap, Kate, Mera, Elizabeth and Martha White, Dorothy Stewart, and Frank Applegate.[18] They set up tents on the Palace of the Governors' patio for exhibits and other tents near city hall to house the Indians who had come to dance or exhibit their crafts. Distance and unpredictable transportation meant that many people from the pueblos stayed in Santa Fe, some of them likely at Kate and Chap's house. Cafeteria-style dinners were organized, and Dietrich offered her bath facilities for the Jemez women who cooked.[19]

For the first time, an effort was made to have potters sign their works at the fair, but the potters found this generally unacceptable, indicating that the "old timers" would never have done so. First place of $5 went to Susanna Aguilar of San Ildefonso and second place to Maria Martinez, who also took home nearly $100 from sales. Other artists who made more than $10 in sales were Julian Martinez ($38.50), Desideria ($53.75) and Anna ($23.50) (Maria's sisters), and Lufina Baca of Santa Clara ($43.25).[20] Chap was pleased with the committee's work, describing its results in the same letter to Brad that Hewett found. "It goes to show as I often told the Director that the way to get cooperation is to hand out responsibility. We couldn't have nicked that bunch for $5.00 apiece when the School ran it (on the museum's money!) But up against it themselves, they pledged $100.00 apiece & got contributions of $25 to $50 without much effort. Looks like we can make a real Fair of it from now on."[21]

The fair's success buoyed Chap. Likewise, his Indian arts class at the university always revitalized him. But in late September, his heart was heavy with news of the death of his beloved Springer. Funeral services were held in Philadelphia, attended only by immediate family, but in Santa Fe, Chap and Hewett came together to honor Springer. Chap helped to organize Springer's memorial service on October 9, 1927, in St. Francis Auditorium. Speakers included Judge O. L. Phillips, Judge A. J. Abbott, Captain W. C. Reid, and Hewett. At a Las Vegas memorial service a few days later,

Hewett and Chap again honored Springer. Chap credited Hewett's kindness for his first teaching job. He then described his work with Springer on the crinoid publications and his enduring affection for his mentor. "This then was the side of his nature that most often revealed itself to me; his kindness, his gentleness, his self-effacement in his search for truth."[22]

Amid grief over Springer's passing, Chap must also have felt a curious relief. While Springer had lived, the bonds among Springer, Hewett, and Chap had been often strained but never broken. Now the triangle that had enmeshed Springer, Hewett, and Chap for so long collapsed. Chap had already taken a step toward autonomy by serving on the laboratory's executive committee, although still a museum staff member. With Springer's death, a freedom of movement emerged for Chap and Hewett.

Even with the promise of liberation, Chap recognized that a difficulty for the new laboratory would be establishing sound internal boundaries. He correctly assessed that cobbling together a patchwork of interests posed a systemic pitfall. He aired his concern to Hodge, a recent appointee to the interim executive committee:

> As I see it, we are in exactly the reverse of the School-Museum fix. Those two institutions were created by the Director, who not only laid the wires but who has pulled them for the past 20 years. On the contrary, in our case, a few individuals who have had the vision, may, if all goes well, be elected to the Executive Committee. From there on I feel that we lack a common understanding of all the ways and means by which the executive end of the proposed combine can function. There are probably a half dozen "patterns" of organization, each of which has its advantages in certain institutions, and which should be thoroughly investigated.
>
> Your experience and knowledge of institutions should prove of the greatest value and I wish I could hop the magic carpet for a little discussion of the subject if we are suddenly handed the responsibility of making the darned thing run.[23]

If Chap was unsure about institutional models, confidence in his work was bolstered by the reception it was receiving. November and December saw the publication of three articles: "Stone Wall Construction in Ancient Pueblos and Cliff Dwellings," "A Feather Symbol of the Ancient Pueblos," and "The Shalako Ceremony at Zuni." Chap's study of the feather symbol, which complemented Fewkes's earlier research, remained a favorite of his.

Chap continued to work out of his museum studio, but his future was centered on the new laboratory. In a strategic move, Hewett and Magoffin had been invited to sit on the board of trustees of the museum-laboratory.[24] Both had accepted. Hewett, however, consistently alienated project leaders by creating thorny triangles—which did not, of course, surprise Chap. Magoffin was already caught between defending Hewett's claim that the new enterprise would compete for resources and duplicate services and assuring Bumpus that he would cooperate. Before the year's end, Hewett enlisted as ally James F. Zimmerman, the young president of the University of New Mexico. When Zimmerman was invited onto the board, he too, having been prompted by Hewett, questioned the new organization. Kidder and Appleget tried to allay his concerns, appealing to his rather precocious political good sense. As Kidder observed to Chapman, "I believe he is a different breed of cats from Hewett and Magoffin."[25]

The beginning of 1928 saw Hewett and Magoffin resigning from the board. In a lengthy letter to Kidder on January 6, Hewett alleged that his own annual reports had been all but plagiarized in the committee's preliminary statement. Magoffin quickly took advantage of the situation to resubmit to Rockefeller—not the foundation—his request for an endowment for the school in Santa Fe on the grounds that a promised cooperative plan had not emerged. However, even as he importuned Appleget, citing the school's record of cooperation with other institutions, its assistance with the revival of Native arts, and its role in securing collections that remained in the Southwest, Hewett's record had already undercut Magoffin's arguments. The Rockefeller people had direct experience of Hewett's 1924 failure of compliance. They were aware that Hewett had illegitimately appropriated a collection of state papers for the school. He was hardly a model of cooperative goodwill in 1927. And as for Native arts, Rockefeller himself had seen the IAF's collection relegated to a basement storage room to which the public, let alone Pueblo people, could hardly have had access. To make matters worse, Magoffin's document also bore Hewett's signature.

Appleget, having protected Rockefeller from political and emotional entanglements so far, gave him the go-ahead on January 12: "I think you may safely give consideration to the whole matter[.] . . . [T]he project seems soundly conceived and organized[;] . . . it is so thoroughly a 'going concern' that it will continue, as best it can, whether you contribute or not; its sponsors are convinced of its importance."[26] They began discussing the details of funding. Optimistically, Kidder wrote Chap to prepare to come to New York in February on short notice. Rockefeller, however, was bothered by Hewett's, Magoffin's, and Zimmerman's objections. In mid-February he halted proceedings until their issues were addressed. He continued, however, to make private contributions through Chap to the IAF.

Appleget and Kidder began a concerted effort to reassure Zimmerman and win over Magoffin, but Hewett remained obstructionist. Frustration was contagious; Kidder wrote to Appleget on February 13, "The more one sees of this matter the more clearly it becomes apparent that it is a one-man job. Both Magoffin and Zimmerman were as nice as pie until they were jacked up by Hewett. . . . Dr. Bumpus, on hearing that Zimmerman's opposition was a serious matter, proposed bringing pressure to bear on him through [Senator Bronson] Cutting. This I very strongly deprecated. We simply must not let politics enter this controversy."[27] Kidder also asked Chap to use his skills to keep the press muzzled in Santa Fe. Editor Dana Johnson's ill will toward Hewett would only inflame the director. At last, the concerted diplomacy achieved results with all but Hewett. By the end of March, Zimmerman accepted membership on the board, representing the state board of regents as well as the university. Magoffin, after an attempt to leverage a publication grant out of the situation, relented and indicated that if differences were resolved he would be happy to serve on the board. He let it be known, further, that Hewett would do as he was told.

While Appleget and Kidder smoothed ruffled feathers, Chap was stretching his wings. Two more articles were published: he was sole author of "Bird Forms in Zuni Pottery Decoration" and coauthor of "Preliminary Survey of the Archaeology of Southwestern New Mexico" with Lansing Bloom and Wesley Bradfield. The latter described investigations into the Mimbres Valley and portions of the Gila and Rio Grande Valleys. The authors endorsed archaeology's trend toward replacing small-scale field trips with a methodology of systematic study.

Chap continued to take comfort in his family life. His children, both in grade school, occasionally stopped by his studio after school. They enjoyed family get-togethers that included their grandmother, who lived with two other elderly women in a house on Grant Avenue. Frank described her as typically dressed in black, her gray hair coiffured, with lace on collar and cuffs. In the evenings, Kate would tell stories about her latest project, remodeling Dietrich's Canyon Road home, now named "El Zaguan" because of the long *zaguán* or corridor that ran from the garden into a patio.[28] Besides Spanish-style fireplaces, Kate added brick walkways to the *zaguán* and the west porch floor.[29] Kate and Dorothy Stewart were also collaborating on a book, *Adobe Notes, or How to Keep the Weather Out with Just Plain Mud*, filled with Kate's advice and illustrated with Stewart's linoleum block prints. Spud Johnson's Laughing Horse Press published it in 1930.[30]

An incident that Frank recounted decades later embodied his parents' flexibility and generosity during this time. Returning home from dinner with their friend Margretta Dietrich, Chap and family literally stumbled over some people who were lying on the living room floor. They turned on the light to discover that the unexpected guests were from Santo Domingo and among them was one of the better potters. She had come "to see Dad for something or other and since he wasn't there, they came in, lay down, and went to sleep. So then they woke up, did their business with Dad and then went off. So that sort of thing happened several times."[31]

Kenneth M. Chapman, 1929. (Courtesy of Palace of the Governors [MNM/DCA], 28131.)

Progress on the laboratory project had once again been stymied by disruptions from Hewett and Magoffin. In May, Kidder met with both and hammered out a statement of boundaries and policies. Magoffin seemed more amenable, but Hewett defended both his own museum-school and the University of New Mexico as well. Kidder conceded that a new Santa Fe institution called a "museum and laboratory," perceived to be redundant and privately endowed, could threaten tax support for the university and the school as the agency responsible for the state museum. Therefore, he agreed to drop the word "museum" from its title. This deletion would clarify the organization's intent to focus on modern humanity and Southwest environmental influences rather than historical and archaeological themes. It would create educational programs focused on different subjects from those of the school or university graduate programs, and it would publicize that it would not duplicate or displace the school's or university's efforts. In return, the AIA, museum-school, and university welcomed the new scientific endeavor (with cautious qualification), and expressed desire for full cooperation.[32]

Some IAF supporters were discouraged by the removal of "museum." Kidder expressed satisfaction to Appleget but warned that despite Magoffin's apparent cooperation, Kidder suspected him of putting Hewett up to bargaining.

Now Kidder hoped for a June decision, again sharing his expectations with Chap and urging continued secrecy. Appleget was leaving New York for the summer, however, and disappointed them with the news that no definite recommendations would be made to Rockefeller until his fall return. Kidder was then beset by doubts regarding his effectiveness. He confided in Chap, asking him to be honest if he felt there was a better man for the job and expressing hope that the more ardent of the trustees would not lose patience with the process.[33]

While awaiting the September decision, Chap occupied himself with fieldwork funded by Rockefeller. He traveled to Acoma, Acomita, and Laguna, collecting for the IAF and ordering for the Indian Fair. He confidently wrote Rockefeller that "we find, as a result of our six years' work, that we have established a sort of bureau of standards, as far as the pottery of the Pueblos is concerned—a collection that is consulted not only by the Indians, but by collectors, dealers, artists, writers, and others who want accurate information." He then penned a zesty description of a serendipitous discovery at Acoma, where the Fox Film Company was making *Redskin*.

We must thank the Famous Players Company for unintentionally bringing one rare old jar to light. I arrived on the scene one morning, just as they were training their cameras on the elaborately staged "wedding feast" in the plaza. Hundreds of Indians were grouped around whole sheep, rotating on spits, heaps of Texas watermelons, loads of California grapes, bunches of bananas hung on tripods, and other delicacies never before seen at Acoma. At the rear of the scene was a group of twenty women, awaiting the signal to walk through the picture with jars on their heads[;] . . . one caught my eye—red instead of the usual Acoma white, and obviously a replica of a pre-Spanish or very early Spanish period jar!

The situation called for some quick thinking. I couldn't afford to wait until the scene was finished, for some member of the Company might take a fancy to it and beat me to it. And I could not walk through the scene to find the owner of the pot while the director was still arranging its last details with a critical eye. So I hit on another scheme, and walking into the edge of the scene, I picked up the jar and carried it out to a safe distance to examine it.

It worked, for the owner spied me and came running over to me to rescue her pot. I bought it and then learned that it had been copied about fifteen years ago by her aunt, from an ancient jar still in her possession. After the "Wedding

Feast" we hunted up the aunt who had just arrived that morning, and I was pleased to recognize old Dolores Ascension, one of the potters from Acomita who has won prizes, year after year, at our Indian Fair. She remembered me and my interest in her work. The rest was easy, and I left that evening with both the replica and the original![34]

Chap also taught a short university course in Indian art during Hewett's summer field session. The students provided a happy distraction, but the session itself was the occasion of an insult that would trouble Chap for nearly thirty years. Magoffin spent several days in camp conferring with Hewett but capped his visit by summoning Chap to his tent and subjecting him to an obviously well-rehearsed speech. Magoffin said he had interviewed several Santa Fe residents on the possibility of Rockefeller funding a new laboratory and had heard that Chap submitted a report that conflicted with Hewett's. He had also queried his informants on Chap taking over as director of the new institution. Chap was ready to push back with facts, but Magoffin slipped in an unexpected slur that Chap did not immediately digest:

> He said I would find considerable opposition; in fact, when he mentioned me, a prominent lawyer had exclaimed, "What—that God-damned Judas?" I thanked Dr. Magoffin for his information but did not add that I had declined the Laboratory offer of the Directorship.
>
> Instead, I told him that I doubted if he had obtained a fair cross section of opinion from the residents of Santa Fe, regarding the conflict between the School-Museum and the proposed Laboratory. I told him that I could provide him with a list of a dozen or more, who would say that in their opinion his Archaeological Institute, through its "School" in Santa Fe, had been using the Museum of New Mexico, for the past twenty years as a meal ticket.
>
> The sun was beating down on his tent, the temperature inside was up to 100 [degrees] and Dr. Magoffin, a 200 pounder, was mopping his brow and neck. "What do you mean?" he demanded. "Look at your annual reports," I said. "Ninety-nine percent, playing up the activities of the School, on Museum money, and only one line saying, 'Received from the State of New Mexico $20,000.'"
>
> "Well," he said, "I must confess that we haven't been doing what we should, all these years, but our Archaeological Institute will soon be in a position to hand over [to] the School, an endowment fund of $250,000." I was tempted to tell him that I had learned from a more reliable source that the Institute's prospective grant from the Rockefeller Foundation would not be forthcoming, but decided to leave that to his friends.[35]

The comparison to Judas, who delivered Christ to the Romans, stung Chap deeply, perhaps finding its mark in "a little grain of conscience."[36] Nusbaum, Kidder, and Brad had each tried to preempt any misgiving of Chap's, for they all reminded him that the past was past and that Hewett could only blame himself. But, in fact, Hewett was wounded, and Chap knew it. At some point, a copy of the telltale letter to Bradfield that Hewett saw made its way back to Chap, with Hewett's penciled comment at the top of the first page. The echo of Magoffin's words reveals that Hewett was aware of the insult and felt the same:

> This is a most interesting character study. The writer of this letter accepted for twenty-five years with ostensibly sincere gratitude, my personal interest in his welfare; the opportunities that I made for him being about all he had with the exception of the work given him from time to time by Mr. Frank Springer. During the hard years when we kept the institution going under extreme difficulties Chap appeared to adapt himself to the conditions most willingly. His real attitude, however, was known to some, as when President Magoffin of the A.I.A. was here making his investigation of the School, Chap was spoken of to him as "a damned Judas." . . . ELH[37]

For Chap, the accusation was a vicious hit. Its sting reverberated long after he left Magoffin's tent. He feared it would tarnish his goodness in the eyes of his descendants, should they learn of it. For the rest of his life, Chap cached multiple copies of documents recording his efforts to remain loyal to Frank Springer and Edgar Hewett as well as detailed, redundant notes on conversations with Rockefeller and copies of their correspondence. He stashed away copies of his various complaints against Hewett. Record keeping was characteristic of Chap's meticulous nature, not to mention grasp of political expediency, but in this case it appears defensive, giving the impression that he "doth protest too much."[38]

That Chap, a person whose sterling character was widely recognized throughout his life, should have felt so vulnerable is somewhat perplexing. However, having sat in quiet judgment against Hewett for nearly fifteen years, Chap apparently found it unnerving to be judged himself and found wanting. This time, Chap had no Springer to offer perspective or to force reconciliation. Given Chap's conscientious character, Magoffin's words compelled him to reexamine every aspect of his behavior with regard to gaining Rockefeller's help for the IAF, including the instigative alliance with Nusbaum. In retrospect, it seems that events had mushroomed far beyond what Chap could ever have imagined and now were beyond his control. Though the number and nature of outside interests did not surprise Chap, who knew the players on the professional field, the stakes involved might have. Like a once-mighty Ozymandias, Hewett was beginning to topple.[39] When Chap recognized that he and his small band of brothers were agents in his downfall, he apparently had pangs of conscience not shared by the others. He quietly began a new collection, not of pottery, but of private papers to prove he had not deliberately set out to betray Hewett.

His return from camp brought a happier counterpoint and a reminder that life goes on. Chap was surprised by the smooth operation of Indian Fair, organized by Dietrich and the White sisters, and that encouraged him to look forward to better times. Tonita Roybal won first prize, Maria, second (Maria also won $10 for being the best-dressed Pueblo woman at the fair).

Kidder finally met with Appleget in September and wrote Chap that Appleget had found that "all requirements in regard to cooperation, brotherly love, etc. were fulfilled, and that he would proceed to lay our request once more before Mr. Rockefeller."[40] But it was still not yet to be. Bumpus wrote Appleget that Hewett was increasingly unpopular in Santa Fe and that therefore state funding for the museum was somewhat jeopardized. Bumpus had tried to advocate on Hewett's behalf so Hewett would not be able to interpret a shortfall to be the result of Rockefeller's imminent funding. Strange bedfellows! Appleget assured Rockefeller that they were above reproach no matter what, and Bumpus braced them for the probability that there was still mischief ahead. As anticipated, the mischief came, and it was Magoffin this time. Having failed to get a $500,000 endowment for the AIA based on Hewett's university courses, he spun more objections, again hammering on endangered state funding. Exasperated, Appleget wrote Rockefeller:

> Strangely enough he does not consider that a gift on your part to the work of the Institute itself would have the same effect. . . . [T]he State's support . . . has already been endangered, not by any possible action on your part, but rather by the growing lack of confidence on the part of State officials in Dr. Hewett. . . .
>
> I am sorry that we have not been able to make a more complete job of winning over Dr. Magoffin and Dr. Hewett. . . . I believe that they are actuated by selfish motives and are behaving in unsportsmanlike fashion. My recommendation is that you authorize me to send the attached letter of pledge to Dr. Kidder, declining at the same time Dr. Magoffin's renewed request in behalf of the work of the Archaeological Institute in the Southwest. Mr. Debevoise and I believe that nothing would do more to clarify the air and stop the undercurrent of intrigue than a definite statement of your intent. The only alternative to this seems to be to drop the whole matter.[41]

On November 5, Hewett accepted his seat on the board of trustees. Perhaps he had resigned himself to the inevitable. Or perhaps he had decided it was best to assume a strategic position in which he could bide his time. Later that month, the Laura Spelman Rockefeller Memorial Fund announced an award of $15,000 to the Laboratory of Anthropology for its first summer field school session, but it gave Kidder no clue of Rockefeller's inclination regarding the larger laboratory funding. He was itching to move forward and again turned to Chap as a safe outlet for venting his discouragement.

At last, in early December, Rockefeller asked Appleget if he could now make the laboratory pledge without incurring enmity. Appleget replied in the affirmative, cautioning that there was always a chance that certain unnamed opponents could make trouble. Appleget penned a formal rejection of Magoffin and Hewett's last proposal; he assured them that it reflected no criticism of their aims but was necessitated by both a lack of close fit with Rockefeller interests and also unavoidable limitations. This communication officially closed the professional books as far as the Rockefeller organization was concerned. Hewett, however, never got over the urge to undermine the lab, as Chap would later see for himself.

On December 7, Appleget transmitted Rockefeller's pledge of $200,000 for buildings and equipment, to be drawn on as needed, and a formula for a five-year annual operating budget of $40,000 that included stipulations that the foundation would decrease outright contributions and expect the laboratory to increase matchables over that period.[42] A safety valve was built in: at the end of the first five years, consideration would be given to possible further assistance, perhaps in the form of an annual gift toward maintenance or a capitalization of the same in the form of an endowment. It was not a permanent endowment as Kidder had desired, but the total pledge of $335,000 was ample, coupled with the Laura Spelman Rockefeller Memorial funding of the summer fieldwork, to launch the laboratory. Kidder called the second annual meeting of the board for December 27, but Chap, felled by the strain and the winter, was down with the flu. Kidder wrote him on Christmas Eve, expressing some regret that Chap would be absent from yet another annual meeting. He informed Chap of his wish to have him appointed as interim director on part-time salary, pending selection of a full-time director, and reiterating their mutual understanding that Chap had his sights on a research/curatorial position. Chap was thus approved as secretary/treasurer of the laboratory and given the authority to act on its behalf in Santa Fe and to requisition funds to implement board-approved measures. As 1930 began, Hewett and Kidder did a bit of horse trading for Chap's time, conducting themselves cordially enough. The lab would have Chap full time for the first half of the year, but he would retain his studio and nominal connection with the museum; what he would do in the second half would be determined later. Chap was to be available for museum duties as needed, easing Hewett's strained staff budget.

Aside from a request to Chap to put in a good word with Cutting to keep up funding for Hewett, Kidder made clear that Chap's time allocation was discretionary: "I am sure that no one connected with the Laboratory has any disposition to hold you to the status of a clock-puncher. You should take what vacation you need and devote such of your time as you wish to research, whether for the Laboratory or the Museum is immaterial." He also raised the first of many boundary problems between the IAF and the laboratory:

> Yesterday Appleget replied to a query by me in regard to matching of funds raised in 1929. He said that such funds would be matched by Mr. Rockefeller for application to the 1930 budget. In other words, anything that we can get in this year will be doubled, and the extra amount will be available for 1930. This brings up the question of Pottery Fund contributions. It seems to me that we ought to be able to make some arrangement with the Fund by which their income could be counted. I shall take this up with Mr. Appleget when I see him January 24th.
>
> Please calm the Fund members in regard to the museum feature. They should understand that this aspect of the Laboratory has in no way been slighted in the Trustees' plans, but has merely not been stressed for obvious reasons.[43]

Events proceeded smoothly until March, when Francis Wilson, acting as the lab's legal representative, blew the whistle on House Bill 32, an Act for the Preservation of the Scientific Resources of New Mexico.[44] A melodrama involving himself, Chap, Kidder, Hewett, and Zimmerman erupted. The bill, sponsored in part by Hewett, was intended to prevent depredation of archaeological sites on state lands. It called for protection in the form of board-issued state permits (a board on which the museum director would sit). Section 2 also contained a provision that no less than 50 percent of all specimens excavated on state lands would be retained as the property of the state of New Mexico—hence, the museum. Chap had read the bill prior to leaving for a lecture tour. Although he recognized that the bill could be construed as harmful to the ability of institutions outside the museum to enlarge their collections, Chap was determined to avoid any involvement with museum-related legislation. He also thought that the bill's wording was so sloppy (the term "state lands" was omitted in some sections) that even if the bill passed, it would be near impossible to enforce and would likely be challenged by legitimate curio dealers. Therefore, after talking it over with Bradfield, he felt he could safely leave town without sounding an alarm on the lab's behalf.

Wilson, however, interpreted the bill as being aimed directly at the lab.[45] He intercepted it after it had passed both houses and was awaiting signature. He deterred the governor from signing, but his notes somehow turned up on Dana Johnson's desk—who promptly published another anti-Hewett piece in the *New Mexican*. Wilson was livid that Chap had left town without apprising him of the bill. He later tried to call Kate, to locate Chap, but "since she and the kids were taking inoculations against rabies (another of life's little pleasantries) she was out at that hour."[46] Wilson took it upon himself to champion the lab against Hewett.

With the brouhaha building, Kate tried to reach Chap by wire and phone, urging him to return. Hewett, now on the defensive, called Kate to explain the bill's purpose in preventing the depredation of sites. On March 5, the *New Mexican* published Chap's calm statement, obtained long distance, that he found nothing to object to. In a reference to Wilson's misplaced zeal, "Mr. Chapman pointed out that while those who have objected to the provisions of the bill are at perfect liberty to do so as expressing their own sentiments, he is in a position to say that the Laboratory as such has no objections to it." He emphasized cooperation between the museum and the lab: "Chapman, while an official of the Laboratory is furnished with a studio in the Museum through the courtesy of Dr. E. L. Hewett."[47]

In Andover, Kidder was bombarded with letters. Wilson's fury was split between Hewett and Chap:

> The first measure which was passed and which was stopped at the Governor's door so to speak, was about as bad a one for us as it could be. Our friend, Kenneth Chapman, to the contrary notwithstanding. I know that he is very sore at me because I presumed to speak for the Museum and Laboratory. However, . . . someone had to, and upon the theory that I was attorney for it I spoke in unmeasured terms as tho I had all the authority in the world. . . . The original bill was drawn innocently enough by everybody who had anything to do with it except Hewett. . . . I am much disappointed that Kenneth did not bring the bill to me as soon as he got a copy of it as he knew about it before it was introduced. Such matters he should not be permitted to pass upon because he isn't competent. He is all right in his own line and all of that but when it comes to legal matters or matters which have to do with our legal status and the future career here he should be told that he must discuss them with me. . . . I find fault with him because he did not do that. . . . You know that I am much attached to Kenneth Chapman but on this occasion he certainly slipped up seriously.[48]

Chap, on the other hand, reported to Kidder that he had criticized the omission of the phrase "state lands" in several sections when he had discussed the bill with Bradfield. He wrote that "I tried to see Wilson for several days before I left. . . . I am sure that I would never have thought of asking him not to represent the Laboratory without the authority of the Executive Committee." He explained that the omission alone would have given Wilson sufficient cause for recalling the bill without involving the lab, and that the subsequent publicity uproar may have hurt the lab more than the bill would have, even if Hewett had intended mischief. He wryly added that on his lecture tour he "visited eight museums and have returned with the conviction that they can be made the most deadly bore on earth, and that it will require nothing short of genius to prevent our perpetrating just another example."[49]

Even Zimmerman became involved in the bill fracas. After Wilson had stopped its passage, Zimmerman worked with him on modifications so the bill could not be used against the lab. But Hewett had rejected compromise, and so Zimmerman expected the original bill, still unsigned by the governor, to die. By now he and Chap recognized each other as kindred souls; their relationship flowered into lifelong professional and personal friendship. Zimmerman wrote Kidder that trouble could have been avoided if Chap had been there. "I assure you that Chapman and I will talk over all points together, and he will come [east] with full authority to represent me in everything that may come before the meeting[.] . . . I really believe that when Chapman and I clear matters here, he can take care of the situation admirably."[50] Ironically, when Hewett wrote Kidder he defended Chap: "Chapman has doubtless written you about the perfectly infamous activities of Frank Wilson. . . . His sole purpose of course is to create all the prejudice he can toward the school and State Museum. . . . Chapman did what he could but the idea seemed very generally accepted that Mr. Rockefeller and his millions were on the point of being driven out of the state."[51]

Kidder empathically responded to each letter. He opined to Chap, "Personally, I think the whole business was a tempest in the teapot. . . . I wish to thunder Wilson had kept out, but I cannot very well tell him so, nor in writing to Zimmerman can I repudiate his action. I have told Zimmerman, however, that I had no hand in objecting to the bill, having been willing to leave matters entirely in your hands. . . . Please don't worry about this business. It will all come out in the wash."[52] Chap's laissez-faire political stance was a quality that Zimmerman and others came to love and respect. Wilson and Chap eventually settled their differences, Chap maintaining "that my fair knowledge of the archaeology of New Mexico and of English, and my insight as to the probable activities of the Laboratory all had some weight even against the legal point of view."[53] To confirm his original position, in typical fashion he quietly researched the number of major untouched archaeological sites on state lands, as compared with those on private lands. He concluded that except for a few such as Pecos, Quarai, and San Diego de Jemez, already controlled by the state through its museum, the great majority were on private lands and not subject to the provisions of House Bill 32. The "tempest" was for naught.

Kenneth Chapman, secretary-treasurer of the Laboratory of Anthropology, had new status. He was no longer Hewett's employee, but peer; representative of the lab to Zimmerman and his university; and professional colleague of Wilson. During the legislative hullabaloo, Chap, whose preferred bailiwick was researching pottery design elements, demonstrated steadiness and political acumen. On March 25, he used new Laboratory of Anthropology stationery to inform Nusbaum that Wilson had turned over the deed to the land. Though the site seemed relatively remote, "citified" improvements had already been made (the water main and sewer were in), and a planned highway relocation would eventually put them on a quiet road leading to what was to become a residential district, down the Lamy road. "I feel that it might be a blessing in disguise, and that what we would lose in numbers of visitors, we would gain in being able to give more attention to those who have sufficient interest in our work to hunt us out."[54] He was glad that Kidder was of like mind.

On April 16, 1929, Chapman terminated his employment with the museum. It must have been a joyful liberation. Hewett's request for an increase in appropriations from the state had failed; ten days earlier he had broached the subject with Chap, who told Hewett he would look out for himself. The next several months found Chap active with the advisory building committee, to which the executive committee appointed him when it was established at a May meeting. Chap was approved as executive secretary at a salary of $300 per month. Discussion was held about the most desirable director: either an eminent anthropologist who would lend scientific stature to the lab or an administrative pragmatist to whom scientific direction/counsel would be given by a committee. This either/or approach to defining the ideal leader reflects a fundamental split among the founding board and would become a haunting leitmotif in subsequent hirings.

While Chap attended to building plans, the Laboratory of Anthropology offered its first summer field training course in anthropology backed by the Spelman Memorial Fund. Fourteen students on scholarship and four volunteers attended the eight-week session organized by Kidder, Fay-Cooper Cole, and R. B. Dixon. The course was so well received that the Spelman Memorial Fund granted an additional $60,000 for the 1930–34 period. Chapman recalled a serendipitous deal that helped to balance the scales after years of the museum housing the IAF pottery:

In 1929, the first year of field training, under the Rockefeller grant, each of the three parties acquired a used Model T.-Ford, which served for the field session, and brought them back to Santa Fe. The flivvers were left back of the Museum until we could decide how to dispose of them.

Meantime Sam Hudelson [sic], custodian at the Museum, inspected them and found that by dissecting the three, he could assemble one useful car, and use it to haul the other two to the dump. He reported this to Dr. Hewett, who asked if the one usable car could not be turned in to the Museum in recompense for facilities, including lights afforded to the Indian Arts Fund in its several years' use of basement storage space. With Dr. Kidder's approval the deal was closed.[55]

After Indian Fair in September, the IAF had to vacate the museum basement. Chap was offered five fireproof ground floor rooms at Sena Plaza, rent free until January 1, after which the lab would pay $175 per month. The deal was approved, and Chap purchased steel shelves and set up the collections there. Appleget was promoted to the Rockefeller Foundation; Chap would soon be dealing with Rockefeller representative Arthur Packard.

In October, Chap went to Mesa Verde to discuss the possibility that Jess would accept the lab directorship. The Nusbaums were torn, as both outdoor lovers were committed to archaeological work. Aileen expressed her fear that if Jess left the Park Service he would find himself tied to petty administrative details in a "glorified janitorship" and passed over for research grants. On the other hand, Nusbaum knew that the demands of the Mesa Verde work were taking a toll on Aileen's health; secretly, he did not rule out taking the position.[56] For now, they proposed a half-time arrangement whereby Jess could do both. Chap related his frustration to Kidder:

The whole situation looks pretty shaky to me, but I assured her that we wanted Jess, some way, even if we have to hunt around for the best man in the country who can be on the job the year round as executive secretary. . . . What are we going to do with all these research yearners like myself? Somehow I have been picturing Jess on the job, putting over big things in the development of the Laboratory, and instead—he wants to grab a trowel![57]

While Chap, Kidder, and Nusbaum were each considering what was best for themselves and the laboratory, the country went into crisis. On Black Thursday, October 24, 1929, stock values dropped rapidly. When stock prices fell again on Monday, stockholders panicked, selling a record 16,410,030 shares of stock. It was rumored that businessmen jumped from office buildings immediately upon hearing the news, but in fact the consequences of the crash took much longer to emerge. Initially, the news from Wall Street, although dramatic, seemed to portend nothing much different from earlier financial panics and depressions. Most citizens had learned to take them in stride. In fact, Chap's first job hunt had occurred shortly after the Panic of 1893, and he had not only found a job but, in a few years, the economy had returned to health. There was no hint, yet, that this event would prove different.

So Chap, Kidder, and Nusbaum remained focused on their situation. After consulting with Rockefeller to ensure there would be no suspicion of an abuse of their friendship, Nusbaum accepted the position, with the consent of the National Park Service.[58] On December 27, the board retroactively approved Kidder's negotiations with Nusbaum and voted to offer him the directorship effective January 1, 1930, at an annual salary of $6,000. Chap began his work with the Laboratory of Anthropology as executive secretary; he was later given the title of curator as well. Nusbaum, even more than Chap, was aware of Rockefeller's feelings about the man so dedicated to Native art. "He is pleased with Chapman's work in the pueblo field." Nusbaum penned to "My Dear Kiddo." "He is very fond of Chap, as is Mrs. R., and that means everything."[59]

Now Chap could awaken each morning with anticipation. Released from Hewett, and certain he had made the right choice, Chap relished each moment. He belonged to the laboratory, an institution that respected and supported his life's passion. With Nusbaum as head of the laboratory, and Mera as colleague, Chap believed the years ahead of him were to bring to fruition his desire to enlarge the IAF collection and conduct his own studies. More than three years earlier, Abby Rockefeller had asked to see the pottery collection. Now the future was his.

CHAPTER 11

THE UNEXPECTED NAVIGATOR

Wooden crates are crammed next to empty shelves in the small office at Sena Plaza. Chap has gently boxed the last of the IAF pots. All is in order for their short voyage to the newly constructed Laboratory of Anthropology. Next door, Mera has been industriously involved in a survey of New Mexico archaeological sites, while Nusbaum, adjusting to his role as director, is overseeing construction and coordinating plans for the laboratory's first programs. Today is moving day. As Chap ponders the twists of fate, the excelsior littered about suddenly absorbs him. The curlicues of shaved wood suggest meandering eddies and currents, and the pots indeed seem as though they have been packed for a long sail. Neither Chap nor anyone else can foresee when and how the lab will drop anchor, given the circumstances: she has been christened not with a champagne bottle but with an economic crash.

Her charter crew—Nusbaum, Chap, and Mera—seemed destined for success. However, she lacked clear board navigation, which forced her into a circuitous route seeking a safe port among local, regional, and national interests, for she was a hybrid from the outset.[1] This conglomerate of interests would have been challenging enough without a national economic downturn. The laboratory had five years to become self-sufficient, but hard times precluded a secure funding strategy. The Great Depression meant recruiting backers at a time when few had an extra dime, much less a dollar. The hope that the downturn would be short was fading by 1931. Eastern New Mexico had become part of the Dust Bowl, and the effect on the state's rural economy was harsh. Even successful businesses throughout the state were affected.

Despite the ominous forecast, Chap was happy to be aboard. Lab construction boosted expectations. The building committee, of which Chap was a member, had chosen to sponsor an architectural competition. It called for a design for a grand complex totaling thirty-eight structures to be built on the Monte Sol site. Firms across the nation responded. John Gaw Meem, the Southwest's preeminent architectural talent, won the contract. Construction began on July 30, 1930, but the grand plan proved ephemeral. Only two buildings were ever erected: the administration-research building and the director's residence. Meem, however, infused them with the enduring qualities of Santa Fe style—a perfect way to house the founders' dreams. The buildings that traced their origins to a broken Pueblo pot were imbued with the integrity of architectural balance and a rooted sense of regional history. The commission established the national reputation of Meem's young firm.[2]

As the laboratory's foundation was poured, the staff and board could only hope that the economy would turn by the expiration of the original grant. Kidder felt more keenly than ever that lack of an assured endowment was a mistake, but he hoped to demonstrate that the lab was worth permanently providing for.[3] Nusbaum and Chap centered their attention on searching out matching funds, at times debating whether a donation should be credited to the laboratory or the IAF. During the commotion of the move-in period, they made an uncharacteristic error and missed the deadline for submitting IAF matching receipts for 1930. Arthur Packard, Appleget's successor, referred the problem to Rockefeller, who forgave the error. But accompanying Packard's check to the lab was a review of the complex matching procedures. Packard's letters reveal an account-minded personality with a knack for gnarled prose and a propensity for a strict interpretation of terms. Chap had the dual task of accounting for lab expenses to Packard and comptroller George Beal and IAF expenditures to Rockefeller. The lab's internal computations, the IAF's ambiguous status, and outside contributions must have caused ledger headaches for Chap.

Until the doors of the new building opened, the lab existed solely in the form of its staff. During 1930, Chap had the exhilarating experience of being able to engage full time in work that touched various aspects of Indian art: he conducted Harvey courier training, taught one day per week at the University of New Mexico, prepared text and photographs for his publication on Pueblo pottery, and made periodic trips to pueblos to pursue his art revival "missionary work" and to acquire specimens for display at Indian Fair. His exuberance encouraged long days. Chap wrote Kidder that "Kate has just reminded me, with all her . . . 'wim and wigor,' of the solemn assurance I gave her that I would begin the new year by cutting out the habit of steadily working overtime[.] . . . I have promised not to smuggle in any more night work."[4] During construction, staff began occupying offices. Furnishings, some designed by Chap and locally crafted, were moved in. Exhibition cases, storage vaults, and study-friendly installations soon encompassed growing collections despite construction that kept life unsettled and plaster dust in the air. Chap's work in the new building began March 1, 1931, when the IAF collections finally arrived from Sena Plaza.

When Rockefeller visited the lab in early April, he was happy with the construction, but concerned about Chap. Perhaps Chap had dust-related respiratory problems or looked unusually gaunt. Rockefeller immediately funded a four-week vacation for him. When Nusbaum told Chap, he acted quickly: *I could not take advantage of a full month for Jesse L. Nusbaum had planned to attend a conference . . . within three weeks and had tagged me to carry on as acting director in his absence. "How soon can you get going?" he asked. I called Kate, who had already had her vacation with the children in and near Tucson, and with her help, boarded an afternoon train to El Paso enroute to southern Arizona, where I spent an enjoyable ten days.*[5]

His thank-you note to Rockefeller included the jubilant news that this interlude had resulted in a weight gain of four pounds—"a most remarkable feat for one of my perverse Chapman physique."[6] He blamed his Wednesday night teaching obligations for the curtailment of his leave, avoiding mention of Nusbaum's upcoming "conference," which was actually a sticky political situation arising from government field investigations into Indian welfare.[7] Congressional committees descended on Santa Fe, the pueblos, and the lab for hearings. John Collier, executive secretary of the American Indian Defense Association, was agitating against the Bureau of Indian Affairs. Nusbaum saw Collier as a relentless propagandist and might have welcomed an opportunity to take him to task. However, when asked to testify publicly against Collier, he declined, fearing that Collier's publicity hounds would drag Rockefeller's name in with the laboratory. Chap had cut his vacation short to cover for Nusbaum, who spent almost two weeks in private meetings at the lab and elsewhere. Their sensitivity to the political aspects may explain the "teaching" dodge in Chap's note, for he, Nusbaum, and Kidder always shielded their benefactor from the press.

Laboratory programs began in earnest in 1931. An exciting team developed as talented staff members were added. Stanley Stubbs was hired as an assistant archaeologist and photographer to help with Mera's archaeological survey, which had identified nearly eleven hundred sites along the Upper and Middle Rio Grande valleys. Mera, the curator of archaeological surveys, documented the distributions of dozens of diagnostic pottery types, which also demonstrated how the prehistoric configurations of cultures changed over time.[8]

As a new institution, the laboratory wanted to be among the first to incorporate technological innovations. Sidney Stallings came aboard to perform a dendroarchaeological survey of the Rio Grande Valley.[9] His wife, Alice, wore a number of hats, assisting wherever needed. Kidder had arranged Carnegie Institute funding for Anna Shepard, a future ceramics expert, who came with her ceramic technology project.[10]

One of Chap's first lab projects was preparing his study of Santo Domingo pottery for publication. He had begun this monograph at the museum, where he had had to wedge research in among a myriad of administrative tasks. Preparing and publishing it were laboratory priorities. He would have to get Hewett's permission to use over three hundred of Chap's drawings from 1920–27, but it was a request well worth making since the study represented the first significant research on post-Spanish pottery characteristics as developed at a particular pueblo. Despite having to overcome the pueblo's concern about people prying into its methods,* Chap selected Santo Domingo because of the comparative simplicity, integrity, and abundance of its pottery. In his monograph (still used by potters), Chap focused on decorative style, citing the extensive use of a few basic, irreducible design elements. The monograph included over seventy pages of design elements, mimicking the "wallpaper" of drawings that graced Chap's office.

Despite Nusbaum's support for Chap, their personality styles differed, so it was almost inevitable that the pressures of construction and accountability would trigger seismic rumblings in their friendship. Nusbaum was frustrated when Chap could not be found, or arrived late, for meetings. The previous year's equipment funds had run out, so Chap had expensed pottery shelves, files, and so forth to the maintenance advance, leaving Nusbaum to cover the balance as he might. On the other side of the fence, Chap expected to be liberated from administrative duties and have latitude to pursue his teaching and studies. He was unhappy when Nusbaum told him that his two-hour evening course at the university did not justify an overnight trip every week—Chap had to change it to afternoons so he could be back the same day. When it came to crediting matchable donations, the lab's interests edged out the IAF's. To top it off, Nusbaum ordered him to hold off photographing more pots for the time being. (As far as Nusbaum could see, he already had over four hundred photos gathering dust.) It was too much for Chap. "Apparently I have hurt him in more ways than one," Nusbaum wrote Kidder. "He cant [sic] see anything but Indian Art, modern stage, and frankly says that is his only interest, and if we cant support that in better way [sic], he might as well quit. . . . I hope that Chap comes around O.K. in time."[11]

Friendship is good medicine, and the two were able to heal the breach—and clarify Chap's job description satisfactorily—before the construction dust settled. The new laboratory formally opened September 1, 1931, creating a local splash. A public ceremony was followed by a three-day conference on Southwest archaeological problems. The fourth annual meeting of the lab trustees wrapped up events. The IAF and fledgling laboratory collections were now on view. Because the laboratory had fiscal responsibility for both collections, the founders expected that the IAF collection would soon merge with the laboratory's. Yet the boundary between the two collections was maintained. IAF supporters felt that their collection represented the impetus for the laboratory's existence. While the new building offered the promise of a first-class exhibition space, some

---

* A friend of Chap's, a young man from Santo Domingo, thought that a book about Santo Domingo pottery was a good idea but had little success when he tried to talk to the council about it. He suggested that if Chap could wait, he'd see what he could do. "How long would that take?" Chap asked. His friend thought a minute and then answered, "Maybe ten or fifteen years" (AC2, 156, KMC-SAR).

still hoped for an IAF-exclusive building, preferring to wait before merging collections. Rockefeller's fondness for the IAF and the fact that it had his primary loyalty occasionally complicated Nusbaum's job.[12]

A case in point arose with an opportunity to acquire six blankets mentioned in Chap's 1928 IAF report. By 1931, the Depression forced trader MacMillan to offer the blankets for sale. Philanthropist/collector Albert Barnes was about to buy them when he learned that Mera had longed for them. Barnes offered Rockefeller a $500 donation toward the $4,800 asking price if the lab picked up the balance; otherwise he would buy them. Rockefeller asked Nusbaum if he should contribute to the IAF for them. Nusbaum reminded him that lab collecting now took precedence. "While there is every reason to believe that the proposed merger will be consummated at the specified time, since the respective directorates are now largely interlocking, I am particularly eager that any further contribution from you towards acquirement of collections, establish a Laboratory title to the material purchased thereunder."[13] The extensive six-month correspondence surrounding the acquisition revealed several incipient problems: complex communication, blended collections, and shared funding sources—the kind of museum-school pitfalls that aroused Chap's concern, as he had written to Hodge. The carefully chartered laboratory/IAF arrangements, enfolding numerous interests, ironically began to mimic some of Hewett's institutional dynamics.

Personal agendas likewise posed potential challenges. On November 30, the Exposition of Indian Tribal Arts was to open in New York. For the exposition catalog, Chap contributed an article about ceramics, in which he stated that pottery is the most comprehensive, authentic, and aesthetically pleasing of all the Native art forms.[14] Organizers of the exposition included Oliver La Farge and the White sisters, who defined it as the first exhibition of Indian art as *art*, not ethnology. But an incident between Chap and Elizabeth White set her against the lab. She requested a loan of weavings from the lab and IAF for the coming show plus the Exposition of Indian Tribal Arts' two-year tour. Chap helped her select two of the lab's most prized blankets and some IAF items, and documented the transaction. When they hadn't arrived in New York by October, she wrote to have them shipped. Chap replied that, given their delicate nature, he would ship them a week before the exhibit. He also conveyed an unexpected IAF reversal not to release their specimens for touring and asked that the blankets be returned at the end of the show. White shot back that the blankets were not needed and then generally let it be known that the lab had turned her down cold, denying the existence of Chap's file to the contrary.[15]

Like the exposition, Chap held Indian art to be *art* and taught it that way. His university class was now housed within the fine arts rather than anthropology department, indicative of the shift in emphasis. In a speech at the university, Chap illuminated the importance of Indian arts, although he imagined that some in the room might question whether there was enough on the subject to cover "even an hour's chatter."[16] He suggested that through an Indian arts class, students would learn that "good taste involves some degree of restraint, that simplicity is more restful and enduring than that which grows out of the instinct to decorate everything in sight."

> I believe that art students may learn from the study of Indian design, perhaps better than from the decorative art of any other culture, to use judgment and moderation in their experiments, and to temper zest with what measure of calm contemplation is still spared to this hectic age. If this contemplation gives some insight into the cultural background of another race; if it leads to even the faintest suspicion that Art, after all, may not be the exclusive heritage of our own much vaunted superior civilization, perhaps something may be planted in the minds of students that will bear fruit in ways unforeseen.[17]

In October, Zimmerman gave Chap permission to use university facilities to teach Indian art to twelve young Indian students (ages sixteen to eighteen, boys and girls) from the Albuquerque Indian School. A critic of this program wrote to the *Taos Valley News* that such a course, being taught by an Anglo, would further taint what was already corrupted by commercialism. The *New Mexican* defended the course, since the sole instructor was the "recognized authority on Indian design, who deals only in ancient Indian patterns and materials found and preserved by the Indian arts fund [*sic*]."[18] Chap's syllabus for both Anglo and Indian students dwelt on designs from each pueblo, and, unwittingly perhaps, presented hand-drawn idealizations beyond those created on actual wares with irregular surfaces.[19]

Closer to home, Chap also conducted a university-accredited night extension course at Santa Fe High School. Though short lived, the *New Mexican* wrote it up as one of the most popular public courses ever offered. It is easy to visualize him presenting well-organized talks with prepared graphics and deft blackboard sketches. He also offered an intensive summer lab course in cooperation with the university, "the most satisfactory course I have given."[20] It attracted art teachers, including Indian Service teachers and field workers, from over twenty states; by 1934, the last year it was offered, the cap of twenty-five students had been raised to fifty. Other teaching included eight full days of instruction at the Santa Fe Indian School, donated by the lab as part of its commitment to the IAF mission.

Chap was well able to manage the parallel but complementary collecting of both the IAF and the lab. Two trends quickly developed. First, the IAF began accepting historic Navajo jewelry, blankets, and other textiles. Second, the number of items donated to or acquired by the lab increased, while IAF donations tapered off. Chap used the Wissler System to identify which field an item belonged to, the IAF system to designate the type of item, and a notation for its ownership (IAF or lab) and source (gift, purchase, expedition). Items were displayed together without distinction, however.

In early 1932, at the behest of Packard, Chap and Nusbaum set off for an urgent investigation of winter-induced hardship on the Navajo reservation to determine if the foundation should intervene. They reported that government programs were adequate to the situation, and Nusbaum noted that he had seen some splendid Navajo silver that traders were not yet willing to part with but which pointed to a gap in lab collections. Packard relayed this to Rockefeller, who gave $5,000 to the lab for purchasing silver. When spring sadly did not remedy the winter's toll, traders were forced to dispose of their "dead pawn" silver, so the donation proved timely. Nusbaum asked Chap to accompany him in acquiring pieces for the lab, and they *conferr[ed] with traders, and banks and mercantile firms in Gallup and elsewhere.*[21]

During the same period, the Indian Service fortunately began reimbursing the lab for Chap's consulting services at $100 per month, converting his donated time to income. Chap thus devoted one paid day per week to promoting Indian art, offering a course of art instruction and supervising at the Santa Fe Indian School, which had recently added a new arts and crafts building. Chap designed a curriculum for unmarried sixteen- to twenty-one-year-olds that focused on their pueblos' designs. He was justly proud when his pupils contributed award-winning works to the annual Gallup Intertribal Indian Ceremonial.

Chap's consistent interest in developing a market for Indian art found expression in his support of local pueblo fairs, beginning that year, and his mentoring relationship with Dorothy Dunn. The decision to hold small fairs at each pueblo rather than the annual fair in Santa Fe originated with Margretta Dietrich, who was now NMAIA vice president under Meem. She and other fair committee members found the town event exhausting to manage. Because most pueblos couldn't send large delegations anyway, Chap supported the change. Local fairs seemed like a good way to enrich and encourage each pueblo's art during the Depression; however, they did not pan out as hoped because ceremony eclipsed craft exhibits.

A more successful enterprise during this time was his association with artist Dorothy Dunn. Like Chap, Dunn had attended the Art Institute of Chicago, where she was introduced to Native art in 1925 through a trip to the Field Museum. During her 1928 sabbatical in Santa Fe she met Chap, who reinforced her determination to teach painting to young Indian artists. In the early fall of 1932, after teaching elementary school at both Santo Domingo and Shiprock, she returned to Santa Fe, where she approached Chester Faris about a position in the Santa Fe Indian School art program overseen by Chap. With Faris's support, Dunn accepted a fifth-grade teaching position and opened an unofficial painting studio where she represented herself not as an educator but a guide. She demonstrated basic painting techniques and acquainted Pueblo students with a range of historical and cultural expressions but encouraged the students to deepen their acquaintance and experimentation with their own art heritage. Bureaucratic response was tepid, and in early 1933 the studio was ordered closed. Dietrich and several local artists rallied to Dunn's defense. As a result, the Bureau of Indian Affairs appointed her teacher of fine and applied arts the following fall.

As Dunn's program evolved, students developed the unique Santa Fe Studio style. Its strong graphic sense and flat style became a model of Southwest Indian painting for decades. Marketing artwork was an important component of Dunn's classes. Along with mentors Chap and Dietrich, she believed that stimulating patronage of Indian art would reduce the influence of traders, who encouraged souvenir production. Yet the education department of the Indian Service pressured her to teach traditional European aesthetics and technique. Discouraged by chronic resistance, Dunn turned to Chap for support. Her journal notes, "Chapman . . . believes in me which is all that counts after all."[22]

In February 1933, Chap had another opportunity to work directly with southwestern Indian artists when the Indian Service organized a landmark four-day conference of rug weavers with the cooperation of the lab and the museum-school. About twenty-four weavers, mostly Navajo, arrived for tours, collection viewing, and dialogue. "They grinned expansively when Mr. Chapman told them, through Interpreter Deschne, 'I have the finest job in the United States; I can handle all these fine old blankets and silver whenever I want to.'"[23] Still, they doubted his math:

> They became very attached to Mr. Chapman, but they left feeling still convinced that moth balls and pest control are a myth and that Mr. Chapman's early education must have been neglected for he never learned to count. Seventy years is too long a life for any one blanket! This viewpoint was new to them. . . . If the life of a rug is to be extended from a few months or two or three years to a hundred years, then of course there is a reason for making a worth while rug. It changed their opinion of why white folks want Indians to make better blankets.[24]

A celebratory air surrounded the encouragement of fine weaving as another source of Native art income.

Chap continued working on his Santo Domingo monograph, helped along by a $2,500 grant from the Carnegie Corporation. Concurrently, he took on a three-year project with publisher C. Szwedzicki in Nice, France, who proposed a two-volume hardbound portfolio of Pueblo Indian pottery with full-color plates. In return for underwriting Chap's text and illustrations, the lab would receive a number of copies at cost. Chap wrote Rockefeller that he enjoyed the project. Nusbaum was less enthusiastic, since the Depression discouraged subscription sales of an expensive work aimed at institutions and collectors.

Locally and nationwide, the Depression relentlessly weakened faith and opportunity. Roosevelt, sworn into office in March 1933, inherited the anguish of fifteen million unemployed Americans. Family stress now preoccupied Chap. His mother had moved to Philadelphia in 1930 to live with Vera and her daughter, Catherine. As a loving son and older brother, Chap sent regular support. But Mary had turned eighty-eight in November 1932, and an illness that began in December was worsening. Chap thought she would not live much longer. On May 31, 1933, Mary Chapman passed away in Philadelphia. Services were held in South Bend, Indiana, and she was buried next to her husband. Chap presumably traveled to join Dwight and Vera at their mother's funeral.

Chap's loss—and perhaps some understandable distraction—occurred as the laboratory hit its halfway point in its five-year guaranteed funding. Concurrently, Nusbaum found himself dealing with personality clashes within the IAF. The previous fall, local trustees George Bloom, Margaret McKittrick Burge, and Alice C. Henderson had identified themselves as "progressives" who felt the lab was neglecting the IAF and ignoring its charter to preserve and stimulate Indian art. White, still steamed at the lab, sided with them. They made their case at the September 1932 laboratory board meeting. (It coincided with Fiesta, where there were always Anglo eggheads and eccentrics mingling amid Hispanic songs and Indian dances.) Kidder's letters to his "Bestest One" Madeleine replayed a soap opera:

Tuesday 8 a.m.—The fiesta, I find to my great relief, is nearly over. It began Saturday & the ball's been bad (I was to have been a judge—narrow escape!). . . . Things are going fine as far as the work of the Lab. goes, but there's a good deal of bickering. . . . There is no fundamental trouble between Lab. & Indian Arts. It's personality clashes, as far as I can see[.] . . . There's a new movement, I hear, against the Arts Fund.

Wednesday a.m.—Our meeting was grand. Proctor, Vay, Margaret [McKittrick] Burge[,] . . . Mary Wheelwright, Mr. Simpson, Zimmerman, Chap, Bronson Cutting, Hewett, Nusbaum & I. Everything went fine. Hewett was friendly, but reserved. . . . I think I smoothed over certain Arts Fund-Lab. roughnesses. . . . The plaza, when we strolled around it after dinner, was jammed[.] . . . A real fiesta & so different from the old forced Hewett ones.

Wed. a.m. [a week later]—Had a long talk with Margaret McKittrick Burge. . . .
Nusbaum & Aileen hate her like poison . . . but I believe she could be handled
if they were tactful. However, that's up to Jess. By & large he's doing a wonderful job.

Thursday before breakfast—I think I've managed to straighten out a few kinks.
An outsider sometimes can do so better than a person who is, like Jess, in constant touch with the kinkers. . . . At teatime I came home to meet Mrs. Mary
Austin who wanted to see me about . . . attaching her Society for the Preservation
of Spanish Art to the Lab. She's tried to work with Hewett, but has been thwarted
at every turn. I do wish a piano would drop on that man.[25]

Kidder feared for his endowment campaign if Rockefeller saw the fledgling organization unraveling. He suggested that the progressives form an ad hoc committee to
define issues and propose solutions. Mera appointed Henderson chair, and its members
included Austin, Burge, and Chap. Mera counted on Chap as a stabilizing force, but most
of the plan was developed without him since he could not make many of the meetings,
an absence possibly connected with his mother's illness at the time.[26] In February 1933,
Nusbaum was shocked at the draft proposal from a "little group that is so desperately
opposed to our scientific projects . . . when their income from memberships and contributions has all but expired."[27] They wanted a new Indian art building that would be supported by the lab but administered by the IAF to house the IAF specimens. At the same
time, the IAF would keep its own share of matching dollars. Adding insult to injury, they
likened the lab to a benevolent parent who houses a child but gives nothing to eat or
wear. Chap's loyalty to the lab kept him from expressing any views he may have shared
with the progressives.

To Nusbaum's relief, Burge and Henderson turned against each other, and the committee self-eroded. He learned that selfish motives had underwritten the demand—
namely, that both Bloom and Burge wanted salaried positions at the new center. Nusbaum
and Kidder needed Chap's input. "We must not at this time allow the I.A.F. to split off
from us and take its collections away, as there is obviously danger of their doing if they
cannot achieve the separate directorship which they desire[.] . . . I am not certain that it
would even be wise to talk of it to Mera, as he is likely to blab or to act unwisely. I should
think it could be discussed safely with Chap."[28]

Chap was sensitive to political machinations with good reason. His emotional invest-
ment in the lab, his friendship with Nusbaum, and Rockefeller's personal interest in himself and the IAF heightened the need to remain well informed and prepared to intervene.
Mera called an informal meeting with six other local conservatives, including Nusbaum

and Chap. They formulated a compromise, proposing that they hire an assistant curator to arrange collection exhibits in conjunction with a special IAF committee. On July 3, Nusbaum wired Kidder, with picaresque familiarity: "Love feast concluded Statement unanimously approved trustees officers unanimously reelected. . . . Unnecessary vote any proxies Airmailed copy approved statement So endeth round two It s [*sic*] a great life if you dont weaken."[29]

Following this drama, Nusbaum wanted clearer board direction. He sent a memo to the executive committee (Kidder, Alfred Lewis Kroeber, and Clark Wissler) soliciting their input on the lab's role in furthering contemporary Indian arts and crafts. It was a hint that the lab needed to capitalize on Indian art, which could attract financial support. He stressed the value of Chap's consultation to Indians and educational programs for Anglos, though they brought no real money. He suggested implementing an Indian art department, for which the IAF would do its share while the lab maintained administration and custody of collections. As to fund-raising, the lab's incorporation terms prohibited soliciting visitors for donations unless they brought it up. "Mr. Rockefeller Jr., has written me several times as to the fact that I have not approached wealthy friends of his when they visited the Lab," Nusbaum wrote. But he noted, "You just cant 'nick' your guests for 'this and that.'"[30] Subtle rifts had emerged between Nusbaum and Kidder. Kidder's endowment drive sprang from his relationship with the board scientists, reinforcing Nusbaum's view that they and Kidder failed to grasp how the "pet colt" could help the "big horse" even if the harness needed occasional adjusting. Kidder must have known that Nusbaum was frustrated, but he was still after permanent funding. When he was reelected chairman at the annual board meeting, he accepted on condition that a replacement would be elected in a year. He felt that his service was unhealthily long and could appear dominant, but hoped he would have achieved his goal by then.

As the laboratory settled into its final year of guaranteed funding, the early winter brought two new federal programs that absorbed more of Chap's time. The first was sponsored by John Collier, now commissioner of the Bureau of Indian Affairs. Nusbaum's opinion notwithstanding, Collier used his new position to achieve reforms in the "Indian New Deal." In 1934, Collier found funding for an arts and crafts study board, chaired by James W. Young, then with the University of Chicago. Collier and Young had been involved with the American Indian Defense Association; both had sponsored unsuccessful Indian art marketing proposals to Congress. They wanted an eclectic board, and Chap was an obvious choice.

Second, a grant from the new Civil Works Administration under the Treasury Department initiated the Public Works of Art project in December, which ran less than six months. In New Mexico, more than sixty-five murals, over six hundred paintings, ten sculptural pieces, and numerous indigenous Hispanic and Native American crafts were created. Regional committees were set up to give unemployed artists mural commissions at $23.50 to $42.50 per week. Nusbaum was asked to direct Southwest Region 13, and he accepted on condition that Chap handle the job as secretary in charge of fieldwork. Faris helped supervise twenty Indian artists, including Pablita Velarde and Allan Houser; artist Gus Baumann was appointed to manage twenty-five Anglo artists, including Raymond Jonson, Gerald Cassidy, and Will Shuster. He found them to be a whining, grasping lot, in contrast to Indian artists who were more serene and whose symbolic expressions transcended outside or dominant cultures.[31] Chap traveled with him to enroll regional artists.

Chap also oversaw the work of seven project artist-copyists, who produced for the lab over two hundred excellent Indian design drawings for Indian Service use as he directed. Possibly during this period, Chap's sense of impishness led to a practical art joke. Stanley Stubbs cherished the tale, which he handed down many years later to archaeologist Edwin Ferdon Jr. Apparently Chap decided to recruit the collective talents of the lab staff to create a "modern art" entry for an upcoming juried show at the art museum. He hung a blank canvas on the wall in the main office hall and set out paints and brushes. He suggested that each member add a few brush strokes as they passed by. The masterpiece was juried in as "a fine piece of modern art—until the truth came out and a few artists got mad."[32]

While Chap applied himself to the federal program, the Rockefeller Foundation responded to the ongoing economic depression by making organizational changes. Rockefeller created the Davison Fund to organize his personal giving, including lab funding, naming Packard as director. This new fund would focus on local needs and assist more broadly with addressing poverty and improving interracial conditions. (It is unclear if Kidder was aware that the fund's definition could be interpreted in such a way that support of a Southwest anthropology institution would be seen to fall outside its purview.) When Rockefeller secretary David Stevens visited the lab in early May, he was struck by Chap's trove of knowledge. Just as Chap cherished a fine old pot, Stevens wanted to preserve Chap's expertise and share it as widely as possible. He suggested making a film record for distribution to institutions beyond New Mexico.[33] Per Stevens's invitation, Chap submitted a grant proposal for film and sound recordings of his lectures. A one-year $5,000 grant for 1934–35 was awarded, giving Chap dedicated time that would theoretically relieve him of some responsibilities as well as ease payroll—by now, all staff took voluntary pay cuts.

In July 1934, conservatives dominated the IAF annual meeting, so there was no threatened schism. They resolved to continue the custodial arrangement, in hopes that the lab might eventually create a separately housed Indian art division and relinquish the IAF collection. Chap and Mera, however, felt that these wishes would disappear with

Kenneth M. Chapman supervising painting of pottery designs, Public Works of Art Project, Laboratory of Anthropology, c. 1935. (Photograph by T. Harmon Parkhurst. Courtesy of Palace of the Governors [MNM/DCA], 73955.)

time and inertia. Contributions to the IAF were by now pathetic. Their matching contribution for 1933 had dropped from the previous year's paltry $53 to an embarrassing $2.12. Meanwhile, Chap's summer was filled with Indian Service and lab teaching. Stubbs took on Chap's curatorial duties for the four thousand catalogued items, over half of which were now lab acquisitions.

In August, Rockefeller stayed at the Nusbaums' home for several days. Nusbaum needed Rockefeller's input on Packard's suggestion to whittle down board size and on how to fill Kidder's place. Rockefeller asked about the IAF's failure to merge collections, and Nusbaum explained that the conservatives felt it best to simply wait; assimilation was inevitable since the well was drying up. Rockefeller seemed satisfied. Nusbaum optimistically anticipated Rockefeller's contribution would be roughly $30,000 in maintenance funds; acquisitions would require separate Rockefeller funds.[34] He drove Rockefeller up to Gallup for the ceremonial, and they camped out that night, with Rockefeller's son David. Nusbaum had ample opportunity to open his heart. Did he share how unhappy he was, cooped up indoors, entangled in administrative knots?[35]

Chap was coincidentally in Gallup for a meeting of Collier's Indian art study committee. Collier had scored a legislative triumph in June with the passage of the Indian
Reorganization Act (Wheeler-Howard Act) protecting landholdings, offering relief, and
favoring self-determination. Encouraged, Collier had wired Young, asking him to get
the committee moving.[36] Their task was to survey Indian arts and crafts and recommend federal protection and promotion in U.S. markets. For three days, they grappled
with the dilemma of a dominant social group intervening in the culture of a weaker one,
which they acknowledged usually was detrimental to both, though they did observe that
the IAF's record was exemplary. They recommended a board to oversee preserving and
marketing Indian art—a job right up Chap's busy alley. They posited that a U.S. mark of
authenticity could protect both artist and consumer.

As winter closed in, Chap wanted to finish his monograph. Nusbaum cautioned
Stevens, "I have not let Mr. Chapman start any work on the [film] project, nor do I
contemplate his commencement of work until he has completed his text for the 'Pottery
of Santo Domingo Pueblo' publication. This has to be completed first and he is making
excellent progress thereon."[37] Nusbaum figured when Chap completed his opus, a travel
break to explore film recording methods would renew him.

By the time the laboratory board convened in New York, Rockefeller had conferred
with his advisors over Nusbaum's input. Harvard-educated Carl Guthe, director of the
Museum of Anthropology at the University of Michigan, was elected chairman, and
Kidder took a seat on the board. The entire board vacillated between research and education priorities.[38] The IAF reluctance to entrust its accessions to the lab resulted in
further indecision. Nusbaum's assessment of Rockefeller's intentions proved wrong. The
Davison Fund pledged only $20,000 of a requested $28,000, and still no endowment.

In time for Christmas, volume 1 of the Szwedzicki *Pueblo Indian Pottery* arrived.
Chap's text earned critical praise. The beauty stored in his heart converted his normally
fine writing into transcendent images of regional nature, the people, and the evolution
of their art. He was humble about it: "I regard my writing only as a means of putting
over my illustrative material."[39] With its gorgeous plates, the original limited edition
was stunning. It was offered by subscription at $35, later reduced to $25 since subscribers were scarce. (Today, a rare signed and numbered copy of both volumes fetches up
to $6,000!) Szwedzicki was unable to sell U.S. subscriptions from France to fund the
second volume. Desperate, he wrote Chap, offering two hundred copies at $12.50 that the
lab could sell at any price. How Chap came up with a check for ₣1,760.00 is a mystery,
but he greatly enhanced Szwedzicki's holiday, and Nusbaum was able to wish Rockefeller
a happy New Year with a copy.

January 1935 opened with another plea from Szwedzicki for the lab to buy books, but
Chap answered, "Mr. Nusbaum finds it more difficult than last year to raise money."[40]

The mail brought other gloomy news. The foundation issued its last grant for summer field education, to cover two years while the lab located other income. "The Rockefeller Foundation no longer regards support of work in cultural anthropology as within the program of social sciences and, therefore, this grant is final."[41] Chap needed a respite and slipped away for a week in Chihuahua, Mexico, while Nusbaum applied for more time on the stalled film project.

In June, Chap was still working on the Santo Domingo monograph text (the plates were done); he was working Sundays, holidays, and late evenings so the piece would be ready for review when the advisory board met in early July. In mid-June, he freed time to travel east to explore recording technologies for the film project, whose deadline had been extended. He spent almost three intense weeks transacting lab business, viewing National Museum of Natural History collections, and interviewing twenty people on motion and still film technologies.[42]

With Rockefeller support dwindling, Nusbaum foresaw the stress of "nicking" lab visitors. A promising light appeared at the end of his darkening tunnel. Demaray, the associate director of the National Park Service, told him confidentially that the Mesa Verde superintendent position would soon be vacant, and he was invited to return. The Nusbaums' private decision was likely immediate, for he was increasingly miserable. Chap was as unaware of their decision as anyone. When the inevitable rumors began, however, Nusbaum wrote Packard who formally spoke to Rockefeller on his behalf. Rockefeller was not surprised; he had anticipated such an outcome. In November, Nusbaum tendered his formal resignation, effective December 31, stating his need for restorative work close to nature.

A week later, the lab's ninth annual board meeting in New York was "an unusually interesting one."[43] With a crisis in leadership and funding, the members' proposed solutions veered from sponsoring adult education to modeling the lab after Woods Hole, as Kidder had first suggested. Chap was named acting director pro tem. Kidder requested a $20,000 matching Davison Fund pledge for 1936, but he was crushed by the defeat of his dream. Had Rockefeller, he wondered, rejected endowing the lab because of more worthy causes in the lean years, or had the lab disappointed him? The latter possibility saddled him with self-doubt for years. Clutching at straws, he tried to leverage a guaranteed personal commitment to secure permanent funding, but Packard rejected it. Construing this as the Davison Fund's loss of faith in the laboratory's purpose, Kidder suggested transferring the lab's assets to the university, museum, or even the National Park Service.[44]

Chap, ignorant of what was transpiring, had some remorse over Nusbaum's departure, for in heeding advice to keep at his own work, he felt he might have indirectly made things harder for Nusbaum. But with pro tem responsibilities looming, Chap worked through his regrets and turned to the present. He shipped off *The Pottery of Santo Domingo* manuscript to the publisher. He was truly bewildered over how it could have taken so long and remorseful "that I could not have foreseen the delay with my monograph[,] for [Nusbaum] has depended, heretofore, on my judgment in furnishing reasonably accurate estimates of the time involved in projects."[45]

After Nusbaum's official resignation, Kidder sent Chap a letter of appointment, apologizing for asking him to shoulder a burden that would supplant more congenial work. "But you understand the situation and will realize, I am sure, that you are the only person who can take the helm. . . . What we need now is the same sort of tact, friendliness and understanding which you gave in such full measure before."[46] Chap replied that he was not at all discouraged, and the sooner he learned the extent of the Davison Fund grant, the better he could plan for it. He confided that the worst of the lab challenges were nothing compared with the hopelessness of his last ten years with El Toro! When Packard learned that Chap had agreed to a one-year directorship, he offered unexpected advice to make it a permanent position:

> "Hold onto it, Chap. Mr. Rockefeller has confidence in you and will be disappointed if you give it up."
>
> I told Arthur that I could not think of abandoning my own projects for an administrative job. His response was, "Why let that bother you[?] Keep both of them going at once. If the job interferes, hand the job to a secretary and hide out."
>
> That might have worked if I had had the direction of a well-financed institution, but where nine-tenths of my time & attention had to be directed to begging, concentration on my own projects was out.[47]

Nusbaum had not yet told Chap that the Davison Fund had pledged a mere $10,000 outright, with up to $10,000 matching, half of what Kidder had asked for. Chap was also unaware of the extremity of Kidder's disappointment. Kidder reconvened the board members to offer four choices: try to make past programs workable, perhaps with a new focus on social science; return to the local group that had originally supported the IAF; affiliate with another New Mexico institution; or turn the plant over to the National Park Service.[48] An elected executive committee (Zimmerman, William D. Strong, and Nusbaum) was pessimistic and ineffectual. Their talk of throwing in the towel drained Kidder. On December 31, 1935, he resigned from the board. The chaotic situation gave rise to rumors that Rockefeller would abandon the project and that the lab would close. The executive committee charged Kidder with telling Chap to get the lab in order for termination. Kidder couldn't bear to deliver the bad news all at once and chose to wait.

Chap and Kate, c. late 1930s.
(Courtesy of School for
Advanced Research Archives,
AC02 805a.)

Over the holidays, then, Chap was blissfully in the dark. He and Kate had recently moved the family into a "hillside casa" above the lab. Helen, now high school age, spent the school year in Colorado Springs at a girls' boarding school. Frank attended the University of New Mexico. Following Kate's expressive lead, he had learned to play the family's Chickering piano, an ability that gave him a social edge among the university coeds. At home, emulating his father's inventive curiosity, Frank figured out a way to divert water from a spring above the house into a tank with a clever float valve mechanism. Kate and Chap weren't sure how much trouble the unimproved road would give before spring, an unknowing metaphor for Chap's new responsibilities. They looked forward to quiet times at their new home, enjoying the garden and the peace of the mountains. Kate's poetry best expressed the landscape of their life:

Old Love

Young love is a mountain
Linking the lowlands to the sky:
An upheaval of the earth's crust that tore, shredded the sunlight of the plains,
Then drew it together again with lacings of purple shadow.

Old love broadens as the mountain weathers,
For Time smoothes the highest aspiring crag to a gentler outline;
Crumbles and grinds the uttermost peak into soil for aspen and hemlock,
Into valley floors where lakes lie, the beginnings of placid rivers:
While always, from year to year, a wider and wider plain becomes
    silt-covered and fertile.

Can this old mountain, then, regret the sky-thrust of an earlier age,
When now its lakes are haven to a million stars,
Their sanctuary forever?[49]

Over the New Year, heavy snows hit. The difficult roads notwithstanding, the Nusbaums loaded their truck and rolled out January 5. In the interim, the Chapman ménage settled in for a few cozy nights with moonlit snow and wintry breezes stirring the piñons. Chap perhaps reflected with Kate on his future now that he was more than five years and less than four miles from where he had toughed it out under El Toro. At age sixty, Chap turned his conviction, creativity, and integrity to navigating the lab, with gusto.

He began by relying on secretary Virginia Jessop to help him manage lab details; Stubbs became acting curator and pitched in with the film project while Chap began charting an interim course. A mysterious message—essentially "after the deluge, what?"—from Tozzer puzzled him. Its full meaning came to light with the mail on January 6. Kidder's resignation arrived, along with personal regrets over the Davison Fund news, Chap's first hint of deep cuts. Kidder understated the mandate to shut the lab down, so Chap assumed it still had a future. He returned his best wishes, as much a believer in Kidder as ever. Next, he wrote Tozzer that his cryptic message was now clear, but having barely begun to capitalize on "our wonderful collections," he was determined to keep them unified "in view of 'el Toro's' oft repeated prediction that in due time the School would sweep up the remains. . . . So we will have frequent discussions with the hope that there may be some way of continuing the Museum feature as is. [The whole situation] was handed to me so suddenly that I have hardly begun to size it up. But I can say that even if I had foreseen this in 1929, I would have made the jump just the same."[50]

Chap was impervious to demoralization. Though he had publicly supported the lab's absorption of the IAF, he may have privately sided with the progressives' prodding for greater autonomy. He would have been cognizant of the growing aloofness of the Rockefeller Foundation and the subtle conflicts between Nusbaum and Kidder. He was now at liberty to overhaul the ship, not knowing she was consigned to dry dock. He wrote Guthe that it "can't be as hopeless as it seems, despite the 'diminishing support' joker in the communication of the Davison Fund." He still felt that the singular lab-IAF combination could make significant contributions. "It is a part of Santa Fe's unique setting and it would be a mistake to warp it into any other pattern. Over 14,000 visitors were given a personally conducted view of the collections last year, and everything points to increased tourist travel for 1936."[51] He could not fathom why Nusbaum had withheld the fact of the reduced pledge, but he busied himself developing a bar graph to analyze past support trends. He saw that he could do no worse and might even do better.

During these first weeks, Jessop accepted a job in California, so Chap had to learn the ropes quickly—she was leaving February 10—and find a replacement. Suddenly, he received shocking news. Stallings, back from visiting the university's anthropology department, reported that Zimmerman had announced the lab's demise. Worse, Zimmerman told the whole department, Hewett included, to go pick through the wreckage, as Chap would probably dispose of it on a first-come basis.

Stunned, Chap rapidly had to piece together the origin of the deadly gossip, which would hurt his credibility with donors. He and Stubbs immediately called on Zimmerman, who described the gloomy board meeting and their unanimous vote to close the lab. Kidder's resignation had convinced Zimmerman the lab had taken its last gasp and that Chap would be detailed to give it a swift, decent burial. *"But," I said, "they have nothing to lose, and I and my staff have, and unless Kidder overrules me I intend to carry on."* He convinced Zimmerman that the lab should keep going at least through the year, while he propped it up financially and Guthe ordered a survey by research councils. Chap's resolve echoed the boyhood spunk he had tapped into when the neighbor had suggested he would not be able to keep up with Dwight: *I said to myself then, "I'll show you."*

Next, with the approval of the staff I wrote Kidder that we were not ready to call it quits. I had in mind particularly the plight of the Indian Arts Fund, which might have made far better progress on its own, than that afforded by its five years of forced subordination under the Laboratory.[52]

He implemented crisis intervention. To counteract rumors, he reframed the same facts that had discouraged the trustees and issued a press release extolling the lab's good fortune in renewed Rockefeller support. He sold the staff on the value of positive publicity. A few days later, Nusbaum sent a hastily written note with the bizarrely belated news about the Davison Fund. By now Chap knew, yet jauntily replied, "It's a great life, but getting out of reach of phone every night has kept me from going under."[53] He was still bewildered and hurt, though, that Nusbaum had withheld the information so long.

With a public relations plan in hand, Chap turned to developing a financial one. He butted heads with Packard, who held to matching terms that Chap felt should no longer apply. Communication was slow. While chafing to begin raising money, he initiated a practice of giving optimistic monthly progress reports to the advisory board. Dietrich helped to polish Chap's popular image. Right before the February *New Mexico Magazine* went to press, she apparently rewrote the opening of her article on Pueblo painters, spotlighting Chap as acting director of the lab though it had little bearing on the rest of the piece.

During Chap's frequent meetings, he and his staff brainstormed over ways to downsize programs. They settled on limiting projects to the Southwest, particularly those with immediate news value. They publicized activities, including a free lecture series by staff and visiting anthropologists. Attendance grew. Chap exulted, "Within a few weeks I had received several applications for jobs, and three unsolicited contributions, one a $1000 bond as the nucleus of an endowment fund! I knew then that we had it licked!"[54] The board approved Guthe's plan to commission an objective study of the laboratory by three social science research councils; the Davison Fund agreed to finance it.

Chap tenaciously intended to return to the film project despite impossible scheduling logistics. He put it to Stevens that any financial help he could arrange in the name of the project would relieve him of that much panhandling, sharing that he was still struggling with giving Nusbaum the benefit of the doubt over the Davison Fund matter. Stevens encouraged Chap to economize with any remaining project monies and reapply for more. He empathized with Chap over the Nusbaum riddle, but Nusbaum himself cleared the air when he visited Chap two weeks later. He said that at the time he had felt bound by confidentiality and had no idea how subsequent events had pressured Chap. Amends were made, and the matter ended.

Meanwhile, the lab turnaround became contagious. Tozzer was pleased that Chap was challenging the board's defeatism and intended to contribute $250 as a matching gift. "You deserve all the support in our power and I only wish it might be more. I am going to show your letter to Mr. Scott and see if I can't get something out of him."[55] They were heading into June—late for Chap to be pursing donations if he were to meet his goals. He still needed Packard's agreement on what qualified as matching funds, and he didn't want to be cornered into leaning desperately on friends. Pinning Packard down via mail was tough. Chap and Guthe went to campaign in person for the broad matching interpretation so Chap could start gunning for victims, as he wryly thought of it. To maneuver into position, he asked if Packard thought it demeaning if he were to solicit memberships as low as $10. Packard declared that to the contrary, leadership was finally getting it. Encouraged, Chap and Guthe went on to hammer out terms that Packard accepted on principle. Chap was back by June 24, eager to capitalize on his gains.

> So the job was up to me. On my return trip I gave much thought to the necessary approach, and singled out several business and professional men who I felt sure would at least listen patiently to my "pitch." . . . Though most of them responded promptly, there were hints of surprise on their part that Mr. Rockefeller had not taken care of our needs.
>
> That prepared me for a better approach[.] . . . I would ask, "Do you know how the Laboratory is supported?" And I was ready for the usual answer, "Why, of course I do. That's Mr. Rockefeller's museum. He puts up the money."
>
> Then I would give him the facts, and add, "If you are contributing $10 per year for a membership, wouldn't you be apt to remember that it is _not_ Mr. Rockefeller's museum? It's one of Santa Fe's institutions, _not_ Mr. Rockefeller's; and it needs support from the people of Santa Fe."[56] (emphasis in original)

During the next few weeks, he interviewed at least one hundred Santa Feans! Having grasped how the assumption of Rockefeller "ownership" had hindered donations, he quickly honed an efficient marketing edge that won seventy-five local and out-of-state visitors who became regular contributors. One of them was James Young, who enthusiastically subscribed and even attended the next annual meeting. He soon became a board member and eventually chairman.

Chap's rapid finesse of $2,500 in matchables convinced him that he could exceed the maintenance budget. He finally realized the film project was a pipe dream and returned the unused balance of the grant.[57] He now awaited the results of the research councils' independent study. The three invited councils had each sent a representative: Frederick Osborn (Social Science Research Council), Leslie Spier (National Research

Council), and Charles Amsden (American Council of Learned Societies). Amsden, who had been chosen to be the field investigator, came in early August to begin several weeks of study.

Even while wrestling with administrative matters, Chap accomplished some tasks close to his heart. In his article "Indian Pottery by the Roadsides," Chap took on the uninformed Anglo tourist market by detailing what to expect at each pueblo as well as identifying how to buy good pottery (for example, by tapping the pot or accepting only those with characteristic earth-tone colors).[58] "If [the traveler] seeks only the cheap, . . . he is sure to find much to satisfy his taste. But if he wishes to select pieces that are beautiful and useful as well—bowls and jars that tell in form and decoration, of the age old importance of pottery in Pueblo Indian life, let him plan his purchase with a few simple points in mind."[59]

The Indian Fair committee hired a young writer, Maria Chabot, for a *New Mexico Magazine* series on Indian art. One result was the Saturday fair. Chabot began a weekly Saturday market throughout the summer months, modeled on fiesta markets she had seen while reporting on Spanish arts in Mexico, where she had first met Kate, Dietrich, and Stewart. The first Saturday fair was held in July 1936. Potters sold their wares under the portal of the Palace of the Governors. Chabot asked previous award winners like Maria to serve as judges, but the Pueblo women said they couldn't judge each other. Instead, some of those whom Chap had trained as Indian Fair judges two years earlier volunteered. The milling crowds made an educational talk impractical, so Chap painted a large sign enumerating characteristics of good pottery. Chabot wisely involved local retailers and the chamber of commerce and arranged for buses to pick up potters from featured pueblos. After the judging, the buses took potters to see the lab collections. This model was followed for four years; the Saturday fair was a precursor of today's annual Indian Market as well as the museum's daily Native American Vendors Program under the portal. Since the weekly fair proved so successful, Dietrich and others decided to reinstate the annual Santa Fe Indian Fair, in conjunction with Fiesta.

Chap and the potters continued to collaborate with regard to new designs. In the mid-1930s, his association with the Aguilar sisters of Santo Domingo resulted in their creating a series of pots with decorative schemes based on Santo Domingo models yet distinct from anything produced there or in other pueblos.[60] Occasionally Frank, Chap's son, would visit the lab and listen in while potters discussed their art with his father. "He'd go down in the basement and locate these pots they were interested in, and I'd go down with him. I think the talk was very definitely artist to artist."[61]

That fall, Amsden, Osborn, and Spier released their report. They saw no immediate need to dissolve or merge the lab with another institution. They stated that during the crisis the board's obligation ought to be less scientific and more proactively fiscal, stressing that the lab should support its own maintenance but apply for outside grants to fund research and other activities. They recommended adding nine lay members to the board, who would each commit $1,000 in support upfront, which would provide an immediate infusion of capital; if these volunteers were local or regional, they would be invested in lab survival and aware of which programs would garner support. In fact, Amsden took it upon himself to start recruiting them. Their report stated that anthropology research was the number one activity, and while museum work might not seem compatible with that, the lab should explore ways to capitalize on its collections. Finally, the study committee felt strongly that the director should be a man of science.

The report's biggest shortcoming was its failure to recognize that in hard times it is easier to open wallets with tangible collections of historic and revitalized pottery than with abstract anthropology studies. The committee had somehow missed the secret to Chap's success. Moreover, suggesting that a scientist ought to be director was a grave miscalculation.

The Davison Fund overseers failed to appreciate the significance of Chap's leadership and maintained distance. They were committed to a policy of diminishing support. Rather than introduce critical consultation ". . . when rather powerful forces of regeneration were at work, we . . . felt that we had to follow a passive role and contribute in a way that would keep the ship afloat without exercising control."[62]

The lab board met on November 21. Despite the study recommendations, they wanted more investigation! They voted to keep the lab open and at the same time commissioned an internal study and appointed a committee to report in a year. They also lopped "acting" off of Chap's title. He was appointed director at his former salary of $500 per month (less $100 from his Indian Service stipend). He accepted provided that prompt attention was paid to appointing a successor, being "more determined than ever before to return to my own work."[63] He and Guthe prepared for critical negotiations with Packard. They compromised on $7,500 outright and the same in matching.

Chap's remaining concern was a $600 shortfall in meeting this year's full matching funds. Back at his desk on December 18, he had one trump card left. Having avoided tapping friends, he now turned to one who came through (probably Meem). Chap had triumphed! He and the staff had created programs that were winning support. He had bumped the number of contributors from 15 to 146, and the lab now qualified for every cent of matchables. On New Year's Eve, he wrote Packard that the lab had gone "way, WAY over the top! But Cheerio! It has been a swell year[.] . . . I will be writing soon . . . particularly in regard to a better interpretation of 'contributions' as distinguished from 'operating revenue.'"[64]

The holidays brought two bonus gifts. Before the year closed, he had taken delivery of copies of his monograph, *The Pottery of Santo Domingo Pueblo*, and the second

Szwedzicki volume of *Pueblo Indian Pottery*. Each uniquely established the importance of post-Spanish pottery.

The lab had turned a corner. "It might be said that in the first period the responsibilities of the Board had not been discovered, in the second period discovery was awakening."[65] In January, Amsden wrote Chap that the lab's infancy was over and it was now entering its adolescence, and that Chap must deal with the problem of keeping the staff on its toes and the trustees interested, for without endowment they could not afford to slacken. "I'm especially glad that you're the Director. Nobody knows better than I what a pretty job you did during that crucial year 1936."[66] Rockefeller also sent praise coupled with personal concern: "I hear splendid things of you in the work which you are doing for the laboratory during this interim period and only hope you are not overtaxing your strength."[67]

To the contrary, as spring crested, Chap had robust energy. When Dwight's son, John, arrived during a road trip with a college buddy, he was struck by his uncle's passion and dedication to Indian art. And—having been raised with his mother Ethel's dim views on his aunt—John was completely unprepared for Kate's enthusiastic embrace. He was instantly enamored of his Santa Fe kin.[68]

Throughout the summer and fall, the lab stayed the course. Outside contributors had dropped a bit but the mean contribution had increased. The $7,000 from the lay board members (they had apparently ended up with seven rather than nine) made a huge difference, and a total of some $12,000 had been obtained in general funds from others. Board makeup was on the cusp of change. The 1937 meeting rehashed the same old question: scientific research or museum appeal? (The more mystifying question is, why did the board straddle this fence for so long?) There was also the matter of a new director, and social anthropologist H. Scudder Mekeel was a strong candidate. He had worked with the Yale Institute of Human Relations and more recently directed the applied anthropology unit of the Bureau of Indian Affairs. Conversant with both social policy and ethnological research, he had the qualifications of a trained anthropologist that the board sought in a director.

Only twelve trustees attended the November 1937 meeting. Guthe reported to Nusbaum, "A number of the Advisory Board and Trustees felt that Mr. Chapman should remain as Director, and yet he very definitely desires to devote more of his time than he now can to his research in Indian art. . . . [T]he Trustees elected Mekeel Director."[69] Mekeel accepted and would take over in January. The board's gratitude toward Chap backfired:

The Board insisted that the Laboratory's $4800 of my salary be continued for a year, to compensate for the lesser amount that I had received in 1936.

> *But that, combined with the $6000 for Mekeel, proved too heavy a load during the depths of the depression. Accordingly, after some months I cooperated by accepting a considerable cut, for the privilege of giving full time to my own work.*[70]

Chap had to surrender his conviction that Indian art was the backbone of the lab. He had private reservations about Mekeel's business sense, but he was hankering to return to his own work. He wanted to be supportive of Mekeel, so he tried to set up favorable conditions for his successor by wringing what he could out of the Davison Fund. He was flying solo in this year's meeting with Packard, which always required a full mental tank. Packard discussed complicated formulas for determining the ratio of matching funds, the idea being to wean the lab off Davison Fund support while reinforcing more aggressive soliciting. He agreed to $7,500 for outright funds and finally hit on a ratio whereby the lab would have to raise $10,000 to qualify for $7,500 matching, for a total budget of $25,000. Having arrived at what he felt was a good plan for 1938, he added a twist: withhold matching funds until the full $10,000 had been raised. This gave Chap pause.

> *I turned it over in my mind and could see some advantages in having the $7500 as bait until <u>bingo</u>, a related idea did for once come out of a side alley—I told Packard that we must remember that a new [director] is to take hold and that he will have his hands full . . . raising confidence in his program.*[71] (emphasis in original)

Packard saw the logic of this and eased up. On his trip home, Chap sacrificed plans to visit Vera to take advantage of an opportunity to speak on "Ten Centuries of Pueblo Indian Arts and Crafts" at the Cleveland Museum of Art. If nothing else, it heralded his return to Indian art and design studies.

With Mekeel about to take charge, Chap began his consulting work for the Indian Arts and Crafts Board (IACB), an outgrowth of the earlier study committee. The Indian Arts and Crafts Bill, another Collier victory, provided for a government mark of genuineness and standards for the use of this mark. It now became a federal misdemeanor, punishable by fine, to manufacture or sell goods as "authentic" without the mark. René d'Harnoncourt, IACB chairman, was a chemist by training whose interest in Mexican folk art had made him a self-taught authority. He was optimistic about generating an appreciative market for handcrafted Native articles. He felt that the problem was not that decline in demand had diminished quality and tradition but rather the opposite. The tasteless fakes, mass-produced Indian goods, and trinkets had stifled interest and sales. Where Chap had been concerned about the deterioration in the art, d'Harnoncourt was worried about the deterioration in the market.

His plan of attack was to educate consumers and gradually infuse the market with fine workmanship.

IACB members, including Chap, published qualifying standards for silver jewelry to bear a stamped mark of genuineness. They started with standards for fine quality slug (untooled coin-quality) silver and then explicitly detailed acceptable production methods and techniques. Dealers would receive printed tags and placards. Use of the mark was optional, but only an IACB agent could apply it. In early December, Chap received a shipment of steel punches for stamping silver to test in preparation for his work as inspector/judge. Problems quickly emerged. Punches broke, and the bracelet punch was too large—stamping the inside ruined the outer designs. Who better than Chap, with his penchant for tinkering, to solve such problems? He happily wrapped up 1937 with manageable concrete tasks, while Mekeel began 1938 with huge theoretical hurdles. In consultation with the Rockefeller Foundation, Mekeel planned a broad program of research that would comprise projects in six social sciences. He envisioned bringing in experts from each field for summer research fellowships. He wanted to network with local institutions, establish a publications fund, and build up the lab's research library over three years.

The government stamp began monopolizing Chap's time. He naturally thought about the mark as a design element. It consisted of "U.S." and an initial for each tribe, but Chap wanted Native symbolism to be used instead of the initial. For the Navajo, he toyed with a mini–squash blossom and crescent rather than "N." He visited the workshop of Navajo silversmith Ambrose Roans (also Roan or Roan Horse) to watch him experiment with stamping. He examined the stamping on manufactured sterling articles and hypothesized that it must be done simultaneously with the outer work, since there were no signs of damage to either. He used the unbroken punches a hundred times each on sheet metal to ensure they would hold up. For the most part, though, he found them inferior to useless. When he turned his attention to the sample paper tags intended for labeling the stamped products for sale, he found they too were unsatisfactory, so he tried linen. All this during one week at the end of January! Time was tight, so d'Harnoncourt asked an acquaintance to consult Tiffany's, who affirmed the difficulty of the task. The punches needed to be much smaller, so a new set was shipped.

In April, the pace of Chap's job as special consultant to the IACB rapidly stepped up. In early April, d'Harnoncourt put out a bulletin that the mark was now available. Within twenty-four hours, dealers were notified that Kenneth M. Chapman had been designated as judging agent and would appear in various cities to determine which pieces qualified for the stamp. D'Harnoncourt informed Collier that Chap, with assistance from Roans, would start marking silver for the traders in Gallup on April 11. Chap, Roans, Dooley Shorty (who taught silversmithing in Albuquerque and who would also serve as a code breaker during WWII), and another judge spent the rest of April making a circuit of New Mexico traders. They inspected 4,000 pieces, of which they stamped 2,322. Once marked, some were sent to National Park stores. When Chap returned, he began developing an instrument to make it easier to detect bracelets made with slug silver, as required, from those made with rolled silver.

The flurry of activity died down, however, as complaints from traders flowed in to the IACB. Higher-bracket retailers wanted a requirement that stores hold a larger stock of the stamped silver than small shopkeepers could afford to purchase so that high-end stores could be the sole displayers of the placard. Their view was that any curio shop with merely a few dollars' worth of stamped goods would sabotage the use of the placard as a mark of distinction. Others felt that most small retailers would make no effort to carry the stamped silver but would boost the sale of inferior yet more ornate designs by "referring disparagingly to the stamped silver as heavy, plain, and set with inferior turquoise."[72] Judging and stamping slowed sales momentum. Although Chap was retained as a special consultant to the IACB through May 1946, his active participation began to diminish by 1940. The IACB's mission, however, proved lasting.[73]

In June, Chap wrote Hodge that things were going well at the lab and that publishing in particular was looking good. Besides the General Series bulletins, he expected that the Santo Domingo monograph could soon be issued for sale as a lab publication. Summer also brought the lab's eighth annual summer Indian arts course.

Once Mekeel had completed his program plan, Chap acquainted him with the financial setup. Operating expenses actually increased in 1938, partly due to Chap's generous salary but also because of Mekeel's decision to commission an analysis by Raymond Rich Associates, a public relations firm specializing in fund-raising for non-profit organizations. The Rich Survey took the wind out of Mekeel's and the board's science-filled sails. The report stressed the public relations possibilities of the collections as well as of Indian art education, conservation, promotion, and social welfare programs. A few years back, Nusbaum had opposed those who had been proposing a separate Indian art center on the grounds that this "progressive" view represented a few petty minds. Ironically, the Rich report now emphasized Indian art and Chap's work as a key asset and recommended an affiliated Indian Arts Center as the best way to raise lab maintenance revenue! The report suggested that for a year or two scientific programs be subordinated to consolidating Chap's gains. This information provoked another surge of board ambivalence. At the annual meeting, they were torn between promoting Mekeel's program and supporting an Indian arts center. The Davison Fund still wavered on whether to intervene.

The calendar rolled over to 1939, but the year began with disappointments. Mekeel's application for a $15,000 Carnegie Corporation grant was rejected and his budget projection was $9,000 over the previous year. He and the board would have to resort to deflationary measures or send the lab spiraling into the red. At last, the Davison Fund trustees decided to step in. Packard was dispatched to Santa Fe to study the situation. He found the mission broad, salaries high, programs confused, thinking wishful, and the IAF/lab relationship shaky. His memo reported on interviews with a potpourri of people, such as Meem, Aileen Nusbaum, and, of course, Chap. Common threads included disappointment that the lab hadn't lived up to expectations, a sense that compared to other local institutions the lab was deadweight, hope that the board could start fresh, and faith in Indian art.

The memo communicated a breathtaking frankness and some surprises. In speaking of Guthe, the memo noted that "he may muddle through but he is not incisive. . . . [I]f the thing rides through to a success he will be a big-shot, if it fails, it will be Mekeel's failure." Of Lansing Bloom, Packard said, "He seems quite stable and thoughtful." Of Mera, "He has an unfortunate manner which may prejudice the soundness of his thinking[.] . . . Aileen Nusbaum says he likes to be the power behind the throne, that he is selfish and primarily interested in the little job that he can have for himself, and that Mekeel is becoming his yes-man. Mera clearly indicated to us that he is very jealous of Chapman. . . . He is potentially dangerous."[74] Scudder Mekeel had few proponents. Raymond Rich said he had withdrawn from further involvement because it would be bad practice for the lab to pay his rates when the lab could hardly manage salaries; further, "he doesn't believe Mekeel can run the institution and he doesn't want to be associated with a failure. . . . He feels the ship is far from being cleared of surplus cargo."[75] If anyone shines in Packard's memo, it's Chap, in a veritable catalog of praise:

He is something of a special character in Santa Fe.

Chapman is universally loved and esteemed in New Mexico.

She has a high regard for Chapman.

Chapman in 1939 conversations feels that Zimmerman would be glad to get him at the University.

Kenneth Chapman is probably the strongest personality factor in the local situation. What, for example, would be the implications in support, auspices, and program if Chapman were Director and a New Mexican were Chairman with a Park Service tie-up? Hindsight indicates that the wise thing would have been to disregard a good deal of the Amsden Report, to have kept Chapman in the saddle, to have reduced the program to one of Indian Arts, and . . . getting some young person with energy to be trained by Chapman to take on the Laboratory.

He says he is ready to step in again if it proves necessary.[76]

The question of the lab being affiliated with the National Park Service was put to interviewees. Generally, it was not well received, but the fact that Packard saw this as a possibility was worrisome. Guthe and Cole therefore asked Chap to act as a personal emissary to Rockefeller. Chap reluctantly agreed. He wrote Rockefeller that he was planning a trip to New York and requested an appointment to discuss past developments and the lab's future in the light of recent progress. Rockefeller responded that it would be a pleasure to see him because of their early days but business matters were Packard's domain. Fearful of jeopardizing their relationship, Chap was hesitant to push. He hoped to gain Rockefeller's ear by simply appealing to his desire to protect all he had invested in the lab.

Chap and Rockefeller met on October 6, 1939. They reminisced—and chuckled— over the grilling Rockefeller had given Chap during the trip to the pueblos. When the philanthropist then remarked how little the lab resembled what they had in mind in 1926, Chap saw his opening. He made an honest admission of his delicate position, and his personal appeal won a guarded response. Rockefeller began by saying that he had been continually apprised of the lab's situation and summarized his understanding of it:

1. We had contemplated an institution much on the lines of the I.A.F. in [1926] that was largely a vision.
2. Later the plans of the Lab intervened. He did not explain how he was won over by them. He said frankly that he was not particularly interested in the plans for so general a program of research, but that he "and all of us" were swayed by the visions of the research group, "which have not materialized as we hoped."
3. "Now we view the situation 10 years later and we find this difference. The I.A.F. has a home, it has vastly increased collections, it has now a certain measure of prestige, but it is faced with the necessity of accepting only its share of whatever measure of success the Lab has achieved."[77]

Chap said he was aware that Rockefeller had been uneasy about the IAF's unwillingness to have the lab absorb its identity and collections. He explained the reasons for the holdout, the integrity of its collection being the primary one. He was now disturbed that the trove might be handed over to the government and dispersed. Rockefeller assured him that lab holdings would be relinquished to the Park Service only as a last resort and that he would deplore breaking up the collections. Rockefeller then ended the meeting, saying that he hoped their pleasant personal relations would continue and that Chap should look him up whenever he was in New York. This assurance of abiding friendship allayed Chap's fears. Three weeks later, Rockefeller sent fraternal afterthoughts:

> It interested me to find . . . that we both seemed to have retained so completely our original ideals for the Laboratory and that we still see eye to eye as to what in our judgment its prime interest and field of service should be[.] . . . I was delighted to find you in such good health and want to tell you again how deeply appreciative I am of what you have done for and been to the Laboratory during all these years since we first dreamed dreams together in regard to the possibility of its creation.[78]

Guthe's and Cole's hopes for the lab faded when Packard reduced Davison Fund support to $5,000 matching. Kidder wrote that the lab's future depended almost entirely on Chap's attitude toward it. Perhaps Kidder's faith in him fortified him and gave him the strength to be assertive when the time came. For now, it was a different board that convened. The inclusion of locally invested lay members had offset the heel dragging of the scientists. Young was elected chairman and brought to it the same intensity that underscored his advertising career.[79] A decision was made to use collections to the lab's benefit and establish a center of Indian art. Though this appeared to be what Chap and Rockefeller—even the IAF progressives—had envisioned, Chap saw it for what it was: an expedient, probably temporary. With enough support among the remaining academics they could undermine it. Worse, deep salary cuts were necessary. Chap's dropped to $1,300 a year. Guthe and Mekeel agreed that if the lab's gross income did not reach $15,000 by July 1, Mekeel would seek other employment. Chap, anticipating that he would be asked to step in, wrote Guthe that he would cover daily operations for a few months at most but would do no fund-raising unless the board overcame its indecisiveness. He wanted board support. "It would not be fair to the board, nor to myself, to undertake as director, to perpetuate a setup in which I could not work to advantage. For I can not [*sic*] conscientiously solicit support, nor direct a major program for Indian arts, with such a kaleidoscopic picture before me."[80]

The board decided to exploit the collections. Mekeel saw no professional future in an Indian art museum, and so he tendered his resignation in early April; Chap again became acting director. He wrote to a friend that the title "acting" indicated that he

Kenneth M. Chapman and
Maria Martinez, 1946.
(Courtesy of School for
Advanced Research Archives,
AC02 821a.)

"hoped to be relieved of the job before I forget what my own work is about."[81] He had a
history of compatibility and good work with Young, who would be a great board ally.

Chap kept up as much contact with the potters as was possible with the lab's difficulties. He had spoken with Maria who said she would be willing to meet with the
Boy Scouts. In fact, she was usually amenable to outdoor demonstrations and would
even allow photos of her and Julian making pots to be taken, if given a few days
notice.[82] Family affairs took priority on September 7, 1940, when Helen and Bob Potter
exchanged marriage vows. The romance had blossomed in Colorado Springs—Bob's
mother owned the boarding school that Helen had attended. No one understood the
joy of a wedding better than Kate, who recognized in young love the link between
earth and heaven. The wedding was celebrated in John Gaw Meem's recently completed
Cristo Rey Church on Canyon Road.

The lab board met in fall in Santa Fe. Chap was offered, and declined, the permanent directorship of the lab. At d'Harnoncourt's suggestion, the board had resolved that the lab would retain its name and form an internal unit, the Institute of Indian Arts. Chap would continue as acting director and simultaneously become director of the institute whereby he would be granted the authority to study possibilities and solicit direct support for its operation. There would be low overhead with the initial single institute, but various institutes could be added (e.g., archaeology, southwestern anthropology) depending on available funds or donors. Packard was as tickled as it was possible for him to be. Privately, he hinted to Young that under these terms the Davison Fund would consider renewing, instead of further diminishing, the current grant. The lab budget was now a lean $15,000. Chap, Mera, and Stubbs were the only program staff, helped by a secretary and a janitor. As 1940 ended, everyone could chance a sigh of relief. Though war had begun overseas, it was distant thunder.

Since Chap had the next nine months to design the institute on paper, he arranged his acting directorship, now salaried at $3,000 a year, to accommodate his IACB consulting. He traveled to New York in January to attend the opening of the 1941 Exhibition of the Indian Arts at the Museum of Modern Art, organized by d'Harnoncourt. The exhibit included objects loaned by the lab, and Chap wrote to a colleague that it was a "grand show."[83] No less than the First Lady, Eleanor Roosevelt, paid homage to the art that he had worked so hard to preserve and promote, acknowledging that the Indians' "heritage constitutes part of the artistic and spiritual wealth of our country."[84] In February, he resumed his weekly university night class, boasting fifty students, and in April attended a conference in Lubbock, Texas, where he delighted in catching up with old friends, sharing news such as Frank's first teaching job in the public schools and Kate's hope that Helen and Bob's first baby would be born on August 4, Santo Domingo day.[85] In July, he happily broadcast that he was a grandfather: Helen and Bob's first child, named Margretta for their dear friend, Sister Piggy, had arrived a little early, on July 22, 1941.

Chap began work on the San Ildefonso monograph and also made frequent field trips to encourage quality production for the Pueblo Indian Arts and Crafts Market in Albuquerque, an offshoot of a trust agreement between the IACB and Tesuque Pueblo. He visited Acoma and Zuni once a month but noted that with few exceptions worthwhile material was scarce; most of the families made tourist trinkets, selling them on the highway.[86] "I enjoy my field trips to the pueblos, but chafe as usual at sidetracking my work on my San Ildefonso volume," he wrote to Guthe. "Buying pottery becomes a strenuous job in some pueblos."[87] Throughout the summer, Chap outlined the proposed institute and solicited feedback from colleagues. When he submitted his draft at the October board meeting, it was approved, with Chap essentially being the sole start-up staff. His path took an unexpected turn, however, and the institute was never pursued.

Shortly after the board meeting, Hewett asked to speak with Chap and the treasurer, Dan Kelly. "He began by warning us of what is ahead for privately conducted institutions (he's telling us!) and then asked if we had ever considered a tie-up with the University."[88] Hewett wanted the university to take over the lab to house its social science graduate programs and asked them to discuss it with Zimmerman. So they did; Zimmerman in turn laughed the idea off but wondered if the lab would consider turning itself over to the museum-school. Kelly and Chap said no for now but did suggest that "such a solution may present itself later on. Then we three got into a huddle and tried to figure out what El Toro had under his sleeve. There was no agreement but the most charitable conclusion was that he hoped to add luster to his career by saving the wreck for the state."[89]

Then Zimmerman put something new on the table. Two years earlier he had told Chap that he could always have a faculty post if he ever wanted it, and in Kelly's presence Zimmerman now offered him one. He said it would entail minimal additional work over Chap's current commitment and that he could finish up his monograph at the location of his choice. A five-year commitment would qualify him for the state pension.[90] The lab had no such safety net—it could barely provide for its survival. Chap began active discussions with Zimmerman about a full-time position at $3,600 a year and informed Young he intended to take it. Zimmerman became more cost conscious when he realized the extent of Chap's unfinished work and how the lab might stand to benefit by its publication and so ended up proposing that the lab bear half of his salary.

On December 7, the Japanese attacked Pearl Harbor, and within days the United States was at war. As Americans worried about what lay ahead, the lab too faced an uncertain future. It would soon be without Chap's guidance and leadership, and without the Davison Fund as well. Packard notified Chap that funding was to be terminated as of December 31. The best he could offer was advice to solicit Rockefeller's personal support, but he gave no guarantees. Before Christmas, Young called Packard with the news that Chap had a five-year teaching offer, at the end of which he could expect a pension. Packard immediately wrote Chap, placing their personal correspondence on a friendly basis by opening it "Dear Kenneth":

> Horace Albright and Mr. Young spoke to me about your plans for the next year at the University of New Mexico. I realize that this step on your part will have a real bearing on the Laboratory's plans for next year. On the other hand, I do not see how you could do other than accept Dr. Zimmerman's offer[.] . . . I hope too that we shall still keep in keep in touch with each other.[91]

Chap was not quite ready to resign as acting director with no one to man the helm. He judged 1941 an economic success. He had guided a trim ship, and attendance was comparable to the previous year despite his having to curtail the free lecture series and close on Sundays. He and the small staff had handled visitor services and maintained the building well, minimizing repairs. Most important, he managed to pull in the necessary $10,000 to receive the $5,000 matching, again making budget.

As for the coming year, it was hard to predict the war's impact. In January, Chap asked Packard to appeal to Rockefeller for the same funding terms. He also asked Young to put Zimmerman's half-and-half terms before the board, as he had an August start-up date with the university. While he waited, he received happy news from Packard that Rockefeller had pledged $5,000 against $10,000 receipts for 1942.

In May, the executive committee agreed on principle that the lab would absorb $1,800 of Chap's annual salary, with the understanding that Chap would continue his IACB consulting at $1,200, leaving only $600 for the lab to cover. They delegated Young and Kelly to work out the exact terms. When the four men sat down together, Zimmerman volunteered to fill in as lab director, at no charge, with Chap's assistance, an act of generosity that made the plan feasible. James Young, *sitting next to him, slapped a sheet of paper and a pencil before him and said, "Sign on the dotted line."*[92] Chap was now free to hand off the baton. Chap would remain on the lab advisory board, retain his IACB duties, and pursue his studies using the lab's facilities as a research fellow, jointly financed by the lab and the university.

Morley was in town during these meetings, aware of what was transpiring. Three days before the announcement, and apparently without Chap's knowledge, friend Vay wrote David Stevens to ask if the Rockefeller Foundation might make a five-year commitment of at least $600 annually to either the lab or the university to cover the lab's shortfall in Chap's wages. He said that given the uncertain future of the lab, it would be a small gift toward a guaranteed future for Chap. Stevens forwarded the letter to Packard, who acknowledged that a guarantee of $3,000 to cover the five-year period would be a "useful and stabilizing factor in the completion of the important contribution which Chapman i[s] uniquely equipped to make in the field of Indian art."[93]

Rockefeller wrote Chap a warm letter, praising his service and contributions, expressing regret that he was withdrawing from active leadership but acknowledging that he fully understood his reasons. This correspondence meant much to Chap, who treasured their mutual esteem and shared vision.

Chap now had June, July, and part of August to indulge in his studies. He and Kate were looking ahead to a new celebration in August, when they would welcome Jennie Kaufman into their lives as Frank's wife. Both teachers, Frank and Jennie had become acquainted in Santa Fe. Their weekly dancing dates at La Fonda and common interests led to a promise to love each other always.

While they celebrated young love at Frank and Jennie's wedding on August 16, Chap could look back over the last decade with calm assurance. Throughout the hard times and prewar years, Chap had steered both the IAF and the lab through straits of scarcity and the doldrums of board paralysis. No matter how dark the skies, like all good navigators he could fix his sights on certain stars: the timelessness of Indian pottery, the delight of friendship, the joy of creativity, the worth of consistency, and the serenity of integrity. He could now leave the ship's wheel to others and enjoy security in fulfilling his life's work on the wide plain of Kate's "old" love, whose lakes were "haven to a million stars."

CHAPTER 12

THE EARTHEN VESSEL

In the fall of 1942, already lean times were made even more spare by war rationing. Sugar coupons had been issued that summer. By December, mandatory gas rationing would take effect. Yet despite the lack of consumables, Chap felt rich. Once again, he was officially assigned to do the work he loved full time. "I am happy to say that I have resigned as Director of the Laboratory and at last am free to work on my books," he wrote in response to an information request in October. "The next one will be on San Ildefonso pottery. . . . I have transferred to the faculty of the University of New Mexico, but am detailed to do my work full time at the Laboratory. . . . So it enables me to keep at my work here without being dragged into Laboratory business—a fine arrangement."[1]

According to Chap, Zimmerman's plan *went smoothly until a year later when in a conference with Dr. Zimmerman the question of age came up. I then learned for the first time that under the University's system, members of the faculty could* <u>*request*</u> *retirement at 60, could* <u>*demand*</u> *it at 65, but it became* <u>*mandatory*</u> *at 70. "How does that affect me?" I asked. When he found out that I would reach 70 at the end of only 3–½ years [of teaching full time] he was stunned, but after a moment's consideration said, "Oh, well, we'll find some way around that, when the time comes."*[2]

Replacing the directorship were three pottery studies—San Ildefonso, Santa Ana, and Cochiti. The material on San Ildefonso was closest to completion. For years, Chap had been gathering information from the potters themselves—Maria and Julian Martinez, Tonita Roybal—as well as from local collections, particularly the laboratory and IAF collections. In addition, he had pages of notes about and sketched designs of pots housed in museums out east. Now he could get down to the business of publishing. The staff had been told not to disturb or distract him from his work on the San Ildefonso publication.[3] By February 1943, he had rearranged his workspace so that he had sufficient room to get the manuscript and drawings ready for publication.[4]

But, as with many wishes that are granted, the gift of time simply revealed that other obstacles stood in the way. To complete the books, Chap was faced with four main tasks. The first two—finishing the drawings and conducting additional research to supplement the text—benefited greatly from additional time because they were labor intensive and fairly straightforward. Nearly all of the drawings for San Ildefonso were finished. At least half of the drawings for Cochiti and Santa Ana were in his hand.

The third and fourth tasks, however—deciding which of the drawings would best represent each design and then mounting the drawings on plates—were amenable to procrastination. Chap was loath to commit to a drawing until all resources had been considered. He wrote to Zimmerman, "it has been desirable to await inspection of every available specimen of pottery before making the final selection of drawings for each plate."[5] In addition, his new status at the laboratory ironically created another obstacle. Being wholly employed by the university—and scrupulous with regard to favors—Chap no longer felt entitled to free use of the laboratory's resources. Thus, photographic work on the plates was postponed until he could arrange for funding from another source.

The largest contributor to continued delays, though, appeared to be a lifetime of administrative distractions that had fashioned a work environment Chap found unable to abandon, regardless of his voiced complaints. Probably no one was surprised then—least of all, Chap—when he allowed additional tasks to impinge almost immediately on publication time. Ruth Underhill, an anthropologist who had studied under Boas and was working for the Bureau of Indian Affairs, had asked Chap to review her manuscript on Pueblo crafts. In March 1943, Chap wrote to apologize for his tardiness:

> Your letter of February 13, enclosing your paper on Pueblo Crafts has lain on my desk these many weeks along with a bale of other correspondence, while I was pushed around in the basement by several things demanding immediate attention.
>
> . . . Among other things keeping me busy I have taken on sole responsibility for distributing the plates of Navajo blankets as set forth in the enclosed. So I am publicity agent, bookbinder, carpenter, shipping clerk, office boy, banker, and scavenger—the latter title earned by weekly visits to Penney's and other stores around the Plaza, hunting out and cutting up paper cartons of the right size for making the flat sides of containers for the portfolios.[6]

Personal affairs intruded, as well, with March 1943 bringing birth and death to his circle. Chap and Kate's second granddaughter, Pamela, was born to Frank and Jennie late that month in El Paso, where Frank was teaching. The happy news eased Kate and Chap's spirits, which had been burdened by the war and, more recently, the agonizing ordeal surrounding the death of Julian Martinez. After a four-day search in early March, Julian's body had been found on a hill near the pueblo, where he had fallen. The news was devastating. A former governor of the pueblo and a nationally recognized artist in pottery and watercolors, Julian had been close to Chap ever since they had shared their excitement over pottery designs at the museum. "I have had so much to ask Julian, but am grateful for all he told me," Chap wrote after Julian's death.[7] Their delight in the pottery motifs had inspired Chap's career. Julian, one of the most creative artists of his time, had simply seen the designs' potential and lived it. Chap noted that "there will never be another Julian."[8]

Maria suffered her loss with quiet fortitude, but Julian's death was a new burden of sorrow for the pueblo, already suffering from war casualties.[9] Two of Maria and Julian's sons, Felipe and Tony, were engaged in the fighting, as were hundreds of other young Pueblo men. Meanwhile, San Ildefonso had acquired the war as neighbor. By early 1943, scientists at Los Alamos, on the hills above the Santa Clara Pueblo, were harnessing the principles of physics to create the world's newest weapon. The site had been a boys' school, which Robert Oppenheimer noticed while horseback riding in the 1920s during a visit with classmate Francis Fergusson. Twenty years later, when the federal government searched for a location for its top-secret atomic research project, code-named the Manhattan Project, Oppenheimer suggested buying the school and surrounding ranch land.

For two years, Oppenheimer managed the scientific program on "the Hill." The actual work remained secret, but Santa Fe residents could not help but notice the Army guards prowling around offices at 109 East Palace Avenue: they were the only men in Santa Fe dressed in three-piece suits.[10] The lack of information only heightened their interest. Lights could be seen from miles away, occasionally fires raged and smoke billowed, and always there were mysterious explosions. Rumors multiplied like "maggots in one of Mel Hagman's garbage cans," according to the *Santa Fe New Mexican*.[11] By war's end, more than five thousand people lived on the Hill or worked on the project, including people who traveled daily from San Ildefonso and other nearby pueblos. According to ethnologist Underhill, "the effect was as though a number of large cities had moved into the desert and the Pueblos had become their suburbs."[12] Chap also noted the difference in a letter to Rose Dougan:

> There are many changes in the pueblos since you were last here—and most of them not what we would have wished. Doubtless you have heard of the Army's hush, hush project which took over Los Alamos School, and has developed a great plant up on the mesa. Great trucks from the road, which is being straightened and improved at a cost of over a half million. Most of the adults of San Ildefonso work at Los Alamos, coming and going in army busses. The women get $3 per day and pottery making is about at a standstill, except for Maria's output. Since Julian's death last March, Santana has taken on the decorating. It might be worse.[13]

The war, with the limitations on travel it imposed, meant fewer donations and visitors to the laboratory. But following England's lead, which encouraged museum activity for morale building, the laboratory continued its regular activities.[14] Supporting the war effort in Chap's own family were Frank, who was teaching ground-school aviation at the University of Texas in El Paso, and Helen's husband, Bob Potter, who was training at Camp Hale. Located just north of Leadville, Colorado, the camp was home to the U.S. Army's Tenth Mountain Division, a special ski unit created immediately after Pearl Harbor and now preparing to fight in northern Italy.[15]

Helen and toddler Peggy remained in Colorado Springs, sharing their apartment with a friend's wife whose name was Helen Siegman. To avoid confusion, Helen Potter suggested that she be called by her family nickname, "Chappie." When possible, Kate traveled to see Helen and Peggy. Siegman's husband, Kenneth, recalled Kate as a wonderful, happy fun-loving person, with a flair for the unexpected. On at least one visit, remembered Siegman, Kate packed her coffee pot and pressure cooker in a suitcase and then wore all her clothes—dresses and coats—one on top of the other![16] Despite difficulties in traveling during the war, Kate assured Helen that she would return to help with the new baby, expected in February.

Chap and Kate spent more time than usual together that winter, as heavy snows discouraged even local travel. The arrangement pleased Chap, who felt that he could accomplish more away from the office, and he envisioned a future where he'd spend even more time at home with Kate. "We have had more than our share of snow and it has been so difficult getting our car up to our place in the foothills that I have spent several days at a time at home, working on my drawings and text," Chap wrote to a colleague in Denver. "I seem to make better headway, away from the Laboratory, and am setting my work in shape so that I can stay away for a week or more at a time."[17] In February, the weather cleared long enough for Kate to travel back to Colorado to help Helen. Amid the general anxiety of war, the Chapman family had cause to celebrate, this time over the Valentine's Day birth of Robert.

Helen and her new baby returned home to Peggy's delight and Kate's attentive care. But two weeks later, Kate, suddenly ill, was admitted for an emergency appendectomy. Chap hurried to Colorado Springs, remaining while she recuperated. As she healed, he probably teased her about his being the caregiver to the caregiver. But each day she gained strength. By mid-March, even the *Santa Fe New Mexican* carried a short article that noted her improvement.[18] Meanwhile, a relieved Chap kissed his family good-bye and left for Santa Fe, expecting Kate to follow soon.

Chap would have been en route when Kate, still in the hospital, unexpectedly developed an embolism and died on March 14, 1944. Presumably Helen knew first and had to wait to share the terrible news with her father, knowing that when he arrived in

Santa Fe, he'd be anticipating arrangements for a joyful reunion. Instead his world shattered. Accustomed to leaning on logic, Chap must have felt betrayed. He had just left Kate, with every sign of a successful recovery. He had just spoken to her. He was expecting her back.

Helen accompanied Kate's body to Santa Fe by train. Already fragile from childbirth and the stress attending her husband's imminent departure, and now imagining her own and her father's life without Kate, Helen must have been exhausted beyond endurance. Frank traveled from El Paso for the funeral and, together, the family suffered a week of shocked grief along with Kate's dearest friends, Dorothy Stewart and Margretta Dietrich. They had just rejoiced in Kate's recovery. Now they were left only with her stories. Although Chap could treasure over twenty-eight years of a happy, joyous marriage, he could not yet look back. She was still too much in his present.

Recalling his father's death, Chap knew that healing would be a long, torturous process. In 1894, he had had to find a job quickly to support his mother and siblings. This time, too, his response was work. Just a week after Kate's death, Chap wrote to a colleague, "I am beginning my Wednesday night class at the University in Albuquerque tonight, my first routine work since the sudden death of my good wife on the 14th. I know from experience that work is the only anodyne at such a time and that she would wish me to keep on."[19]

Chap focused again on his publications, telling a correspondent that he was working on several books "each of which will show the decorative art used by the potters in one pueblo. While there is a greater need for more general studies, I am concerned first with finishing of studies begun over twenty years ago. When they are published I hope to get at something more useful to the general public."[20] His work was the only laboratory project still funded by the Rockefeller Foundation. David H. Stevens, who assessed Chap's projects annually for the foundation, described the San Ildefonso monograph as Chap's most important work.[21]

Helen and her children spent a month with Chap that spring. Chap wrote to Nusbaum that Helen had helped him to "clear the house of a load of non-essentials. It seemed a cruel and hard boiled procedure . . . but I bless her for her nerve and foresight in making a clean sweep." They wrote nearly a hundred thank-you notes to Kate's friends, many of whom Chap scarcely knew by name but who seemed genuinely touched at her passing. Trying to busy himself every minute, Chap suffered a nearly complete collapse in early summer and was forced to spend several weeks recuperating.[22]

Fall brought Indian Market, as it was now called, which served as a helpful distraction as Chap judged alongside Bertha Dutton, Olive Rush, Eugenie Shonnard, and Edith Ricketson. But even the market was preoccupied with death. Service Flags, created by the NMAIA, hung along the walls above the market. Stars on each flag signified the number of young men and women from each pueblo who were fighting in the war, been taken prisoner, or died.

Death seemed relentless. In October, James Zimmerman, only fifty-seven, died of a sudden heart attack while attending a dinner party in Albuquerque. At the time of his death, he was president of the university, a member of the museum's board of regents, a member of the school's managing board, and director of the laboratory. In recalling Zimmerman's zeal regarding the laboratory, James Young, then president of its board, said, "His personal welfare was always placed behind the demands on his time and his strength. . . . [His] interest in all phases of laboratory work was constant and unflagging."[23]

Chap, who greatly admired Zimmerman, felt the loss keenly. The crescendo of such emotional events—the war, Julian's appalling death, the shocking loss of Kate, Zimmerman's sudden heart attack—might have persuaded some to look toward home and family for comfort. Chap, faced with loneliness, chose to wed himself to work. Despite the laboratory's precarious state, it felt more like a refuge than the empty house he returned to each night. Without Kate to come home to and unwilling himself to drive back and forth, Chap decided to make it his home. In November, he moved out of his house and into a small room at the back of the laboratory. In a letter to Stevens, Chap wrote that "with the first snow, I gave up my daily commuting and spent my nights at the Laboratory, making only week end trips up the hill by taxi or, if the snow was too deep, by Shank's mare[.] . . . I can recommend the setup to any hermit who wants to hole in for the winter—actually within the city limits!"[24] Few staff members were there to notice or comment, as only Elizabeth Wesley, executive secretary, Marian Bond, part-time receptionist, and Stanley Stubbs remained on staff. Those who knew probably thought that the arrangement was temporary, expecting it to end in spring.

Chap did return to his house for a time that summer when Helen and her children arrived. Bob Potter's homecoming was eagerly anticipated after Germany's surrender in May 1945. Yet war still raged in the Pacific, spurring the Manhattan Project staff on to an even more feverish pace. As Chap celebrated his seventieth birthday, Oppenheimer and his staff were en route to the Trinity site on the White Sands Proving Ground near Alamogordo, New Mexico, for the detonation of the nation's first atomic bomb. In the early morning hours of July 16, the blast from the test touched people for hundreds of miles around. Nearby residents swore the sun rose twice.[25] Still, despite whispers, Chap and the rest of Santa Fe learned of the new weapon only after the military dropped the bomb on Hiroshima, Japan, three weeks later. A second bomb brought surrender. Along with news articles, the *Santa Fe New Mexican* finally was able to publish the many rumors that had circulated about the Hill. "The news of Los Alamos had scarcely raced about the Plaza this morning when the membership of the 'I-Knew-It-All-Along' club began growing by leaps and bounds. . . . Gas warfare, rockets, jet propulsion, death rays and—atomic bombs—were among the guesses most frequently voiced [before learning about the bomb]. During the last Presidential campaign, Alamos—no foolin'—was sometimes a Republican internment camp."[26]

The end of the war found Chap, now seventy years old, not only still working—and living—at the laboratory, but also continuing to teach his class at the University of New Mexico one evening per week. Uncertain of the status of his university retirement pay, he had met with acting president Thomas Popejoy, who had served as executive assistant to Zimmerman.[27] He had good news. Chap would receive retirement pay prorated to the years spent teaching full time. In addition, faced with an astonishing boost in enrollment from returning GIs, Popejoy offered a stipend if Chap would continue with his Indian arts class. It was a pleasing outcome, as Chap found contact with the students "most stimulating."[28]

At the laboratory, Zimmerman's death had resurrected the issue of direction, which Chap did his best to ignore, focusing on his monographs and letting the energetic and persuasive James W. Young, chairman of the laboratory's board, search for the new director. Since 1942, Young had partnered with Zimmerman to return the laboratory to a mission that was national in scope. As president of the laboratory's board, Young had sent elaborate invitations to high-class prospects, envisioning thousands of "Cadillac" members supporting their work nationwide. The list flowered into a membership of one thousand. Although Chap's inclination was to preserve the regional focus, he admired Young and his work. *He often told us, "I would consider myself stupid if, with the Laboratory's splendid plant and collections, I could not expand Chap's own little local, $10, membership list into the thousands." His idea was simple, "Don't beg for money, but give the members something for their money."*[29] Young devised a series of silk-screen prints of specimens from the collections, called "Masterpieces of Indian Art."

In June 1945, Young hired a new laboratory director, Maurice Ries, a former government official in inter-American affairs. Ries and Young proposed a new program that emphasized the educational functions of the laboratory. In this role, the laboratory was charged with interpreting, for the public, scientific findings in general. Three months after Japan's surrender, Ries organized a series of public lectures and radio programs that included the first talks by scientists who produced the atomic bomb, "proving that the Laboratory of Anthropology was an important instrument in bringing scientific knowledge to laymen."[30]

Chap's own ideas about the direction the laboratory should take sharply diverged from the vision that gave primacy to science, but he continued to disregard management concerns and placed his energies squarely on his books. "Now that three years have passed since I got to work on my books I doubt if I shall ever have occasion to take part in the management beyond that as a member of the board of trustees," he wrote to Stevens. He reasserted his focus, saying, "There is plenty here to keep me going but I often feel the need of a good library, and will be hunting one when travel and subsistence get back to normal."[31]

In Santa Fe, without Kate's social ties, work absorbed Chap; indeed, he was so consumed by his work that he decided to make the move to the lab permanent. He lived and slept in a small room at the back of the building that was equipped with inventions of his own design. To outwit a sore back, he hung a trapeze from the ceiling's vigas to help pull himself out of bed.[32] He also created an easel that allowed him to draw while lying in bed.[33] Stanley Stubbs, a close friend as well as IAF curator, appointed himself as Chap's lookout. Thirty years Chap's junior, Stubbs was a revered member of the staff and a laboratory veteran, having joined in its founding year. Highly respected, Stubbs "probably knocked fresh experimental chips in more potsherds, unraveled more alleged bayeta, and critically examined more worn old Indian silver, than any other museum man in the country."[34] Yet each day at noon, Stubbs drove Chap to the plaza for his main meal; Chap would then return by taxi. For his morning and evening meals at the laboratory, Chap used a hot plate in the basement on which he also performed experiments. Occasionally he'd let the kettle go dry while cooking his tansy or Rocky Mountain bee plant. As terrible smells seeped upstairs, Stubbs—fearful that the place was on fire—would walk down to the basement to investigate and, in a very gentle way, take care of the whole thing.[35]

Precious to Chap were his children and grandchildren, loved for themselves and also because they were reminders of happier times with Kate. He celebrated Thanksgiving and Christmas with Frank and Jennie's family in Albuquerque, driving down with her parents, also Santa Fe residents. Each spring, Chap took advantage of his teaching schedule to spend one night a week at Frank's house, having taken the bus or hitched a ride to Albuquerque in the lab van. Every other week, Frank and family would visit in Santa Fe.[36] Helen often lived out of state, with Bob in the Army, so Chap mailed letters covered with doodles and sketches.[37] When Helen and the children lived in Santa Fe during the Korean War, they often dropped in on Chap at the laboratory after work hours. His granddaughter, Margretta "Peggy" Potter Harnisch, remembers a great big key stuck in the door that Chap would turn two or three times before opening. "He'd be towering over us, and it became quite a family joke. Every time he would greet us at the door, he would say 'Well, well, well,' and then invite us in. We spent many hours there with him at the museum, just roaming around."[38]

Chap did occasionally meet with friends, joking with Helen about invitations to teas from all the "old cutes."[39] A young seventy, accomplished and admired, Chap would have been a most eligible bachelor. He was a regular at meetings of the Atalaya Garden Club, which was, according to one of its members, very social—people used to meet, and then once in a great while people would mention a garden.[40] Most were Chap's longtime friends, such as Margretta Dietrich and Leonora Curtin. Catherine Rayne, companion to Elizabeth White for thirty years, recalled that when Chap promised to talk about his garden, she had wondered, "Now, how could he talk about his garden, since he lived at the Lab?" Meanwhile, she had spotted a Campbell's soup can sticking out of his back pocket and thought, "Oh, poor Chap, he has to bring his own food." Instead, he pulled out a can that held sixteen different varieties of morning glories![41]

Even at parties—Santa Fe was famous for its parties, such as the White sisters' grand costume affairs at El Delirio[42]—Chap preferred a quiet talk, one on one, to more gregarious socializing. In October 1946, he had a new tale to share with his friends. As he was patching the roof of his house one Saturday, he had wondered about band music coming from the plaza. Later, he read that huge crowds had gathered to celebrate the first-day issuance of the General Stephen Watts Kearny commemorative stamp. Among the celebrants was Joseph J. Lawler, third assistant postmaster general, who declared the new three-cent stamp—which featured a drawing commemorating the one hundredth anniversary of Kearny's entry into Santa Fe—to be one of the most beautiful and appropriate that could be issued, according to a contemporary news article.[43] What the newspaper did not report—nor did the celebration's hosts appear to know—was that the drawing's creator was only a few miles away . . . patching his roof![44] Chap had prepared the illustration originally for Twitchell's 1909 publication (see plate 5).

For the most part, though, work trumped social events. Rockefeller continued to fund Chap's project, although his work on San Ildefonso, which he appeared so close to finishing in 1942, was still not complete. Chap let other tasks claim his time—talking with Pueblo artists who came to view the lab's collections, for example, or corresponding with younger researchers who depended on his expertise—justifying the diversion by citing the laboratory's inadequate numbers of staff. In the 1946 annual report, Ries reported that Chap continued to be the bulwark of the laboratory's research activities even though he was not officially a member of the staff. In fact, the situation was becoming desperate. With Mera now retired, the lab was reduced to only one salaried scientist, Stanley Stubbs, a museum technologist and a field archaeologist by training. Despite their close friendship, the fact that Stubbs was the only salaried employee occasionally prompted Chap to say, in a spirit of frustration, that "the Laboratory of Anthropology is the only anthropological institution in the country without an anthropologist on its staff."[45]

In early December 1946, the laboratory's dire condition became public when the executive committee acknowledged a deficit of approximately $11,500 (nearly half its

expenses). Once again, a change in policy was the proposed cure. The formal statement issued by Ries stressed the laboratory's concern with the "whole science of man."
Although the phrase sounded disconcertingly like the one Hewett used when describing his original purpose in establishing the School of American Research, director Ries
asserted that the laboratory was "unique in every respect, from its broad name to its
opportunities for service to anthropology and mankind."[46]

In fact, however, the ambitions and the supporters of the laboratory and the museum-
school had begun to merge in theory if not in reality. While financial obstacles had
thwarted the laboratory's initial mission, the museum, through programs like its Hall of
Ethnology, had begun to address the very problems that had fueled Chap's frustration
many years earlier. Chap had noted that Hewett's fury about the laboratory "proved indirectly a distinct gain for his Museum. He cut out most of his outside activities and settled
down to renovate and expand its exhibits and activities."[47] In addition, several museum-
school board members sat on the laboratory's board. Among them was Sylvanus Morley,
who was not only Chap's friend but also Hewett's chosen successor. Interestingly, Morley
encouraged the idea of the laboratory merging with the museum complex, along the
lines of Kidder's 1935 plan. Out of respect for Hewett, however, Morley made no overt
effort to initiate such a union.

On this subject, at least, Chap and Hewett agreed. Chap's years of anguish at the
museum-school had cemented his aversion to such a complex organization. For him, a
merger should be considered only as a last resort. For his part, Hewett remained deeply
antagonistic toward the laboratory. Chap often thought that Hewett "would have been
pleased to see the laboratory's building leveled to the ground, and burros grazing over
the site."[48]

Between the men themselves, however, the bitterness had begun to fade. When
they met on campus, Chap reported that Hewett "always had interesting bits of information regarding our mutual friends of early days, but not once did he ever bring up
any of our unsettled differences."[49] Later, when Hewett's overtaxed heart forced bed rest,
Chap was a frequent visitor. "By then the acute phase of our differences had passed; he
loved to recall the happier past and I spent many hours with him, but always with my
fingers crossed."[50]

As luminarias brightened Santa Fe during Christmas of 1946, both Hewett's health
and the laboratory were failing. Hewett, eighty-one, soldiered on until the last day of
1946, when he passed away in an Albuquerque hospital. The laboratory lasted as an
independent entity only days longer. Although the official merger would not occur for
several months, Chap reported that as soon as the news of Hewett's death was received,
the promerger factions acted at once and within a week the laboratory and museum
were made one.[51]

To Chap, who embodied the spirit of the laboratory, the merger felt like failure. Joining the museum-school meant admitting publicly that Hewett's institution was stronger. Chap briefly resisted, traveling east in January to interview an elderly supporter, who had promised a significant contribution to the laboratory. On the same trip, he met with Packard, to whom he indicated that he "was not sure that any fundamental change in the [laboratory's] situation would be brought about as a consequence [of Hewett's death]."[52] But the facts told otherwise, and Chap no longer had the energy or will to fight. "I believe I could have led the Board to swing back again to my more conservative regional plan . . . and by taking over once more as Director on a full-time basis, I believe I could have built up added support for my projects. But that would have meant the end of my own work, for which I had just received another Rockefeller Foundation grant. The sacrifice was too great; I said nothing, but helped to save something of the Laboratory's prestige—its corporate name and purpose, and its separate budget which enables us to receive and expand contributions in the Laboratory's name."[53]

The only possible silver lining here was Morley's leadership, which Chap knew could be trusted. Despite Morley's relationship with Hewett, Morley thought of himself as a museum man rather than a schoolman.[54] Since 1914, Morley had been spending six months in Central America and six in Santa Fe. He was an expert on Mayan sites, particularly in hieroglyphic texts and calendar inscriptions. Morley was also renowned for his efforts in communicating information to both the professional and lay public. In addition, Morley's ability to maintain good relations with Hewett while pursuing a career as an "eastern" archaeologist through the Carnegie Institute made him the perfect candidate for managing the soon-to-be-merged museum-school and laboratory. The school's board appointed Morley acting director of the school—and, ex officio, museum director—in June. Official acceptance would come in August, during the annual board meeting of the museum and school. The merger would then require ratification by the legislature, scheduled to meet in January 1949.

Meanwhile, in private discussions, Morley fashioned a plan. The results were reflected in a July proposal, presented by James Young and approved by Francis Wilson and Chap. The document, which formally initiated the merger, proposed that the laboratory transfer its buildings, grounds, and collections to the museum, with the exception of the laboratory's director's residence. The latter would be deeded to the school in return for an immediate $8,000 mortgage loan. At the same time, the laboratory board attempted to pare down its operations so it could survive the eighteen-month period until the legislature would meet. Ries, who had earlier enthusiastically supported the merger, now found his program cut and angrily resigned.

At the same time, Rockefeller was discreetly queried concerning his views. Having learned that the merger would not affect Chap's position at the laboratory or at the

University of New Mexico, Rockefeller indicated that he would prefer not to express his opinion on the consolidation although he did make it clear it was important that the collections continue to be available for educational exhibition.[55] During these developments, Chap learned of the death of Abby Rockefeller and promptly sent his condolences. In his thanks, Rockefeller told Chap that "The letter which you wrote me at the time of Mrs. Rockefeller's going and your beautiful tribute to her are deeply appreciated. . . . May I extend to you my understanding sympathy in your own loneliness these past years. Because you know so well what I am going through, your thought of me at this difficult time is the more helpful."[56]

By August 23, 1947, the plan had crystallized. At the annual meeting, the school's board named Morley as its director and then approved the merger in principle. They increased the size of the board from twenty-eight to thirty-six members so as to be able to bring people on who were sympathetic to the laboratory's goals.[57] Chap and Stubbs were chosen to head the Indian art and the anthropology departments at the laboratory in a revamped operational structure.

With regard to the proposal, some members questioned the gift of the director's residence in exchange for the loan. However, Morley was faced with several problems, among them the laboratory's need for an immediate $8,000 loan, an eighteen-month delay before the legislature would meet, and the inadvisability of offering the state property encumbered by mortgage. Thus, the exchange of the director's residence for an urgently needed loan seemed reasonable. In the final proposal, approved by the school, museum, and laboratory boards in September, the director's residence, plus about eight acres of land, was offered as a gift to the school. The laboratory building, the remaining forty-two acres of land, and the collections were to be offered to the state. Two deeds and a bill of sale were put into escrow in the First National Bank of Santa Fe.[58]

Before then, though, the two organizations were symbolically joined during Hewett's memorial services held the weekend of the annual August board meeting. Perhaps Hewett's ghost was tempted to disrupt the proceedings, but the ceremony proceeded smoothly. Hodge, museum board president Daniel T. Kelly, and Morley spoke at the service. Most symbolic, though, was Chap's unveiling of the memorial plaque over the niche that contained Hewett's ashes. Under the circumstances, Chap may have felt that discretion was the better part of valor, for the newspaper reported that the ceremony was performed "in respectful and sympathetic silence."[59]

With the appointment official, Morley enthusiastically plunged into the task of bringing all factions together. In February, Chap's project was still the mainstay of the laboratory. But, by summer, when Morley moved his offices to the laboratory, it could boast of at least eight different research projects under the auspices of organizations ranging from the IAF to the University of Chicago. Everyone anticipated official approval of the merger by the legislature, but to pave the way, *El Palacio* prepared a promotional issue for its January edition that included an article by Chap on the laboratory's accomplishments.

But the atmosphere of hope abruptly evaporated when Morley passed away from a sudden heart attack on September 2, 1948. All who knew Morley mourned him. Chap was devastated and, at the new museum complex, the loss of Morley seriously demoralized the staff. But, with the legislative session looming, there was little time to grieve. The board quickly sought and approved a new director, Boaz Long.

Long, a diplomat since 1913, had known Morley in Guatemala. With the legislature scheduled to meet in only four short months, many saw Long's diplomatic experience as a godsend. By the time it met, Long was prepared but faced an unexpected challenge in accommodating a new project—Florence Bartlett's interest in establishing a folk art museum. Bartlett was considering the director's residence, which had been promised to the school, as a possible site. Thus, during the session, Long pushed not only for the museum-school-laboratory merger but also for continuing the negotiations for a folk art museum. By session's end, he had approvals for both.

The approvals had come at great cost to the museum, however. Although largely unpublicized at the time, the wording of House Bill 82 differed significantly from the proposal approved by all three boards in September 1947. In that proposal, the state was to receive the laboratory building, its collections, and about 42 acres of land; the school was given the director's residence and about 8 acres. House Bill 82, however, offered the state only the laboratory building and 26.65 acres of land; the laboratory's Indian arts collection would not be transferred to New Mexico. More damning, when the items were removed from escrow in August 1949, the three items placed there in 1947 had "spontaneously" transformed themselves into four: (1) A deed for the laboratory building plus 26.65 acres, *instead of the 42.3 acres agreed upon in 1947*; (2) a deed for the director's residence to the school for 23.6 acres, *instead of the 7.9 acres agreed upon in 1947*; (3) a bill of sale from the laboratory to the state for the laboratory building's furnishings and equipment, *instead of the collections agreed upon in 1947*; and (4) a bill of sale from the laboratory to the school for *all* collections. Thus, the assets of the AIA's school—and not New Mexico's museum—suddenly increased as it gained extra acreage and the laboratory's entire Indian arts collection. All documents were signed by Boaz Long and Daniel T. Kelly (secretary) and thus considered binding according to the Lab Inc. bylaws.[60]

Although it would be nearly twenty years before proof was offered that named Long as the main author of this deception, both Chap and Stubbs saw it for what it was: robbery.[61] Chap's attitude toward Long visibly stiffened, a sentiment that was both noticed and defended. When Chadbourne Gilpatric of the Rockefeller Foundation wrote of his visit to Santa Fe, he mentioned the "tireless and tiring efforts" of Long. Gilpatric noted that although Chapman "was the man to talk with," only two hours were set aside for their meeting. "While amicable, the relationship between C[hapman] and L[ong] is clear. The former is a serious artist and a man of strong and admirable character; he has no use for administrative finaglings or casual social dealings. L, on the other hand, acts like the retired Foreign Service officer old style that he is. He delights in contact and promotional activities and seems to have no feel for either art or science."[62]

Battered by his losses and deeply disillusioned, Chap became even less visible with regard to management and more devoted to his private projects. In the summer of 1950, he realized that the time spent teaching his class at the university would be better applied at the laboratory and so told the dean of fine arts that "I would rather have him ask why I was quitting, than to hang on until he asked why I was not!" Living in the back room and writing, often until midnight, Chap became an almost ghostlike presence in the laboratory. A glimpse of Chap in the halls by new staff evoked only awe. In 1950, Gilpatric and Stevens of the Rockefeller Foundation provided a grant for an assistant to Chap. He favored Bruce Ellis, husband to archaeologist Florence Hawley Ellis and a graduate of the University of New Mexico, whom Chap knew from his Indian arts class.[63] His instincts were well rewarded. "They were like two peas in a pod," remembered Fred Wendorf, a contemporary of Ellis. "Their personalities were very similar, and to Bruce Ellis—Chapman was god, that's all."[64]

Ellis and Chap worked together for nearly six years, during which time Ellis prepared illustrations for the Santa Ana and San Ildefonso publications, expanded Chap's line-break paper, and accompanied him to the pueblos and fairs. In 1952, Chap wrote to Neil Judd, "My choice of an understudy, two years ago, was one of the happiest decisions of my life, for I don't know how I ever got along without Bruce Ellis."[65] For his part, Ellis wrote to Gilpatric of the Rockefeller Foundation that "in the Laboratory, on field-trips and even during our lunch-hours together on nearly every week-day of the year I have tried to absorb as much as possible of his [Chapman's] knowledge of and 'feeling' for the subject. In spite of the fact that my questions sometimes must have interfered with his digestion, we remain on good terms."[66]

Bolstering his legendary status, Chap received honorary doctorates from three institutions: the University of Arizona (1951), the University of New Mexico (1952), and the Art Institute of Chicago (1953), the last particularly prized by Chap. "Having received two honorary doctorates, Arizona, 1951, and New Mexico, 1952, I was glad to call it quits," Chap wrote to Judd. "But two weeks ago I received notice of another from the Art Institute of Chicago, where I studied a few months as a kid, just 60 years ago. . . . Having spent so many years in a sort of no man's land between Anthropology and Art, and exposed to the sniping of both camps, it is gratifying to receive this recognition from

Kenneth M. Chapman (right), recipient of an honorary doctorate by the University of New Mexico (UNM), with his son, Frank Springer Chapman, UNM math instructor at that time, 1952. (Courtesy of School for Advanced Research Archives, AC02 805f.)

the artists."[67] In reporting on the degrees, *El Palacio* suggested that Chap's finest contribution was "not to white students of Indian art but to the Indian artists themselves" through his participation in the revitalization of potterymaking at San Ildefonso Pueblo. "Surely it should not be hard to imagine that among the congratulations offered to 'Chap' for his new laurels are some being murmured in Tewa."[68]

Chap may well have received such compliments in person, for he still traveled to San Ildefonso and other pueblos, ostensibly to gather more data for his monograph but also to visit. Lambert recalled that "the Indians loved him[;] . . . it was a family thing with them. You could tell that Chap was looked on as part of the family. Maria would be so happy to see him, her sisters would be so happy to see him. . . . There was a really good relationship between him and these old people, the younger ones too."[69] Chap's rapport with the potters was a bridge between cultures that had been raised in friendship and had weathered the decades. In 1945, artist Fred Kabotie of the Hopi Reservation thanked Chap for his friendship and support in helping him receive a year's fellowship, stating "Both my wife and I felt proud, but without the willing support of my friends this is not possible for the Hopi Reservation Indian."[70] Indian Art expert Francis "Frank" Harlow noted that "[Chap] went [to the pueblos] to try to understand, to be with them. . . . And they understood him, I think."[71] At a 1954 meeting of the IAF, where Chap received a standing ovation, Maria herself paid high tribute to Chap in her remarks.[72]

While Chap's work with the Pueblo potters and his research in Indian arts—work that had defined the laboratory for twenty-five years despite persistent attempts to shift its focus—was celebrated, the laboratory suddenly defied its decades of false starts by establishing a new niche. In the early 1950s, Jesse Nusbaum, then consulting archaeologist for the U.S. Department of the Interior, seized on a new opportunity. When the El Paso Natural Gas Company began to lay pipelines, Nusbaum, citing the Federal Antiquities Act of 1906, urged the company to take action to locate and excavate archaeological sites in the pipelines' paths. This time, the gods smiled. The laboratory, in conjunction with the Museum of Northern Arizona, recorded over three hundred potentially endangered prehistoric and historic sites in New Mexico, Arizona, and Colorado, excavating forty-five of them.[73]

The success of this enterprise transported the laboratory into a new and, ultimately, enduring scientific phase. In 1954, the laboratory persuaded New Mexico's highway department and the U.S. Bureau of Public Roads to participate in the first nationwide, cooperative Highway Archaeological Salvage Program.[74] An immediate outcome was that, suddenly, Stanley Stubbs and Chap were no longer the lone lab scientists. Instead a young energetic scientific staff shared the hallways. Stewart Peckham (salvage archaeology), Edwin Ferdon (anthropology), Fred Wendorf (anthropology), Nancy Fox (curator, collections), Marjorie Lambert (museum staff member since 1937), and Ellis now enlivened the laboratory with intellectual zeal and a passion for the laboratory's goals. Most were in awe of "Dr. Chapman," whose formality contrasted with their generation's tendency toward the casual. But Sally Lewis Rodeck, who worked at the laboratory in the early 1950s, recalled "everyone respected [Chap], everyone. . . . And he had a wonderful laugh."[75]

A 1954 trip to Deming, New Mexico, with Ellis, Lambert, and another researcher, Elizabeth Davis, provides a whimsical view of Chap's analytical and somewhat solitary nature. They had traveled there to look at the Alex Thompson collection, the sale of which Lambert later successfully negotiated. Then they decided to cross into Mexico for dinner. "The real attraction was a great big back room that was absolutely full of booze," recalled Lambert. "People use to go there to get liquor very cheaply and come back across the border to the United States. That was a revelation to Chap, who in a way was absent-minded, the absent-minded professor and in many ways very naïve, I guess, one of the things I liked about him." While the others made purchases, Chap was studying the shelves of liquor, pen in hand. "'Marjorie,' he said, 'it's just like learning your pottery types[.] . . . I'm learning and I'm counting,' he said, 'I just can't believe it,'" Lambert recalled. "But you know he didn't condemn us, he didn't think we were a bunch of drunks or anything, he was just scientifically interested."[76]

Another of Lambert's stories illustrates her perception of Chap as a man who coupled innocence with stubborn resilience. She recalled that one weekend he disappeared from the lab without telling anyone where he was going. When he didn't come back after a couple of days, she asked her husband to drive up to Chap's house in the foothills.

> We got up there, and I was hoping we wouldn't find a dead body or a man with a broken leg. There he was up on the roof of this house, which was being regularly vandalized—and eventually it was vandalized to the point of no return—and there he was, with some mud that he had mixed up, and a little kettle he set up. And he had some tar that he had melted—why he didn't set himself on fire, I don't know. . . . I said I thought that we better take him back to town, because, I said, how are you going to get back? He said, well, I told the taxi to come and get me at the end of the week. So you can see what I mean by being an innocent.[77]

For Chap's eightieth birthday, Lambert, along with other members of the IAF, planned an elaborate celebration at her and her husband's home. They decorated with Indian artifacts, including Wide Ruins rugs ("we put them right out on the ground"), a cake decorated with potsherds, and appetizers skewed by bone awls ("which Stanley [Stubbs] said I could have from the collection of bone pins"). "I never saw anyone have such a good time as he [Chap] did," Lambert recalled. Laughing, she confessed: "We had a great big bowl of punch, and Jack and I had made it, and it was a combination of tea, and spices, and rum. I don't think any of them knew that it had rum in it, all these elderly people, but they certainly had a good time."[78]

Some of the younger staff members—for example, Lambert and Ellis—now judged alongside Chap at Indian Market, which remained his focus throughout the 1950s, although the event was merely holding its own rather than growing.[79] "He encouraged all the Indian women," Lambert recalled, "and if he saw something particularly good in the Indian Market, he would take extra pains with this person to tell what she should do, and how to make it better maybe and so on. He was really wonderful."[80]

In the 1950s, Indian Market was only one of many Fiesta celebrations, which began with the burning of Zozobra, Old Man Gloom, and continued—for many—both day and night. The Fiesta drew carloads of tourists to Santa Fe for its four event-filled days, which ended in a swirl of street dancing. As in the heyday of the 1920s art colony, Santa Fe was considered an exotic destination where the lifestyle was considerably more liberal than most. Tourists reveled in the atmosphere. Taking advantage of the economic prosperity that flowed across the nation after the war, Santa Fe developed two new attractions—a ski basin and an opera house—to entice even more tourists. Many stayed on, much as they had in the 1880s.

However, along with economic good times came Cold War paranoia, which not even liberal Santa Fe completely escaped. Nationwide, sportsmen signed loyalty oaths to acquire fishing licenses, high school students signed them to receive their diplomas, and tenants of public housing projects sent them in with their rent.[81] In Santa Fe, residents' fears were fueled by the case of Oppenheimer, then scientist-adviser to the government on atomic energy. In the mid-1950s, Oppenheimer, who had led the Manhattan Project to success against all odds, was accused of associating with Communists two decades earlier and questioned about his opposition to the newly developed hydrogen bomb. After month-long hearings, Oppenheimer was charged with treason in 1954, declared a security risk, and stripped of his clearance. The *Santa Fe New Mexican* reported that Los Alamos scientists found the decision particularly frightening, as they considered the possibility that charges would be leveled next against those who had worked with Oppenheimer.[82]

In this climate, Chap's own fears of being called a traitor surfaced. Haunted by Ralph Magoffin's 1928 accusation of having been "that God-damned Judas," he worried about that epithet emerging from a set of Hewett's papers recently donated to the museum. *For the first time I realized what a risk I had taken all those years, in not asking Mr. Rockefeller to review my statements regarding our first meeting.*[83] So in February 1954 he wrote to Rockefeller, a paragon of business ethics, for confirmation that he had behaved honorably—one elderly gentlemen to another:

> In my correspondence and in my rare visits with you, I had never thought of recalling any of the incidents of my first meeting with yourself and Mrs. Rockefeller, in 1926, or of mentioning the complications that arose shortly after in my conferences with Dr. Hewett. Viewed through the haze of so many years, those stormy scenes had seemed hardly worth recounting, even though

the sting of some of them lasted for several years. I was well aware that Dr. Hewett had given his associates his own version of my differences with him, for by some I was branded as a traitor who had betrayed his chief. But as the years passed most of them had relented and eventually, during my directorship of the Laboratory, several had gladly accepted memberships on our Board. . . .

So the matter rested until a few weeks ago when in a casual conversation with the executive secretary of the Museum he volunteered the information that an employe [sic] of Dr. Hewett's widow had recently sent to the Museum a considerable package of manuscripts which they believe will provide material for one or more additional volumes of the memoirs. . . .

For myself, I might decide to dismiss the whole matter, but since it may mean much to my children in years to come, I feel that I should try to clear these three points that lent me such assurance in the long-drawn-out controversy that followed. I would prefer to spare you the trouble of reviewing them but if you are willing to do so, let me assure you, Mr. Rockefeller, that I will gladly accept your decision and advice in the entire matter.[84]

When Rockefeller indicated his assent, Chap sent his notes that brought three main points to Rockefeller's attention: (1) that Abby Rockefeller had asked to see the Indian pottery ("whatever comes of this, always remember, I asked if we might see the pottery"), (2) Rockefeller himself showed only the slightest interest in Hewett's work and concentrated instead on the general museum situation in Santa Fe, and (3) Rockefeller told Chap that he had asked Hewett for a statement concerning the Santa Fe institutions but had not received a reply.[85]

Rockefeller, per usual practice, turned the matter over to associates to collect and read the pertinent files. In early summer, Rockefeller himself read everything and then composed the following:

I have been a long time in replying to your letter of March 28th with its interesting enclosures. I hope the delay has not inconvenienced you. It has not been due to a lack of sympathetic understanding of your reasons for writing me as you have, but rather to the pressure of other things.

Your Memorandum entitled "Memorandum of My Meetings with Mr. and Mrs. John D. Rockefeller, Jr., June 10 and 11, 1926" would seem to cover the facts as I recall them. Whether this is true in every minute detail, I could not say under oath. That it is so, however, is my very definite impression.

I can see no reason why this Memorandum should not be used by you should the occasion arise in any way that would be helpful to you. It certainly could do me no harm nor can I see why it should be in any way disturbing to those who survive Dr. Hewett.

Re-reading these various memoranda of yours, recalls so vividly my interest, with you, in the Laboratory of Anthropology and all that led up to its establishment. How I wish I might sometime be in Santa Fe again and have the opportunity of seeing you and laboratory. If ever you are in the east be sure to let me know that I may have the pleasure of a visit with you in New York.[86]

Before sending the letter, Rockefeller turned to a trusted adviser, Tom Debevoise, who recalled his own discussions with Appleget. Rockefeller asked him to scrutinize all pertinent documents, including the above letter, to ensure that sending it would do no harm. Rockefeller noted, "Mr. Kenneth M. Chapman was the man whom I met in Santa Fe and to whom I made various pledges and through whom my cooperation in the establishment of the Laboratory was channeled. He is a fine man and I have every confidence in him. Dr. Hewett . . . I knew and had various contacts with[.] . . . I never had the same feeling, however, for Dr. Hewett that I had, and have continued to have, for Mr. Chapman. Dr. Hewett was a good deal of a politician, quite self-centered and I am inclined to believe, jealous of Mr. Chapman."[87]

Chap would have been tremendously gratified had he ever been privy to the above note or to Debevoise's assertion that "If further facts come to light I am sure they will be in favor of Mr. Chapman."[88] As it was, on August 9, 1954, Chap expressed his "deepest satisfaction" over Rockefeller's "most cordial letter."

It is most gratifying to have your assurance that it would seem to cover the facts as you recall them. Considering the many hundreds, if not thousands, of such incidents in your long and useful career, it is most remarkable that you have so clear impression of the items stressed in my statement.

That my own recollection of them is so clear is, as I have stated, due very largely to the fact that I found them at the time so unusual and meaningful that for once I saw the importance of making full notes of them at once, item by item.

I am placing your letter with my copy of the memorandum and accompanying correspondence in my safe-deposit box and . . . as possible insurance in behalf of my children, they will be invaluable.[89]

Satisfied with the outcome, Chap turned his attention to a new task for the Rockefeller Foundation: preparing his memoirs. David Stevens of the foundation had urged Chap to capture his experiences on paper, so during the mid-1950s, Chap set down in longhand his memories of a midwestern childhood, his years working with Frank Springer, and his career at the museum and, later, the laboratory. As Chap admitted, he "had no use for dictating to a secretary or machine. Nor am I a competent typist. As Jess Nusbaum once said, I did my dictating with a soft pencil."[90] Ellis typed the drafts and edited some of the sections on Chap's childhood. Chap acknowledged that "each incident has been recorded regardless of its interest to others, and in many cases perhaps too much in detail."[91] For historians with an interest in Santa Fe's colorful society of writers and painters or in Chap's interactions with the potters, the memoirs are instead maddeningly thin. One suspects that Chap was wary of setting down opinions about his contemporaries on paper. Not so with his grievances concerning Hewett, however; these he catalogued as if expecting a jury instead of a publisher.

Chap and Ellis refined the ever-present San Ildefonso monograph as well. The book continued to be anticipated by the Rockefeller Foundation as a "most important contribution," but its completion remained out of reach more than a decade after Chap was released to work on it full time. Although Chap was receiving pressure to finish it, it was clearly difficult for him to let go. Stewart Peckham, who headed the lab's salvage archaeology projects, remembered that Chap would always want to go someplace to see one more San Ildefonso pot.[92] In 1956, Chap reported that the introduction now included "the latest information regarding several ceramic types of the Tewa area, preceding the earliest known San Ildefonso wares."[93] He set 1957 as the completion date. But in 1958, he described the San Ildefonso Pueblo monograph as "a work that still grows as new possibilities unfold."[94]

The collections at the lab remained a constant pleasure for Chap, who treasured the opportunity for talking with the Pueblo artists when they came to view them. In 1958, Lucy Lewis of Acoma Pueblo arrived at the lab with her daughters and photographer Laura Gilpin to meet Chap. During their visit, Chap showed them pottery from various prehistoric cultures, including examples from Mimbres, Chaco, and Mesa Verde, with the result that all of these influences were soon expressed in Lewis's exceptional work. In particular, the Lewis family pioneered the use of the Mimbres-inspired designs—novel styles at the time—that so appealed to tourists and collectors.[95] Chap's role—by way of showing them to Lewis—is another example of his support for innovation within the context of tradition.

Searching out decorations not in the lab's collection, Chap toured thirty-six museums in 1958 to view material and arrange for photographs for the San Ildefonso monograph. The fact that so much southwestern material was deposited outside the state remained a source of irritation. He blamed Hewett, particularly, not only for his "gifts" of pottery to other museums but also for the irresponsible handling of the Normal University collection, which continued to rankle.[96] Thus when the Shermack

Lucy Lewis of Acoma Pueblo and Kenneth M. Chapman, c. 1958.
(Courtesy of School for Advanced Research Archives, AC02 805b.)

report and the Rockefeller-backed Mitchell Wilder report abruptly awoke New Mexican politicians to the fact that their museum was funded by the state but managed by a private organization over which they had no power, Chap was relieved. And he could not have been more pleased by what this knowledge resulted in—their desire to separate the organizations.

"No doubt you have kept up with the changes in the School-Museum setup," Chap wrote to Harold S. Colton, Museum of Northern Arizona director. "I was in favor of the split, but we are held in suspense by the delay of our new Governor. . . . Some say he has been awaiting the next fiscal year, which begins tomorrow. We shall see."[97] As Chap predicted, the connection between the museum and the school was officially severed on July 1, 1959, when the legislature voted to make the Museum of New Mexico a state agency, with a board appointed by the governor. Without the museum as its showpiece—and its funding source—the school was left to its own resources: "a staff of two, an unclear mission, and an uncertain future."[98] Hewett's early failures to establish a private, sustainable funding source were painfully evident.

On paper, the boundaries in the legislation seemed clear, but when it came to shelves of pottery, ownership was anything but obvious. The school claimed 7,117 items of textiles, jewelry, and pottery, a total that included not only the ill-gotten laboratory collection but also items originally acquired by the museum. The IAF owned 5,254 items. The museum had obtained a relatively small number of archaeological materials during the salvage projects.

Chap and the other members of the IAF board were infuriated by the politics that had placed the laboratory's collection and most of the museum's property in the hands of the school and anxious about the fate of their collection. The issue that the board faced was whether to leave their collection with the museum and, if so, whether they should stipulate that they would maintain control over exhibitions. Emotions ran high. At the October 1959 IAF board meeting, as Chap reviewed the history of the fund, he may have been reminded of the personality conflicts that had surfaced in the 1930s. William J. Keller, chairman of the museum's board of regents, openly declared that "decadent views and selfish interests on both sides must be discarded. The Board will have no sympathy for pressure groups, for pet projects, pet theories or pet ideas."[99] When a member of the IAF board questioned what type of cooperation they could expect from the museum, Keller replied that the board of regents would accept nothing with strings attached.

A week later, however, the museum seemed more amenable to negotiating, having heard that there was a good possibility that the IAF would pull out. The fund negotiated terms that included a one-year contract (rather than five), a curator assigned to the collection (they proposed Stanley Stubbs), and control over acquisition of future items. Realistically, however, there were few options when it came to storing and exhibiting the collection. Then, before negotiations were complete, Stubbs, curator of the collection, died from a sudden heart attack. IAF board members were shocked and devastated. Thus, funeral arrangements for Stubbs occurred just as the fund was conducting final arrangements of its own. In Stubbs's place, Chap agreed to curate the collection and also recommended that Betty Toulouse's catalog of items be duplicated and placed in a vault when complete.

It was left to the anthropology division of the museum to determine ownership of the remainder. Owing to storage issues, the museum chose to integrate all of its anthropological holdings with those already housed at the laboratory building. Nancy Fox and Albert Ely, representing the museum, and Betty Toulouse, representing the school, conducted a physical inventory of all the specimens, a process that ultimately took over ten years to complete. Artifacts housed at the laboratory that were found to belong to the school were placed on long-term loan to the museum.

In October 1960, the museum moved forward with its plan to found a department of Indian art under the administration of the art museum. As a result, in 1962, the IAF collection was right back where it started: in the basement of the Museum of Fine Arts, housed in a newly remodeled exhibition gallery for the new department of Indian art. At the opening, the IACB presented certificates of appreciation to Chap, Elizabeth White, and the IAF in recognition of their services.

Soon to follow was the merger of Lab Inc.—the corporation that had been formed to show Rockefeller that it was "a going concern"—with the school. Officially joined in May 1963, Lab Inc. and the school declared they agreed to merge when they discovered they had virtually the same board of directors and purposes. The laboratory collection, still on long-term loan to the museum, remained in the basement of the Laboratory of Anthropology building for at least three decades more, however. The arrangement was an ongoing source of aggravation for the laboratory-museum, which found itself responsible for caring for the collection but bound to assign credit to the specimens—in its inventory or when it sent them out on loan—to the school, which had never collected, curated, or housed them.[100] Two years later, the fund's board agreed to merge its organization with the school, thus reuniting—in theory at least—the laboratory and IAF collections. The IAF remained an active entity, however, and in 1966 celebrated forty years with an exhibit at the Amon Carter Museum in Fort Worth, Texas. At the opening, which nearly eighty-five hundred people attended, Chap spent almost three hours answering questions.[101]

Among IAF members, one question recurred: have we accomplished our mission? Time and again, its board answered with an emphatic "no." But evidence of the IAF's accomplishments could be seen at Indian Market. The conservative potters—those who could be depended on to exhibit traditional designs and shapes—were showing pieces that were quite unusual. Lambert and Toulouse felt that the ideas were based on the IAF collection because many of the new pieces were reminiscent of older modes of pottery-making. In weaving, Lucy Lowden of Jemez Pueblo won an award for an embroidered manta with the designs and colors of early mantas, which she had seen in Mera's pueblo embroidery publication.[102] And the Amon Carter booklet, *Quiet Triumph* concluded that the IAF's record was indeed complete: "The former urgency of finding and preserving has long since passed, while the educational mission has become the responsibility of the U.S. Indian Service." That same year, the IAF began to deed its collection to the school, and in 1972 dissolved its corporation after fifty years.[103]

Chap probably appreciated better than anyone the ironic twists and turns that had brought the two collections together again under the auspices of the school. From the time of Elizabeth Shepley Sergeant's dinner party through the 1960s, he had held the IAF close to his heart. He had elicited the first donation from John D. Rockefeller Jr. He had initiated the sequence of events that had transformed the proposed exhibition space

Indian Arts Fund Group of first members: Andrew Dasburg, Amelia Elizabeth White, Kenneth M. Chapman, and Jesse L. Nusbaum, c. 1965. (Photograph by Laura Gilpin. P1979.149.77. Dye coupler print [type C], c. 1965, 7 15/16 x 10 inches. © 1979 Amon Carter Museum, Fort Worth, TX, bequest of the artist.)

for the fledgling collection into a laboratory of anthropology. He had watched as the laboratory tested its wings and then succumbed to the Depression . . . and meanwhile observed that Hewett's museum-school expanded exactly those programs for which he had lobbied. After personally willing the laboratory into life through the 1940s, he was forced to witness its collapse during the merger with the museum-school. Then, he stood by not only as the laboratory's collections fell to the school, but also as Lab Inc.—which he believed he had saved as an independent entity—joined it, and the IAF collection as well. Rationally, he must have realized the advantages. Emotionally, he surely wept.

The laboratory's soul proved remarkably resilient, however—grounded, as it was, in Chap's own valiant spirit. Chap would not be alive to savor the blossoms, but, in fact, the laboratory's powerful force would emerge intact and thriving. Its first reincarnation was as the Museum of Indian Arts and Culture, created in 1988 as the answer to a sixty-year dilemma: was the lab to be primarily a research institution or a public museum?[104] Chap had always championed the latter, and today the museum magnificently fulfills that goal. It offers both exhibits and educational displays of southwestern Indian culture that are developed in active participation with advisory groups and the expertise of its Native American staff.

The laboratory's second reincarnation took the form of the Indian Arts Research Center, designed to preserve the IAF collection and completed in 1978 as part of the School of American Research (now School for Advanced Research), under the direction of Douglas Schwarzt. The center is located at El Delirio, Elizabeth White's estate, which she bequeathed to the school in 1972. It is dedicated to the very programs that Chap had long advocated: involvement with Native American artists and students who wish to study traditional arts and crafts. The center exquisitely houses the pottery collection, still arranged by pueblo as first envisioned and organized by Chap himself.

Finally, Indian Market, which stagnated after World War II, saw unprecedented growth beginning in the late 1960s as part of a renewal in interest nationally about Native American cultures.[105] Today, the popularity and prominence of Indian Market as a venue of fine art is undisputed. Each third weekend in August, nearly a thousand exceptional artists display and sell their own works, generating several million dollars in sales overall. Over one hundred thousand people converge in Santa Fe's plaza, eager to catch a glimpse of a revered artist's latest works or to discover a new favorite. Prize-winning artists, whose reputation and sales immediately increase once they have won an award, all meet the Southwest Association of Indian Artists' rigorous regulations and artistic standards.[106] Chap's indelible mark, according to Indian art expert Bernstein, can be seen in the manner in which Indian Market has endured into the twenty-first century. "Everybody's still working on the same formulas that this man, working with Maria Martinez and Tonita Roybal, really established."[107]

Chap, of course, could not divine such fruit. So he concentrated instead on events over which he had some control. Acknowledging his own mortality, he began in 1962 to organize his possessions at the laboratory even as he continued to refine his San Ildefonso monograph. During the day, he began to purge his files and gradually disposed of his books and collections by either selling them or giving them away. *Then at five o'clock I am suddenly left alone with no excuse for not getting at writing and other work toward finishing my long overdue volume on the Pottery of San Ildefonso. Once I get going, I seldom find a good stopping place before midnight.*[108]

When frail health compelled him to move out of the laboratory and into an apartment, the San Ildefonso monograph remained a perpetual work in process. Yet, in January 1962, Chap wrote to Neil Judd that "I am giving considerable time to one other that I hope to see in press before the grim reaper taps me." Curiously, the second book to which he referred was fiction: *Nazarus*. Self-published in 1964, it purported to be a translation of a manuscript written in the first century AD by a Greek named Atticus, who served as tutor, companion, and trusted assistant to Pontius Pilate. Chap portrayed Pilate in a favorable light, similar to the way he was figured in stories written by early Christians, before Pilate's fortunes fell into steep decline, and he became a villain. Chap was "amazed at the increasing tendency, particularly among writers of fiction, to represent the Procurator as besotted, corrupt, and either an overbearing tyrant, or the week-kneed [*sic*] tool of the High Priests."[109]

But why *Nazarus*, when the San Ildefonso monograph remained so long overdue? In her book about Pilate, Ann Wroe suggested that those who write about Pilate ceaselessly project their own ideas and anxieties on him, often revealing in the process as much about themselves as they reveal about him.[110] Chap's detour thus might be seen as something that allowed him to reexamine his own role as someone who had been labeled traitor. (Chap's impish humor may also have been amused by the connection between Pilate's official title, Procurator, and one of his own titles, curator.) Like the early stories of Pilate, Chap shows the real man as well meaning—he was a man with excellent principles who found himself caught in a tragedy. But whatever the psychological factors that may have motivated Chap's authorship, *Nazarus* proved him to be an excellent storyteller.

Other projects competed for Chap's attention. For several years, Chap had sent reprints of the postcards he had sold to tourists in Las Vegas, New Mexico, as Christmas cards—each postcard delivered fifty years after its original printing. Since sending the last of those cards in 1959, he began to sketch new greetings. In 1962, his Christmas wishes were particularly charming: a self-portrait—pen in one hand, two Cochiti Pueblo cloud-flowers in the other—with a pottery bird pecking at the table. The accompanying description both instructed and delighted:

> For this year's card I have chosen a concept of the Pueblo Indian pottery makers which expresses their best wishes, not for Christmas alone, and not for their families and friends alone, but for "all the year and all the people."
>
> Naturally in the arid Southwest their wishes have long been, and are still expressed by symbols of the blessings of rain. In my drawing this is shown by triple cloud clusters. That at the left, with the fringe of pendent rain-lines, is "rain for ourselves." The other represents clouds far off, where often the "rain for others" seems to reach the earth at a point.
>
> In many instances the clouds are used in bands, though occasionally they are associated with leaves, to indicate their beneficence for growing crops. But particularly at Cochiti Pueblo I have found pottery decorated with a more poetic

Kenneth M. Chapman, self-portrait, 1962. (Courtesy of School for
Advanced Research Archives, AC02 11a.)

concept—the clouds actually growing on stems. The potter, an aged woman
from whom I acquired the design, said, "I like to paint these little cloud-flowers
for ourselves and for others. Then when the real clouds come they will feel sorry
for the little flowers and will send them the good rain."

While musing over this I was surprised by the arrival of a prehistoric pottery bird. . . . [H]e stood for some time at my elbow, commenting on the clever
use of rain symbols by the potters of today. "In our time," he said, "the rain priest

would not have permitted it, for fear that the women potters might make mistakes that would bring lightning down upon all the people. But now I see that they have learned the right way to paint them on their large storage jars, where they may be seen, not for just a few hours of a rain dance, but every day during their long years of use."

Here I come back with a jolt, from A.D. 1500 to 1962, to wish you and all yours a Merry Christmas and a Happy New Year.[111]

Imagination and scholarship informed his days throughout his eighties and into his nineties. He changed little over the years. He was still tall—just a hint of a stoop—and remarkably thin. At eighty-three, he complained that he wished his head were as "nimble" as his legs, which benefited from their repeated trips to retrieve forgotten items. He noticed that he accomplished most when concentrating on only one thing but had no need of hearing aids as he was "temperamentally adjusted to ignore what I would rather not hear."[112] At his ninetieth birthday, celebrants honored him as a "Gentleman, scholar, and perhaps best of all, a wise and witty companion."[113] The La Posada party found him surrounded by friends, though most of the guest list was assembled from members of the new generation, such as Marge Lambert, Bruce Ellis, and Laura Gilpin. Several contemporaries had died since his eightieth birthday celebration: John D. Rockefeller in 1960, Margretta Dietrich in 1961, and Ted Kidder in 1963.

Knowing his own time was limited, how much harder then for Chap to have to bear the heartbreak of his daughter passing away before him. In October 1965, Chap learned that Helen had cancer. Mother of six and stationed at a U.S. Army base in Germany, she returned to the States for medical care, where she received a prognosis of only a month to a year. "I refuse to give in by one iota until I've planted a garden, and seen it grow and bloom!" Helen wrote to family. Summoning courage of her own, she added "When I last saw Uncle Dwight [Chap's brother] in the Chicago airport, I tried, in my fumbling way, to tell him that the courage and humor he and Dad maintained through the years were always a source of great strength to me." She saw her garden bloom but succumbed to cancer in the fall. Too frail to travel to the funeral, Chap struggled at home with the pain.

The following spring, Chap moved to a cabin at Der Kleine Heim, a communal rest home located near Lamy, New Mexico. He no longer cooked—no fear of burning hot plates!—but still went out walking and, occasionally, entertained visitors. A favorite was Frank Harlow, who worked in the theoretical division of Los Alamos Laboratory by day but was an artist, historian, and writer by night. He liked to pick Chap's brain, and he especially sought advice when he was preparing several books on Pueblo pottery in the mid-1960s. Tall and thin, like Chap, Harlow's broad interests were more than a match for

Chap's varied pursuits. Harlow's doctorate was in mathematical physics, a field in which he published extensively, but according to his wife, he used his so-called free time like a career.[114] His first foray—again mirroring Chap's—was fossils. He had hunted them, drawn them, and published on the subject before plunging into a study of Pueblo Indian pottery. In 1967, when he was writing *Historic Indian Pueblo Pottery*, he often visited Chap to look over drawings or query him about a particular pot or sherd. "I remember that I was very impressed with his powers of observation," Harlow said. "He taught me a lot about the idea that when you look at individual Indian pots you are trying to think about the establishment of the typology . . . and [that] it is often the little tiny details that are important."[115]

Chap, too, recognized a kindred spirit. During a visit, Chap mentioned the still unpublished San Ildefonso monograph to Harlow and asked if he would finish it. "Not because he thought it was bad," Harlow remembered, "quite the opposite, he was very pleased with what he had done and for good reason, of course." Chap admitted he did not want to complete the book. "It was such a poignant discussion," Harlow remembered. "I don't recall precisely the words, but I remember the essence of what he said. He thought that when he finished it, it would be like finishing his life." Chap told Harlow to complete the book in whatever way seemed right. When the time came, Harlow purposely tried to simulate Chap's writing style, using notes that he had written verbatim, providing transitions, and adding a chapter on historical background. "It was a lovely commission if you wish," he said. "I never got paid anything for it, it was just the fun of doing it."[116]

In February 1968, Chap suffered a second heart attack, and he was sent off to St. Vincent's Hospital by ambulance. When his son, Frank, visited there on February 23, Chap asked him to get the mail and phone the laboratory to let his friends know of his condition. Having accomplished this task, Frank returned and visited for a while. Later that day, Chap passed away. In a memorial tribute, John Gaw Meem outlined Chap's accomplishments—his work with the artists from the pueblos, the preservation of the IAF collection, the founding of the Laboratory of Anthropology, and Chap's own talents as an artist—noting also that he "possessed extraordinary charm as a person. He had a gentle integrity and a beguiling sense of humor that made him beloved by the Indians of the surrounding pueblos and by his very many friends in Santa Fe."[117]

But words that Frank Harlow wrote for his own book, *Modern Pueblo Pottery*, though not originally intended as such, may serve as an even more fitting tribute. In the preface, Harlow wrote, "A brand-new pot may be dazzling in its virtuoso creation from the simplest materials of earth and vegetation. But let it age with dignity, acquire the chips and fractures of loving use, be rubbed by countless hands and permeated with the sweat and toils of human labor; let it assist in all the mysteries of prayer and supplication to the gods for rain, for appeasement and thanksgiving, for celebrations of joy and beauty, for relief from suffering; let its familiar appearance burn into the hearts and memories of half a dozen generations; then the vessel and the people and the village and all the surrounding fields and rivers and mountains become one being, and if you can sense all this you are close to understanding the real essence of Pueblo Indian pottery."[118]

Or, you could say, "the essence of Chap."

Appendix: A Taos Creation Myth

by Kenneth Milton Chapman

Day before Yesteryears in the Expansive Old Southwest[1]

A Taos Creation Myth

As related by old Yoquesabe, the venerable Cacieque [*sic*] of that pueblo, with the correct dope concerning the origins of the Indians, and the colonizing of the Taos Art Foundry—pardon us!—we mean the founding of the Taos Art Colony.

Many, many years ago, my grand children, when the world was very young, there were no Taos Indians on earth, for then our people lived far down beneath the ground. They were like fishes, swimming about in the dark. Their children and their children's children complained because they could not be like Indians. They could not sing, they could not dance, it was worse than being in an Indian school, says Yoquesabe.

So the All-Father took pity on them and allowed them to wiggle up into the world above where they could grow arms and legs.

But soon they began to complain again that the roof of their new world was so low that they were compelled to squat on the floor.

Then the All-Father told them to get all together and to push up with their shoulders at the roof above them. They did so and broke up into a larger world, and soon they were standing up like men.

But one of them had squatted so long that he could never stand up, and his children's children have been crouching ever since as you can see in many of the Taos picture writings today.[2]

But this new world was cold and dark, and so they complained again. Then the All-Father told them to make a ladder by standing one on the shoulder of another until one of them could break a hole through the roof of their dark world. This they did and their war captain, who was the topmost man, gave a mighty heave with his shoulder and sure enough he broke through the roof and let the light of our world stream in upon them.

Then our people down below cried: "Tell us, what do you see outside?" He raised himself up and looked about him, and he saw a beautiful mountain and a little river flowing among trees, through a wide, green valley. Then, looking the other way he saw a man close by, with a tablita of many colors in his hand, writing a picture of the mountain.

The man turned when he heard the noise, and called out "Good morning! Do you want a job, posing?"

The war captain said: "Wait a minute and I will call up my people to talk with you." So he thrust a pole down into the hole and all our people—men, women and children—climbed up on it.

"How much you pay," they asked.

"Well," the man said, "I haven't any good money now, only Mexican dinero, because the United States isn't started yet, and we will have to wait until George Washington can make some good money for us."

"Oh, that is all right, Mr. Sharp," our people said. "We know you are all right, and we would rather go to work now and wait for the good money. Can you give us all a job?"

"Not now," said Mr. Sharp, "but Phillips and Blumy are learning to write pictures and pretty soon they will be coming out with Kit Carson, and other artists will come, and then there will be jobs for everybody."

"Well," our people said, "maybe we had better look around now and find a good place to live." But Mr. Sharp said, "Listen! I have been writing pictures all over the world, and believe me, there is no place on earth so beautiful as this valley! I call it Taos. So you had better stay here and wait for the artists."

"All right," our people said, "then we will stay and build us a pueblo so that we can be ready for them when they come."

And that is how our people came to live here at Taos. And now Mr. Sharp looks as young as he did when our old people first came out of the ground and our pueblo looks almost as good as new, and the grandchildren of the grandchildren of the grandchildren of our old people now got jobs posing for the artists.

This is a true story, so it must end, for if the truth is stretched too far it becomes as thin as a store blanket, and that, my grand children, would never, never do.

—MYTHOLOGIST

NOTES

* The source of the book's epigraph is "San Ildefonso—Supplement to Notes Accompanying San Ildefonso Butterfly Designs: An Experiment with Pueblo Pottery Decoration," in AC2.179, KMC-SAR.

CHAPTER 1 NOTES

1. Rose Naranjo, Santa Clara, as quoted and described by Trimble (1987, 13).

2. From an anonymous document, "People and Points of View," 1939, Collection OMR, Record Group III 2E, Series Cult. Inst., Subseries Lab/Anthr., Box 18, Folder 175, KMC-RF.

3. AC2.145, KMC-SAR.

4. AC2.145, KMC-SAR.

5. AC2.134, KMC-SAR.

6. AC2.145, KMC-SAR.

7. Diary of John Milton Chapman, 1865–66, KMC-PP.

8. Personal papers of Westley White, AC2.2, KMC-SAR.

9. From Jane Skinner White to John White, September 28, 1844, AC2.2, KMC-SAR.

10. Personal papers of Mary Cordelia White Chapman, AC2.4, KMC-SAR.

11. Personal papers of Mary Cordelia White Chapman, AC2.4, KMC-SAR.

12. Personal papers of Mary Cordelia White Chapman, AC2.4, KMC-SAR.

13. AC2.145, KMC-SAR.

14. AC2.139, KMC-SAR.

15. AC2.145, KMC-SAR.

16. AC2.145, KMC-SAR.

17. AC2.145, KMC-SAR.

18. AC2.142, KMC-SAR.

19. AC2.145, KMC-SAR.

20. AC2.142, KMC-SAR.

21. AC2.145, KMC-SAR. The factory itself was one of many along the bend in the St. Joseph River, which Chapman noted was *probably an attractive woodland spot when La Salle and Marquette found an Indian village there . . . [but] a half century of bustling middle-western progress had left it innocent of charm. . . . A mile or so beyond the river the campus and middle-western-Gothic brick buildings of Notre Dame University lent a note of culture more reputed than actually heard in the city itself, for the good brothers and their students took little part in community affairs.*

22. Personal papers of Mary Cordelia White Chapman, KMC-PP.

23. AC2.141, KMC-SAR.

24. AC2.142, KMC-SAR.

25. AC2.142, KMC-SAR.

26. AC2.142, KMC-SAR.

27. AC2.141, KMC-SAR.

28. AC2.142, KMC-SAR.

29. Fowler (2000, 80); Snead (2001, 8); our sources for the development of anthropology in the United States primarily include Fowler's and Snead's excellent studies. Fowler details the development of Southwest anthropology between 1846 and 1930, providing biographical vignettes of the anthropological pioneers and histories of the major contributing institutions. Snead explores the historical development of archaeology in the

Southwest (1890–1920), contrasting the motives of the major eastern museums with those of regional archeological societies.

30. As described by Fowler (2000), Morgan, like others of his time, assumed that all human social and cultural forms were developed from a few panhuman elementary ideas. Environmental and historical factors affected how quickly human groups passed through these phases, which accounted for "living savages," but progression was inevitable. Morgan believed that humans' course of development began with primitive communism and promiscuity and culminated in nineteenth-century Victorian and American civilization. (Imagine! Corsets as pinnacles of civilized society!)

31. Fowler (2000, 107–11); Jonaitis (1992, 44).

32. AC2.142, KMC-SAR.

33. AC2.141, KMC-SAR.

34. AC2.142, KMC-SAR.

35. AC2.142, KMC-SAR.

36. AC2.142, KMC-SAR.

37. AC2.142, KMC-SAR.

38. AC2.142, KMC-SAR.

39. AC2.139, KMC-SAR.

40. AC2.141, KMC-SAR.

41. AC2.145, KMC-SAR.

42. AC2.142, KMC-SAR.

43. Pierpont (2004, 48).

44. Fowler (2000, 207).

45. AC2.145, KMC-SAR.

46. Snead (2001, 22–24); Fowler (2000, 209).

47. Pierpont (2004, 48).

48. Fowler (2000, 209–10).

49. Fowler (2000, 209–10).

50. Pierpont (2004, 48).

51. AC2.145, KMC-SAR.

52. AC2.145, KMC-SAR.

Chapter 2 Notes

1. KMC to family, November 11, 1893, AC2.6, KMC-SAR.

2. AC2.147, KMC-SAR.

3. John H. Vanderpoel, biographical information, *www.askart.com*, January 2005.

4. Irving (1980, 5).

5. KMC to family, November 11, 1893, AC2.6, KMC-SAR.

6. Irving (1980, 5).

7. Maxon (1970, 9).

8. Kuh (1980, 10).

9. Falk (1990).

10. Maxon (1970, 5).

11. Kuh (1980, 10–12).

12. Falk (1990, 9).

13. AC2.147, KMC-SAR.

14. AC2.147, KMC-SAR.

15. AC2.147, KMC-SAR.

16. AC2.147, KMC-SAR.

17. KMC to his family, January 8, 1894, AC2.6, KMC-SAR. (Note: the letter is dated Chicago, January 8, 1893, but since it refers to events that could only have taken place in 1894, the authors presume that he had misdated the letter.)

18. Smith (1933, 114).

19. AC2.147, KMC-SAR.

20. KMC to Vera, March 30, 1894, AC2.6, KMC-SAR.

21. KMC to family, January 8, 1894, AC2.6, KMC-SAR.

22. KMC to mother, March 8, 1894, AC2.6, KMC-SAR.

23. KMC to mother, March 28, 1894, AC2.6, KMC-SAR.

24. AC2.147, KMC-SAR.

25. AC2.134, KMC-SAR.

26. AC2.147, KMC-SAR.

27. AC2.147, KMC-SAR.

28. AC2.148, KMC-SAR.

29. KMC to mother, St. Louis, Wednesday evening (June 1894), AC2.6, KMC-SAR.

30. Pollack (1967, xxxviii).

31. Hofstadter (1955, 99).

32. AC2.148, KMC-SAR.

33. Primm (1981, 357).

34. Primm (1981, 357).

35. KMC to family, St. Louis, Friday morning (mid-June 1894), AC2.6, KMC-SAR.

36. AC2.148, KMC-SAR.

37. KMC to Vera, July 11, 1894, AC2.6, KMC-SAR.

38. KMC to Dwight, June 28, 1894, and mother, July 1, 1894, AC2.6, KMC-SAR.

39. KMC to mother, July 1, 1894, AC2.6, KMC-SAR.

40. AC2.148, KMC-SAR.

41. AC2.148, KMC-SAR.

42. AC2.148, KMC-SAR.

43. AC2.148, KMC-SAR.

44. AC2.148, KMC-SAR.

45. AC2.148, KMC-SAR.

46. AC2.148, KMC-SAR.

47. AC2.150, KMC-SAR. While the two friends discussed job possibilities, Champe also asked Chap's opinion of some drawings that an artist had left with him; according to Chap, they were highly individualistic renditions of femininity, as unreal as the most ethereal fashion plates of those days but with a whimsical quality that might appeal to many. Chap and Champe found it hard to pass judgment on them, but Champe's editor decided for them—he told Champe to purchase the work. Afterward Champe made the artist's acquaintance, bought more of the drawings, and suggested that Chap might enjoy meeting her. But before that could take place, Rose Cecil O'Neill had moved with her mother to New York, where O'Neill's

work began to earn her fame as the creator of intriguing infants called kewpies!

48. AC2.150, KMC-SAR.

49. AC2.150, KMC-SAR.

50. Latham (1972, 2).

51. AC2.150, KMC-SAR.

52. AC2.134, KMC-SAR.

53. AC2.152, KMC-SAR.

54. AC2.152, KMC-SAR.

55. AC2.152, KMC-SAR.

56. AC2.152, KMC-SAR.

57. Fowler (2000, 154).

58. Powell (1900, xiii).

59. "A Tape Recorded Interview with Dr. Kenneth Chapman, Secretary of Region 13 PWAP," interviewed by Sylvia Loomis at his residence, 313 Camino Alire, Santa Fe, NM, December 5, 1963, 2, KMC-PP.

60. AC2.152, KMC-SAR.

61. AC2.152, KMC-SAR.

CHAPTER 3 NOTES

1. AC2.156, KMC-SAR.

2. AC2.156, KMC-SAR.

3. "The Springer Memorial Services" (1927, 370).

4. Chauvenet (1983, 80).

5. Traube and Mares (1983, 1–21).

6. "A Tape Recorded Interview with Dr. Kenneth Chapman, Secretary of Region 13 PWAP," interviewed by Sylvia Loomis at his residence, 313 Camino Alire, Santa Fe, NM, December 5, 1963, 2, KMC-PP.

7. AC2.156, KMC-SAR.

8. "Ralph Emerson Twitchell" (1926, 79).

9. "Ralph Emerson Twitchell" (1926, 80).

10. AC2.156, KMC-SAR.

11. Cuban (1984, 19).

12. Chauvenet (1983, 80).

13. AC2.156, KMC-SAR.

14. AC2.156, KMC-SAR.

15. *The New Mexico Normal School* (1898–99, 9).

16. Hewett (1943, 126).

17. Chauvenet (1983, 38).

18. *The New Mexico Normal School* (1898–99, 13).

19. Hewett, foreword (1903), "Syllabus of Lectures on Anthropology," School of American Research #2, NMSA.

20. AC2.156, KMC-SAR.

21. "Necrology: Dr. Frank Springer" (1927, 386–93); Springer's father had the reputation of being the best *nisi prius* judge (*"nisi prius"* refers to a trial court in which civil cases were heard before a judge and jury) Iowa had ever had.

22. Fowler (2000, 221).

23. Gillispie (1970, 72).

24. "The Springer Memorial Services" (1927, 365–66).

25. Pearson (1961). The story of the Maxwell Land Grant, on which Springer's fortunes were built, has its beginnings in the mid-nineteenth century, when Guadalupe Miranda and Charles Hipolite Trotier de Beaubien, under Mexican law, petitioned Governor Manuel Armijo of Santa Fe on January 8, 1841, for a tract of land that covered much of northern New Mexico. Since the seventeenth century, land grants had been routinely awarded to Spanish settlers as an incentive to settle the territory and, ultimately, enrich Spain's coffers, and the awards continued when the territory passed to Mexico in 1821. In 1846, as the territory changed hands once more, Miranda chose to return to Mexico and sold his interest to Beaubien. Nearly twenty years later, in 1864, Lucien B. Maxwell, Beaubien's son-in-law, became sole owner. In 1870, Maxwell sold the grant, which ended up in the hands of English and Dutch investors, who incorporated as the Maxwell Land Grant and Resources Company.

26. Pearson (1961, 66).

27. Pearson (1961, 92). Springer deserves praise for his integrity and brilliance. As he argued for the company and the right to the patent, he also revealed, however, the extent to which he was a man of his time. The justices before whom he argued, too, were men of their time. Nowhere in the Supreme Court's opinion is there mention of the Indian people, who still believed they had rights to the grant (indeed, whose ancestors did not even recognize the concept of property), or of the many Spanish-American and American settlers who still were claiming rights on the grant. Nor did the opinion note the original purpose behind the Mexican government's issuance of grants, which was to serve as a means of encouraging settlement instead of personal gain. Nevertheless, the opinion stood, and with United States law firmly behind it, the company began to enforce its rights.

28. Caffey (2006, 55); according to a letter from Springer to his wife, Josephine, the town was named without his knowledge and against his wishes.

29. Caffey (2006, 129).

30. "The Springer Memorial Services" (1927, 382).

31. Caffey (2006, 104). Caffey provides a detailed account of Springer and Wachsmuth's relationship as coauthors of the crinoid studies.

32. "Necrology: Dr. Frank Springer" (1927, 390).

33. Crinoids are members of the group of echinoderms that make up one of the great branches of the animal kingdom. They are related to the sea urchin and starfish but, unlike them, each creature grows a long stem that attaches itself by roots to the bottom of the sea.

34. "The Springer Memorial Services" (1927, 389–90).

35. AC2.156, KMC-SAR.

36. "ELH, 1899–1929," KMC-PP.

37. AC2.156, KMC-SAR.

38. AC2.156, KMC-SAR.

39. "Vera's Account with ELH," KMC-PP.

40. AC2.155, KMC-SAR.

41. AC2.161, KMC-SAR

42. McNary (1956, 30).

43. AC2.156, KMC-SAR.

44. AC2.156, KMC-SAR.

45. Fowler (2000, 196).

46. Snead (2001, 56–57).

47. History of Plains Indian ledger art, http://www.redpanda.net (accessed January 2, 2005); Fowler (2000, 350). The Plains Indians' ledger art was created in the early 1860s, when paper from accountant ledger books, acquired in trade or as spoils from war or a raid, replaced buffalo hide as a canvas. Instead of traditional paints, bone, and stick brushes, the Plains artists used colored pencils and crayon. Initially, the painters drew military exploits and important acts of personal heroism as in traditional Plains art. But as the federal government forced the Plains people onto reservations, their artists also began drawing scenes of traditional ceremony and daily life. In the Southwest, however, such paintings were rare. Several Hopi men had created colored pictures of kachinas in the 1890s for Jesse Walter Fewkes, and a few Pueblo and Navajo artists were drawing pictures based on their own experience, using whatever materials were at hand.

48. AC2.156, KMC-SAR.

49. AC2.156, KMC-SAR.

50. Fowler (2000, 345). By 1900, traders Thomas Keam, Lorenzo Hubbell, J. B. Moore, and Aaron and Jake Gold had established a market for Indian "curios." Navajo, Hopi, and Zuni people produced silver jewelry or weaving, the designs of which the traders controlled. Nampeyo and others at Hopi were involved in the Sikyatki pottery revival, and Hopi kachina dolls were marketed as well. The Rio Grande Pueblo people made a variety of pottery bowls, ollas, effigy pots, and figures. Fred Harvey saw an opportunity and began to sell curios at his outlets, and he also hired Indian craftsmen to demonstrate their craft.

51. Fowler (2000, 218).

52. Cohodas (1992, 90).

53. Brody interview, 2006.

54. "A Tape Recorded Interview with Dr. Kenneth Chapman, Secretary of Region 13 PWAP," interviewed by Sylvia Loomis at his residence, 313 Camino Alire, Santa Fe, NM, December 5, 1963, 2, KMC-PP.

55. Winship (1903).

56. Chauvenet (1983, 39).

57. Fowler (2000, 262–63).

58. Handwritten note in scrapbook related to "Annual Meeting Normal Regents," *Las Vegas Record*, June 28, 1902, Frank Springer, 1889–1913, personal scrapbook, NMSA.

59. AC2.156, KMC-SAR.

60. Handwritten note in scrapbook related to "Annual Meeting Normal Regents," *Las Vegas Record*, June 28, 1902, Frank Springer, 1889–1913, personal scrapbook, NMSA.

61. "Springer Resigns" (1903).

62. AC2.156, KMC-SAR.

63. Caffey (2006, 131–35)

64. Chauvenet (1983, 47).

65. Chauvenet (1983, 58).

66. "ELH, 1899–1929," KMC-PP.

67. "ELH, 1899–1929," KMC-PP.

68. AC2.156, KMC-SAR.

69. "The Springer Memorial Services" (1927, 392).

70. AC2.155, KMC-SAR.

71. Twitchell (1909).

72. "The Springer Memorial Services" (1927, 393).

73. AC2.155, KMC-SAR.

74. "The Springer Memorial Services" (1927, 393).

75. "ELH, 1899–1929," KMC-PP. About this time (1907), Springer made substantial investments in the St. Louis, Rocky Mountain and Pacific Company (coal field development and transport) and the Cimarron Valley Land

Company (Eagle Nest dam project), according to Caffey (2006, 142, 172), which may explain Springer's request that Chap wait for a settlement.

76. AC2.155, KMC-SAR.

77. "The Springer Memorial Services" (1927, 395–96).

78. "The Springer Memorial Services" (1927, 403); Springer's scientific emphasis was on classification. In his tribute to Springer, Hewett tells of the time that Springer visited the British Museum and asked permission to inspect the crinoid collections. He was told by the keeper of that division that the entire crinoid section had been dismantled. It was being restudied and rearranged to conform to Springer's classification. It would not be possible to see it. "Would Mr. Springer himself be permitted to see the collections?" he modestly asked. "Well, that could hardly be refused." Then he introduced himself to the astonished keeper.

79. "The Springer Memorial Services" (1927, 391).

80. Springer (1920, 15).

81. "The Springer Memorial Services" (1927, 392).

82. "The Springer Memorial Services" (1927, 395–96).

83. Fowler (2000). In the Southwest, where Hewett hoped to make his mark, several groups of anthropologists, all with ties to Powell's Bureau of Ethnology, had been at work since the 1880s. Additional institutions became involved in the following decade, including Frederick Ward Putnam's Peabody Museum of Archaeology and Ethnology at Harvard as well as his programs at the American Museum of Natural History in New York City and at the University of California at Berkeley. The Field Museum of Natural History in Chicago, where Franz Boas had hoped to become employed after the 1893 fair, was directed for a short time by William Henry Holmes (Boas never forgave him). Meanwhile Boas, a Putnam protégé, organized a graduate program at Columbia University that was then attended by such future bright lights of U.S. anthropology as Alfred Kroeber and Margaret Mead. Boas believed that

a top priority was to develop a group of anthropologists trained in rigorous research methods in both university and museum settings around the country.

84. Fowler (2000, 263); see also Snead (2001, 80).

85. AC2.161, KMC-SAR.

86. Chauvenet (1983, 52).

87. Chauvenet (1983, 53).

88. Chauvenet (1983, 54).

89. Chauvenet (1983, 55–56).

90. Kidder (1960, 3).

91. Kidder (1960, 3, 12).

92. Kidder (1960, 12–13).

93. Hewett (1943, 152).

94. Hewett (1943, 153).

95. Bandelier ([1890] 1960, 3–4).

96. Guthe (1925, 13–14).

97. At that time, Byron Cummings was dean of the school of arts and sciences at the University of Utah. He had led his first archaeological expedition in 1906 at Nine Mile Canyon in central Utah for the AIA. A friend of Hewett's through the AIA, Cummings led several more expeditions for its Utah Society. After 1915, Cummings was associated with the University of Arizona, where he was an important influence on the development of archaeology there through the 1950s. (See also Bostwick, 2006.)

98. AC2.160, KMC-SAR.

99. AC2.160, KMC-SAR.

100. AC2.161, KMC-SAR.

101. AC2.160, KMC-SAR; the drawing is reproduced in Hewett (1909, 66).

102. AC2.161, KMC-SAR.

103. AC2.161, KMC-SAR.

104. Fowler (2000, 267–68).

105. Fowler (2000, 80).

106. Chauvenet (1983, 77).

107. Fowler (2000, 268).

Chapter 4 Notes

Lambert (n.d., 155).

1. KMC to Judd, April 19, 1952, Neil M. Judd, nine letters, 1927, 1953, AC2.80, KMC-SAR. In 1952, Chapman wrote to Judd that Holmes "was my hero—the only one of his generation who had the artist's and draftsman's approach to Indian design, and his work is as sound today as the day it was written."

2. Lummis (1918, xvii).

3. Hewett (1918, 62).

4. Hewett (1918, 62).

5. Hewett (1918, 64).

6. Aitken (1950, 1).

7. Nusbaum (1980, 43).

8. Nusbaum (1980, 10).

9. Judd (1960, 3).

10. Harrington (1950, 71).

11. Lambert (n.d., 167).

12. Nusbaum (1980, 36).

13. Nusbaum (1980, 36).

14. Nusbaum (1980, 36).

15. Nusbaum (1980, 37).

16. Lambert (n.d., 167).

17. Nusbaum (1980, 35–36).

18. Laird (1975, xv).

19. Judd (1968, 142).

20. Marriott (1948, 155).

21. FS to Fletcher, August 25, 1909, ELHP.

22. Amended House Bill No. 100, Territory of New Mexico, February 19, 1909.

23. Snead (2001, 94).

24. Hewett (1918, 23).

25. AC2.158, KMC-SAR.

26. AC2.158, KMC-SAR.

27. Marriott (1948, 195–96).

28. Chauvenet (1983, 76).

29. Nusbaum (1978, 85–87).

30. AC2.158, KMC-SAR.

31. Nusbaum (1980, 43).

32. AC2.158, KMC-SAR.

33. FS to Fletcher, August 25, 1909, ELHP.

34. Nusbaum (1978, 87).

35. Nusbaum (1978, 88).

36. Nusbaum (1978, 88–89).

37. KMC to ELH, February 20, 1910, ELHP.

38. Rice (1987, 24–25).

39. Fowler (2000, 282).

40. Fowler (2000, 179).

41. Fowler (2000, 285).

42. AC2.162, KMC-SAR.

43. KMC-PP.

44. AC2.339, KMC-SAR.

45. Marriott (1948, 196).

46. AC2.156, KMC-SAR.

47. Lambert (n.d., 161).

48. KMC to ELH, March 18, 1910, ELHP.

49. KMC-PP.

50. KMC to ELH, April 16, 1910, ELHP.

51. AC2.162, KMC-SAR.

52. "ELH, 1899–1929," KMC-PP.

53. KMC to ELH, June 16, 1910, ELHP.

54. AC2.162, KMC-SAR.

55. AC2.161, KMC-SAR.

56. Snead (2001, 139–40).

57. Hewett (1918, 85).

58. AC2.157, KMC-SAR.

59. Comfort and Comfort (1959).

60. AC2.157, KMC-SAR.

61. Hewett (1918, 85).

62. Judd (1968, 140–41).

63. Reyman (1992, 74). Hewett and Arizona's Byron Cummings both encouraged women in the field of archaeology, which was generally considered a male-dominated discipline, especially before World War II.

64. J. Fox (1993, 301).

65. AC2.158, KMC-SAR.

66. Rice (1987, 246–47).

67. Rice (1987, 248).

68. AC2.158, KMC-SAR.

69. KMC to ELH, February 17, 1911, ELHP.

70. FS to ELH, January 6, 1911, ELHP.

71. FS to ELH, January 6, 1911, ELHP.

72. ELH to KMC, November 14, 1909, ELHP.

73. Huntington (1912, 117).

74. "My First Quarter Century in the Southwest, 1899–1926," KMC-PP.

75. "My First Quarter Century in the Southwest, 1899–1926," KMC-PP.

76. AC2.152, KMC-SAR.

77. AC2.160, KMC-SAR.

78. AC2.160, KMC-SAR.

79. AC2.160, KMC-SAR.

80. AC2.160, KMC-SAR.

81. AC2.157, KMC-SAR.

82. Bolgiano (1997, 54).

83. Bolgiano (1997, 54).

84. AC2.157, KMC-SAR.

85. Snead (2001, 147–48).

86. AC2.160, KMC-SAR.

87. Fowler (2002, 272).

88. Fowler (2002, 272).

89. A. M. Tozzer to Hodge, quoted in Fowler (2000, 267).

90. AC2.160, KMC-SAR.

Chapter 5 Notes

1. "The Paintings of Charles Hawthorne" (1968).

2. JLN to ELH, May 28, 1912, ELHP.

3. AC2.156, KMC-SAR.

4. AC2.157, KMC-SAR.

5. Landgren (1940, 18).

6. Landgren (1940, 17).

7. Efland (1990, 62). Ironically, the National Academy of Design had itself been formed by a group of dissident students who had rebelled against the policies of the New York Academy.

8. Art Students League of New York (2000–2001, 5).

9. "History," New York Public Library web site, www.nypl.org/admin/pro/history.html (accessed June 2001).

10. "My First Quarter Century in the Southwest, 1899–1926," KMC-PP.

11. KMC to Hodge, February 22, 1913, MS.7.EIC.1.36, HP.

12. AC2.156, KMC-SAR.

13. Meeting of the managing committee of the American School, National Museum of Natural History, January 3, 1913, ELHP.

14. Chauvenet (1983, 98).

15. Hodge to Carroll, December 8, 1911, quoted in Fowler (2002, 272).

16. KMC to ELH, January 6, 1913, ELHP.

17. KMC to ELH, February 9, 1913, ELHP.

18. KMC to ELH, February 9, 1913, ELHP.

19. Nusbaum (1950, 163).

20. Purdy (1979).

21. Nusbaum (1950, 164).

22. Nusbaum (1950, 165).

23. Kidder (1950, 97).

24. Wilson (1997, 122). In *The Myth of Santa Fe*, Wilson explores the invention of the Santa Fe tradition, which Morley, Chapman, and others were

25. Nusbaum (1950, 165–66).

26. "Old New Santa Fe" (1912, 1).

27. Santa Fe's architecture was labeled "the Santa Fe style" largely as a result of the research undertaken by Nusbaum and Morley in preparation for the New-Old Santa Fe exhibit. However, the revival in New Mexico had actually started in Albuquerque, in 1905, when the central heating plant at the University of New Mexico was constructed with a flat roof, a stepped-up profile, and second-story porticoes. The UNM Board of Regents summarily dismissed university president William George Tight in 1909 for adopting this innovative approach (Purdy [1979]).

28. Nusbaum (1978, 88).

29. AC2.157, KMC-SAR.

30. AC2.156, KMC-SAR.

31. Howard and Pardue (1996, 75–76).

32. Wilson (1997, 129).

33. FS to JLN, March 30, 1915, from East Las Vegas, NM, #01-0072, NMNH.

34. KMC to ELH, February 9, 1913, ELHP.

35. ELH to KMC, April 5, 1913, ELHP.

36. KMC to ELH, April 18, 1913, ELHP.

37. KMC to ELH, May 19, 1913, ELHP.

38. Kidder (1962, 89).

39. KMC to ELH, February 24, 1913, ELHP.

40. KMC to ELH, no date, ELHP.

41. AC2.157, KMC-SAR.

42. AC2.157, KMC-SAR.

43. AC2.157, KMC-SAR.

44. ELH to KMC, June 19, 1913, ELHP.

45. ELH to KMC, May 9, 1913, ELHP.

46. Lambert (n.d., 164–65). Curiously, a similar story is found in Frederick Hodge's papers, although the driver was Sylvanus Morley and the passengers included Mitchell Carroll (AIA secretary), Carroll's young son, and Carlos Vierra. In Hodge's version, it is Vierra who falls from the car (see File MS-7, Frederick Webb Hodge Papers, Heard Museum).

47. Lambert (n.d., 164–65).

48. ELH to Dr. Paton, February 15, 1913, ELHP.

49. Hewett (1918, 139).

50. ELH to KMC, July 25, 1913, ELHP.

51. ELH to KMC, July 25, 1913, ELHP.

52. Chauvenet (1983, 40).

53. Gaither (1957, 38); Chauvenet (1983, 89–90).

54. AC2.158, KMC-SAR.

55. Morley (1915, 295).

56. Nusbaum (1950, 171).

57. Morley (1915, 294–95).

58. Sheppard (1989, 63).

59. Chapman, quoted in Sheppard (1989, 64–65).

60. FS to ELH, April 14, 1914, ELHP.

61. FS to ELH, May 21, 1914, EHLP.

62. Carlson (1958, 10).

63. Landgren (1940, 86).

64. AC2.156, KMC-SAR.

65. AC2.157, KMC-SAR.

66. ELH to FS, July 7, 1914, ELHP.

67. FS to ELH, October 27, 1914, ELHP.

68. "Chapman-Mueller Wedding" (1915, 8).

69. FS to ELH, no date, ELHP.

70. FS to ELH, October 27, 1914, ELHP.

71. "Splendid Art Exhibit Opened in Old Palace," December 14, 1914, clipping, newspaper unknown, KMC-PP.

72. Note on reverse side of painting, KMC-PP.

73. Vierra to sister Mabel, August 14, 1907, Carlos Vierra folder, NMSA.

74. Robertson and Nestor (1962, 24–27).

75. Obituary, Carlos Vierra Folder, 3, NMSA.

76. FS to ELH, October 27, 1914, ELHP.

77. FS to ELH, October 27, 1914, ELHP.

78. Laws of New Mexico, chap. 95, 1915.

79. "Chapman-Mueller Wedding" (1915, 8).

80. Fowler (2000); Snead (2001).

81. Kidder (1962, 89).

82. Fowler (2000); Snead (2001).

83. "Chapman-Mueller Wedding" (1915, 8).

84. AC2.157, KMC-SAR.

85. "Weddings, Santa Fe Style," Margretta S. Dietrich folder, NMSA.

86. "Chapman-Mueller Wedding" (1915, 8).

87. AC2.157, KMC-SAR.

CHAPTER 6 NOTES

1. AC2.199, KMC-SAR.

2. "ELH Complaints," KMC-PP.

3. Walter (1916, 59).

4. Springer's notes indicate that he personally contributed $5,000 of the money he put up for the museum. The remaining $25,000 came from friends, and was secured by Springer (Caffey 2006, 182–83).

5. AC2.157, KMC-SAR.

6. See Beauregard's sketch of *The Renunciation of Santa Clara* as shown in Sheppard, *Saint Francis Murals of Santa Fe: The Commission and the Artists*, 86, and Chap's rendition, 54. Then compare Beauregard's sketch *Preaching to the Mayans and the Aztecs* to the final painting by Vierra, 51 and 90.

7. Sheppard (1989, 88).

8. Robertson and Nestor (1962, 28).

9. FS to JLN, July 3, 1915, Box 7, "Frank Springer, Ada Davis, Museum," NAA.

10. La Farge (1959, 231).

11. La Farge (1959, 235).

12. Caffey (2006, 153).

13. "Records of the Past" (1916, 6).

14. KMC to Hodge, November 14, 1916, MS.7.EIC.1.36, HP.

15. AC2.158, KMC-SAR.

16. Robertson and Nestor (1962, 53); Snead (2001, 161).

17. "Museum Dedication Exercises" (1917, 5).

18. "The Springer Memorial Services" (1927, 397–98).

19. "New Museum" (1917, 1).

20. La Farge (1959, 231).

21. Robertson and Nestor (1962, 47–50).

22. Robert Henri, letter to Henry Lovins, quoted in Robertson and Nestor (1962, 53–54).

23. See Gibson (1983, 71), Laughlin (1994, 115), and Snead (2001, 160).

24. *The Artists of New Mexico* (1935).

25. Snead (2001, 148).

26. Snead (2001, 122).

27. "Sixty Years of Art—Among Other Things," 12, AC2.198, KMC-SAR.

28. Peckham (1990, 15).

29. Brody interview, 2006; interview [anon.] with KMC, December 20, 1960, 89LA6.012, ALAB.

30. "SW Indian Art Chapman Notes," undated, provided to Janet Chapman by Sally Rodeck, July 17, 1996.

31. AC2.204, KMC-SAR.

32. Bernstein (1993a, 121).

33. Holmes (1888, 246).

34. Chapman (1917a).

35. Chapman (1917b, 6).

36. Interview [anon.] with KMC, December 20, 1960, 89LA6.012, ALAB.

37. AC2.156, KMC-SAR.

38. AC2.198, KMC-SAR.

39. Chauvenet (1983, 127).

40. Ellis (1971, 3).

41. Wesley Bradfield had moved from a position with the U.S. Forest Service to work as a Santa Fe curio dealer. Following the 1915 San Diego Exposition, he continued as Hewett's employee at the Museum of New Mexico. In the mid-1920s, Hewett sent him back to San Diego as assistant director of the Museum of Man. He returned to Santa Fe for health reasons after Chap left the museum and took over as curator (Bernstein 1993, 37).

42. Chauvenet (1983, 128).

43. Hewett's nickname, first earned at Rito, was now in common use, though usually behind his back.

44. AC2.198, KMC-SAR. While Chapman identifies Arizona as a target for Hewett's ambition, there is no post-1915 mention of this in the archives of Byron Cummings (Todd Bostwick, private communication, March 2007). By then, Cummings was professor of archaeology and director of the Arizona State Museum at the University of Arizona. Having cut his ties with Hewett after leaving the University of Utah in 1915, Cummings himself aspired to control Arizona archaeology and museums.

45. AC2.198, KMC-SAR.

46. AC2.158, KMC-SAR.

47. AC2.161, KMC-SAR.

48. Lambert (n.d., 157).

49. The incident occurred after Hewett verbally supported Morley's application for a grant that would allow him to supervise a Maya ruins research expedition. Hewett subsequently wrote to W. H. Holmes requesting that he supervise Morley's project. Morley's vociferous protest got the immediate attention of Springer, who then had words with Hewett in private, and the project was subsequently approved without amendment (AC2.161, KMC-SAR).

50. Bernstein (1993a, 70–71).

51. Elliott (1987, 14); Dauber interview, 1994.

52. "The Springer Memorial Services" (1927, 397–98).

53. Frank S. Chapman interview, 1994.

54. "Third Year Book Santa Fe Society" (1918, 6–7).

55. Laughlin (1994, 120).

56. La Farge (1959, 241–42).

57. Bernstein (1993a, 45).

58. Bernstein (1993a, 47).

59. Her name was also spelled "Verra," as Fricke (2003, 143) points out.

60. AC2.158, KMC-SAR.

61. Marriott (1948, 234–35).

62. Marriott (1948, 217–18). In Brody's study on Indian art and Anglo patronage, he points out that "the role of Maria Martinez as a seeker of lost techniques has been dramatized, probably to the detriment of her very real accomplishments as a creative craftsman" (1990, 68). According to Brody, Maria and Julian's own heritage as well as the nearby Pueblos of Santa Clara and Nambé provided them with access to the technique of polished black ware.

63. Marriott (1948, 217–18).

64. Gonzales interview, 1995.

65. *Los Cinco Pintores* (1975).

66. Elliott (1987, 18).

67. Shuster, quoted in Robertson and Nestor (1962, 86–87).

68. Fricke (2003, 69); according to Fricke, Kabotie, Awa Tsireh, and Herrera were employed as custodians at the museum. Chap provided them with materials and a working space so that when they weren't carrying out their duties, they could continue their artwork.

69. AC2.157, KMC-SAR.

70. Rushing (1995, 39).

71. Reeve (1982, 23); Rushing (1995, 41–60); Dauber interview, 1994.

72. Hartley (1920, 14).

73. Paul Burlin, quoted in Udall (1984, 20).

74. Fenyes (n.d.).

75. For the concept of cultural broker, see *Between Indian and White Worlds*, ed. Margaret Connell Szasz (1994).

76. Fewkes to KMC, February 15, 1918, AC2.71, KMC-SAR.

77. Snead (2001, 161).

78. Chapman (1927d, 529).

79. Letter dated March 27, 1921 (Fenyes [n.d.]).

80. "The Nusbaum Accounts," KMC-PP.

81. JLN to FS, May 27, 1918, Correspondence Box 41, Nusbaum Folder, ELHP.

82. FS to JLN, September 4, 1918, Box 7, "Frank Springer, Ada Davis, Museum," NAA.

83. AC2.161, KMC-SAR.

84. KMC-PP.

85. Dauber interview, 1994.

86. AC2.158, KMC–SAR.

87. AC2.158, KMC–SAR.

CHAPTER 7 NOTES

1. Bradfield to JLN, February 19, 1922, NAA.

2. AC2.157, KMC-SAR.

3. "Jabs in the Solar Plexus," *SFNM*, March 27, 1926, 4, KMC-PP. The clipping has penciled corrections on it and is initialed "KMC."

4. "Jabs in the Solar Plexus," *SFNM*, March 27, 1926, 4, KMC-PP.

5. Frank S. Chapman interview, 1994. When Naranjo had asked Chap if there was anything unusual about Frank's birth, Chap told him that Frank at his mother's breast for his first meal was "just like a snapping turtle" (Frank S. Chapman interview, 1994).

6. "An Artistic Chronology" (1967, 2).

7. Coe (1986, 24–25); Harlow interview, 1995; Lambert interview, 1995.

8. Coe (1986, 24–25). Coe visited American Indian groups and individuals across the United States and Canada between 1977 and 1985 as he assembled contemporary/traditional arts and crafts for the exhibition Lost and Found Traditions: Native American Art, 1965–1985. The exhibition itself, as well as his discussions with the artists, explored whether a viable traditional American Indian art still exists.

9. Dunlap interview, 1995.

10. Dunlap interview, 1995.

11. AC2.158, KMC-SAR.

12. AC2.158, KMC-SAR.

13. In asking potters the meaning of elements, Chap must have encountered the same problem identified by his contemporary, Ruth Bunzel, of nomenclature that seems arbitrary and based on subjective realities. While there was general agreement that the designs were deeply significant, the explanations varied (Bunzel [1929, 69–71]). Decades later Maria's son, Popovi Da, explained that the secret meanings of symbols were "only secret because they are within and cannot be easily expressed. This symbolism is perpetuated through memory alone, because we have no written language" (quoted in Spivey [1979, xvii]).

14. KMC to Hewett, undated, KMC-PP. The document refers to preparing a budget for 1921.

15. "Dougan, Rose & ELH c. 1920, incidents E & F," KMC-PP.

16. Chap's action was discovered after he left the museum in 1929. Hewett told the new curator of archaeology, Paul Reiter, to transfer collections to the school. Reiter modified Chap's work by substituting or adding the initials SAR along with the school's code system, and subsequent curators apparently made other unauthorized decisions to disperse specimens (AC2.161, KMC-SAR). This curatorial chaos was to come back to haunt everyone forty years later, when the tangling and untangling of various Santa Fe public and private institutions and collections resulted in animosities over what belonged to whom.

17. Fowler (2000, 262); Snead (2001, 53).

18. "Currelly Collection," KMC-PP.

19. ELH to Charles T. Currelly, September 9, 1920, ROM.

20. AC2.160, KMC-SAR.

21. AC2.161, KMC-SAR.

22. KMC-PP.

23. Chauvenet (1983, 199).

24. AC2.156, KMC-SAR.

25. AC2.161, KMC-SAR.

26. AC2.161, KMC-SAR.

27. "Nusbaum's Unpaid Claims," ELHP.

28. "Nusbaum's Unpaid Claims," ELHP.

29. AC2.161, KMC-SAR.

30. Lambert (n.d., 157).

31. AC2.160, KMC-SAR.

32. AC2.160, KMC-SAR.

33. KMC to Hodge, November 19, 1921, MS.7.MAI.1.121, HP.

34. AC2.161, KMC-SAR.

35. Chapman (1921, 44).

36. AC2.158, KMC-SAR.

37. Hayes and Blom (1996, 38).

38. Berlo and Phillips (1998, 48); Bernstein (1993a, 85); Brody (1990, 23–26, 46); Bunzel (1929, 5, 41); Dauber (1993, 78–79; 167–68); Fricke (2003, 46–47); Frank and Harlow (1974, 5–14); Toulouse (1977, 14–15).

39. John S. Chapman interview, 2002.

40. KMC to Hewett, undated, KMC-PP.

41. Bunzel (1929, 56).

42. AC2.158, KMC-SAR.

43. Bradfield to JLN, February 19, 1922, NAA.

44. ELH to KMC, April 19 1922, KMC-PP.

45. Chapman (1922, 122).

46. Guthe (1925, 14).

47. Lew Wallace Springer to Ada Springer, September 19, 1922, "Correspondence 1897, 1922," MSS. 222 BC, Box 1, Folder 1, FSC.

48. Quoted in Coe (1986, 46).

49. AC2.158, KMC-SAR.

50. La Farge (1959, 273–74).

51. Fewkes to KMC, December 6, 1923, 89LA2.004, ALAB.

52. Bernstein (1993a, 105).

53. Dauber (1993, 183 ff.).

54. Cohodas (1992, 89).

55. Horgan (1957, 319–20).

56. Dauber (1990, 1993).

57. Spivey (2003, 64).

58. Clipping from the *Rocky Mountain News*, April 5, 1925, KMC-PP.

59. Draft of speech delivered at the Art Institute of Chicago, June 12, 1950, KMC-PP.

60. AC2.158, KMC-SAR.

61. KMC to Dr. C. Evernham, July 18, 1955, AC2.105, KMC-SAR.

CHAPTER 8 NOTES

1. Stark and Rayne (1998).

2. AC2.43, KMC-SAR. During his early medical visits to regional communities, Mera undertook amateur investigation of archaeology sites, which awakened his recognition of potsherds. He had continued this work throughout the 1920s, marking roadmaps, collecting small sherd samples, and tracking where he found them.

3. Interview [anon.] with KMC, December 20, 1960, 89LA6.012, ALAB; although Fricke (2003, 77) states that Chapman and Bradfield were also at the gathering, Chapman does not specify this in his memoirs. The authors infer his absence from the 1960 interview with Chapman.

4. Interview [anon.] with KMC, December 20, 1960, 89LA6.012, ALAB.

5. Chapman (1936d, xiii).

6. Amon Carter Museum of Western Art (1966, 10).

7. Fricke (2003, 189).

8. Bernstein (1993a, 93); Dauber (1993, 167).

9. Bernstein (1993a, 107); in this study, Bernstein examines the interactions between Tewa and Anglo cultures that specifically led to the establishment of the Indian Market. Additional information about the effects of Anglo patronage in Santa Fe with regard to Indian art can be found in Brody (1990), Dauber (1993), and Fricke (2003).

10. Amon Carter Museum of Western Art (1966, 10–12).

11. Chapman (1936d, xiii).

12. KMC-FA.

13. Dauber (1990, 591).

14. Dauber (1990, 582–83); Wilson (1997, 149–50).

15. Sando (1992, 117).

16. Dauber (1990, 583).

17. "The Indian Bill" (1922, 4).

18. Dauber (1993, 123).

19. Chapman (1924a).

20. "Report of Talk by KMC, 1954," KMC-PP.

21. Museum of Indian Arts and Culture (1990).

22. "Art Policy of Museum and School" (1921, 2).

23. "Modernists Create Real Sensation with Exhibit" (1924, 3).

24. "Spud, Laffin Hoss Editor, Takes Brief Look at the Modernists" (1924, 6).

25. "Astigmatic Expressionists" (1924, 6).

26. Clipping, self-identified with initials "KMC," KMC-PP.

27. "Every Day in Every Way" (1924, 5). The reference to Chicago is to a well-received Taos/Santa Fe group show in the galleries of Carson, Pirie, Scott, and Co. there.

28. AC2.157, KMC-SAR.

29. KMC to James P. Munroe, April 9, 1924, AC2.91, KMC-SAR.

30. KMC to James P. Munroe, April 9, 1924, AC2.91, KMC-SAR.

31. KMC to Hodge, December 13, 1926, MS.7.MAI.1.121, HP.

32. After the first 4 pots, the number of pots added to the fund's collection by year was 83 (1923), 242 (1924), and 144 (1925). The collection totaled 473 by the end of 1925 (Fricke [2003, 276]).

33. AC2.166A, KMC-SAR.

34. Chauvenet (1983, 166).

35. R. V. D. Magoffin to ELH, June 27, 1924, ELHP.

36. Smith (2002).

37. AC2.166, KMC-SAR.

38. AC2.166, KMC-SAR.

39. "Rockefeller Visit to Mesa Verde," NAA.

40. Twitchell to Hodge, July 8, 1924, MS.7.MAI.1.701, HP.

41. Artist Will Shuster, creator of Zozobra, recalled that Kate Chapman and Dorothy Stewart tried to "revive an affair similar to the Mummers parade" from Kate's native Philadelphia. (AAA, interview with Sylvia Loomis, July 30 1964.)

42. SFNM, clipping hand-dated "1926," AC2.143, KMC-SAR.

43. KMC to E. Irving Couse, October 10, 1924, AC2.63, KMC-SAR.

44. KMC to Anna Lalor Burdick, March 1, 1924, AC2.120, KMC-SAR.

45. AC2.131, KMC-SAR.

46. AC2.157, KMC-SAR.

47. KMC to W. D. Gates, 89LA2.006, ALAB.

48. FS to ELH, June 13, 1925, ELHP.

49. Funds from a New York patron later enabled Austin and Applegate to form the Society for the Revival of Spanish Colonial Arts, a title later shortened to the Spanish Colonial Arts Society. It never flourished as did the Indian Arts Fund.

50. IAF chronology, compiled from minutes of IAF meeting, c. 1962, 1, KMC-PP; in addition to Mera, Chapman, and MacMillan, the board also included artists Frank Applegate, Andrew

Dasburg, B. J. O. Nordfeldt; writers Mary Austin, Alice C. Henderson, Mabel Luhan, Elizabeth Sergeant; anthropology/archaeology colleagues Samuel Guernsey, Frederick W. Hodge, Alfred V. Kidder, Sylvanus Morley and Jesse Nusbaum; patrons Mrs. M. Hare, Mrs. M. Wertheim, Mary Wheelwright, Amelia White; politicians/activists Mary Conkey, Herbert Hagerman, Irene Lewisohn, Margaret McKittrick, Charles Springer; trader James Seligman; and George Bloom, Mrs. R. Pfaffle, Mrs. M. Robinson, Mrs. J. L. Smith, and Nathan Stern.

51. KMC to Hodge, September 15, 1925, MS.7.MAI.1.121, HP (permission courtesy of the Braun Research Library, Autry National Center).

52. Johnson (1925).

53. AC2.185, KMC-SAR.

54. Bernstein (1993a, 93).

55. Dauber (1993, 194).

56. FS to ELH, no date, ELHP.

57. Chapman (1926).

58. Lambert interview, 1994.

59. Frank S. Chapman interview, August 1994.

60. "No 'Chautauqua'" (1926), "Like Eastern Chautauqua" (1926), "Chautauqua a Misfit" (1926), "No New Attitude" (1926).

61. Bernstein (1993a, 67).

62. Howard and Pardue (1996,124). Fergusson, a granddaughter of Albuquerque's esteemed citizens, Franz and Ernestine Huning, was born in "Castle Huning" and grew up in an adobe home a mile or so east of Old Town plaza. She traveled to New York for a master's degree in history from Columbia University after receiving a pedagogy degree from the University of New Mexico in 1913 (Gish [1997, 9]).

63. 89LA2.013, ALAB.

64. Frank S. Chapman interview, July 1995.

CHAPTER 9 NOTES

1. AC2.166.1, KMC-SAR.

2. AC2.162, KMC-SAR.

3. KMC-PP.

4. JLN to KMC, June 23, 1926, AC2.96, KMC-SAR.

5. By this time in his life, Nusbaum was convinced that "Dr. Hewett is his own greatest enemy in many respects" (unidentified document dated "Friday, July 21," 13, Box 1, Notebook LAB, NAA).

6. Amon Carter Museum of Western Art (1966, 10).

7. AC2.166.2, KMC-SAR.

8. FS to ELH, August 17, 1926, Box 600, no. 4, ELHP.

9. KMC to FS, September 1, 1926, AC2.114, KMC-SAR.

10. KMC to Hodge, September 22, 1926, MS.7.MAI.1.121, HP.

11. AC2.163, KMC-SAR.

12. KMC to Hodge, October 14, 1926, MS.7.MAI.1.121, HP.

13. The extra curatorial chore was the result of a decision to merge the historical society's archaeology collections with the museum's, though both would be cut about 30 percent.

14. KMC to FS, October 28, 1926, AC2.114, KMC-SAR.

15. Fowler (2000, 368). Founded in 1906, the American Association of Museums was dedicated to promoting excellence within the museum community by assisting museum staff, boards, and volunteers across the country to better serve the public. In early spring of 1926, Bumpus chaired the association's executive committee on museums in national parks.

16. Rockefeller to KMC, December 10, 1926, KMC-PP.

17. Snead (2001, 164).

18. AC2.158, KMC-SAR.

19. Copy of letter from Bradfield to KMC, November 20, 1926, AC2.155, KMC-SAR.

20. Copy of telegram, n.d., AC2.164, KMC-SAR.

21. Appleget to Bumpus, December 4, 1926, Collection OMR, Record Group III 2E, Series Cult. Inst., Subseries Lab/Anthr., Box 17, Folder 172, KMC-RF.

22. Bumpus to KMC, December 1926, AC2.56, KMC-SAR.

23. In the 1880s the Zuni bestowed on Hodge this affectionate nickname (Fowler [2000, 304]). Hodge's closest friends, including Nusbaum, addressed him so. While Chap's correspondence with Hodge conveys relaxed familiarity, he never writes to "Dear Téluli." Nusbaum, however, was a member of the "Téluli" circle.

24. Hodge to KMC, January 5, 1927, MS.7.MAI.1.121, HP.

25. AVK to KMC, January 10, 1927, AC2.82, KMC-SAR.

26. KMC to Hodge, January 15, 1927, MS.7.MAI.1.121, HP.

27. KMC to FS, January 31, 1927, AC2.114, KMC-SAR.

28. Kate and Dorothy Stewart had recently left with Helen and Frank, who was suffering from a kidney infection, for a rest in Arizona, driving Stewart's Model T Ford truck, known as the "Conestoga PackFord" because of its resemblance to an old Conestoga wagon.

29. KMC to FS, January 31, 1927, AC2.114, KMC-SAR.

30. KMC to John D. Rockefeller Jr., February 11, 1927, Collection OMR, Record Group III 2E, Series Cult. Inst., Subseries Lab/Anthr., Box 17, Folder 172, KMC-RF.

31. AC2.159, KMC-SAR.

32. Bumpus to Appleget, February 15, 1927, Collection OMR, Record Group III 2E, Series Cult. Inst., Subseries Lab/Anthr., Box 17, Folder 172, KMC-RF.

33. Bumpus to Appleget, February 15, 1927, Collection OMR, Record Group III 2E, Series Cult. Inst., Subseries Lab/Anthr., Box 17, Folder 172, KMC-RF.

34. Appleget to John D. Rockefeller Jr., February 18, 1927, Collection OMR, Record Group III 2E, Series Cult. Inst., Subseries Lab/Anthr., Box 17, Folder 172, KMC-RF.

35. Snead (2001, 165).

36. AVK to KMC, February 21, 1927, AC2.82, KMC-SAR.

37. Appleget to John D. Rockefeller Jr., January 12, 1928, Collection OMR, Record Group III 2E, Series Cult. Inst., Subseries Lab/Anthr., Box 17, Folder 172, KMC-RF.

38. "Rockefeller Visit to Mesa Verde," Nusbaum Papers, Box 7, NAA. The writer of the typed note may have been Rosemary Nusbaum, Jesse Nusbaum's second wife, who compiled many of his recollections and letters.

39. "Memo: Conversation," March 8, 1927, Collection OMR, Record Group III 2E, Series Cult. Inst., Subseries Lab/Anthr., Box 17, Folder 172, KMC-RF.

40. KMC to Alexander, March 16, 1927, AC2.50, KMC-SAR.

41. KMC to A. S. Riggs, March 16, 1927, 89LA2.003, ALAB.

42. Fosdick (1956, 292); Fricke (2003, 202).

Chapter 10 Notes

1. AVK to KMC, April 22, 1927, AC2.82, KMC-SAR.

2. Bumpus to KMC, May 10, 1927, AC2.56, KMC-SAR.

3. KMC to Bumpus, May 14, 1927, AC2.56, KMC-SAR.

4. Stocking (2001, 7); Fowler (2000, 369).

5. Bumpus to Appleget, May 27, 1927, Collection OMR, Record Group III 2E, Series

Cult. Inst., Subseries Lab/Anthr., Box 17, Folder 172, KMC-RF.

6. Bumpus and Kidder (1927); attendees included Franz Boas, Columbia University; Hermon C. Bumpus, Brown University and American Association of Museums; Fay-Cooper Cole, University of Chicago and Field Museum of Natural History; Roland B. Dixon, Harvard University; Pliny E. Goddard, American Museum of Natural History and Columbia University; Carl E. Guthe, University of Michigan; Frederick W. Hodge, Museum of the American Indian; Chauncey J. Hamlin, Buffalo Academy of Sciences and President, American Association of Museums; Alfred V. Kidder, National Research Council, Phillips Academy, and Carnegie Institution of Washington; Marshall H. Saville, Museum of the American Indian and President American Anthropological Association; Herbert J. Spinden, Peabody Museum, and Clark Wissler, American Museum of Natural History and Yale University. Invited but unable to attend were: Isaiah Bowman, American Geographical Society; Kenneth M. Chapman, New Mexico Museum and treasurer of Indian Arts Fund; Neil M. Judd, U.S. National Museum; Arthur Lithgoe, Metropolitan Museum of Art; R.V. D. Magoffin, New York University and president of the Archaeological Institute of America; and Frank G. Speck, University of Pennsylvania.

7. "A Communication From Dr. Kidder," 89LA2.015.1, ALAB.

8. Chapman (1927b, 479).

9. AC2.109, KMC-SAR.

10. "Confidential Statement to Members," undated, 89LA2.015.1, ALAB.

11. AVK to John D. Rockefeller Jr., December 19, 1927, Collection OMR, Record Group III 2E, Series Cult. Inst., Subseries Lab/Anthr., Box 17, Folder 172, KMC-RF.

12. Stocking (2001, 5).

13. JLN to John D. Rockefeller Jr., two pages dated July 31, intended for inclusion in letter dated August 5, 1929, but subsequently eliminated according to Nusbaum's handwritten note, Jesse

Nusbaum Papers, Box 1, Notebook . . . LAB, NAA.

14. Fowler (2000, 315); see also Woodbury (1993). A few of the Pecos participants were directly involved in the laboratory's formation, including Chap, Judd, and Spinden. But most participants knew each other from decades of rooting around together in southwestern soil: Byron Cummings, Harold and Mary-Russell Colton, Walter Hough, Ann and Earl Morris, Jesse Nusbaum, and Frances and Sylvanus Morley. Hewett attended the conference, as well. Kidder's invitation was not extended merely as an olive branch; it also was meant to acknowledge Hewett's importance in the Southwest. Strengthened by his attachments to so many of the guests, Hewett's perception of himself as "Dr. Archaeology" was probably not diminished. During discussions of issues pertinent to the new archaeology, however, he may have glimpsed yet another hint of his waning influence.

15. Fowler (2000, 315–17).

16. KMC to Bradfield, September 19, 1927, AC2.55, KMC-SAR.

17. KMC to Bradfield, September 19, 1927 (undated note penciled later by Hewett at the top of the first page), AC2.55, KMC-SAR.

18. Bernstein (1993a, 161).

19. Dietrich, n.d.. On one notable occasion, the seasonal monsoons generated a flash flood that engulfed the Indian campground. All were moved with their belongings into the armory. To cheer them up, Martha White offered all the ice cream they could eat. Though the freezers of every restaurant and drugstore in town were cleaned out, there wasn't enough to fill them up. The fair committee expected their Pueblo guests to be tired and ill humored, but instead they cleared the floor and danced through the night for their own pleasure (Dietrich, n.d.).

20. Bernstein (1993a, 166).

21. KMC to Bradfield, September 19, 1927, AC2.55, KMC-SAR.

22. "The Springer Memorial Services" (1927, 397–98).

23. KMC to Hodge, October 27, 1927, MS.7.MAI.1.121, HP.

24. Another strategic board invitee was Byron Cummings, a largely political appointment to acknowledge him as a major figure in Southwest archaeology. He attended one or two early meetings (Todd Bostwick, private communication).

25. AVK to KMC, January 12, 1928, AC2.82, KMC-SAR.

26. Memo, January 12 1928, Collection OMR, Record Group III 2E, Series Cult. Inst., Subseries Lab/Anthr., Box 17, Folder 172, KMC-RF.

27. AVK to Appleget, February 13, 1928, Collection OMR, Record Group III 2E, Series Cult. Inst., Subseries Lab/Anthr., Box 17, Folder 173, KMC-RF.

28. Sze (1997, 26). Dietrich had purchased the house from Senator Bronson Cutting when he foreclosed on the property, thus saving it from developers. The property, known as the Baca house or the Johnson Place, had been built in the early 1800s and, at one time, was considered one of the finest villas in the city. Dietrich intended to turn it into an elite summer hotel, though that plan was short-lived.

29. Sze (1997, 26).

30. Chapman and Stewart (1930).

31. Frank Chapman interview, May 1994.

32. "Memorandum of Conference," May 22, 1928, AC2.82, KMC-SAR.

33. AVK to KMC, June 9, 1928, AC2.82, KMC-SAR.

34. KMC to John D. Rockefeller Jr., March 25, 1929, KMC-RF.

35. AC2.102, KMC-SAR.

36. Tennyson, *The Vision of Sin* (1842, sec. 5).

37. KMC to Bradfield, September 19, 1927, AC2.55, KMC-SAR.

38. "The lady doth protest too much, methinks" (Shakespeare, *Hamlet*, 3.2.242).

39. **Ozymandias**
I met a traveller from an antique land
Who said:—Two vast and trunkless legs of stone
Stand in the desert. Near them on the sand,
Half sunk, a shatter'd visage lies, whose frown
And wrinkled lip and sneer of cold command
Tell that its sculptor well those passions read
Which yet survive, stamp'd on these lifeless things,
The hand that mock'd them and the heart that fed.
And on the pedestal these words appear:
"My name is Ozymandias, king of kings:
Look on my works, ye mighty, and despair!"
Nothing beside remains: round the decay
Of that colossal wreck, boundless and bare,
The lone and level sands stretch far away.
　　—Percy Bysshe Shelley, 1817

40. AVK to KMC, September 25, 1928, 89LA2.023, ALAB.

41. Appleget to John D. Rockefeller Jr., October 17, 1928, Collection OMR, Record Group III 2E, Series Cult. Inst., Subseries Lab/Anthr., Box 17, Folder 173, KMC-RF.

42. Though well documented in other works, it is useful to review the terms of the five-year operating budget since it had a bearing on Chap's later negotiating when he became acting director: for 1930 and 1931, $20,000 outright and $10,000 matching ($30,000 each year); for 1932, $15,000 outright and $12,500 matching ($27,500); for 1933, $10,000 outright and $15,000 matching ($25,000); for 1934, $5,000 outright and $17,500 matching ($22,500).

43. AVK to KMC, January 9, 1929, 89LA2.0026, ALAB.

44. In 1927, Cummings had passed an Antiquities Act in Arizona. It contained language that included federal and private lands, but the state legislature deleted the private lands provision shortly before passage, and the U.S. Attorney General ruled that the federal lands portion was unconstitutional. Cummings's legislation was the first of its kind in the West, serving as the basis for the current Arizona Antiquities Act, and was likely the basis for Hewett's idea in 1929 (Todd Bostwick, private communication).

45. Wilson to AVK, March 9, 1929, 89LA2.017, ALAB.

46. KMC to AVK, March 15, 1929, 89LA2.026, ALAB.

47. "Anthropology Laboratory Is Not Protesting" (1929, 6).

48. Wilson to AVK, March 9, 1929, 89LA2.017, ALAB.

49. KMC to AVK, March 13, 1929, 89LA2.026, ALAB.

50. Zimmerman to AVK, March 13, 1929, 89LA2.018, ALAB.

51. ELH to AVK, March 25, 1929, AC8.29, KMC-SAR.

52. AVK to KMC, March 18, 1929, 89LA2.026, ALAB.

53. KMC to AVK, March 15, 1929, 89LA2.026, ALAB.

54. KMC to JLN, March 25, 1929, 89LA2.024, ALAB.

55. AC2.159, KMC-SAR.

56. JLN to John D. Rockefeller Jr., August 5, 1929, Jesse Nusbaum Papers, Box 1, Notebook . . . LAB, NAA.

57. KMC to AVK, October 21, 1929, 89LA2:026, ALAB.

58. JLN to John D. Rockefeller Jr., August 5, 1929, Jesse Nusbaum Papers, Box 1, Notebook . . . LAB, NAA.

59. JLN to AVK, February 13, 1929, Box 4, Ted Kidder Correspondence, NAA.

Chapter 11 Notes

1. Stocking (1981, 15).

2. Bunting (1983, 78).

3. Stocking (2001, 232).

4. KMC to AVK, May 17, 1930, Kidder correspondence, AC2.82, KMC-SAR.

5. AC2.163, KMC-SAR.

6. KMC to John D. Rockefeller Jr., May 20, 1931, AC2.163, KMC-SAR.

7. Both the NMAIA and EAIA had cooperated with the Bureau of Indian Affairs' field health programs. In contrast, John Collier, noted for polarizing activists and bureaucrats, used his influence against the Bureau. Nusbaum got caught between the bureau and Collier when the NMAIA asked him to testify on their behalf.

8. Peckham (1990, 13).

9. Nash (1999, 188). Through this method of tree-ring dating, Neil Judd had been able to "bridge the gap" in his chronology just a year before, providing, for the first time, common era dates for prehistoric Southwest sites. In 1930, Stallings and other young archaeologists, such as Emil Haury and Florence Hawley, were among the earliest initiates when they attended the first class given on the subject, taught by A. E. Douglass, who had discovered the "missing" specimen.

10. Cordell (1993, 208).

11. JLN to AVK, June 25, 1930, Box 3, Laboratory of Anthropology, NAA.

12. Stocking (2001, 232).

13. JLN to John D. Rockefeller Jr., June 3, 1931, Jesse Nusbaum Papers, Box 1, Notebook . . . LAB, NAA.

14. Chapman (1931b, 123).

15. If the show resulted in a local grudge, on a national level it may have offered positive reinforcement for the passage of the 1932 Revenue Act exempting Indian-made articles from taxation to alleviate hardship. This legislation would have been a bonus for Maria who was now making over $5,000 annually, motivating other potters to develop greater skills. The Indian Service also paid her $1 per hour to offer classes at the Santa Fe Indian School.

16. 89KC0.033, ALAB.

17. 89KC0.033, ALAB.

18. SFNM, clipping hand-dated October 22, 1930, KMC-PP.

19. Brody interview, 2006.

20. "A Project for the Production of Motion and Still Film Studies . . . ," June 8, 1934, Record Group 1.1, Series 234, Box 1, Folder 9, KMC-RF.

21. AC2.163, KMC-SAR.

22. Quoted in Bernstein and Rushing (1995, 10). When Dunn resigned in 1937, she published a tribute to Chapman in School Arts magazine. Ultimately, Dunn's studio painting established its own legacy. The museum held annual school exhibits, and artists like Pablita Velarde and Harrison Begay became prominent. Some alumni joined the founding faculty of the Institute of American Indian Art in 1962— a ripple effect of Dunn's studio.

23. "Weavers At Laboratory," SFNM, February 14, 1933, clipping in Collection OMR, Record Group III 2E, Series Cult. Inst., Subseries Lab/Anthr., Box 17, Folder 174, KMC-RF.

24. Navajo rug conference project, Collection OMR, Record Group III 2E, Series Cult. Inst., Subseries Lab/Anthr., Box 17, Folder 174, 8–9, KMC-RF.

25. AVK to his wife, no date, letters marked nos. 1, 2, 4, and 5, Boaz W. Long Papers, no. 210, NMSA.

26. JLN to Packard, May 14, 1933, Box 1, Notebook . . . LAB, NAA.

27. JLN to AVK, February 24, 1933, Box 1, Notebook . . . LAB, NAA.

28. AVK to JLN, April 28, 1933, Box 1, Notebook . . . LAB, NAA.

29. JLN to AVK, July 3, 1933, Box 1, Notebook . . . LAB, NAA.

30. Nusbaum memo, September 26, 1933, Box 1, Notebook . . . LAB, NAA.

31. Baumann (1934).

32. Ferdon interview, 1995.

33. Stevens loved and esteemed Chap; his devotion to him was similar to Rockefeller's deep personal loyalty toward Nusbaum. Stevens steered his own children to education and work resources in the Southwest, especially to organizations Chap was involved with. His daughter Barbara eventually attended a class of Chap's at the University of New Mexico, retaining fond memories of it. It was Stevens who later arranged funding to cover Chap's needs so he could write his memoirs.

34. JLN to AVK, September 7, 1934, Box 3, NAA.

35. Although Nusbaum felt that Kidder was unable to secure effective board cooperation, apparently he did not disclose this at the time, revealing it only much later ("Significant Aspects of the Historical Background," Collection OMR, Record Group III 2E, Series Cult. Inst., Subseries Lab/Anthr., Box 18, Folder 175, KMC-RF).

36. Members included Chap, Thomas Dodge (Navajo Tribal Council chairman), Oliver La Farge, Charles Elkus (president of a California division of the American Indian Defense Association), Burton Staples, (Crafts del Navajo), trader Lorenzo Hubbell, Mrs. William Denman (San Francisco), and Isleta artist Diego Abeyta.

37. JLN to Stevens, November 7, 1934, Record Group 1.1, Series 234, Box 1, Folder 9, KMC-RF.

38. Stocking (2001, 15).

39. KMC to Mr. W. S. Campbell, August 9, 1945, 89C04.044.1, ALAB.

40. KMC to C. Szwedzicki, February 1, 1935, Collection OMR, Record Group III 2E, Series Cult. Inst., Subseries Lab/Anthr., Box 18, Folder 181, KMC-RF.

41. Edmund E. Day to AVK, February 19, 1935, Record Group 1.1, Series 234, Box 1, Folder 3, KMC-RF.

42. KMC to Stevens, July 10, 1935, Record Group 1.1, Series 234, Box 1, Folder 9, KMC-RF. One of the interviewees, Captain John G. Bradley, chief of the newly organized division of motion picture and sound recordings of the National Archives, turned out to be a former tenant of Chapman's. He had rented Kate and Chap's "little black house" for a few months in 1933 prior to taking a publicity job in Mexico. "Fortunately we had parted most amicably and there was no awkward

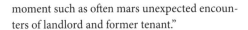

moment such as often mars unexpected encounters of landlord and former tenant."

43. AVK to Packard, November 21, 1935, Collection OMR, Record Group III 2E, Series Cult. Inst., Subseries Lab/Anthr., Box 18, Folder 175, KMC-RF.

44. AVK to Packard, November 21, 1935, Collection OMR, Record Group III 2E, Series Cult. Inst., Subseries Lab/Anthr., Box 18, Folder 175, KMC-RF.

45. AVK to Packard, November 21, 1935, Collection OMR, Record Group III 2E, Series Cult. Inst., Subseries Lab/Anthr., Box 18, Folder 175, KMC-RF.

46. AVK to KMC, November 22, 1935, Record Group 1.1, Series 234, Box 1, Folder 9, KMC-RF.

47. AC2.159, KMC-SAR.

48. Stocking (1981, 12).

49. AC2.18, KMC-SAR.

50. KMC to Tozzer, January 9, 1936, AC2.19, KMC-SAR.

51. KMC to Guthe, January 15, 1936, AC2.73, KMC-SAR.

52. AC2.159, KMC-SAR.

53. KMC to JLN, January 22, 1936, Jesse Nusbaum Papers, Box 2, KMC and JDR, NAA.

54. "Sixty Years of Art—Among Other Things," AC2.198, KMC-SAR.

55. Tozzer to KMC, May 20, 1936, AC2.119, KMC-SAR.

56. "Memoirs: LAB," AC2.159, KMC-SAR.

57. Motivated by Stevens's faith in him, as well as the potential to educate a wider audience, it had been hard for Chap to give up the film project, but it was even harder for the foundation to let go. A memo at the end of the year still held out hope that Chap would request another grant in 1938 when his administrative duties were up. In 1939, all parties—Chap included—conceded it was a dead end.

58. Chapman (1936b, 26).

59. Chapman (1936c, 26); note also that Fricke (2002) provides a discussion of Chapman's writings.

60. Brody (1970, 68).

61. Frank S. Chapman interview, February 1995.

62. "Significant Aspects of the Historical Background," Collection OMR, Record Group III 2E, Series Cult. Inst., Subseries Lab/Anthr., Box 18, Folder 175, KMC-RF.

63. AC2.159, KMC-SAR.

64. KMC to Packard, December 31, 1936, AC2.97, KMC-SAR.

65. "Significant Aspects of the Historical Background," Collection OMR, Record Group III 2E, Series Cult. Inst., Subseries Lab/Anthr., Box 18, Folder 175, KMC-RF.

66. Charles Amsden to KMC, January 25, 1937, AC2.51, KMC-SAR.

67. Collection OMR, Record Group III 2E, Series Cult. Inst., Subseries Lab/Anthr., Box 18, Folder 81, KMC-RF.

68. John S. Chapman interview, June 2002.

69. Guthe to JLN, November 22, 1937, 89LA3.008.2, ALAB.

70. AC2.159, KMC-SAR.

71. KMC to Guthe, handwritten memo and letter, November 30, 1937, 89LA3.008.2, ALAB.

72. KMC, "Notes on Use of the Placard," May 5, 1938, RG 435, Box 4, Records of IACB, NAA.

73. Chap's stamping activities for the Indian Arts and Crafts Board ended, but the board continued its mission of preserving tribal culture and protecting authentic Native art. It sponsored numerous exhibits and eventually erected three museums, focusing on consumer education as a way to guarantee authenticity. Eventually, these proved inadequate to the task of protecting Indian artists. Encouraged by Native activists, Congress passed the Indian Arts and Crafts Act in 1990, essentially a truth-in-advertising law, with civil and criminal penalties for abuses.

74. "People and Points of View," Collection OMR, Record Group III 2E, Series Cult. Inst., Subseries Lab/Anthr., Box 18, Folder 175.

75. "People and Points of View," Collection OMR, Record Group III 2E, Series Cult. Inst., Subseries Lab/Anthr., Box 18, Folder 175, KMC-RF.

76. "People and Points of View," Collection OMR, Record Group III 2E, Series Cult. Inst., Subseries Lab/Anthr., Box 18, Folder 175, KMC-RF.

77. "Memoirs—JD Rockefeller Jr. Reports & Memos Regarding Meetings," AC2.166A, KMC-SAR.

78. John D. Rockefeller Jr. to KMC, November 26, 1939, AC2.163, KMC-SAR.

79. As vice president of the James Walter Thompson Advertising Company, Young would declare at a trade conference in November 1941 that advertising "ought to be the servant of music, of art, of literature and of all the forces of righteousness." As a direct result of his speech, the conference members approved the formation of an organization—called the Ad Council—dedicated to such ideals. When Pearl Harbor was attacked the following month, the council, quickly renamed the War Ad Council, shouldered the task of rallying Americans to war. "Rosie the Riveter," one of the council's more famous campaigns, evokes feelings from those war years even today.

80. KMC to Guthe, December 19, 1939, AC2.73, KMC-SAR.

81. KMC to Mrs. Dam, July 2, 1940, 89C04.045, ALAB.

82. KMC to H. R. Pollock, November 22, 1939, 89C04.059, ALAB.

83. KMC to W. W. Postlethwaite, February 12, 1941, 89C04.059, ALAB.

84. Cassidy (1941, 21).

85. KMC to Guthe, June 16, 1941, 89C04.050, ALAB.

86. KMC to Rice, June 21, 1941, 89C04.061, ALAB.

87. KMC to Guthe, June 16, 1941, 89C04.050, ALAB.

88. KMC to Judd, November 13, 1941, AC2.80, KMC-SAR.

89. KMC to Judd, November 13, 1941, AC2.80, KMC-SAR.

90. KMC to Judd, November 13, 1941, AC2.80, KMC-SAR.

91. Packard to KMC, December 29, 1941, Collection OMR, Record Group III 2E, Series Cult. Inst., Subseries Lab/Anthr., Box 18, Folder 175, KMC-RF.

92. AC2.159, KMC-SAR.

93. Packard to Stevens, May 29, 1942, Record Group 1.1, Series 234, Box 1, Folder 11, KMC-RF.

Chapter 12 Notes

1. KMC to Louise H. Everhardy (Kansas State College), October 10, 1942, 89KC0.006, ALAB.

2. AC2.159, KMC-SAR.

3. Mrs. J. W. Chapman to Carl Guthe, June 11, 1941, 89C04.050, ALAB.

4. KMC to Mrs. Buck, February 1943, 89KC0.054, ALAB.

5. KMC to Zimmerman (regarding grant), July 8, 1944, Record Group 11, Series 234, Box 1, Folder 11, KMC-RF.

6. KMC to Dr. Ruth Underhill, March 19, 1943, 89KC0.002, ALAB.

7. KMC to Elizabeth Shepley Sergeant, June 17, 1943, 89C04.063.2, ALAB.

8. KMC to unknown recipient, n.d., 89C04.044.1, ALAB.

9. Marriott (1948, 277).

10. Steeper (2003, 72–73).

11. "Now They Can Be Told Aloud" (1945, 1).

12. Underhill (1946, 155–59).

13. KMC to Rose Dougan, October 6, 1943, 89C04.045, ALAB.

14. "Monthly Reports, 1936–1942," December 1941, 89LA0.007, ALAB.

15. Kenneth Siegman to Bob Potter III, February 24, 2001, Albuquerque, NM. Kenneth "Sieg" Siegman, who met Helen's husband, Robert Potter II, there, recalled that their training "was extreme to say the least, especially during the winter months. The temperature hovered around the thirty below mark and we would spend weeks . . . without benefit of fires or hot food."

16. Kenneth Siegman to Bob Potter III, February 24, 2001, Albuquerque, NM.

17. KMC to Mr. McMechen, January 24, 1944, 89C04.055.1, ALAB.

18. "Mrs. Chapman Improved Following Operation" (1944, 3).

19. KMC to Dr. W. C. Holden, March 22, 1944, 89C04.051, ALAB.

20. KMC to Mr. Harry B. Buckley, March 20, 1944, 89C04.043, ALAB.

21. Stevens memo regarding KMC and lab, May 20, 1944, Collection OMR, Record Group III 2E, Series Cult. Inst., Subseries Lab/Anthr., Box 18, Folder 176, KMC-RF.

22. KMC to JLN, August 3, 1944, HFC.

23. "J. F. Zimmerman" (1944, 1).

24. KMC to Stevens, August 27, 1945, Record Group 1.1, Series 234, Box 1, Folder 11, KMC-RF.

25. Roberts and Roberts (1988, 192).

26. "Now They Can Be Told Aloud" (1945, 1).

27. During the last five years that Zimmerman was president, Popejoy, a native New Mexican, was a prominent participant in almost all major decisions concerning the university. After Zimmerman's death, however, he was passed over for the presidency because he lacked a doctorate; instead, the board of regents chose Harvard professor, John Philip Wernett, who served until the summer of 1948. At that time, the board reconsidered Popejoy, who officially took office July 1, 1948. Popejoy is credited with guiding the university through two decades of phenomenal growth (Davis [2005, 24]).

28. KMC to Stevens, August 27, 1945, Record Group 1.1, Series 234, Box 1, Folder 11, KMC-RF.

29. "Sixty Years of Art—Among Other Things," AC2.198, KMC-SAR.

30. Ries to Manuel Lujan, March 6, 1946, 89C04.055.1, ALAB.

31. KMC to Stevens, August 27, 1945, Record Group 1.1, Series 234, Box 1, Folder 11, KMC-RF. January 1946 gave Chap the opportunity to satisfy that yearning when he traveled to New York as member of the IACB to attend the opening of the Indian Arts Exhibit at New York's Museum of Modern Art (MoMA). Chap, who had corresponded frequently about the exhibit with its codirectors—Frederick H. Douglas, curator of Indian art at the Denver Museum, and Rene d'Harnoncourt, now of MoMA—attended its opening as well as a dinner honoring Douglas and himself.

32. Peckham interview, 1995.

33. Harnisch interview, 1995.

34. "Stanley A. Stubbs, 1906–1959" (1959, 213).

35. Lambert interview, 1994.

36. Jennie Chapman, personal communication, June 2006.

37. Harnisch interview, 1995.

38. Harnisch interview, 1995.

39. Harnisch interview, 1995.

40. Rayne interview, 1995.

41. Rayne interview, 1995.

42. Stark and Rayne (1998, 106–12).

43. "Kearny Covers Near 400,000" (1946, 1).

44. Harnisch interview, 1995.

45. KMC, memo filed by Packard, January 24, 1947, Collection OMR, Record Group III 2E, Series Cult. Inst., Subseries Lab/Anthr., Box 18, Folder 177, KMC-RF.

46. Press release citing "Lab Will Have 1947 Deficit of $11,000" SFNM, December 11, 1946, KMC-PP.

47. "Sixty Years of Art—Among Other Things," AC2.198, KMC-SAR.

48. "Memoirs A to Z," KMC-PP.

49. "Sixty Years of Art—Among Other Things," AC2.198, KMC-SAR.

50. "Sixty Years of Art—Among Other Things," AC2.198, KMC-SAR.

51. "Sixty Years of Art—Among Other Things," AC2.198, KMC-SAR.

52. KMC, memo filed by Packard, January 24, 1947, Collection OMR, Record Group III 2E, Series Cult. Inst., Subseries Lab/Anthr., Box 18, Folder 177, KMC-RF.

53. "Sixty Years of Art—Among Other Things," AC2.198, KMC-SAR.

54. Ellis (1971, 38).

55. Arthur Jones (for Packard) to John D. Rockefeller Jr., August 14, 1947, Collection OMR, Record Group III 2E, Series Cult. Inst., Subseries Lab/Anthr., Box 18, Folder 177, KMC-RF; Jones to James Young, August 22, 1947, Collection OMR, Record Group III 2E, Series Cult. Inst., Subseries Lab/Anthr., Box 18, Folder 177, KMC-RF.

56. John D. Rockefeller Jr. to KMC, July 26, 1948, AC2.163, KMC-SAR.

57. Chauvenet (1983, 221).

58. Ellis (1971, 19).

59. "Hewett Memorial Rites Held" (1947, 6).

60. Reports by Bruce Ellis in the 1960s and 1971 detail the discrepancies between the original proposal and that signed into law (Ellis, 1971). Ellis provides definite proof that the escrow items had been effectively forged; the descriptive pages had been replaced for the first three items (the two deeds and bill of sale), but the signature and notary page had been left. The fourth item (bill of sale of collections to school) was fabricated in the fall of 1948. Ellis surmised that the escrow items were exchanged because Long was concerned about the location of the Museum of International Folk Art. Because Bartlett was leaning toward the director's residence, Long added more acreage to that deed. With regard to changing the ownership of the collections from the museum to the school, Ellis believed that Long might have thought of it as a sort of trade—because in the event the folk art museum was located on the director's residence property, it was likely that the school would have to give it back to the state. However, a second conjecture is that Long simply decided to keep the collections in private hands, as Hewett had done during his tenure.

61. Ellis (1971, 1–42).

62. Gilpatric, memo, March 10–11, 1950, Record Group 1.1, Series 234, Box 1, Folder 13, KMC-RF.

63. Florence Hawley Ellis was a student of Cummings at the University of Arizona, receiving her BA with distinction in 1927. She earned a PhD from the University of Chicago in 1934 and then taught at the University of New Mexico for more than thirty-six years (Bostwick [2006, 207–9]).

64. Wendorf interview, 1995.

65. KMC to Judd, April 19, 1952, Neil M. Judd, nine letters, 1927, 1953, AC2.80, KMC-SAR.

66. Ellis to Gilpatric, May 22, 1951, Record Group 1.1, Series 234, Box 1, Folder 14, KMC-RF.

67. KMC to Judd, May 14, 1953, Neil M. Judd, nine letters, 1927, 1953, AC2.80, KMC-SAR.

68. "Dr. K. M. Chapman" (1951, 290–91).

69. Lambert interview, 1994.

70. Fred Kabotie to KMC, April 16, 1945, 89C04.054, ALAB.

71. Harlow interview, 1995.

72. "Standing Ovation" (1954).

73. Peckham, Fox, and Lambert (1981, 34).

74. Peckham, Fox, and Lambert (1981, 35).

75. Rodeck interview, 1996.

76. Lambert interview, 1994.

77. Lambert interview, 1994.

78. Lambert interview, 1994.

79. Bernstein (1994a, 70).

80. Lambert interview, 1994.

81. Fariello (1995, 42).

82. "Hill Scientists Lash AEC Decision" (1954, 1).

83. AC2.102, KMC-SAR.

84. KMC to John D. Rockefeller Jr., February 11, 1954, AC2.163, KMC-SAR.

85. "Memorandum of My Meetings with Mr. And Mrs. John D. Rockefeller, Jr.," June 10 and 11, 1926, AC2.163, KMC-SAR.

86. John D. Rockefeller Jr. to KMC, July 26, 1954, Collection OMR, Record Group III 2E, Series Cult. Inst., Subseries Lab/Anthr., Box 18, Folder 177, KMC-RF.

87. John D. Rockefeller Jr. to T. M. Debevoise, July 26, 1954, Collection OMR, Record Group III 2E, Series Cult. Inst., Subseries Lab/Anthr., Box 18, Folder 177, KMC-RF.

88. Debevoise to John D. Rockefeller Jr., July 30, 1954, Collection OMR, Record Group III 2E, Series Cult. Inst., Subseries Lab/Anthr., Box 18, Folder 177, KMC-RF.

89. KMC to John D. Rockefeller Jr., August 9, 1954, Collection OMR, Record Group III 2E, Series Cult. Inst., Subseries Lab/Anthr., Box 18, Folder 177, KMC-RF.

90. AC2.139, KMC-SAR.

91. AC2.139, KMC-SAR.

92. Peckham interview, 1995.

93. "Department of Indian Arts, Kenneth M. Chapman, *Head Associate in Charge (emeritus)* with Bruce Ellis," AC2.1, KMC-SAR.

94. "Department of Indian Arts, Kenneth M. Chapman, *Head Associate in Charge (emeritus)* with Bruce Ellis," AC2.1, KMC-SAR.

95. Dillingham (1992, 25); Maxwell Museum of Anthropology (1974, 9).

96. In 1952, on one of his eastern tours to gather additional information for his monographs, Chap had visited the Royal Ontario Museum to view the collection of pieces from the Normal University collection that had been loaned in 1911. In his memoirs, Chap wrote that *Dr. Currelly was then on vacation, but I found their portion of the collection on exhibition. It looked out of place, so far from home, and the assistant curator told me frankly that it was of little interest to visitors or students. . . . Yet, his portion* *of the collection does have a distinct archaeological value, as a link in the sequence from ancient to modern pottery wares of the Upper Rio Grande. . . . Nothing would please me more, than to see the Normal University's portion of the collection at Toronto returned to the State of New Mexico and, possibly, a collection of equal value but of more general interest assembled to replace it at the present New Mexico Highlands University* (AC2.161, KMC-SAR).

97. KMC to Colton, June 30, 1959, 89C05.002, ALAB.

98. "History of School of American Research," http://www.sarweb.org/home/history.htm (accessed January 15, 2008).

99. "Minutes of the Annual Meeting of the Indian Arts Fund," October 22, 1959, AC1.4, KMC-SAR.

100. In the late 1990s, a real effort was made to divide the collections. Representatives from both the school and the Museum of Indian Arts and Culture/Laboratory of Anthropology took turns selecting undeclared items. To the relief of almost all involved, the "divorce" was made final at that time (Laura Holt, personal communication, 2004).

101. "Meeting of the Board of Trustees of Indian Arts Fund," February 18, 1966, AC1.6, KMC-SAR. Pueblo potters arrived in Fort Worth to demonstrate their craft, though they had to make do with makeshift tools, as their own tools had not arrived because of Santa Fe Railway regulations. Meem stated for the record that he thought the idea of the Indians' demonstration "somehow seemed not quite dignified."

102. "Curator's Annual Report," October 11, 1962, AC1.5, KMC-SAR.

103. Wolf (1988, 33).

104. Fox (1988, 44).

105. Bernstein (1994a, 70). For additional information about the Indian Market, including how Chapman's ideas have influenced it over time, see also Bernstein (1993a, 1993b, and 1994b).

106. "Indian Market" (1997, 10).

107. Interview with Bernstein, 1995.

108. "Teocentli," October 10, 1962, AC2.1, KMC-SAR.

109. "Editor's Statement," 1, KMC-PP.

110. Wroe (1999, 4).

111. AC2.11, KMC-SAR. The archive's collection also includes an earlier version of this drawing, sketched in 1942.

112. Memoirs—addenda, AC2.169, KMC-SAR.

113. "Dr. Chapman Toasted Upon 90th Birthday," July 16, 1965, KMC-PP.

114. Hassenzahl (1975, 6).

115. Harlow interview, 1995.

116. Harlow interview, 1995.

117. "A Tribute to Dr. Chapman" (1968, A-2).

118. Harlow (1977, vii).

APPENDIX NOTES

1. *SFNM*, January 5, 1929 (clipping found in Chapman's personal papers with handwritten notes); although this article was published several years after the Harvey Detours staff dinner that was noted in Joseph Sharp's letter to Chapman (cited in chapter 10), the details of the Taos Creation Myth as published coincide with the observations in Sharp's letter.

2. At the end of the sentence, Chapman hand-wrote in parentheses the word "Couse." This probably refers to a painting by E. I. Couse, depicting a squatting Indian painting pictographs.

BIBLIOGRAPHY

ABBREVIATIONS

AAA Archives of American Art. Smithsonian Institution, Detroit, Michigan, branch.

ALAB Archives, Laboratory of Anthropology. Museum of Indian Arts and Culture, Santa Fe, NM.

ELHP Edgar Lee Hewett Papers. Division of History, Museum of New Mexico, Santa Fe, NM.

FSC Frank Springer Collection. Center for Southwest Research, University of New Mexico, Albuquerque, NM.

HFC Nusbaum-Chapman Correspondence, 1942–47. Jesse Nusbaum Collection. National Park Service, Harpers Ferry Center, Harpers Ferry, WV.

HP Frederick Hodge Papers. Braun Research Library, Autry National Center, Los Angeles, CA.

KMC-FA Kenneth M. Chapman File. Museum of Fine Arts, Museum of New Mexico, Santa Fe, NM.

KMC-PP Kenneth M. Chapman, Personal Papers. Margretta Potter Harnisch (Helen Chapman Potter family), Santa Fe, NM.

KMC-RF Kenneth M. Chapman File. Rockefeller Archive Center, Pocantico Hills, Sleepy Hollow, NY.

KMC-SAR Kenneth M. Chapman Papers. Archives. Catherine McElvain Library, School for Advanced Research, Santa Fe, NM.

NAA Jesse Nusbaum Papers. National Anthropological Archives, Washington, DC.

NMHR *New Mexico Historical Review.* Albuquerque, NM.

NMNH Natural Museum of Natural History, Washington, DC.

NMSA New Mexico State Archives. Santa Fe, NM.

ROM Royal Ontario Museum. Toronto, Canada.

SFNM *Santa Fe New Mexican.* Santa Fe, NM.

INTERVIEWS

Bernstein, Bruce. By Janet Chapman. February 1995. Santa Fe, NM.

Brody, J. J. By Janet Chapman. April 7, 2006. Edgewood, NM.

Chabot, Maria. By Janet Chapman. September 10, 1998. Albuquerque, NM.

Chapman, Frank S. By Janet Chapman. August 1994. Albuquerque, NM.

———. By Janet Chapman and Karen Barrie. July 1995. Albuquerque, NM.

Chapman, Frank S., and John S. Chapman. By Janet Chapman. May 1994. Albuquerque, NM.

Chapman, John S. By Karen Barrie. July 16 and 21, 1995. Wilmette, IL.

———. By Karen Barrie. June 16, 2002. Wilmette, IL.

Chiba, Kay. By Janet Chapman and Karen Barrie. July 1995. Tesuque, NM.

Dauber, Kenneth. By Karen Barrie. May 24, 1994. Evanston, IL.

Dunlap, Carmelita. By Karen Barrie. July 16, 1995. San Ildefonso Pueblo, NM.

Ferdon, Edwin. By Karen Barrie. May 15, 1995. Telephone interview.

Fox, Nancy. By Janet Chapman. July 24, 1994. Santa Fe, NM.

Gonzales, Barbara. By Karen Barrie. July 16, 1995. San Ildefonso Pueblo, NM.

Harlow, Francis H. By Janet Chapman. May 20, 1995. Los Alamos, NM.

Harnisch, Margretta "Peggy" Potter. By Janet Chapman. February 1995. Santa Fe, NM.

Hering, Michael. By Janet Chapman. February 1995. Santa Fe, NM.

Lambert, Marjorie. By Janet Chapman. June 1994. Santa Fe, NM.

Martinez, Adam, and Santana. By Karen Barrie. July 21, 1995. San Ildefonso Pueblo, NM.

Monroe, Barbara. By Karen Barrie. March 1, 1995. Telephone interview.

Parezo, Nancy. By Karen Barrie. May 13, 1994. Tucson, AZ.

Peckham, Stewart. By Janet Chapman. May 5, 1995. Santa Fe, NM.

Rayne, Catherine. By Janet Chapman. October 6, 1995. Santa Fe, NM.

Rodeck, Sally Lewis. By Janet Chapman. July 17, 1996. Northglenn, CO.

Ross, Mary Lou. By Karen Barrie. October 27, 1995. Telephone interview.

Schmidt, Margaret. By Karen Barrie. May 15, 1995. Telephone interview.

Wendorf, Fred. By Karen Barrie. October 25, 1995. Telephone interview.

SOURCES

Aitken, Barbara. 1950. "A Bird Moving." In School of American Research 1950, 1.

Amon Carter Museum of Western Art. 1966. *Quiet Triumph: Forty Years with the Indian Arts Fund, Santa Fe*. Ft. Worth: Amon Carter Museum of Western Art with the cooperation of School of American Research, Santa Fe.

"Anthropology Laboratory Is Not Protesting." 1929. *SFNM*, March 5, 6.

"An Artistic Chronology." 1967. *The New Mexican Special Supplement*, November 12.

The Artists of New Mexico: An Attempted Listing of the Artists of the "Sunshine State." 1935. Pamphlet for seminar in southwestern literature, New Mexico Normal University, Las Vegas, NM.

"Art Policy of Museum and School." *El Palacio* 10(5): 2–3.

Art Students League of New York. 2000–2001. One hundred twenty-fifth anniversary edition catalog.

"Astigmatic Expressionists." 1924. *SFNM*, February 16, 6.

Austin, Mary. 1932. *Earth Horizons: Autobiography*. New York: The Literary Guild.

Bandelier, Adolph F. [1890] 1960. *The Delight Makers*. New York: Dodd, Mead.

Baumann, Gustave. 1934. "PWAP Reports." Microfilm no. D155, AAA.

Benes, Rebecca C. 2004. *Native American Picture Books of Change*. Santa Fe: Museum of New Mexico Press.

Berke, Arnold. 2002. *Mary Colter: Architect of the Southwest*. New York: Princeton Architectural Press.

Berlo, Janet C., ed. 1992. *The Early Years of Native American Art History: The Politics of Scholarship and Collecting*. Seattle: University of Washington Press.

Berlo, Janet C., and Ruth B. Phillips. 1998. *Native North American Art*. New York: Oxford University Press.

Bernstein, Bruce D. 1993a. "The Marketing of Culture: Pottery and Santa Fe's Indian Market." PhD diss., University of New Mexico.

———. 1993b. "From Indian Fair to Indian Market." *El Palacio* 93(3): 14–18, 47–54.

———. 1994a. "Potters and Patrons: The Creation of Pueblo Art Pottery." *American Indian Art Magazine* 20(1): 70–79.

———. 1994b. "Pueblo Potters, Museum Curators, and Santa Fe's Indian Market." *Expedition* 36(1): 14–23.

Bernstein, Bruce D., and J. J. Brody. 2001. *Voices in Clay: Pueblo Pottery from the Edna M. Kelly Collection.* Oxford, OH: Miami University Art Museum.

Bernstein, Bruce D., and W. Jackson Rushing. 1995. *Modern by Tradition: American Indian Painting in the Studio Style.* Santa Fe: Museum of New Mexico Press.

Bloom, Lansing B., Wesley Bradfield, and Kenneth M. Chapman. 1928. "Preliminary Survey of the Archaeology of Southwestern New Mexico." *El Palacio* 24(6): 99–112.

Bolgiano, Chris. 1997. "Lost Diaries Reveal Bandelier's Storied Past." *New Mexico Magazine* 75(5): 50–55.

Bostwick, Todd W. 2006. *Byron Cummings: Dean of Southwest Archaeology.* Tucson: University of Arizona Press.

Brody, J. J. 1970. *Indian Painters and White Patrons.* Albuquerque: University of New Mexico Press.

———. 1990. *Beauty from the Earth: Pueblo Indian Pottery from the University Museum of Archaeology and Anthropology.* Philadelphia: University of Pennsylvania Museum of Archaeology and Anthropology.

———. 1997. *Pueblo Indian Painting: Tradition and Modernism in New Mexico, 1900–1930.* Santa Fe: School of American Research.

Bumpus, Hermon C., and Alfred V. Kidder. 1927. "A Statement as of June 6, 1927—To the Members of the Committee on Outdoor Recreation and to Those Interested in the Establishment of an Anthropological Laboratory and Museum at Santa Fe, and to Those Who Have Already Assisted in the Project." ALAB.

Bunting, Bainbridge. 1983. *John Gaw Meem, Southwestern Architect.* Santa Fe: School of American Research.

Bunzel, Ruth L. 1929. *The Pueblo Potter: A Study of Creative Imagination in Primitive Art.* New York: Columbia University Press.

Burton, Henrietta K. 1936. *The Re-Establishment of the Indians in Their Pueblo Life through the Revival of Their Traditional Craft.* New York: Columbia University Teachers College.

Caffey, David L. 2006. *Frank Springer and New Mexico: From the Colfax County War to the Emergence of Modern Santa Fe.* College Station: Texas A&M University Press.

Carlson, John F. 1958. *Carlson's Guide to Landscape Painting.* New York: Sterling.

Cassidy, Ina Sizer. 1941. "Art and Artists of New Mexico." *New Mexico Magazine* 19(10): 21, 35–36.

———. 1955. "Art and Artists of New Mexico: The Man Who Revived Indian Art." *New Mexico Magazine* 33(10): 30, 47.

Chapman, Kate Muller, and Dorothy N. Stewart. 1930. *Adobe Notes, or How to Keep the Weather Out with Just Plain Mud.* Taos, NM: Laughing Horse Press.

Chapman, Kenneth M. 1916a. "The Evolution of the Bird in Decorative Art." *Art and Archaeology* 4(6): 307–16.

———. 1916b. "Graphic Art of the Cave Dwellers." *El Palacio* 3(2): 37–42.

———. 1917a. *The Cave Pictographs of the Rito de Los Frijoles N.M.* Papers of the School of American Archaeology, no. 37. Santa Fe: School of American Archaeology, Archaeological Institute of America.

———. 1917b. *Conservatism in the Evolution of Decorative Art.* Papers of the School of American Archaeology, no. 37. Santa Fe: School of American Archaeology, Archaeological Institute of America.

———. 1921. "What the Potsherds Tell." *Art and Archaeology* 11(1–2): 39–44.

———. 1922. "Life Forms in Pueblo Pottery Decoration." *Art and Archaeology* 13(3): 120–22.

———. 1923. "Casas Grandes Pottery." *Art and Archaeology* 16: 25–34.

———. 1924a. "Pottery Decorations of Santo Domingo and Cochiti Pueblos." *El Palacio* 16(6): 87–93.

———. 1924b. "The Indian Fair (Santa Fe Fiesta)." *Art and Archaeology* 18(5–6): 215–24.

———. 1926. "An Archaeological Site in the Jornada Del Muerto, New Mexico." *El Palacio* 20(6): 118–22.

———. 1927a. "Chance Forms Derived from the Meander (Summary)." *El Palacio* 22(14): 354–59.

———. 1927b. "Post-Spanish Pueblo Pottery." *Art and Archaeology* 23(5): 207–13; *El Palacio* 22(21–22): 469–82.

———. 1927c. "Stone Wall Construction in Ancient Pueblos and Cliff Dwellings." *El Palacio* 23(17): 479–85.

———. 1927d. "A Feather Symbol of the Ancient Pueblos." *El Palacio* 23(21): 526–36.

———. 1927e. "The Shalako Ceremony at Zuni." *El Palacio* 23(25): 622–27.

———. 1928. "Bird Forms in Zuni Pottery Decoration." *El Palacio* 24(2): 23–28.

———. 1930. "Ceremonial Lighting Stones of the Upper Rio Grande Pueblos." *Museum Notes, Museum of Northern Arizona* 2(11): 4.

———. 1931a. "America's Most Ancient Art." *School Arts* 30(7): 386–402.

———. 1931b. "Indian Pottery." In *Introduction to American Indian Art: To Accompany the First Exhibition of American Indian Art Selected Entirely with Consideration of Esthetic Value*, ed. Frederick Webb Hodge, Herbert Joseph Spinden, and Oliver La Farge. New York: The Exposition of Indian Tribal Arts.

———. 1932. *Decorative Art of the Indians of the Southwest: A List of Publications Containing Illustrations from Basketry, Costume and Ornament, Pottery, Textiles, etc. of Especial Value in the Study of Design*. Santa Fe: Laboratory of Anthropology.

———. 1933–36. *Pueblo Indian Pottery: 50 Reproductions in Color from Specimens in the Famous Collection of the Indian Arts Fund*. 2 vols. Nice, France: C. Szwedzicki.

———. 1936a. "Zuni Silversmithing." *Indians at Work* 4(3): 16–19.

———. 1936b. "Roadside Shopping." *New Mexico* 14(6): 20–21.

———. 1936c. "Indian Pottery by the Roadsides." *Indians at Work* 4(4): 23–27.

———. 1936d. *The Pottery of Santo Domingo Pueblo: A Detailed Study of Its Decoration*. Memoirs of the Laboratory of Anthropology. Vol. 1. Santa Fe: Laboratory of Anthropology.

———. 1937. "Decorative Design." *New Mexico* 15(7): 18–19, 50.

———. 1938a. *Pueblo Indian Pottery of the Post-Spanish Period*. General series, bulletin no. 4, Laboratory of Anthropology, Santa Fe.

———. 1938b. "Pajaritan Pictography: The Cave Pictographs of the Rito de los Frijoles." In *Pajarito Plateau and Its Ancient People*, 139–48. Albuquerque: University of New Mexico Press.

———. 1949. "The Laboratory of Anthropology." *El Palacio* 56(1): 21–24.

———. 1951a. "Harry P. Mera, 1875–1951." *American Antiquity* 27(1): 47–48.

———. 1951b. "Bird Forms in Zuni Pottery Decoration." *El Palacio* 58(10): 316–24.

———. 1961. "New Light upon a Rare Southwestern Pottery Type." *El Palacio* 68(4): 214–17.

———. 1963. *Nazarus*. Santa Fe: Kenilton Press.

———. 1966. "Three Ceremonial Objects." *El Palacio* 73(3): 31.

———. [1970] 1977. *The Pottery of San Ildefonso Pueblo.* Albuquerque: University of New Mexico Press for School of American Research.

Chapman, Kenneth M., and Bruce T. Ellis. 1951. "The Line Break, Problem Child of Pueblo Pottery." *El Palacio* 58(9): 251–89.

"Chapman-Mueller Wedding Unusually Felicitous." 1915. *SFNM*, September 30, 8.

"Chautauqua a Misfit." 1926. *SFNM*, April 15.

Chauvenet, Beatrice. 1983. *Hewett and Friends: A Biography of Santa Fe's Vibrant Era.* Santa Fe: Museum of New Mexico Press.

Los Cinco Pintores. 1975. Pamphlet for the Museum of New Mexico. Albuquerque: University of New Mexico Printing Plant.

Church, Peggy Pond. 1960. *The House at Otowi Bridge: The Story of Edith Warner and Los Alamos.* Albuquerque: University of New Mexico Press.

Coe, Ralph T. 1986. *Lost and Found Traditions: Native American Art, 1965–1985.* New York: The American Federation of Arts in association with University of Washington Press.

Cohodas, Marvin. 1992. "Louisa Keyser and the Cohns: Mythmaking and Basket Making in the American West." In *The Early Years of Native American Art History*, ed. Janet C. Berlo, 88–133. Seattle: University of Washington Press.

Coke, Van Deren. 1963. *Taos and Santa Fe: The Artist's Environment, 1882–1942.* Albuquerque: University of New Mexico Press for the Amon Carter Museum of Western Art, Ft. Worth.

Collier, Peter, and David Horowitz. 1976. *The Rockefellers.* New York: Holt, Rinehart and Winston.

Comfort, Charles Haines, and Mary Apolline Comfort, eds. 1955. *This Is Santa Fe: A Guide to the City Different.* Santa Fe: Comfort and Comfort.

———. 1959. "Dr. Kenneth Chapman, Too Busy to Retire." *The Santa Fe Scene* 2(19).

Conron, John. 1997. *The Laboratory of Anthropology: Historic Structure Report for the State of New Mexico.* Santa Fe: Ellis/Browing Architects.

Cordell, Linda S. 1993. "Women Archaeologists in the Southwest." In Parezo, ed. 1993, 202–20.

Cuban, Larry. 1984. *How Teachers Taught: Constancy and Change in American Classrooms, 1890–1980.* New York: Longman.

Dale, Edward Everett. 1949. *The Indians of the Southwest: A Century of Development Under the United States.* Norman: University of Oklahoma Press.

Dauber, Kenneth W. 1990. "Pueblo Pottery and the Politics of Regional Identity." *Journal of the Southwest* 32(4): 576–96.

———. 1993. "Shaping the Clay: Pueblo Pottery, Cultural Sponsorship and Regional Identity in New Mexico." PhD diss., University of Arizona.

Davis, William E. 2005. "Looking at Tom Popejoy." *Mirage Magazine* 23(2): 22–26.

Dechart, Phoebe. 1978. "Community Theater: Santa Fe's Oldest Surviving Drama Group." *SFNM*, March 19, 12–14.

D'Emilio, Sandra, and Suzan Campbell. 1991. *Visions and Visionaries: The Art and Artists of the Santa Fe Railway.* Salt Lake City: Peregrine Smith Books.

Dietrich, Margretta. N.d. Chapter 2, organizational work. History File #101 (NM Recollections 1). NMSA.

Dillingham, Rick, with Melinda Elliott. 1992. *Acoma and Laguna Pottery,* Santa Fe: School of American Research Press.

"Dr. K. M. Chapman." 1951. *El Palacio* 58(9): 290–91.

Dozier, Edward P. 1970. *The Pueblo Indians of North America.* New York: Holt, Rinehart and Winston.

Dunn, Dorothy. 1936. "An Introduction to Kenneth Chapman." *School Arts* 36(3): 133–36.

———. 1968. *American Indian Painting of the Southwest and Plains Areas.* Albuquerque: University of New Mexico Press.

Efland, Arthur D. 1990. *A History of Art Education: Intellectual and Social Currents In Teaching the Visual Arts.* New York: Teachers College Press.

Eldredge, Charles C., Julie Schimmel, and William H. Truettner. 1986. *Art in New Mexico, 1900–1945: Paths to Taos and Santa Fe.* New York: Abbeville Press, published for the National Museum of American Art, Smithsonian Institution, Washington, DC.

Ellen, Mary, and Laurence R. Blair. 1986. *Margaret Tafoya: A Tewa Potter's Heritage and Legacy.* West Chester, PA: Schiffer Publishing.

Elliott, Melinda. 1987. *Exploring Human Worlds: A History of the School of American Research.* Santa Fe: School of American Research Press.

Ellis, Bruce. 1971. "Narrative Report on the 1947–1949 Division of Assets of the Laboratory of Anthropology, Inc., between the School of American Research, Inc., and the Museum of New Mexico, November 1971." 89LA4.022.3. ALAB.

"Every Day in Every Way Art Critics Grow Jazzier and Jazzier." 1924. *SFNM*, February 21, 5.

Falk, Peter H., ed. 1990. *The Annual Exhibition Record of the Art Institute of Chicago: 1888–1950.* Madison, CT: Sound View Press.

Fariello, Griffin. 1995. *Red Scare: Memories of the American Inquisition, an Oral History.* New York: Norton.

Fenyes, Eva. N.d. Scrapbook of Santa Fe art colony, 1870–1921. Microfilm no. D160, AAA.

Ferdon, Edwin N. 1956. "Long—Long Ago and Today." *El Palacio* 63(11–12): 324–31.

Fergusson, Erna. 1940. *Our Southwest.* New York: Knopf.

———. [1951] 1964. *New Mexico: A Pageant of Three Peoples.* New York: Knopf.

Flynn, Kathryn A., ed. 1995. *Treasures on New Mexico Trails: Discover New Deal Art and Architecture.* Santa Fe: Sunstone Press.

Fosdick, Raymond. 1956. *John D. Rockefeller, Jr.: A Portrait.* New York: Harper and Brothers.

Fowler, Don D. 2000. *A Laboratory for Anthropology: Science and Romanticism in the American Southwest, 1846–1930.* Albuquerque: University of New Mexico Press.

Fox, Jennifer. 1993. "The Women Who Opened Doors: Interviewing Southwestern Anthropologists." In Parezo, ed. 1993, 294–310.

Fox, Nancy. 1983. "Collections of the Laboratory of Anthropology, Museum of New Mexico." *American Indian Art Magazine* 8(2): 56–63.

———. 1988. "The Museum of Indian Arts and Culture." *American Indian Art Magazine* 13(4): 42–47.

Frank, Larry, and Francis H. Harlow. 1974. *Historic Pottery of the Pueblo Indians, 1600–1880.* Boston: New York Graphic Society.

Fricke, Suzanne Newman. 2003. "Institutionalizing Taste: Kenneth Milton Chapman, the Indian Arts Fund, and the Growth of Fine Art Pueblo Pottery." PhD diss., University of New Mexico.

Frisbie, Theodore R. 1974. "A Biography of Florence Hawley Ellis." In *Collected Papers in Honor of Florence Hawley Ellis,* ed., T. R. Frisbie. Papers of the Archaeological Society of New Mexico, no. 2. Norman, OK: Published for the Archaeological Society of New Mexico by Hooper Publishing.

Gabriel, Kathryn. 1991. *Roads to Center Place: A Cultural Atlas of Chaco Canyon and the Anasazi.* Boulder, CO: Johnson Books.

Gaither, James M. 1957. "A Return to the Village: A Study of Santa Fe and Taos, New Mexico, as Cultural Centers, 1900–1934." PhD diss., University of Minnesota.

Garmhausen, Winona. 1988. *History of Indian Arts Education in Santa Fe.* Santa Fe: Sunstone Press.

Gibson, Arrell Morgan. 1983. *The Santa Fe and Taos Colonies: Age of the Muses, 1900–1942*. Norman: University of Oklahoma Press.

Gillispie, Charles Coulston, ed. 1970. Vol. 1 of the *Dictionary of Scientific Biography*. New York: Scribner.

Gish, Robert. 1997. "Enchanting Citizen: Erna Fergusson, '13 BA, Pedagogy." *Mirage* 15(1): 9.

Givens, Douglas R. 1992. *Alfred Vincent Kidder and the Development of Americanist Archaeology*. Albuquerque: University of New Mexico Press.

Gratton, Virginia L. 1992. *Mary Colter: Builder Upon the Red Earth*. Grand Canyon, AZ: Grand Canyon Natural History Association.

Guthe, Carl E. 1925. *Pueblo Pottery Making: A Study at the Village of San Ildefonso*. New Haven: Yale University Press.

Haeuser, Michael J. 2002. *With Grace, Elegance, and Flair: The First 25 Years of Gustavus Library Associates*. St. Peter, MN: Gustavus Adolphus College (http://www.hwwilson.com/jcdawards/about_jcd.htm, accessed January 1, 2008).

Halseth, Odd. 1926. "Revival of Pueblo Pottery Making." *El Palacio* 21(6): 135–54.

Harlow, Francis H. 1977. *Modern Pueblo Pottery: 1860–1960*. Flagstaff, AZ: Northland Press.

Harr, John E., and Peter I. Johnson. 1991. *The Rockefeller Conscience*. New York: Charles Scribner's Sons.

Harrington, John P. 1950. "Little Hummingbird." In School of American Research 1950, 71–72.

Hartley, Marsden. 1920. "Red Man Ceremonials: An American Plea for an American Esthetics." *Art and Archaeology* 9(7): 7–14.

Hassenzahl, Jeanne. 1975. *Harlow*. Los Alamos, NM: Jeanne Hassenzahl.

Hatcher, Evelyn P. 1985. *Art as Culture*. Lanham, MD: University Press of America.

Hayes, Allan, and John Blom. 1996. *Southwestern Pottery: Anasazi to Zuni*. Flagstaff, AZ: Northland Publishing.

Hecht, Robert A. 1991. *Oliver La Farge and the American Indian: A Biography*. Metuchen, NJ: Scarecrow Press.

Hewett, Edgar Lee. 1909. *The Excavations at El Rito de Los Frijoles in 1909*. Papers of the School of American Archaeology, no. 10. Santa Fe: School of American Archaeology, Archaeological Institute of America.

———. 1917. *Santa Fe in 1926*. Papers of the School of American Archaeology, no. 39. Santa Fe: School of American Archaeology, Archaeological Institute of America.

———. 1918. *Organic Acts and Administrative Reports of the School of American Archaeology: 1907–1917*. Papers of the School of American Research, n.s., no. 6. Santa Fe: School of American Research, Archaeological Institute of America.

———. 1927. *Two Addresses on the Life of Frank Springer*. Papers of the School of American Research, no. 21. Santa Fe: School of American Research, Archaeological Institute of America.

———. 1938. *Pajarito Plateau and its Ancient People*. Albuquerque: University of New Mexico Press for the School of American Research.

———. 1943. *Campfire and Trail*. Albuquerque: University of New Mexico Press.

———. 1946. *Two Score Years*. Albuquerque: University of New Mexico Press.

"Hewett Memorial Rites Held at St. Francis Auditorium." 1947. *SFNM*, August 25, 6.

"Hill Scientists Lash AEC Decision." 1954. *SFNM*, June 30, 1.

Hofstadter, Richard. 1955. *The Age of Reform: From Bryan to F.D.R.* New York: Knopf.

Holmes, William Henry. 1888. "A Study of the Textile Art in its Relation to the Development of Form and Ornament." In *Sixth Annual Report of the Bureau of Ethnology to the Secretary of the Smithsonian Institution, 1884–85*. Washington, DC: Government Printing Office.

Horgan, Paul. 1957. *The Centuries of Santa Fe.* London: Macmillan.

Howard, Kathleen L., and Diana F. Pardue. 1996. *Inventing the Southwest: The Fred Harvey Company and Native American Art.* Flagstaff, AZ: Northland Publishing, in cooperation with the Heard Museum.

Huntington, Ellsworth. 1912. "Studies of the Primitive Mind." *Literary Digest*, January 22.

Hyer, Sally. 1994. "Remembering Santa Fe Indian School, 1890–1990." PhD diss., University of New Mexico.

"The Indian Bill." 1922. *SFNM*, September 20, 4.

"Indian Market." 1997. *SFNM*, August 21, 10.

Irving, Donald J. 1979. "History of the School." In School of the Art Institute of Chicago 1979, 5–7.

Jeançon, J. A. 1923. *Excavations in the Chama Valley, New Mexico.* Bureau of American Ethnology, bulletin 81. Washington, DC: Government Printing Office.

"J. F. Zimmerman, NMU Head, Dies Suddenly at Age 57." 1944. *SFNM*, October 21, 1.

Johnson, Willard. 1925. "Indian Arts Fund: Introduction by Willard Johnson." *Indian Arts Fund Bulletin* (1).

Johnson, William Templeton. 1916. *The Santa Fe of the Future.* Papers of the School of American Archaeology, no. 31. Santa Fe: School of American Archaeology, Archaeological Institute of America.

Jonaitis, Aldona. 1992. "Franz Boas, John Swanton, and the New Haida Sculpture at the American Museum of Natural History." In *The Early Years of Native American Art History: The Politics of Scholarship and Collecting*, ed. Janet C. Berlo, 22–61. Seattle: University of Washington Press.

Judd, Neil M. 1960. "Reminiscences in Southwest Archaeology." Pt. 2. *Kiva* 26(1): 1–6.

———. 1968. *Men Met along the Trail: Adventures in Archaeology.* Norman, OK: University of Oklahoma Press.

"Kearny Covers Near 400,000 on 1st Day." 1946. *SFNM*, October 17, 1.

Kelly, Lawrence C. 1983. *The Assault on Assimilation: John Collier and the Origins of Indian Policy Reform.* Albuquerque: University of New Mexico Press.

Kidder, Alfred V. 1915. *The Pottery of the Pajarito Plateau and of Some Adjacent Regions in New Mexico.* Memoirs of the American Anthropological Association 2:6.

———. 1950. "Sylvanus Griswold Morley, 1883–1948." In School of American Research 1950, 93–101.

———. 1960. "Reminiscences in Southwest Archaeology." Pt. 1. *Kiva* 25(4): 1–32.

———. 1962. *An Introduction to the Study of Southwestern Archaeology.* New Haven: Yale University Press.

Knee, Ernest. 1942. *Santa Fe, New Mexico.* New York: Chanticleer Press.

Kochendoerfer, Violet. 1998. *Santa Fe in the Fifties.* Santa Fe: Western Edge Press.

Kramer, Dorothy Dunn. 1977. "The Studio, 1932–1937: Fostering Indian Art as Art." *El Palacio* 83(4): 5–9, 16.

Kuh, Katharine. 1979. "100 Artists 100 Years." In School of the Art Institute of Chicago 1979, 10–13.

La Farge, Oliver. 1959. *Santa Fe: The Autobiography of a Southwestern Town.* Norman: University of Oklahoma Press.

Laird, Carobeth. 1975. *Encounter with an Angry God: Recollections of My Life with John Peabody Harrington.* Banning, CA: Malki Museum Press, Morongo Indian Reservation.

Lambert, Marjorie F. N.d. "Bits and Pieces from the Past." In *Clues to the Past: Papers in Honor of William M. Sundt*, ed. Meliha S. Duran and David T. Kirkpatrick, 155–71. Albuquerque: Archaeological Society of New Mexico.

Landgren, Marchal E. 1940. *Years of Art: The Story of the Art Students League of New York.* New York: Robert M. McBride.

Latham, Frank B. 1972. *1872–1972: A Century of Serving Consumers; the Story of Montgomery Ward*. Chicago: Montgomery Ward.

Laughlin, Ruth. 1994. "Santa Fe in the Twenties." In Weigle and Fiore, 113–21.

Layton, Robert. 1993. *The Anthropology of Art*. 2nd ed. Cambridge: Cambridge University Press.

Ledes, Allison Eckardt. 1990. "Current and Coming: Native American Pottery." *Antiques* 138(3): 378.

LeFree, Betty. 1975. *Santa Clara Pottery Today*. Albuquerque: University of New Mexico Press for the School of American Research.

Lewis, Nancy Owen, and Kay Leigh Hagan. 2007. *A Peculiar Alchemy: A Centennial History of SAR, 1907–2007*. Santa Fe: School for Advanced Research.

"Like Eastern Chautauqua." 1926. *SFNM*, April 15.

Lister, Robert H., and Florence C. Lister. 1983. *Those Who Came Before: Southwestern Archeology in the National Park System*. Globe, AZ: Southwest Parks and Monuments Association.

Luhan, Mabel Dodge. 1935. *Winter in Taos*. New York: Harcourt, Brace.

———. 1937. *Edge of Taos Desert: An Escape to Reality*. Vol. 4 of *Intimate Memories*. New York: Harcourt, Brace.

Lummis, Charles F. 1918. "In Memory." In Bandelier, *The Delight Makers*, xiii–xvii.

———. 1925. *Mesa, Cañon and Pueblo*. New York: Century.

Marriott, Alice. 1948. *María: The Potter of San Ildefonso*. Norman: University of Oklahoma Press.

Maxon, John. 1970. *The Art Institute of Chicago*. New York: Harry N. Abrams.

Maxwell Museum of Anthropology. 1974. *Seven Families in Pueblo Pottery*. Albuquerque: University of New Mexico Press.

McLuhan, T. C. 1985. *Dream Tracks: The Railroad and the American Indian, 1890–1930*. New York: Harry N. Abrams.

McNary, James. 1956. *This Is My Life*. Albuquerque: University of New Mexico Press.

Mera, H. P. [1939] 1991. *Style Trends of Pueblo Pottery 1500–1840*. Albuquerque: Avanyu Publishing.

Mercer, Bill. 1995. *Singing the Clay: Pueblo Pottery of the Southwest Yesterday and Today*. Cincinnati: Cincinnati Art Museum.

"Modernists Create Real Sensation with Exhibit." 1924. *SFNM*, February 12, 3.

Morley, Sylvanus G. 1915. "Santa Fe Architecture" *Old Santa Fe* 2(3): 298.

"Mrs. Chapman Improved Following Operation." 1944. *SFNM*, March 13, 3.

"Museum Dedication Exercises Will Open Next Saturday; Preparation Soon Complete." 1917. *SFNM*, November 17, 5.

Museum of Indian Arts and Culture. 1990. *From this Earth: Pottery of the Southwest*. Santa Fe: Museum of Indian Arts and Culture.

Nash, Stephen Edward. 1999. *Time, Trees, and Prehistory: Tree-Ring Dating and the Development of North American Archaeology 1914–1950*. Salt Lake City: University of Utah Press.

"Necrology: Dr. Frank Springer." 1927. *NMHR* 2(4): 386–93.

Nelson, Mary Carroll. 1972. *Maria Martinez*. Minneapolis, MN: Dillon Press.

The New Mexico Normal School at Las Vegas. 1898–99. East Las Vegas: Las Vegas Publishing Company.

"New Museum the Noblest, Simplest and Most Impressive Type of Christian Architecture Originating on This Continent." 1917. *SFNM*, November 26, 1.

"No 'Chautauqua.'" 1926. *SFNM*, April 15.

"No New Attitude." 1926. *SFNM*, April 15.

"Now They Can Be Told Aloud, Those Stoories [*sic*] of 'the Hill.'" 1945. *SFNM*, August 6, 1.

Nusbaum, Jesse L. 1950. "Vay Morley and the Santa Fe Style." In School of American Research 1950, 162–73.

Nusbaum, Rosemary. 1978. *The City Different and the Palace*. Santa Fe: Sunstone Press.

———. 1980. *Tierra Dulce: Reminiscences from the Jesse Nusbaum Papers*. Santa Fe: Sunstone Press.

"Old New Santa Fe Will Be Pictured in Assembly Room." 1912. *SFNM*, November 18, 1.

"The Paintings of Charles Hawthorne." 1968. Museum of Art, University of Connecticut.

Parezo, Nancy J., ed. 1993. *Hidden Scholars: Women Anthropologists and the Native American Southwest*. Albuquerque: University of New Mexico Press.

Pearson, Jim B. 1961. *The Maxwell Land Grant*. Norman, OK: University of Oklahoma Press.

Peckham, Stewart. 1990. *From This Earth: The Ancient Art of Pueblo Pottery*. Santa Fe, NM: Museum of New Mexico Press.

Peckham, Stewart, Nancy Fox, and Marjorie Lambert. 1981. "The Laboratory's Modern Era: 1947–1981." *El Palacio* 87(3): 33–42.

Peterson, Susan. 1977. *The Living Tradition of Maria Martinez*. Tokyo: Kodansha.

Pettit, R. Fred. 1950. "A Man of Parts, All of Them Lovable." In School of American Research 1950, 198.

Pierpont, Claudia Roth. 2004. "Annals of Culture: The Measure of America." *New Yorker*, March 8, 48–63.

Pollack, Norman, ed. 1967. *The Populist Mind*. Indianapolis, IN: Bobbs-Merrill.

Powell, John Wesley. 1900. *Nineteenth Annual Report of the Bureau of American Ethnology to the Secretary of the Smithsonian Institution, 1897–98*. Pt. 1. Washington, DC: Government Printing Office.

Price, Sally. 1989. *Primitive Art in Civilized Places*. Chicago: University of Chicago Press.

Primm, James N. 1981. *Lion of the Valley: St. Louis, Missouri*. Boulder, CO: Pruett Publishing.

Prucha, Francis P. 1984. *The Great Father: The United States Government and the American Indians*. Lincoln: University of Nebraska Press.

Purdy, James H. "The Carlos Vierra House." 1979. *The Historical Santa Fe Foundation Bulletin* 5(1).

"Ralph Emerson Twitchell." 1926. *NMHR* 1(1): 79–85.

"Records of the Past; Old Palace Notes." 1916. *SFNM*, October 20, 6.

Reeve, Kay Aiken. 1982. *Santa Fe and Taos 1898–1942: An American Cultural Center*. El Paso: Texas Western Press, University of Texas.

Reyman, Jonathan E. 1992. "Women in American Archaeology: Some Historical Notes and Comments." In *Rediscovering Our Past: Essays on the History of American Archaeology*, ed., J. E. Reyman, 69–80. Avebury, UK: Aldershot.

Rice, Prudence M. 1987. *Pottery Analysis: A Sourcebook*. Chicago: University of Chicago Press.

Roberts, Susan A., and Calvin A. Roberts. 1988. *New Mexico*. Albuquerque: University of New Mexico Press.

Robertson, Edna, and Sarah Nestor. 1962. *Artists of the Canyons and Camino: Santa Fe, the Early Years*. Salt Lake City: Gibbs and Smith.

Ruch, Marcella J. 2001. *Pablita Velarde: Painting Her People*. Santa Fe: New Mexico Magazine.

Rushing, W. Jackson. 1995. *Native American Art and the New York Avant-Garde*. Austin: University of Texas Press.

Rushing, W. Jackson, ed. 1999. *Native Art in the Twentieth Century*. New York: Routledge.

Sando, Joe S. 1992. *Pueblo Nations: Eight Centuries of Pueblo Indian History*. Santa Fe: Clear Light Publishers.

School of American Research. 1950. *Morleyana: A Collection of Writings in Memoriam Sylvanus*

Griswold Morley, 1883–1948. Santa Fe: School of American Research.

———. 1940. *Representative Art and Artists of New Mexico.* Santa Fe: School of American Research.

School of the Art Institute of Chicago. 1979. *100 Artists 100 Years: Alumni of the School of the Art Institute of Chicago, Centennial Exhibition.* Chicago: The School of the Art Institute of Chicago.

Schrader, Robert F. 1983. *The Indian Arts and Crafts Board.* Albuquerque: University of New Mexico Press.

Sheppard, Carl. 1989. *The Saint Francis Murals of Santa Fe: The Commission and the Artists.* Santa Fe: Sunstone Press.

Simmons, Marc. 1988. *New Mexico: An Interpretive History.* Albuquerque: University of New Mexico Press.

Smith, Duane. 2002. "The Nusbaum Years." In *Mesa Verde: Shadows of the Centuries*, 105–28. Boulder: University of Colorado Press (http://www.cr.nps.gov/history/online_books/smith/index.htm, accessed January 1, 2008).

Smith, Henry J. 1933. *Chicago's Great Century: 1833–1933.* Chicago: Consolidated Publishers.

Snead, James Elliot. 2001. *Ruins and Rivals: The Making of Southwest Archaeology.* Tucson: University of Arizona Press.

Spivey, Richard L. 2003. *The Legacy of Maria Poveka Martinez.* Santa Fe: Museum of New Mexico Press.

Springer, Frank. 1920. *The Crinoidea Flexibilia.* Washington, DC: The Smithsonian Institution.

———. 1927. *Educational Addresses of Dr. Frank Springer.* Papers of the School of American Research, n.s., no. 17. Santa Fe: El Palacio Press.

"The Springer Memorial Services." 1927. *El Palacio* 23(14–16): 362–411.

"Springer Resigns." 1903. *The Daily Optic*, January 1.

"Spud, Laffin Hoss Editor, Takes Brief Look at the Modernists." 1924. *SFNM*, February 13, 6.

"Standing Ovation Given Chapman by SRO Audience." 1954. *SFNM*, March 1.

Stark, Gregor, and E. Catherine Rayne. 1998. *El Delirio: The Santa Fe World of Elizabeth White.* Santa Fe: School of American Research.

Steeper, Nancy Cook. 2003. *Dorothy Scarritt McKibbon: Gatekeeper to Los Alamos.* Los Alamos, NM: Los Alamos Historical Society.

Stocking, George W., Jr. 1981. "Anthropological Visions and Economic Realities in the 1930s Southwest." *El Palacio* 87(3): 14–17.

———. 1982. *Race, Culture, and Evolution: Essays in the History of Anthropology.* Chicago: University of Chicago Press.

———. 2001. "The Santa Fe Style in American Anthropology." In *Delimiting Anthropology, Occasional Essays and Reflections*, 218–43. Madison: University of Wisconsin Press.

Stuart, David E. 1989. *The Magic of Bandelier.* Santa Fe: Ancient City Press.

"Stanley A. Stubbs, 1906–1959." 1959. *El Palacio* 66(3): 213.

Szasz, Margaret Connell, ed. 1994. *Between Indian and White Worlds: The Cultural Broker.* Norman: University of Oklahoma Press.

Sze, Corinne P. 1997. *El Zaguán: The James L. Johnson House.* Santa Fe: Historic Santa Fe Foundation.

"Third Year Book Santa Fe Society." 1918. *El Palacio* 5(1): 6–7.

Toulouse, Betty. 1977. *Pueblo Pottery of the New Mexico Indians.* Santa Fe: Museum of New Mexico Press.

———. 1980. "Maria, the Right Woman at the Right Time." *El Palacio* 86(4): 3–7.

———. 1981a. "Prelude: Founding the Laboratory of Anthropology." *El Palacio* 87(3): 4–6.

———. 1981b. "The Laboratory's Early Years: 1927–1947." *El Palacio* 87(3): 7–13.

Traube, Alex, and E. A. Mares. 1983. *Las Vegas, New Mexico: A Portrait*. Albuquerque: University of New Mexico Press.

Trennert, Robert A. 1987. "Fairs, Expositions, and the Changing Image of Southwestern Indians, 1876–1904." *NMHR* 62(2): 127–50.

"A Tribute to Dr. Chapman." 1968. *SFNM*, February 25, A-2.

Trimble, Stephen. 1987. *Talking with the Clay: The Art of Pueblo Pottery*. Santa Fe: School of American Research.

Twitchell, Ralph E. 1909. *The History of the Military Occupation of the Territory of New Mexico from 1846 to 1851*. Denver, CO: Smith-Brooks.

Udall, Sharyn Rohlfsen. 1984. *Modernist Painting in New Mexico, 1913–1935*. Albuquerque: University of New Mexico Press.

———. 1987. *Santa Fe Art Colony, 1900–1942*. Santa Fe: Gerald Peters Art Gallery.

Underhill, Ruth Murray. 1944. *Pueblo Crafts*. Washington, DC: U.S. Department of the Interior, Bureau of Indian Affairs.

———. 1946. *First Penthouse Dwellers of America*. 2nd ed. Santa Fe: Laboratory of Anthropology.

Vierra, Carlos. 1917. *Our Native Architecture in Its Relation to Santa Fe*. Papers of the School of American Archaeology, no. 39. Santa Fe: School of American Archaeology, Archaeological Institute of America.

Wade, Edwin L., ed. 1986. *The Arts and the Native American Indian: Native Traditions in Evolution*. New York: Hudson Hills Press.

Wadsworth, Beula M. 1949. "He Revived the Art of the Ancients." *Desert Magazine*, April, 10–13.

Walter, Paul. 1916. "Annual Museum Report." *El Palacio* 3(2): 59–60.

Weigle, Marta, and Kyle Fiore. 1994. *Santa Fe and Taos: The Writer's Era, 1916–1941*. Santa Fe: Ancient City Press.

Whitman, William. 1947. *The Pueblo Indians of San Ildefonso: A Changing Culture*. New York: Columbia University Press.

Wilcox, David R. 1993. "Pueblo Grande as Phoenix: Odd Halseth's Vision of a City Museum." In *Archaeology of the Pueblo Grande Platform Mound and Surrounding Features*, vol. 1, ed. Christian E. Downum and Todd W. Bostwick, 97–138. Phoenix, AZ: Pueblo Grande Museum.

Wilson, Chris. 1997. *The Myth of Santa Fe: Creating a Modern Regional Tradition*. Albuquerque: University of New Mexico Press.

Winship, A. E. 1903. "New Mexico Annual Meeting. Looking About. Fifth Series, 17. [Editorial.]" *Journal of Education* 57(4).

Wolf, Arthur H. 1988. "The Indian Arts Fund Collection at the School of American Research." *American Indian Art Magazine* 4(1): 32–37.

Woodbury, Richard B. 1973. *Alfred V. Kidder*. New York: Columbia University Press.

———. 1993. *Sixty Years of Southwestern Archaeology: A History of the Pecos Conference*. Albuquerque: University of New Mexico Press.

Wroe, Ann. 1999. Pontius *Pilate*: New York: Random House.

INDEX

The initials "KMC" in entries stand for Kenneth Milton Chapman.
Italicized page numbers indicate photographs or other illustrations.
All locations are in New Mexico unless otherwise specified.

AAM. *See* American Association of Museums

Abbott, A. J., 46, 66, 92, 235

Abbott, Jane, 92

Acoma Pueblo, 16, 184; visited by Hodge, 36; photographic record of pottery, 161; visited by KMC, 183, 240–41, 282; economic difficulties of, 191–92; KMC and Lucy Lewis, 306

Adams, J. P. "Jack," 73, 85, 87, 103, 105

Adobe Notes, 238

Agassiz, Louis, 16, 58; influence on Springer, 45–46

Aguilar, Susanna, 235

AIA. *See* Archaeological Institute of America

Aitken, Barbara Freire-Marreco, 70, 82, 84, *87*

Albright, Horace, 283

Albuquerque Indian School, 256

Alex Thompson collection, 302

Alexander, Hartley B., 129, 225

American Association of Museums (AAM), 220, 333n15; early interest in laboratory, 215; outdoor education committee, 215, 221, 232; Bumpus as representative for, 218, 225, 228; Bumpus and Hewett prepare report for, 221; proposes anthropological institute in Santa Fe, 231

American Council of Learned Societies, 272

American Indian Defense Asso-ciation, 174, 177, 253, 261

American Museum of Natural History, 67, 119, 126

Amon Carter Museum, 309

Amsden, Charles, 272–74

Apache, 167

Applegate, Frank, 136, 180, 190, 235; and Spanish colonial arts and crafts, 185, 193; as IAF founder, 193; trains Harvey couriers, 200

Appleget, Thomas B., 249, 305; as Rockefeller's secretary, 214, 217, 218, 231, 237; negotiates with Hewett, 215, 220, 224; opinion of Hewett, 218, 243

Archaeological Institute of America (AIA), 44, 59; supports Hewett, 60–61; parent organization of School of American Archaeology, 62, 75; and local archaeological societies, 185; proposal to Rockefeller Foundation, 185, 207, 209

Archaeological Society of New Mexico, 44, 59, 63

archaeology: growth in field of, 16, 19–20, 49, 51, 126–27, 319n29, 324n80

Armory Show (1913), 138

Art and Archaeology, 128, 129, 159, 225

Art Institute of Chicago, 22–26, 48, 97, 165, 257, 299 arts and crafts movement, 52, 127

Art Students League, 35, 91, 97–98, 111–12

Ascension, Dolores, 241

Atalaya Garden Club, 294

Atchison, Topeka, and Santa Fe Railway, 38, 104, 125

Austin, Mary, 162, 177, 199, 222; and community theater, 132–33; and Spanish colonial arts and crafts, 185, 193, 260

Awa Tsireh (Alfonso Roybal), 137, 177

Baca, Lufina, 169, 235

Bakos, Jozef, 136, 137, 180, 190

Balink, Henry C., 125, 190

Bandelier, Adolph, 44, 59, 69, 115, 189; *The Delight Makers*, 43, 63

Bandelier National Monument, 86–87

Barnes, Albert, 255

Bartlett, Florence, 298

Baumann, Gustave, 133, 137, 158, 189, 190

Beal, George, 252

Beauregard, Donald, 87, 110, 120

Begay, Apie, 51

Bellows, George, 125, 137

Berninghaus, Oscar, 124

Beymer, George II (great-great-grandfather), 6

Beymer, Harriet (great-grandmother), 6

Bloom, George, 259, 260

Bloom, Lansing, 278; assistant to Hewett, 144, 161; fieldwork with KMC, 165, 178, 196, 238

Blumenschein, Ernest, 98, 124, 318

Boas, Franz, 19, 59, 232, 287; opinion of Hewett, 61, 82, 94, 131, 157; member of school's managing committee, 62; concerned about school location, 66

Bond, Marian, 291

Bowditch, Charles, 60, 66

Boyle, Cecily Myrtle, 116, 121, *122*

Bradfield, Wesley, 129, 144, 180, 242, 329n41; and Dougan–von Blumenthal initiative, 133–35, 166; member of museum staff, 137, 154, 161, 163, 196; and prehistoric pottery, 165, 192; and Pueblo Pottery Fund, 174, 184; correspondence with KMC, 216–17, 234–35, 242; coauthor with KMC, 238

Bridgman, George, 98, 112

Bumpus, Hermon C.: member of school's managing committee, 67; enthusiasm for trailside museums, 215; opinion of Hewett, 215, as Rockefeller's agent, 217–19, 221–25; and KMC, 219, 221–22, 231; 222–25, 231; as AAM representative, 225–32

Bunzel, Ruth, 160, 184

Burdick, Anna, 182

Bureau of Ethnology, 16, 65, 115, 130; and Hodge, 36, 67, 82, 99, 100; and Fewkes, 168

Bureau of Indian Affairs, 253, 258, 274, 287

Burge, Margaret McKittrick. *See* McKittrick, Margaret

Burke, Charles H., 179, 192

Burlin, Paul, 125, 137, 138

Burlington, Iowa, 46, 47, 55, 80; museum, 55–59

Bursum Bill, 176–78

Bursum, Holm O., 176

butterfly designs (San Ildefonso), 126, 148–49

Bynner, Witter, 162, 189

Carlson, John, 111–12

Carnegie Institute, 228, 253

Carroll, Mitchell, 80, 100

Cartwright, Sam G., 101

Casas Grandes pottery, 164

Caskie, John, 31, 98

Cassidy, Gerald, 110, 125, 137, 190, 262

Cassidy, Ina Sizer, 125

cave paintings, 116, 121, 128

ceramic technology project, 253

Ceremonial Cave (Bandelier), 66, 84, *86*

Chabot, Maria, 272

Chaco Canyon, 50–51, 151–52, 306

Chamberlin, Adelaide, 140

Champe, Charles, 27–30, 32, 321n47

Chapel Studio, 137, 149, 158

Chapman, Dwight (brother), 2, 3, 8–13, 17–20, 27; KMC resolves to keep up with ("I'll show you"), 11; in contrast to KMC, 14, 17, 162–63; marriage and family, 49, 81, 314

Chapman, Frank Springer (son), xii, xiii, 132, 238, 267, 287, 289, *300*; birth of, 121; on family life, 131, 293; "Oku" as nick-name, 146, 330n5; on KMC's relationship with potters, 146, 238, 272; childhood of, 187, 198, 201; wedding of, 285; and death of mother, 290; and death of KMC, 315

Chapman, George Washington (grandfather), 4, 36

Chapman, Helen (daughter). *See* Potter, Helen Chapman

Chapman, Jennie Kaufmann (daughter-in-law), 285, 287

Chapman, John Milton (father), 2, 3, 4–6, *12*, 19, 21; health of, 5, 10; journal entry of, 5; marriage, 8; owner of Economist Plow Company, 11; travels with KMC to Smithsonian, 16; death of, 26

Chapman, John Sheffield (nephew), xiii, 160, 162, 274

Chapman, Katherine "Kate" Muller, *83*, 85, 104, *109*, *122*, 220, 235, *267*, 272, 334n28; family history, 82–83; at lectures, 82; unladylike behavior of, 82, 162–63; at Rito, 92–93; as assistant to Hewett and Hodge, 97; and New-Old Santa Fe architectural movement, 103; as renovator, 103,

132, 198, 215, 238; studio at museum, 113; field-work, 116, 121; wedding of, 117; contributes idea for Pasatiempo, 189, 332n41; poems of, 198–99, 268; friendship with Dorothy Stewart, 198, 233; against chautauqua, 199–200; *Adobe Notes*, 238; emergency appendectomy, 289; death of, 289

Chapman, Kenneth Milton, *3*, *12*, *34*, *53*, *239*, family history, 2–8; nicknames, 8, 22, 29, 50; childhood, 9–16; in high school, 16–19; and death of father, 26; in St. Louis, MO, 27–32; in Milwaukee, WI, 33–36; in Las Vegas, 38–49, 56–57; in Burlington, IA, 55–59; and Burlington romance, 56, 57; in Province-town, MA, 96–97; in New York, NY, 97–99, 112; jury duty, 105; in Woodstock, NY, 111–12; at 615 Acequia Madre, 132, 136, 144, 187, 199, 201, 220–21; purchases Chapel Studio, 137; at house in foothills, 267–68, 289–91, 302; moves into laboratory, 291, 293; eightieth birthday, 302; writes memoirs, 305–6; ninetieth birthday, 314; death of, 315

—appearance: as youth, 17, 25, 31; as adult, *1*, 38, 144, 253, 314

—as artist: *124*; initial art studies, 15; at Art Institute of Chicago, 22–26; paintings, 32, 104, 113, 125, 126; at Art Students League, 97–98, 111–12; exhibits art, 113, 124, 126, 262; designs furniture, 121, 188, 252; defines art, 127; defends modernism, 180–81, 332n27. *See also* St. Francis murals

—character: conscientious, 17, 88, 120, 242; curious, 77, 127–28; determined, 11, 25–26, 268–75; diplomatic, 88–89, 246, 260; inventive, 17, 105–6, 276, 293; jack-of-all-trades, 79–80, 287; loyal, 127, 142, 205; precise, 130, 154; reserved, 17–18, 24, 31, 48, 147–48; self-conscious, 13–14, 17, 38; sensitive to criticism, 17–18, 242–43, 303–5; square dealer, 33–35, 93–94, 104–5; swayed by friends, 9–10, 71–72; witty, 145, 180–81, 233, 314, 317–18

—fieldwork: at Chaco Canyon, 50–51, 151–52; at Rito, 62–66, 69–74, 84, 107, 241; Pecos ruins survey, 105; at Quarai, 107; Springer expeditions, 116, 121, *122*; in southern Chihuahua, 164; at Jornada del Muerto, 196; in southern Arizona, 253

—health: 30–31, 58, 99, 244, 290, 315; stomach ailments, 11, 73n, 158, 192, 196; hemorrhage, 35–37

—honors: as art student, 24; for house design, 110; honorary doctorates, 299; from IAF, 301; from IACB, 309, 341n31

—Indian art: *160*, *263*, *310*, *313*; early interest in, 9, 14, 15, 16; initial design studies of, 77–79, 85–89,

99, 108; presents chicken-and-egg theory, 90; mentioned in Harper's, 90; and Normal University collection, 91–92, 151–53, 306; studies bird designs in, 99; research at national museums, 99, 247, 265, 282, 306; at Panama-California Exposition, 104, 115; studies meander, 105, 201, 232; decides on career in, 118–19, 126; creates butterfly designs, 126,148–49; influences on his approach to, 127–28, 139; interested in universals of, 128; studies symbols of, 128–29, 164, 330n13; studies post-Spanish pottery, 129, 159–60, 178, 226, 232, 253–54, 273–74; gains recognition, 129, 140; advises Tonita Roybal, 134–35; supports innovation in, 136, 146–47, 306; encourages painters, 137; shift in his awareness toward, 138–40; on Indian art as *art*, 138–39, 255; sees need for local collection of, 148–49, 172; theorizes on design style per pueblo, 160, 167; prepares decorative art survey of, 160; photographs pottery, 161, 179, 184, 254; educates Anglos about, 169–70, 272; sets standards for, 169; shows independence of purpose toward, 171; criticized by next generation of anthropologists, 171; supports art in schools, 179, 183, 256–58; travels on collecting trips, 183–84, 240, 256–57, 282; acts as design clearinghouse for, 184; speaks on importance of, 255. *See also* Indian art, Pueblo pottery

—as illustrator: *122*, *313*; interested in humor magazines, 18, 20, 31, 32; on yearbook staff, 18–19; for *Vox Populi*, 27–31; for Montgomery Ward, 32–33; at Illinois Engraving Company, 32–33; at Cramer Engraving Company, 33–35; sells drawings to tourists, 38; for Twitchell, 40–41, 56; for Springer's crinoid monographs, 47–48, 55, 58, 75, 96, 178, 220; of novelty cards, 54–55, 57, 312–14; at Rito, 65–66; at School of American Research, 77; for railway, 125; for U.S. postage stamp, 294

—at Laboratory of Anthropology: directorship, 233, 244, 265–74, 280, 282, 296; concerned about organizational structure, 236; as officer, 244, 248; on House Bill 32, 245–48; Public Works of Art project, 261–62; film project, 262, 264–65, 268, 270–71, 339n57; on initial merger plan, 296. *See also* Laboratory of Anthropology

—marriage and family life, *109*, 132, *197*, *267*, *300*; meets Kate, 82; social life, 116, 132–33, 198–99, 233, 267–68, 293–94, 338n42; wedding, 117; birth of children, 121, 133; children and grandchildren, 132, 238, 281, 287, 293; response to death of Kate, 290; and Helen's death, 314

—at Museum of New Mexico: as administrator, 74–75, 80, 85, 100, 104–5, 123, 150, 201, 333n13; recognizes importance to Springer, 74, 81, 91, 94, 213; prepares exhibits, 77, 161; resigns from, 94, 248; catalogs collections, 150–51, 330n16. *See also* KMC, professional relationships (Hewett); Museum of New Mexico

—professional relationships: 40–41, 63, 98, 126–27, 158, 230; with Rockefeller, 187–88, 202–6, 209, 212–13, 252, 274, 279, 284, 297, 303–5; mentors Dunn, 257–58

—with Hewett: 49, *87*; respect for, 43, 48, 50–51, 65, 82; distressed by financial practices, 75, 80–81; Hewett-Springer-KMC triangle, 81, 91, 94, 100, 127, 157–58, 192, 196, 201, 212, 236; frustrated by lack of research support, 89, 130, 163–64; and Normal University pottery collection, 90–92, 151–53; discouraged by museum neglect, 100, 129–30, 142, 295; concerned about museum mismanagement, 123, 157, 184; on Nusbaum's accounts, 140–41, 154–55; reacts to "favorite rut," 164; tension regarding Rockefeller, 187–88, 206–17, 225, 231, 234, 241–43, 295, 303; fading bitterness, 295; at memorial service, 297

—with Nusbaum: introduced to, 63; and Tuxtla incident, 71–72; in New York, 96; and unpaid accounts, 140–41, 154–55; and Rockefeller connection, 186–87, 207–9, 212, 218, 226, 234, 242; difference in management styles, 254; tensions during lab transition, 266, 270

—with potters: 195–96, 238, 272; Julian Martinez, 73n, 78–79, 134–35, 287–88; Maria Martinez, 73n, 79, 134–36, 148–49, *281*, 300–301; Tonita Roybal, 134–35; sensitive to norms of Pueblo social culture, 146–48; at Indian Market, 303; Lucy Lewis, 306, *307*

—with Springer: initial impression of, 41; formal introduction to, 44; father-son-like relationship, 48, 55, 58, 131–32; financial agreement with, 57, 91, 323n75; Hewett-Springer-KMC triangle, 81, 91, 94, 100, 127, 157–58, 192, 196, 201, 212, 236; mentored by, 89–91, 108, 110–12, 118–19, 192, 196

—as teacher: 104, 256, 277; in Las Vegas, 43; uses Indian art in class, 52; trains Harvey couriers, 200, 252; at University of New Mexico, 201, 255, 283, 286–87, 290, 292, 299; at Santa Fe Indian School, 256, 257; at Albuquerque Indian School, 256

—written works: "The Evolution of the Bird in Decorative Art," 115, 128; "Graphic Art of the Cave Dwellers," 116, 128; *Conservatism in the Evolution of Decorative Art*, 128; "What the Potsherds Tell," 159; "Life Forms in Pueblo Pottery," 164; "The Pottery Decorations of Santo Domingo and Cochiti Pueblos," 178; "Post-Spanish Pueblo Pottery," 226, 232; "Chance Forms Derived from the Meander," 232; "Taos Creation Myth" (spoof), 233, 317–18; "A Feather Symbol of the Ancient Pueblos," 236; "Stone Wall Construction in Ancient Pueblos and Cliff Dwellings," 236; "The Shalako Ceremony at Zuni," 236; "Bird Forms in Zuni Pottery Decoration," 238; "Preliminary Survey of the Archaeology of Southwestern New Mexico," 238; *Pottery of Santo Domingo Pueblo*, 253–54, 264, 266, 273, 277; Exposition of Tribal Arts catalog, ceramics article, 255; *Pueblo Indian Pottery*, 258–59, 264, 274; "Indian Pottery by the Roadsides," 272; *Pottery of San Ildefonso Pueblo*, 282, 286, 290, 294, 306, 311, 315; *Nazarus*, 311

Chapman, Mary Cordelia White (mother), 3, 6, 7–8, *12*, *197*, 238; as painter, 2, 8; marriage, 8; bird lore, 12–13; in Las Vegas, 49, 56, 81; in Santa Fe, 95, 122, 132; moves to Philadelphia, PA, 259; death of, 259

Chapman (Summers), Pamela (granddaughter), 287

Chapman, Vera (sister), 3, 10, *12*, 13, 101; in Las Vegas, 49, 56, 81; and daughter, 95, 259; in Santa Fe, 95; at Museum of New Mexico, 95, 101; at Panama-California Exposition, 113; in Philadelphia, PA, 259

Chetro Ketl, 151, 159

Chicago World's Fair, 19–20

Chihuahua, Mexico, 43, 61, 164, 265

Civil Works Administration, 261

Cleveland Museum of Art, 275

Cochiti Pueblo, 52, 161, 178, 286–87, 312

Cole, Fay-Cooper, 248, 279

Collier, John, 253, 261, 275, 276

Colter, Mary Jane, 104

Colton, Harold S., 307

community theater. *See under* Santa Fe, New Mexico

Corwin, R. C., 186–88, 209–12

Couse, E. Irving, 124, 190, 344n2

Cramer Engraving Company, 33–35

crinoid research. *See under* KMC, as illustrator; Springer, Frank

Cristo Rey Church, 281

Cruz, Juan, 193

Cummings, Byron, 63, 67, 151, 326n63, 329n44, 336n24

Currelly, Charles T., 105, 151–52, 161

Curtin, Leonora, 294

Cushing, Frank Hamilton, 16, 20, 115

Cutting, Bronson: and city planning, 101; owner of *Santa Fe New Mexican*, 108, 162, 206, 238, 245, 259; donates land to laboratory, 222

Czaplicka, Maria Antoinette, 157

Dasburg, Andrew, 137, 180, 190, 193, *310*

Davey, Randall, 137, 190

Davis, Elizabeth, 301

Davison Fund: created, 262; diminishing support for laboratory, 264, 269, 273, 275, 280; finances research council study, 270, 273; considers intervention in laboratory affairs, 277; Packard studies laboratory situation, 278–79; supports Institute of Indian Arts, 282; terminates laboratory funding, 283

Debevoise, Thomas, 243, 305

DeHuff, Elizabeth, 179

DeHuff, John D., 178–79

Delight Makers, The (Bandelier), 43, 63

Deming, New Mexico, 301

Denver and Rio Grande railway, 63

Denver National Bank, 179

Der Kleine Heim, 314

d'Harnoncourt, Rene, 275, 276, 282

Dietrich, Charles, 198

Dietrich, Margretta Stewart, 294, 336n28; friendship with Kate and KMC, 198, 233, 238, 272; and Indian Fair, 235, 243, 257, 335n19; and NMAIA, 257; supports laboratory, 270; death of, 314

Dixon, Roland B., 63, 131, 248

Dorman, H. H., 101

Dougan, Rose, 288; and Dougan–von Blumenthal initiative, 133–36; and conflict over museum-school collections, 150; and Indian Fair

proposal, 165, 166, 172; as integrationist, 171; and Indian art education fund, 179, 182

Dougan–von Blumenthal initiative, 133–36

Dunlap, Carmelita, xiii, 148

Dunn, Dorothy, 257–58; and KMC, 257

Dunton, W. Herbert, 124

Dutton, Bertha, 290

Eastern Association on Indian Affairs (EAIA), 177, 183

Eastern Woodlands tribe, 2

Economist Plow Company, 11, 26, 33

El Delirio, 294, 311

Ellis, Bruce, 299, 301, 306, 314, 342n60

Ellis, Florence Hawley, 299, 342n63

Ellis, Fremont, 136, 137, 190

El Palacio: first issue, 108; Walter, editor of, 108, 161; lacks funds for illustrations, 109; KMC publishes in, 116, 128, 129, 178, 196, 225; promotes Santa Fe, 125; announces Dougan proposal, 165; defends open-door policy, 180; supports laboratory-museum-school merger, 298; on relationship of KMC with potters, 300

El Paso Natural Gas Company, 301

Ely, Albert, 308

El Zaguan, 238

Engle, William J. (step-grandfather), 7

Exhibition of the Indian Arts, Museum of Modern Art, 282

Exposition of Indian Tribal Arts, 255, 337n15

Fall, Albert B., 176

Famous Players Company, 240

Faris, Chester, 171, 257–58, 262

Federal Antiquities Act of 1906, 59–60, 301

Federal Board for Vocational Education, 182

Fenyes, Eva, 140

Ferdon, Edwin, Jr., 262, 301

Fergusson, Erna, 200, 333n62

Fergusson, Francis, 288

Fewkes, Jesse Walter, 36, 236; at Chicago's World Fair, 20; member of school's managing committee, 62; authors articles on ancient pottery, 65,

115; commends KMC for design analysis, 140; credits Nampeyo with pottery revitalization, 168–69

Fiesta (Santa Fe), 133, 165, 189, 235, 259, 303

Fletcher, Alice Cunningham, 84; founding member of AIA, 59; and Hewett, 61, 62, 70; on location of school, 66; chair of school's managing committee, 67, 69

Fletcher, John Gould, 61–62

Fox Film Company, 240

Fox, Nancy, 301, 308

Fred Harvey Company, 38, 104, 175, 200–201, 233, 252

Freire-Marreco, Barbara. *See* Aitken, Barbara Freire-Marreco

Gallup, New Mexico, 183, 184, 212, 257, 263, 264, 276

Garcia, Marcelino, 101

Garrison, W. E., 70

General Federation of Women's Clubs, 177

Gilpatric, Chadbourne, 298–99

Gilpin, Laura, 306, 314

Goldsmith, Nathan, 87

Granville Female Seminary, 8

Guthe, Carl, 278; studies Pueblo pottery, 184; chairman, laboratory board, 264, 271, 273, 274, 280; correspondence with KMC, 269; orders research council survey, 269; requests KMC to visit Rockefeller, 279

Halseth, Odd, 180, 184

Hano Pueblo, 168

Hanszen, Oscar, 42–43

Harlow, Francis, 301, 314–15

Harnisch, Margretta "Peggy" Potter (granddaughter), xiii, 282, 289, 293

Harrington, John P.: at Rito, 63, 69, 72, 87, 93; member of museum staff, 75, 82, 100; tended by KMC during illness, 79–80

Hartley, Marsden, 138

Harvey Detours. *See* Indian Detours of Fred Harvey Company

Hawthorne, Charles, 96–97

Hayden, T. A., 103

Henderson, Alice Corbin, 125, 136; and NMAIA, 177; trains Harvey couriers, 200; as IAF progressive, 259, 260

Henderson, Junius, 87

Henderson, William Penhallow, 125, 133, 177, 190

Hennings, E. Martin, 125

Henri, Robert, 125, 137

Hewett, Cora Whitford, 43, 50–51, 60

Hewett, Donizetta Wood, 75, 85, 94–95, 152

Hewett, Edgar Lee, 42, 87, 211; teaching theories of, 41–43, 62; as teacher, 43, 65, 84, 150; and death of Cora, 60, 129–30; "El Toro," 84, 129, 329n43; and St. Francis murals, 110–12; mentoring relationship with students, 126–27, 131, 142, 151, 234; sabbatical, 178, 182, 196; death of, 295; memorial service for, 297

—archaeology: early interest in, 43–44; and science of man, 43; supports regional archaeology, 44, 51, 59, 149, 185–86, 228; fieldwork in Chaco Canyon, 50–51, 151–52; and Federal Antiquities Act of 1906, 59–60; fieldwork at Rito, 61–62, 66, 69–74, 82, 84, 107, 241; interest in historical murals, 74, 85, 89; plans for expansion, 74, 93, 100, 129–30, 185–86, 212; AIA lecture tours, 75, 80, 185; fieldwork in Central America, 79, 85; interdisciplinary study with Hodge, 82, 100; diminished reputation in, 82, 94, 131; provides opportunities for women, 84, 326n63; believes in historic pageantry, 133, 189; on artists as researchers, 136; claims credit for Indian Fair, 172; initial response to Pueblo Pottery Fund, 185; and Rockefeller, 187–88, 207–15, 223–25; reacts to laboratory, 228–31, 234, 237–44, 283, 295; sponsors House Bill 32, 245, 247

—leadership positions: president of Las Vegas Normal University, 39, 41–44, 52–54; director of School of American Archaeology, 61, 67; director of Museum of New Mexico, 67, 80; director of Panama-California Exposition, 93, 99, 104; director of Museum of Fine Arts, 115; professor of San Diego State College, 141, 150; director of San Diego Museum, 149; chair of UNM anthropology department, 201

—relationship with KMC: in Las Vegas, 41–44; on Chaco Canyon trip, 50–51; offers position in Santa Fe, 67; on Normal University pottery collection, 91–92, 151–53; on Nusbaum's accounts, 140–41, 154; offers position in California, 141–42; response regarding curatorship, 163–64; and Painters of the Southwest exhibit, 189–90; on report for Rockefeller, 207, 209–12; opinion of KMC as traitor, 242. *See also under* KMC, professional relationships (Hewett)

Hickey, Ethel, 200

Higgins, Victor, 125, 138

Highway Archaeological Salvage program, 301

Hillers, John K., 16

History of Military Occupation (Twitchell), 56, 294

Hodge, Frederick Webb, 36, *87*, 94, 214, 327n46; and Bureau of Ethnology, 36, 67, 82, 99, 100; member, school's managing committee, 67; interdisciplinary study with Hewett, 82, 100; mentors KMC, 99, 105, 158, 183, 219–20; relationship with Nusbaum, 140, 219, 334n23; opinion of Hewett, 158; invited to IAF board, 193–94; supports laboratory, 230

Holmes, William Henry: at Chicago's World Fair, 20; chief of Bureau of Ethnology, 59; supports Hewett, 60; KMC's lifelong hero, 69, 325n1; member of school's managing committee, 69; mentors KMC, 99; authors articles on ancient pottery, 115, 128; supports laboratory, 230

Hopi, 16, 20, 137, 168–69, 185, 301

Hough, Walter, 36, 115

House Bill 32 (NM, Site Preservation Bill), 245–48, 336n44

House Bill 82 (NM, Merger Bill), 298

Houser, Allan, 262

Hrdlicka, Aleš, 230

Huddleson, Sam, 137, 161, 180, 249

Huntington Southwest Survey, 126

Huntington, Ellsworth, 90

Hyde Expedition, 51, 151

Hyde, Benjamin Talbot, 199

IACB. *See* Indian Arts and Crafts Board

IAF. *See* Indian Arts Fund

Illinois Engraving Company, 32–33

Indiana: Albion, 9–11; Jefferson Township, 6; Noble County, 6; South Bend, 11–19, 319n21

Indian art: commercial potential for, 52, 135–36, 275–76, 323n50, 337n15; preservation of, 126, 149, 165–71, 232; and Dougan–von Blumenthal initiative, 133–36; shift in national consciousness about, 138, 177, 311; in Arts Club exhibit, 146–47; at Indian Fair, 165–72; promotion of

Pueblo embroidery, 192; weaving conference, 258; in Santa Fe Saturday fair, 272. *See also* Indian Arts Fund; Indian painting; Pueblo pottery; Pueblo Pottery Fund; *and under* KMC, Indian art

Indian art education fund, 179, 182

Indian Arts and Crafts Bill, 275

Indian Arts and Crafts Board, 261, 264, 275–77, 309, 338n36, 339n73; KMC as special consultant for, 276–77; sets standards for silver jewelry, 276–77

Indian Arts and Crafts Study Board, 261, 264

Indian Arts Fund (IAF), *310*; as result of dinner party, 174–75, 331n3; KMC as curator of, 174–75; as example of cultural intervention, 175, 264, 332n9; potters' attitude toward, 175, 195, 306, 309; incorporates, 193; recruits trustees, 193, 332n50; enlarges scope, 193; organizational structure of, 194, 196; mission of, 194, 309; as extension of Indian Fair, 195; objectives of, 195; KMC accountable for funds of, 209; and Kidder, 216; concerned over boundary with laboratory, 226, 232, 240, 245, 254, 259–61, 263, 279; collections, 234, 240, 243, 248–49, 252, 256, 257, 280, 308, 332n32; progressives v. conservatives, 259–62; discussions on its fate, 308; fortieth anniversary of, 309, 343n101. *See also* Pueblo Pottery Fund

Indian Arts Research Center, 311

Indian Detours of Fred Harvey Company, 200–201, 233

Indian Fair: initial (1922), 165–72, *167*; and Twitchell, 166; objectives of, 168; labeled as revival, 168; Hewett's attitude toward, 168; opportunity for KMC/potter collaboration, 169–70; influences pottery style, 170; credit for, 172; annual fairs, 178–79, 182, 189, 193, 212, 235, 243; local fairs at pueblos, 257; reinstated after 1936, 272

Indian Market, 290–91, 302–3, 309, 311, 343n105

Indian painting: Apie Begay, 51; KMC encourages painters, 137, 329n68; Pueblo painters, 137, 146–47, 177, 323n47; program by Dorothy Dunn, 257–58; Santa Fe studio style, 258, 338n22

Indian Service, 184, 192, 257, 258

Institute of Indian Arts, 282

integrationists v. preservationists, 170–71

Isleta Pueblo, 183

Jaffa, Nathan, 80

Jeançon, J. A., 109

Jemez Pueblo, 50

Jessop, Virginia, 268, 269

Johnson, E. Dana, 162, 180, 206, 238, 246

Johnson, Eleanor Hope, 116, 121, *122*

Johnson, Willard "Spud," 162, 180, 194–95, 238

Jones, William A., 52, 159

Jonson, Raymond, 190, 262

Judd, Neil M., 63, 70–71, *87*, 151, 299; at Rito, 84; on National Museum staff, 93; supports laboratory, 230

Kabotie, Fred, 137, 177, 301

Kearny, Stephen Watts, 75, 294

Keller, William J., 308

Kelly, Daniel T., 283, 297, 298

Kelsey, Francis, 60, 62

Kidder, A. V. "Ted," *64*, 106, 109, 151, 183, 229; early fieldwork, 61–62, 69; relationship with KMC, 63–64, 88–90, 116, 206, 216, 220, 224, 242; at Pecos, 89, 115–16, 234–35; *Pottery of the Pajarito Plateau*, 115; contributions to archaeology, 116, 126; on KMC and pottery revitalization, 166; early supporter of laboratory, 216; opinion of Hewett, 224; on laboratory endowment, 226, 244, 252, 261, 265; principal negotiator for laboratory, 228–44; as chairman of laboratory board, 247, 259, 261, 280; on future options for laboratory, 264–66; resigns from laboratory board, 266; death of, 314

Kroeber, Alfred Lewis, 261

Kroll, Leon, 125

Laboratory of Anthropology: national organizational meeting for, 232, 335n6; executive committee of, 232, 266; incorporates, 233; mission of, 233; agreement with IAF, 234; negotiates with Hewett, 236–40, 243–44; Zimmerman joins board of, 237; Rockefeller's pledge to, 244, 336n42; location of, 248; construction of, 248, 251–52; and field training, 248–49; and lack of clear board direction, 251, 261, 264, 273, 274, 277, 280; founding staff of, 252; and Indian welfare, 253, 337n7; formal opening of, 254; collections of, 254–57, 308–9, 343n100; and suggestion to focus on Indian Arts, 261, 277;

research council survey, 269–73; Rich Survey, 277; response to World War II, 289; James W. Young as chairman of board, 292; merges with museum-school, 295–98; merger deception, 298, 342n60; Highway Archaeological Salvage Program, 301; Lab Inc. merges with school, 309. *See also under* KMC, at Laboratory of Anthropology

—directors: KMC, 233, 244, 265–74, 280, 282, 396; Jesse Nusbaum, 249–65; H. Scudder Mekeel, 274–80; James F. Zimmerman, 284–91; Maurice Ries, 292–96; Sylvanus "Vay" G. Morley, 296–97; Boaz Long, 298–99

Lacey, John F., 59–60, 67

LaFarge, Oliver, 120, 124, 255

La Fonda Hotel, 144, 163, 200

Laguna Pueblo, 36, 183, 191, 240

Lambert, Marjorie, 69, 84, 199, 301–2, 314

Las Vegas, New Mexico, 38–49, 52–56, 81

Las Vegas Normal University: Hewett as president, 39, 41–44, 52–54; teaching standards of, 43, 52–53; potential for regional museum at, 44; board controversy over Hewett, 53–54; pottery collection of, 81, 90–92, 151–53, 306, 343n96

Laughing Horse, 162, 194

Laughing Horse Press, 238

Laughlin, Ruth, 104, 105

Laura Spelman Rockefeller Memorial Fund, 215, 244, 248

Lawler, Joseph J., 294

League of Women Voters, 198

Lewis, Lucy, 306, *307*

Liljevall, Georg, 47

Long, Boaz: as director of laboratory, 298–99; involved in merger deception, 298, 342n60

los cinco pintores, 136

Lotave, Carl G., 75–77, 85, 89

Loudon, Elsie, 192

Luhan, Mabel Dodge, 162, 177

Lummis, Charles, *86*; member of Archaeological Society of New Mexico, 44, 59; member of school's managing committee, 62, 67, 69; member of museum board of regents, 69; at Rito, 84, 92; supports Hewett, 93

MacMillan, James, 175, 193, 255

Magoffin, Ralph V. D., 185–86, 230; president, AIA, 228; supports Hewett, 228, 236–40, 243–44; refers to KMC as traitor, 241, 303

Maier, Herbert, 222

Manhattan Project, 288, 291–92, 303

Ma-Pe-Wi, 137

Martinez, Crescencio, 137, 177

Martinez, Julian, 70, *147*, 148, 235, at Rito, 69, 72–73; at Museum of New Mexico, 75, 78–79, 85, 107; at Panama-California Exposition, 104, 113, 139; and Dougan–von Blumenthal initiative, 134; creates black-on-black pottery, 136; paintings of, 177; use of design motifs, 184; death of, 287–88

Martinez, Maria, *147*, 172, *281*, 288; at Rito, 69–70, 72–73; at Museum of New Mexico, 75, 78–79, 85, 107; at Panama-California Exposition, 104, 113, 139; and Dougan–von Blumenthal initiative, 134–36; creates black-on-black pottery, 136, 329n62; sells pottery at pueblo, 139, 190–91; exhibits pottery, 148; reacts to KMC butterfly designs, 148–49, 172; at Indian Fair, 171, 235, 243; signs pots, 171–72; praises KMC, 301

Martinez, Santana, xiii, 148, 288

McFie, John R., 44, 59, 66, 67, 153

McKittrick, Margaret: as NMAIA Chair, 177, 179, 182, 183; as IAF progressive, 259–60

McNary, James G., 50–52

McNary, Margretta, 50–52

McQuarrie, Marion, 84

Meagher, Josephine Chapman (aunt), 10, 19, 20, 26, 33

Meem, John Gaw, 200, 251–52, 257, 281, 315

Mekeel, H. Scudder, 274–80

memoirs, xi, xii, 4n, 305–6

Mera, Harry, 180, 235, 255, 278, 331n2; and IAF, 174–75, 193, 232, 260, 262; curator of archaeological survey, 251, 253, 282

Mesa Verde, 85, 157, 186–87, 207, 249, 265, 306

Mimbres ware, 165, 306

Mitchell Wilder Report, 307

modernists, 138, 161–62, 180–81

Monhoff, Fred, 137

Montgomery Ward, 32–33

Montoya, Anna (Maximiliana Martinez), 235

Montoya, Desideria, 235

Moore, Flora, 84

Moran, Thomas, 138

Morgan, Lewis Henry, 16, 78, 320n30

Morley, Sylvanus "Vay" G., 75, 78, *87*, *102*, 151, 284; fieldwork in Southwest, 61–62, 65, 69, 71–72; and Tuxtla incident, 71–72; fieldwork in Central America, 71, 79, 85, 93, 101; outburst over Hewett's broken promises, 89, 130, 329n49; and New-Old Santa Fe architectural movement, 101–3, 109; and La Bajada incident, 106–7; at Carnegie Institute, 113; contributions to archaeology, 126; supports merging laboratory with museum-school, 295; as director of merged institution, 296–97; death of, 298

Morris, Earl, 151

Mruk, Walter, 136, 180, 190

Muller, Katherine "Kate." *See* Chapman, Katherine "Kate" Muller

Munroe, James P., 182

murals. *See* St. Francis murals; *also under* Museum of New Mexico

Museum of Fine Arts, 119–26; Springer's influence on, 115, 328n4; construction of, 120–23; dedication ceremonies for, 122–24; open-door policy of, 124–25, 180; artist's description of, 125–26, 136–37; KMC as curator of, 126, 161–64, exhibits Maria Martinez pottery, 148; modernist exhibit, 180; self-expressionist exhibit, 180

Museum of Folk Art, 298

Museum of Indian Arts and Culture, 310–11

Museum of New Mexico: founded, 67; Hewett, named director of, 67; original board of regents, 67, 69, 70; original charter, 74; KMC as administrator, 74–75, 80, 85, 100, 104–5, 123, 150, 201, 333n13; Palace of the Governors renovations, 75–77; historical murals of, 76–77, 85; collections of, 92, 150, 308–9; New-Old Santa Fe exhibit, 103; Paul Walter as acting director of, 108; artist studios in, 137; catalog of collections, 150, 308; state support for, 154; Rockefeller vision for, 188; Rockefeller requests report on, 205–15; Hall of Ethnology, 295; Sylvanus "Vay" Morley as director of, 296; separates from school, 306–7; negotiates with IAF, 308

Museum of Northern Arizona, 301, 307

museums: museum age (1875–1920), 9; life-group and culture approach, 20; Hewett's early interest in regional, 44; Aggasiz's opinion of,

45–46; Springer's opinion of, 74; as educational resource, 74, 186, 215; Rockefeller's vision of, 186; code of ethics, 194; and trailside exhibits, 215; Bumpus's vision of, 215; KMC's opinion of, 247. *See also* American Association of Museums; *and individual museums*

museum-school. *See* Museum of New Mexico; School of American Research

Musgrave, Arthur F., 125

Myers, Ralph, 125

Nampeyo, 20, 168–69

Naranjo, Santiago, *86*, 116, 146, 330n5

Nash, Willard, 136, 137, 190

National Museum of Natural History, 16, 91, 93, 96, 99, 151

National Research Council, 216, 228, 271

Native American art. *See* Indian art

Native American painting. *See* Indian painting

Native American Vendors Program, 272

Navajo, 51, 104, 257; silver, 20, 150, 167, 256, 276; textiles, 167, 255, 256, 258, 287

Nave, Gabrielita, 167

Nelson, Nels, 119, 126, 216

New Mexico Association for Science, 128, 158, 178, 215

New Mexico Association on Indian Affairs (NMAIA), 177, 179, 182–83, 190, 257

New Mexico Educational Association, 158

New Mexico Magazine, 272

New-Old Santa Fe architectural movement, 103, 120

New York Public Library, 98–99

Nordfeldt, B. J. O., 137, 161, 180, 190

Normal University. *See* Las Vegas Normal University

Norton, Charles Eliot, 60

Nusbaum, Aileen, 154, 186, 249, 278

Nusbaum, Jesse L., 70–71, *87*, 186, *217*, *310*; and Southwest fieldwork, 62, 69–70; at Mesa Verde, *64*, 85, 157, 186–87, 207, 249, 265; at Normal University, 70; and Tuxtla incident, 71–72; relationship with KMC, 71–72, 106–7, 206, 207–8, 217–18, 242, 254; renovates Palace of the Governors, 75–77, 120; fieldwork, Central America, 79, 101; at National Museum, 93, 96; New-Old Santa Fe exhibit, 103; Panama-

California Exposition, 104, 113; and La Bajada incident, 106–7; renovations at Pecos, 115; construction of Museum of Fine Arts, 120–23; relationship with Springer, 140, 156; at Heye Museum, 140; Hewett and unpaid accounts, 140–41, 154–56; relationship with Rockefeller, 186, 263; trains Harvey couriers, 200; encourages KMC to ally with Rockefeller, 207–9, 212, 218–19, 234, 242, 333n5; as director of laboratory, 249–65; reacts to IAF progressives, 260–61; requests clear board direction, 261, 338n35; and Public Works of Art project, 261–62; member of laboratory executive committee, 266; consultant for U.S. Department of Interior, 301. *See also under* KMC, professional relationships (Nusbaum)

Old Santa Fe group, 102–3. *See also* New-Old Santa Fe architectural movement

Old Santa Fe Association, 199–200, 206

Oppenheimer, Robert, 288, 291, 303

Osborn, Frederick, 271, 272

outdoor education committee (American Association of Museums), 215, 221, 232

Packard, Arthur: as Rockefeller representative, 249, 252, 262, 270, 275; advises KMC, 266, 283; on laboratory situation, 278–79; supports Institute of Indian Arts, 282; on future options for laboratory, 296

Painted Desert Exhibit, 104, 113

Painters of the Southwest exhibit, 189–90

Pajarito Plateau, 43, 44, 49, 63–66, 69–74, 88

Palace of the Governors: declared national monument, 66; home of Museum of New Mexico, 67; home of School of American Archaeology, 67; renovated, 75, 120; pottery demonstrations at, 107, 166; artist studios in, 137

Panama-California Exposition, 93, 99, 104–5, 113, 115, 139; Painted Desert Exhibit in, 104, 113; and KMC, 104, 115

Parsons, Sara, 125, 138

Parsons, Sheldon, *124*, 125, 190; considered for St. Francis murals, 110; and community theater, 133; at Museum of Fine Arts, 137, 161–62

Pasatiempo, 189, 332n41

Pearl Harbor, 283

Peckham, Stewart, 301, 306

Pecos conference, 234–35, 335n14

Pecos site, 89, 105, 115, 216

Phillips, Bert, 125, 318

pictographs. *See* cave paintings

Pilate, Pontius, 312

Pope, William H., 105

Popejoy, Thomas, 292, 341n27

Potter, Helen Chapman (daughter), 133, *197*, 267, 282, 289–91, 293; childhood of, 187, *198*–99, 201; wedding of, 281; death of, 314

Potter, Robert (grandson), xiii, 289

Potter, Robert (son-in-law), 281, 289, 293, 341n15

pottery. *See* Pueblo potters; Pueblo pottery

Powell, John Wesley, 20, 59

preservationists v. integrationists, 170–71

Provincetown, MA, 96–97

Public Works of Art project, 261–62, *263*

Pueblo Bonito trading post, 51

Pueblo Indian Arts and Crafts Market (Albuquerque), 282

Pueblo potters. *See* Aguilar, Susanna; Ascension, Dolores; Baca, Lufina; Dunlap, Carmelita; Lewis, Lucy; Martinez, Julian; Martinez, Maria; Martinez, Santana; Montoya, Anna; Montoya, Desideria; Roybal, Tonita

Pueblo pottery: sent out of Southwest, 16, 44, 51, 59, 105, 184; traditional standards of, 52, 166, 167–69, 195–96, 226, 330n8; within context of arts and crafts movement, 52; commercial potential of, 52, 166–70, 177, 181, 190–91, 195; anthropological significance of, 77–78, 159; as index artifacts, 77; classification approach to, 77–78, 234; Pajaritan, 88–89, 97, 108; preservation of, 126, 148–49, 165–71, 232; connection between textile and pottery design, 128; persistence of symbols over time, 128–29, 164; and Dougan–von Blumenthal initiative, 133–36; shift in national consciousness on, 138, 177, 311; research vocabulary of, 139; Casas Grandes ware, 164; KMC collects data on, 165; and Indian Fair, 165–72; revitalization of, 168–71; Anglos setting standards for, 170, 178, 240, 272; signed, 171–72, 235; political significance of, 176; and Bursum Bill, 176–78; as factor in regional identity, 177; effect of Manhattan Project on, 288. *See also* Indian art

Pueblo Pottery Fund: founded, 174–75; first catalogued item of, 175; goals of, 175; artistic merit as acceptance criteria, 175; provides inspirational models, 175; shares membership with NMAIA, 178; moves to Museum of Fine Arts basement, 184–85, 332n32; considers enlarging scope, 185; incorporates as Indian Arts Fund, 193. *See also* Indian Arts Fund

Putnam, Frederic Ward, 19, 59–62, 66, 73

Puyé, 50, 69–70, 72, 76–77, 80, 85, 117; visited by Nelson and KMC, 119; KMC on Hewett excavation at, 158

Rapp and Rapp, 120

Raymond Rich Associates, 277–78

Rayne, Catherine, 294

Raynolds, Ruth, 50–52

regional archaeology, 158, 251; and Hewett, 44, 51, 59, 149, 185–86, 228

Reid, W. C., 36, 39–40

Reifsnider, C. K., 27, 29–30

Remington, Frederick, 138

Rice, Roscoe, 184, 191

Richey, Frank E., 27–30

Rich Survey, 277–78

Ricketson, Edith, 290

Ries, Maurice, 292–96

Rito de los Frijoles, 116, 121–22, 128, 141; field sessions at, 62–66, 69–74, 82–84, 92–93, 107; Ceremonial Cave, 66, 84, *86*

Roans, Ambrose, 276

Robbins, W. W., *87*

Rockefeller Foundation, 185, 207, 210, 241, 276, 290, 298, 299

Rockefeller, Abby, 203, 205, 206, 297, 304

Rockefeller, David, 263

Rockefeller, John D., Jr., 186, *211*, 225, 263; and interest in integrated museum experience, 186; with Nusbaum at Mesa Verde, 186; discusses museums with Hewett, 188; meets KMC, 202–6; requests report from KMC, 206; values ethics, 206; initial pledge to IAF, 209; compares reports from Hewett and KMC, 214, 218; opts for anthropology lab, 219; funding policy of, 226; relationship with KMC, 252, 274, 279, 284, 297, 305; opinion on museum-school-laboratory merger, 296; correspondence regarding 1926 events, 303–5; death of, 314

Rodeck, Sally Lewis, 301

Rollins, Warren, 133, 137, 190

Rolshoven, Julius, 125, 137

Rough Riders, 36, 40–41

Royal Ontario Museum of Archaeology, 105, 151, 161

Roybal, Alfonso. *See* Awa Tsireh

Roybal, Tonita, *135*, 165, 172; advised by KMC to specialize, 134–35; and Indian Fair, 168, 169, 193, 243

Rush, Olive, 190, 290

San Diego Exposition. *See* Panama-California Exposition

San Diego Museum, 149

San Diego State College, 150

San Francisco World's Fair, 93

San Ildefonso Pueblo, 79, 104, 107, 133–35, 184, 190, 205, 226; workers at field sessions, 63, 66, 70, 72–73; visited by KMC, 73n, 146, 300; painters, 137, 147; butterfly designs, 148–49; photographic record of pottery, 165; and drought, 178; pottery studies by Ruth Bunzel and Carl Guthe, 184; pottery study by KMC, 282, 286, 290, 294, 306, 311, 315; and World War II, 288

San Juan Pueblo, 135

Santa Ana Pueblo, 286, 287, 299

Santa Clara Pueblo, 50, 146, 159, 171, 235; visited by KMC, 117; and drought, 178; and World War II, 288

Santa Fe, New Mexico, 76, 96, 120, 136, 144, 161–63, 174, 206, 294; plaza, 76, 82, 145–46, 259, 311; and city planning, 103; and tourism, 103, 125–26, 189–90, 222, 303; community theater in, 132–33, 233; and chautauqua, 199–200; and the "Hill," 288, 291–92; and Cold War, 303

Santa Fe Art Colony, 119; KMC as founder of, 126; modernists, 136, 161, 177, 180; traditionalists, 136; neighborhoods of, 136, 161–62; seeks uniquely American aesthetic, 138; preservationists, 138, 170; defends genius of Native expression, 138; incorporates Indian symbols in art, 138; KMC as complement to, 138; as political factor, 176, 177, 199; as economic factor in Santa Fe, 189; organizes Pasatiempo, 189

Santa Fe Fiesta. *See* Fiesta (Santa Fe)

Santa Fe Indian School, 255, 256, 257

Santa Fe New Mexican, 44, 101, 108, 180; as anti-Hewett, 94, 101, 162, 206, 246; and society news, 116, 117, 289; on Indian art, 122, 177, 185, 256; on Los Alamos, 288, 291, 303

Santa Fe studio style, 258

Santa Fe style (architecture), 103, 114, 120, 251, 326n24, 327n27

Santo Domingo Pueblo, 52, 257, 272, 282; photographic record of pottery, 161; pottery studies by KMC, 178, 253–54, 258, 264–66, 273, 277; visitors at KMC's house, 238

School of American Archaeology. *See* School of American Research

School of American Research: founded as School of American Archaeology, 62; summer school sessions, 62–69, 71–74, 82–84, 92–93, 107, 126, 151–52, 241; decision regarding location, 66–67; Hewett named director of, 67; funding for, 67, 80, 153; KMC on founding staff, 67, 69, 77; and Rito excavations, 107; pottery demonstrations at, 107; and Quarai excavations, 107; name change of, 129; granted museum property, 129; Bumpus's opinion of Hewett's management, 223; merges with laboratory, 297–98; separates from museum-laboratory, 306–7; Indian Arts Research Center, 311; School for Advanced Research, 311

Schwarzt, Douglas W., 311

Schweizer, Herman, 104, 175

self-expressionist exhibit, 180–82

Seligman, Arthur, 101

Seligman, James L., 101, 175

Sena, Jose D., 119

Sergeant, Elizabeth Shepley, 174, 176, 177, 194, 309

Sharp, Joseph, 125, 233, 318

Shepard, Anna, 253

Shermack Report, 306–7

Shonnard, Eugenie, 290

Shorty, Dooley, 276

Shuster, Will, 136, 137, 190, 262

Siegman, Kenneth, 289

Sioux, 167

Skinner, James (great-grandfather), 6, 7, 8

Skinner, Jane. *See* White, Jane Skinner

Skinner, Rueben (great-great-grandfather), 6

Sloan, Dolly, 189

Sloan, John, 125, 137, 190

Smithsonian Institution, 16, 20, 36, 45, 67, 99, 115; visited by KMC and father, 16

Social Science Research Council, 271

Southwest Association of Indian Artists, 311

Spanish and Indian Trading Company, 175

Spanish colonial arts and crafts, 185, 332n49

Spier, Leslie, 271, 272

Spinden, Herbert J., 98, 158, 183

Springer, Edward, 140

Springer, Eva, 47, 125

Springer, Frank, 45, 46, 86, 122, 322n28; and Maxwell Land Grant, 39, 46, 322n25, 322n27; in Las Vegas, 44–48; meets KMC, 44; researches crinoids, 45–47, 322n31, 324n78; fatherlike relationship with KMC, 48, 55, 58; health of, 56–57, 192, 220, 233; proposes financial agreement with KMC, 57, 91, 323n75; *Crinoidea Flexibilia*, 58, 123, 131; *American Silurian Crinoids*, 58, 220; fieldwork, 63, 116, 121; member of museum board of regents, 74; interest in historical murals, 76, 85, 89; mentors KMC, 89–91, 108, 110–12, 118–19, 192, 196; at National Museum, 91, 96, 100; supports St. Francis murals, 110–12; and Museum of Fine Arts, 115, 119–20; on Nusbaum's accounts, 141, 154–55; on Rockefeller situation, 218; death of, 235. *See also under* KMC, professional relationships (Springer)

Springer, Wallace, 140, 156, 172

Stallings, Alice, 253

Stallings, Sidney, 253, 269, 337n9

Stevens, David, 264, 284, 290, 291, 293, 338n33; supports KMC film project, 262, 270; funds assistant for KMC, 299; encourages KMC memoirs, 305

Stevenson, James, 16, 115

Stevenson, Matilda Coxe, 16

Stewart, Dorothy, 162, 235, 272, 290; friendship with Kate, 198, 233; against chautauqua, 199–200; illustrates *Adobe Notes*, 238

St. Francis murals, 119; Springer and Hewett support, 110–11; KMC and Vierra as team, 110–11, 114; Hewett suggests KMC as artist, 111; KMC prepares for, 112–14; KMC and Vierra paint, 119–20, 328n6

stock market crash (1929), 249–50

Strong, William D., 266

Stubbs, Stanley, 262, 301; member of laboratory staff, 253, 282, 291, 294, 297; as IAF curator, 263, 268; consults Zimmerman with KMC, 269; relationship with KMC, 293; attitude toward Long, 298; death of, 308

Sun House project, 150

Sunmount Sanitarium, 125, 199

Szwedzicki, C., 258, 264, 274

"Taos Creation Myth" (spoof), 317–18

Taos Society of Artists, 189, 190, 233, 317–18

Tesuque Pueblo, 135, 178, 198, 282

Texas Federation of Women's Clubs, 199

Thompson, Alex. *See* Alex Thompson collection

Toulouse, Betty, 308–9

Tozzer, Alfred M., 60, 61; at school's summer session, 63; criticizes Hewett, 65, 94, 131; concerned about school's location, 66; relationship with KMC, 98, 158, 183, 268, 270

traditionalists, 136

True, Allen, 172, 179

Tsirege, 49, 52

Tuxtla, 71–72

Twitchell, Ralph Emerson, 119, 133, 145, 189; as Rough Riders advertising chairman, 40–41; *History of Military Occupation*, 56, 294; and Indian Fair, 166, 172

Underhill, Ruth, 287, 288

University of Arizona, 299

University of Chicago, 261, 297

University of Michigan: Museum of Anthropology, 264

University of New Mexico (UNM), 256, 267; Zimmerman as president of, 201; establishes anthropology department, 201; Indian arts class taught by KMC at, 201, 252, 254; and laboratory, 237–239, 265, 269, 283; moves Indian arts class to fine arts, 255; KMC on faculty of, 283, 286–87, 292, 299; awards honorary doctorate to KMC, 299–300

Ute, 167

Vanderpoel, John H., 22, 24, 26, 48

Van Soelen, Theodor, 125

Van Stone, Bertha, 150, 166, 190

Velarde, Pablita, 262

Vierra, Ada, 116

Vierra, Carlos, 114, *122*, *124*, 125, 133, 190; fieldwork, 101, 116, 121; New-Old Santa Fe exhibit, 103; and St. Francis murals, 110–11, 114, 119–20; at Panama-California Exposition, 113

von Blumenthal, Vera, 133, 329n59

Wachsmuth, Charles, 47, 48, 55, 322n31

Walter, Paul A. F., 66, 130, 161; editor of *Santa Fe New Mexican*, 44; member of Archaeological Society of New Mexico, 44; administrator of museum-school, 108, 151; editor of *El Palacio*, 119

Wendorf, Fred, 299, 301

Wesley, Elizabeth, 291

Wetherill, Richard, 20, 151; and Hyde Expedition, 51

Wheeler-Howard Act, 264

Wheelwright, Mary, 259

White, Abby, 108

White, Amelia Elizabeth, 174, 294, *310*, 311; and Santa Fe Art Colony, 162; and NMAIA, 177; donates land for laboratory, 222; and Indian Fair, 235, 243; and Exposition of Indian Tribal Arts, 255; as IAF progressive, 259; honored by IACB, 309

White, Jane Skinner (grandmother), 6

White, John II (great-grandfather), 6–7

White, Martha, 162, 235, 243, 255, 294

White, Westley (grandfather), 6–7

White, Wilson "Witt" (uncle), 6, 8

Williams, J. Insco, 8

Williamsburg, VA, 186

Wilson, Francis C., 193, 222, 225, 233; and House Bill 32, 245–48; and merger, 296

Wilson, Olive, 133, 134, 166

Wissler, Clark, 261

Wood, Donizetta. *See* Hewett, Donizetta Wood

Woods Hole Marine Biological Laboratory, 216, 226, 265

World's Columbian Exposition (1893), 19–20

World War II, 277, 283, 288, 289, 291–92

Woy, Maud, 84, *87*

Yale Institute of Human Relations, 274

Young, James W., 261, 271, 282, 283, 340n79; chairman of laboratory board, 280, 284, 292; and Zimmerman, 291; and merger, 296

Zia Pueblo, 16, 51, 137, 161, 184

Zimmerman, James F., 245, 259, 286; president of University of New Mexico, 201; member of laboratory board, 237–238; on House Bill 32, 247; member of laboratory executive committee, 266; announces laboratory's demise, 269; consulted by KMC, 269; offers faculty position to KMC, 283, 286; on future options for laboratory, 283; director of laboratory, 284–91; death of, 291–92

Zozobra, 189

Zuni Pueblo, 16, 20, 161, 183, 184, 282; studies by KMC, 236, 238